GLOBAL SOUTH ASIA

Padma Kaimal
K. Sivaramakrishnan
Anand A. Yang
SERIES EDITORS

LAHORE CINEMA

Between Realism and Fable

IFTIKHAR DADI

UNIVERSITY OF WASHINGTON PRESS
Seattle

Publication of this open monograph was the result of Cornell University's participation in TOME (Toward an Open Monograph Ecosystem), a collaboration of the Association of American Universities, the Association of University Presses, and the Association of Research Libraries. TOME aims to expand the reach of long-form humanities and social science scholarship including digital scholarship. Additionally, the program looks to ensure the sustainability of university press monograph publishing by supporting the highest quality scholarship and promoting a new ecology of scholarly publishing in which authors' institutions bear the publication costs.

Funding from Cornell University made it possible to open this publication to the world.
www.openmonographs.org

Copyright © 2022 by the University of Washington Press

Composed in Minion Pro, typeface designed by Robert Slimbach

The digital edition of this book may be downloaded and shared under a Creative Commons Attribution Non-Commercial No Derivatives 4.0 international license (CC-BY-NC-ND 4.0). For information about this license, see https://creativecommons.org/licenses/by-nc-nd/4.0. This license applies only to content created by the author, not to separately copyrighted material. To use this book, or parts of this book, in any way not covered by the license, please contact University of Washington Press.

UNIVERSITY OF WASHINGTON PRESS
uwapress.uw.edu

LIBRARY OF CONGRESS CATALOGING-IN-PUBLICATION DATA
Names: Dadi, Iftikhar, author.
Title: Lahore cinema : between realism and fable / Iftikhar Dadi.
Description: Seattle : University of Washington Press, [2022] | Series: Global South Asia | Includes bibliographical references and index.
Identifiers: LCCN 2022015152 (print) | LCCN 2022015153 (ebook) | ISBN 9780295750798 (hardcover) | ISBN 9780295750811 (paperback) | ISBN 9780295750804 (ebook)
Subjects: LCSH: Motion pictures—Pakistan—History—20th century. | Motion pictures—Pakistan—Lahore—History—20th century. | Motion pictures—Urdu-speaking countries.
Classification: LCC PN1993.5.P3 D33 2022 (print) | LCC PN1993.5.P3 (ebook) | DDC 791.43/095491—dc23/eng/20220722
LC record available at https://lccn.loc.gov/2022015152
LC ebook record available at https://lccn.loc.gov/2022015153

♾ This paper meets the requirements of ANSI/NISO Z39.48-1992 (Permanence of Paper).

CONTENTS

Preface vii
Acknowledgments xv
A Note on Translation and Transliteration xxi

Introduction: The Lahore Effect 1

1 Between Neorealism and Humanism: *Jago Hua Savera* 29

2 Lyric Romanticism: Khurshid Anwar's Music and Films 56

3 Cinema and Politics: Khalil Qaiser and Riaz Shahid............. 104

4 The *Zinda Bhaag* Assemblage: Reflexivity and Form.............. 142

Notes 165
Bibliography 203
Index 221

PREFACE

Cinema in Pakistan emerged as an influential industrial and cultural form during the twentieth century. Film production in Lahore dates back to the 1920s silent film era, and consequently its history extends much earlier than the founding of the country in 1947. By the mid-1950s, Karachi and Dhaka also emerged as important centers of production, leading to the rising numbers of films released in many languages, including Bengali, Punjabi, and Urdu, and later in Pashto and Sindhi. This book focuses primarily on Urdu cinema from Lahore from 1956 through 1969, a period I designate as constituting *the long sixties*. An era of relative political stability that witnessed considerable economic, social, and infrastructural development, this stretch of about a dozen years extends across the reign of the military ruler Mohammad Ayub Khan (1958–69).[1]

Lahore Cinema: Between Realism and Fable is a formal and contextual analysis of social and experimental Urdu films from Lahore made during the long sixties. The final chapter focuses on a recent Punjabi film that revisits many of the concerns of the earlier cinema. The films I analyze in this book traverse realism and fable, history and fantasy, narrative and lyric, and marshal diverse cultural lineages from South Asia. These include premodern orality, colonial-era theater, progressive writing, and Hollywood genre conventions and tropes. An important concern of this study is the evocation of a public sphere by cinema and its effects, which traverse social hierarchies and are discrepant with nationalist political horizons.

Lahore Cinema has been informed by the growing scholarship on the cinema of South Asia, but it must be stressed that the focus of this work remains uneven. In the last two decades, research on Indian—and especially Bombay—cinema has substantially contributed various approaches to diverse bodies of film and its institutions. This work is salient for my analysis because I examine films whose industrial practices, themes, and forms have many parallel and shared developments between Lahore and Bombay. Ravi Vasudevan's writings on midcentury Bombay cinema's formal values and their relation to society have been valuable, including his analysis of the rise of the "Muslim social" film from the mid-1930s, which, this study argues, continued to flourish in Lahore in the fifties and sixties.[2] This study has also gained from many other scholars' works on Indian films and filmmaking.[3] Indeed, the complex and resonant relays between cinematic genres and tropes between India and Pakistan is a vital consideration for this book.[4]

I have worked on cinema from Pakistan and South Asia for many years, as an artist and a scholar. As a member of the Editorial Advisory Board of the journal *BioScope: South Asian Screen Studies* since its founding in 2010, I have kept abreast of emerging scholarship and key methodological developments in the field of South Asian cinema studies. Increasingly, there is growing scholarly awareness that cinema in South Asia, precisely due to its complex regional interconnections from the very beginning, cannot be solely situated within national frameworks. Film historian Ashish Rajadhyaksha has underscored the degree to which midcentury Bombay cinema was shaped by a diasporic sensibility produced by migrants who had been inhabitants of territories that mostly became part of West Pakistan after 1947: "It has often been said that Bombay's Hindi cinema itself is nothing but a cinema of a Punjabi diaspora, with its sagas of twins separated at birth."[5] Rajadhyaksha has also proposed that a "Lahore effect" resulting from the shared aesthetics between Bombay and Lahore characterized many of the most celebrated productions of Bombay during the mid- to later forties, both before and after the Partition of 1947. This capacious and suggestive conception, which encompasses lineage, form, fable, and reflexivity, is valuable in understanding the Lahore social film during the long sixties and beyond, and its significance is elaborated on in the introduction.[6]

From the outset, cinema in Pakistan was beset by extended crises: paucity of capital, inadequate distribution networks, lack of trained industry personnel, and competition from Bombay films. It has been disparaged for being vulgar and commercial, for failing to achieve artistic value or enact critical consciousness among its viewers, for having low production values, for making recourse all too often to stereotypes and typage, for relying on melodramatic hooks and popular plot schemas, and for being unable to shake off a parasitic dependence on Bombay cinema.[7] These generalizations remain largely unchallenged because of the paucity of scholarship on the cinema of the fifties through the seventies.[8] Additionally, the potential to analyze the important medium of commercial cinema for its complex and multiple effects on questions of cultural memory, the public sphere, and engagement with modernity has remained mostly unaddressed.

While scholarship on Bombay cinema is far more developed than the study of the social film from Pakistan or other South Asian locations and countries, an emerging body of work is partly redressing this imbalance.[9] This study draws from and aims to contribute to this body of scholarship whose primary focus is on the lesser-examined developments in South Asian cinemas. Significant new work on Pakistani cinema includes Kamran Asdar Ali's essays on the social and cultural meanings of the social film in Pakistan during the sixties and their relation to transformations in social and cultural life, Lotte Hoek's writings on the multifarious linkages between Dhaka and Lahore industry personnel before and after 1971, and Salma Siddique's work on exchanges between India and Pakistan and infrastructural developments during the first decade following the Partition.[10]

Lahore Cinema engages with emerging methodologies for the analysis of South Asian cinema in several specific ways. Firstly, by analyzing an experimental neorealist film from Lahore as being inextricably South Asian, it moves the analysis of neorealism beyond national contexts. This is in keeping with recent efforts in cinema studies to theorize "global neorealism"—where neorealist cinema in various sites is not simply seen as a reflection of Italian cinema but is evaluated comparatively with attention to its own context of production, circulation, and social and aesthetic value. Recent work on melodrama in cinema has also situated this mode in analogous frameworks. Secondly, by examining relays between realism and fable, it situates reflexivity and political awareness across genres, and in doing so questions the assumption that experimental cinema is endowed with criticality and popular cinema is primarily apolitical and a distraction. Commercial cinema draws from both popular and high cultural registers, as exemplified by major Urdu poets and writers who contributed lyrics and dialogue to feature films. Consequently, this study draws from cultural studies' theorizations that understand popular cultural forms as sites for contestation over collective memory and aspiration.

This study also situates Urdu rhetorical forms and cultural valences as being foundational to Lahore as well as much of midcentury Bombay cinema. Until now, scholarship on the latter has neglected to ask a key question of its major films—the evocations of enunciation and lyric in the making of meaning.[11] Bombay cinema itself is deeply habituated to the universe of tropes and symbols from the broad North Indian linguistic register, in which "Urdu" plays a major role. It's worth stressing that the linguistic resources and cultural resonances associated with Urdu in this study are not proposed as being elite or purist. As a language of a popular commercial form always seeking to expand its audience, "Urdu" here is understood in an expansive register that embraces aspects of neighboring language registers from North India and the Deccan. Hindi, Hindi-Urdu, and Hindustani have also been variously deployed to characterize this cinema. It is certainly not my intention here to assume a partisan stance among long-standing Hindi/Urdu rivalries, especially as popular cinema largely overcomes this by not having to rely on either the Hindi or the Urdu script, and through broader accessibility in its choice of diction. But since my subject is Lahore cinema and its legacies, I seek to investigate the historical, cultural, and affective landscape that emerges from this capacious conception of Urdu for both Bombay and Lahore cinemas.

Moreover, the significance of language in Lahore cinema bears methodological lessons also for a full reckoning of the midcentury Bombay film and its meaning-making as it draws upon a vast reservoir of cultural references. The resilience of the commercial film in the mid- to later twentieth century in both cities owes a great deal to its participation in this larger world, which evokes a cinematic public sphere across and beyond existing social groups, communities, and ethnicities. Indeed, the midcentury social films of both Bombay and Lahore draw from and contribute to a shared and transnational mediatized universe, reiterating analogous narrative tropes, lyrics, and characterization. This is often the case also for the Hindi and Urdu films made in Calcutta, Dhaka, and Karachi. Among the most powerful vectors of social and aesthetic modernization in South Asia, the commercial film provides complex affective and imaginative resources for its audiences to navigate an accelerating modernity and fraught politics by anchoring social change across the terrain of deeper cultural imaginaries.

This book focuses primarily on the Urdu cinema of Lahore during the long sixties (apart from chapter 4)—analyzing a small number of exemplary films that possess formal and narrative depth, evoke multiple cultural resonances, and are largely original works.[12] This is primarily not a study that tackles reception history or stardom. And although gender is a focus of some of the analysis presented here, and scholars such as Kamran Asdar Ali, Nasreen Rehman, and Salma Siddique have contributed to the subject, Lahore's melodramatic social film of the long sixties awaits a fuller analysis from this perspective.[13] My readings are based neither on an overarching national framework nor on solely foregrounding issues of identity, typage, and representation. But while Lahore cinema as a cultural form cannot be understood without taking its complex linkages with Bombay and larger South Asia into account, the production and circulation of films have also been shaped by country-specific policies and reception.[14] The national social and infrastructural context therefore needs to be assessed accordingly. I have striven to maintain a judicious balance between the specificities of the national circumstances and the larger cultural aspirations and imaginaries of the cinematic form.

While this study examines a later era than the periods Vasudevan and Rajadhyaksha have discussed above, the distinctive genres and cinematic tropes that had developed in earlier periods, especially the Muslim social, and the resonances these evoke across time, space, and mediums remain salient, as they reverberate across the long sixties. Although I analyze exemplary films in relation to transformations in society and political economy, it is primarily the aesthetic problems of form, narrative, and language that I am concerned with, and what they enable in their capacity for sensory stimulus and in their social address in the "cinematic public sphere."[15] Above all, I foreground reflexivity as it evokes historical events and inherited fragments of cultural memory that incorporate fable, or the "cinema-effects" of this promiscuous medium, as it enacts recursive instantiations in form, narrative, and affect.[16] These qualities have arguably rendered commercial cinema in much of South Asia as the most significant cultural form in its capacity to address diverse publics during the twentieth century.

This volume's introduction begins by sketching the background of Lahore cinema before the midfifties, situating especially the transformations in the wake of the Partition of 1947, which led to the exodus of numerous important personnel but also brought many migrants to Lahore with prior experience in Bombay cinema. A brief account of the development of the film song in Bombay during the forties and fifties follows, as the song constitutes a most significant element of the fifties and sixties social film from Bombay and Lahore. Next, I trace the cultural politics of the Ayub Khan era, salient for understanding how filmmakers negotiated this period of military rule. I subsequently analyze the putative parasitic dependence of Lahore cinema on Bombay by thinking through their mutually constitutive relationship across 1947. An elaboration of the concept of the Lahore effect, a significant and resonant formulation for this study, follows. Finally, I reflect on the consequences of the absence of an official archive for the cinema of Pakistan and of a parallel amnesia among the younger generations with regard to its complex legacy.

Chapter 1 examines the appeal of neorealism for thoughtful filmmakers during the fifties in South Asia and specifically in Lahore. *Jago Hua Savera* (A new day dawns, 1959), directed by A. J. Kardar, with the screenplay and lyrics contributed by leftist poet Faiz Ahmed Faiz, is the only prominent example of a neorealist Urdu film from Pakistan during the long sixties. Its team included personnel from the cultural left in Calcutta, and its elements included dialogue and songs drawn from the Bengali folk background. Set in East Bengal, *Jago Hua Savera* shuttles between a humanist vision of traditional rural life as timeless and perennial and a progressive understanding of rural exploitation and poverty as having become unsustainable. For its local release, it included a color song-and-dance sequence, thus also venturing into a melodramatic register. Rather than analyze the film as a unified totality, I see it as a riven and divided form that is potentially productive as instigation for continued engagement and experimentation.

The focus of chapter 2 is on Khurshid Anwar (1912–84), who began his career as a music director and later worked on several important films during the fifties and sixties as writer and director. In his youth, Khurshid Anwar had been involved in anticolonial activities in Lahore inspired by the revolutionary Bhagat Singh (1907–31) but disavowed Marxism, instead embracing a lyric romanticism in his later film work. Anwar's Lahore films weave centrally around the conflict between the "East" and the "West." They render this tension distinctive by the role music plays in its invitation to heal the unbearable consequences of this divide. In a further twist, the "East" here has a prelapsarian evocation that harks back to a conception of India before its dismemberment at the Partition in 1947. In this sense, this elegiac body of work is suffused with melancholic romanticism and offers an implied address that is sharply at variance with the claims of Pakistani nationalism.

I return again to filmmakers inspired by a broadly leftist vision in chapter 3. An important branch of the All-India Progressive Writers' Association was in Lahore, where many prominent writers were affiliated with this movement since the midthirties. The filmmakers who emerged from this matrix include the directors Khalil Qaiser and Riaz Shahid, and lyricists Habib Jalib and Faiz Ahmed Faiz, who are leading figures in Urdu poetry. These directors and writers made several significant films that tackle imperialism and everyday exploitation in a social and melodramatic register. Their efforts can be understood as enacting a cinematic public sphere that participates in but is also discrepant with nationalist projections. The focus in this chapter is on their social films—including one directed by Iqbal

Shehzad based on a short story by Saadat Hasan Manto—that foreground the broad leftist examination of modern everyday life and address exploitation through melodramatic tropes and lyric poetry.

Finally, chapter 4 jumps several decades ahead to examine a 2013 Punjabi-language production directed by Meenu Gaur and Farjad Nabi. The film narrates the story of three young men who attempt fatal encounters with their lives to leave a society that presents little possibility for forward movement. *Zinda Bhaag* (Run for life) is highly intermedial and reflexive. It returns in many ways to earlier cinema, by juxtaposing realism and fable and activating lineages of cultural memory in oral and cinematic mediums from across South Asia. Its fabling draws on other imaginative modes—literature, poetry, and theater—to transform them into new, fantastic modes of aspiration promised by neoliberal entrepreneurial effort, participation in shadowy economic schemes, and physical migration. This film, made decades after the others examined in the previous chapters, nevertheless serves as an important recapitulation of the salience of the Lahore effect into the present and makes for an appropriate finale to this study.

ACKNOWLEDGMENTS

This book has taken a very long time to research and write, and I have accumulated innumerable debts that this short note cannot adequately acknowledge.

Over the years, Kamran Asdar Ali's friendship and his abiding encouragement and feedback have been most valuable for my engagement with Urdu cinema. He has been a vital interlocutor in cinema studies of Pakistan, which essentially did not exist as an academic field until a few years ago and in whose establishment he has played a pioneering role. His scholarship on the organized left in Pakistan and its cultural manifestations has been crucial for my own thinking about commercial cinema as a form and its entanglements with society and politics. Lotte Hoek and Sanjukta Sunderason have provided detailed and generous feedback on *Jago Hua Savera* in workshops in Edinburgh in 2016 and Austin in 2017, and subsequently. Hoek's work on cinema in Bangladesh/East Pakistan before and after 1971 and her study of industrial exchanges between Dhaka, Karachi, and Lahore have been deeply illuminating. Ravi Vasudevan's writings on midcentury Bombay cinema have been extremely salient for my own thinking about the social film in Lahore. Moreover, his indefatigable initiative as founding editor of the leading journal *BioScope: South Asian Screen Studies* has immeasurably enriched the study of cinema across South Asia since its founding in 2010. Vasudevan kindly invited me to serve as an editorial advisor of *BioScope* at its launch, and over the years I have greatly benefited from this association. A central formulation for this work draws from Ashish Rajadhyaksha's conception of the Lahore effect. Rajadhyaksha elaborated on this at the Lahore Biennale 01 Academic Forum I had organized in 2018 in Lahore, and in our subsequent communication. I deeply appreciate Lalitha Gopalan's advice and counsel over many years. Her influential analysis of Bombay action cinema has been formative for the discipline and for my own thinking. Aamir Mufti's perspective on Faiz's Urdu lyric poetry has shaped my understanding of the central role of the song in the social film. Zahid

Chaudhary read parts of this manuscript and offered incisive suggestions. He has been unfailingly generous with his feedback over the years and also counseled on the title of this study. Sonal Khullar has been gracious with her thoughtful advice and has offered ongoing methodological and practical guidance in bringing this project to completion.

I have presented aspects of this work in multiple venues. At the Beyond Crisis: A Critical Second Look at Pakistan workshop at Johns Hopkins University in 2006, I received thoughtful advice from organizer Naveeda Khan, respondent Aamir Mufti, and several of the other participants. Kamran Asdar Ali has made it possible for me to present on multiple occasions at the University of Texas at Austin. Ravi Vasudevan invited me to present at the conference The Many Lives of Indian Cinema: 1913–2013 and Beyond: Disciplines, Histories, Technologies, Futures at the Centre for the Study of Developing Societies (CSDS), New Delhi, in 2014, which proved to be an opportunity to meet many established and emerging scholars. I thank Vazira Zamindar and Asad A. Ahmed for including me in the program of the film festivals on Pakistani cinema they organized, at Brown University in 2014 and at Harvard University in 2015. I thank the organizers of the plenary session of the forty-eighth Annual Conference on South Asia in Madison, Wisconsin, in 2019 for inviting me to present on *Zinda Bhaag*. Meenu Gaur has been most helpful in answering my queries on the making of *Zinda Bhaag*, at the film festival at Brown and later at Princeton University on Zahid Chaudhary's invitation. Ali Khan and Ali Nobil Ahmad's publishing initiatives on scholarship on Pakistani cinema (and including my own work) have enabled the field to become more established. My conversations with Salima Hashmi on Lahore cinema of the sixties and seventies have been insightful in gaining a sense of the ethos of that period.

Others who have offered advice and support at various junctures or whose work I have drawn from include Tariq Omar Ali, Isabel Huacuja Alonso, Shaina Anand, Anjali Arondekar, Nilanjana Bhattacharjya, Moinak Biswas, Arif Rahman Chughtai, Raza Ali Dada, Manishita Dass, Esha Niyogi De, Madhuri Desai, J. Daniel Elam, Haris Gazdar, Durba Ghosh, Will Glover, Zebunnisa Hamid, Rabia Hassan, Syed Akbar Hyder, Usha Iyer, Ayesha Jatoi, Nadeem Khalid, Naveeda Khan, Gwendolyn Kirk, Khalid Mahmood, Naila Mahmood, Parvez Mahmood, Ranjani Mazumdar, Monika Mehta, Rini Bhattacharya Mehta, Farina Mir, Chris Moffat, Debashree Mukherjee, Madhuja Mukherjee, Hira Nabi, Tejaswini Niranjana, Asif Noorani, Hoori Noorani, Rauf Parekh, Mustapha Kamal Pasha, Geeta Patel,

Nasreen Rehman, Yousuf Saeed, Salma Siddique, Harleen Singh, Layli Uddin, Hasan Zaidi, and Mazhar Zaidi.

The appeal of Pakistani films from the 1950s through the 1970s can be gleaned from the recollection and career of two friends, whose later work is not normally associated with this cinema. Both are now unfortunately deceased. In many conversations, Saba Mahmood, a leading scholar of anthropology and religion, would fondly recall her cinephilia for Urdu cinema when she was living in Karachi during her early years. And it is not generally known that I. A. Rehman, a foremost public advocate for human rights in Pakistan, was a film critic for about a decade, writing a weekly column in *Pakistan Times* from the mid-1950s, and whose writings addressed Hollywood, Indian, and Pakistani films.

Abdul Ghaffar ("Ghaffar bhai") at Rainbow Center, Karachi, made available DVDs of many of the films discussed in this work. Anjum Taseer kindly supplied me with a DVD copy of *Jago Hua Savera*. Khawaja Irfan Anwar, Guddu Khan, and Haroon Siddiqui provided rare archival materials. In Lahore, Qudsia Rahim has generously enabled my research on multiple occasions. I thank Aimon Fatima and others at the Lahore Biennale Foundation for procuring hard-to-find publications. I express deep thanks to Naila Mahmood in Karachi for her encompassing help in multiple field research trips and in sourcing materials, and for supervising Asim Muhammad Ameen, who assisted me in fieldwork. Ateeb Gul has transliterated the Urdu text, and Harris Khalique and Aamir Mufti have offered valuable advice on translating key terms and lyrics.

I thank the Global South Asia series editors, Padma Kaimal, K. Sivaramakrishnan, and Anand A. Yang for their support of this project. Comments by the two anonymous reviewers on an earlier draft of the manuscript have greatly improved the book in numerous ways. Lorri Hagman, Joeth Zucco, and the team at the University of Washington Press that includes Chad Attenborough, Beth Fuget, Kait Heacock, and David Schlangen have expertly brought this project to realization. Carole Stone copyedited an early draft of this manuscript, and Elizabeth Mathews carefully did the final copyediting. I thank Lisa DeBoer for preparing the index. This volume has been made available in open access format with the support of a TOME ("Towards an Open Manuscript Ecosystem") award from Cornell University Library.

Colleagues at Cornell University's Institute for Comparative Modernities (ICM) have provided sustained encouragement and advice over the years. Friend, mentor, and colleague Salah Hassan has been unfailing in his support for my academic, scholarly, and artistic work for over two decades. My colleagues at ICM, especially Esra Akcan, Fouad Makki, Natalie Melas, and Viranjini Munasinghe, have been enthusiastic in their support. I thank Daniel Bass, manager at the Cornell South Asia Program, for his work in bringing speakers and performers on South Asian music and cinema to campus. Bass is also a DJ of *Monsoon Radio* on WRFI 88.1 FM, keeping the South Asian film song regularly on air in Ithaca. Colleagues at the Department of History of Art have been very supportive of my research for many years and have provided a most hospitable environment for faculty and graduate students to research neglected and emerging areas in art and visual culture.

Research for this project was financially supported at Cornell by the Department of History of Art, the South Asia Program, and the Society for the Humanities. I am deeply grateful to Cornell University Library for making available materials from their own collections and through interlibrary services. Their services have been essential in finding rare publications from their own collections and those scattered in various libraries across North America. The American Institute of Pakistan Studies has assisted me in numerous ways in conducting research in Pakistan.

Above all, Elizabeth Dadi has been a constant partner in a scholarly and artistic engagement with cinema. Our collaborative art practice for over two decades owes much to our understanding of the cinematic as a mode of production and perception and as it unfolds in diverse genres and global sites. A selection of these projects can be found at our artistic website www.dadiart.net. Rehan Dadi assisted in multiple ways in research and over the years has enjoyed his exposure to the social and the *masala* film.

My mother, Dr. Shamim Dadi, was born in Bareilly and educated in Lucknow and at the Aligarh Muslim University, before moving to Karachi, where she attended Dow Medical College in the wake of the Partition in 1947. She worked for many years as a physician at the Lady Dufferin Hospital and subsequently established a private practice serving largely low-income and Afghan refugee communities. She was also a serious student of Hindustani classical music, with *ustads* who would come to our house every afternoon during the week for many years. She was also a devoted fan of cinema songs from the golden age of Bombay and Lahore. Throughout her adult life, she remained a vociferous critic of the destructive and divisive effects the Partition has had on society and culture in South Asia. This book is dedicated to her memory.

Chapter 1 (with minor changes) has been previously published in Lotte Hoek and Sanjukta Sunderason, eds., *Forms of the Left: Left-Wing Aesthetics and Postcolonial South Asia* (London: Bloomsbury, 2021). Chapter 4 is an expanded and revised version of the essay published earlier in Vazira Zamindar and Asad Ali, eds., *Love, War & Other Longings: Essays on Cinema in Pakistan* (Karachi: Oxford University Press, 2019).

A NOTE ON TRANSLATION AND TRANSLITERATION

This book is intended for a wide readership. Accordingly, I have broadly adopted the following conventions in order to offer a simplified and readable transliteration of Urdu terms:

- Song lyrics, dialogue, and concepts follow the Library of Congress guidelines, with the exception of using *ch* instead of *c* for the letter *ch*.
- In most cases, the final *h* is omitted (*qiṣṣa* instead of *qiṣṣah*).
- Hindi and Urdu terms in wide usage in English are spelled according to their common usage (*ghungroo, munshi, qawwali,* et cetera).
- Titles in the citations and the bibliography omit all transliteration characters except for the *'ain* as ' and the *hamza* as '.
- Proper names of people and film titles are sometimes listed in English with variant spellings. I have aimed for consistency based on the most common usage and guided by IMDb listing but have generally retained variant spellings in quotations, citations, and bibliography.

Unless otherwise noted, all translations from the Urdu are mine.

LAHORE CINEMA

INTRODUCTION

The Lahore Effect

CINEMA HAS AN IMPORTANT HISTORY WELL BEFORE 1947 IN Lahore, and the close relation between Bombay and Lahore from the early period has been most significant. Many actors, music directors, and film directors from Lahore, Punjab, and regions west of Punjab had gone on to have prominent careers in Bombay and Calcutta during the thirties and forties. With the coming of sound to Bombay cinema in 1931, the need for actors and playback singers with facility in Urdu/Hindi/Hindustani was needed in Bombay, as this diction consolidated itself as the linguistic register of the Bombay film subsequently.[1] Speakers of Urdu, the official provincial language of Punjab, spoken by and written by its residents—whether they were Hindu, Muslim, or Sikh—thus possessed an important advantage in Bombay cinema, as did the residents of the Hindko- and Pashto-speaking regions west of the Punjab, who were familiar with Urdu.[2] Another important lubricant in the relays between Lahore and Bombay was the rise of speculative and informal capital during the thirties and forties. During this period, financiers from the Punjab who were unable to legally invest in agricultural land now turned to other ventures, including backing cinema productions.[3]

In Lahore, the Bhatti Gate location in the old city has been nicknamed "Lahore's Chelsea" because it produced a remarkable number of writers, poets, and singers, as well as cinema professionals, many of whom had moved to Bombay in the thirties and forties to work in its growing film industry.[4] Prominent examples include the director Abdul Rashid Kardar (1904–89), who had directed a silent film in Lahore in 1929 before moving to Calcutta during the thirties and subsequently moving permanently to Bombay, and who mentored important actors, writers, music directors, and playback singers, many of whom migrated to Lahore after 1947.[5]

Lahore had produced numerous films in Urdu and Punjabi before 1947.[6] Historian Ishtiaq Ahmed notes that "Lahore's reputation as a filmmaking centre was established firmly when Roop Lal Shori . . . began to produce films such as *Qismat Ke Her Pher* [The twists of fate] (1931). . . . Later,

D. M. Pancholi, a Gujarati, set up a studio in Lahore, and suddenly the Lahore industry began to be viewed as an up-and-coming competitor to Bombay."[7] During the early forties especially, commercially successful productions included *Khazanchi* (The treasurer, 1941), *Khandan* (Family, 1942), and *Dasi* (The maid, 1944). The singer and actress Noor Jehan (1926–2000), the writer Saadat Hasan Manto (1912–55), and music director Khurshid Anwar (1912–84) are among the major figures from Lahore or the Punjab associated with Bombay cinema who moved during or after 1947 to Lahore, where they made vital contributions to its cinema.[8]

POST-1947 DEVELOPMENTS

The studios in Lahore before 1947 were owned primarily by Hindu families—the Pancholis and the Shoreys.[9] Their exodus to postcolonial India in 1947 along with many experienced personnel, and the violence and chaos at the time, left the infrastructure of film production in the city in shambles. It took some time to again furnish its studios, train technical personnel, and promote a new ensemble of actors and actresses.[10] While Bombay had many recognized film stars whose charisma and media presence resonated with a large and loyal film audience, in Lahore in the early years after 1947, there were hardly any recognizable stars, the exception being the celebrated actress and singer Noor Jehan.[11] The fledgling Lahore-based filmmakers lacked access to the scale of capital that the Bombay filmmakers enjoyed, nor could they draw on a pool of experienced field personnel with expertise in camerawork, editing, sound, lighting, and publicity.[12] All of these needed time to develop, namely about a decade after independence.

The city's film industry post-1947 was primarily developed by migrants with experience in the film industry of Bombay and Calcutta.[13] The directors W. Z. Ahmed (1916–2007), Sibtain Fazli (1914–85), Anwar Kamal Pasha (1925–87), and Shaukat Hussain Rizvi (1914–99) are among the pioneer directors of the postindependence era.[14] They were supplemented by those already in Lahore, including "talented people like Hakim Ahmed Shuja, Imtiaz Ali Taj, Qateel Shifai, Baba Alam Siaposh, Shatir Ghaznavi, Deewan Sardari Lal, Asha Posley."[15] Noor Jehan and her husband, director Shaukat Hussain Rizvi, set up the first postindependence film studio in Lahore, and "Anwar Kamal Pasha rose as the country's first total film maker who scripted, produced and directed his own films. He also had his own distribution office at Lahore. The son of dramatist Hakim Ahmad Shuja, Anwar Kamal was ... cultured and cultivated. He ... promoted young talent.

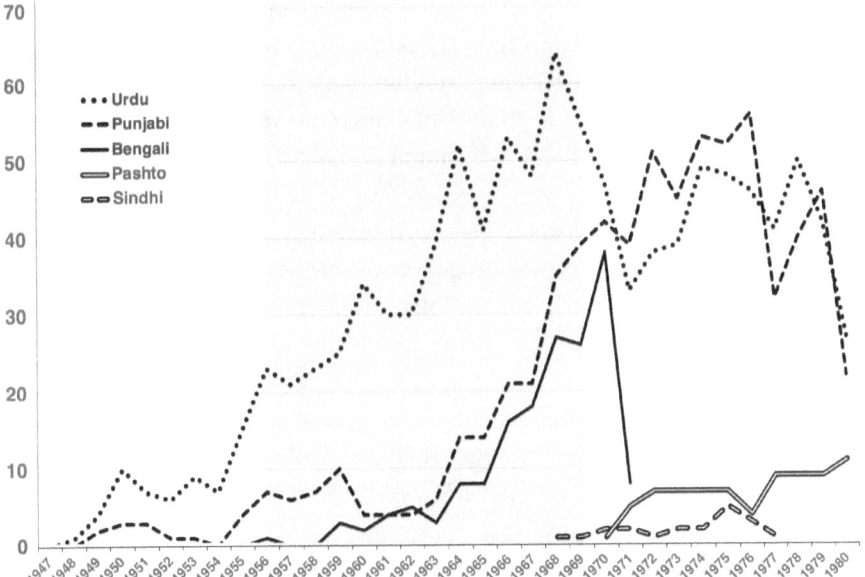

FIG. I.1. Films released in Pakistan in the major languages, 1947–1980. The shaded area demarcates the long sixties (1956–69). Data from *Pakistan Film Magazine*, https://pakmag.net/film/, accessed October 25, 2021. Films released in two languages are added to both graphs.

Dozens of assistant directors, actors and composers graduated under his guidance."[16] Agha A. G. Gul (1913–83), owner of Lahore's Evernew Studios, emerged as the "first mogul of Pakistan," while Jagdish Chand Anand (1922–77) became an important producer and distributor.[17]

Notable Urdu films made in the first decade include *Beqarar* (Restless, 1950, dir. Nazir Ajmeri), *Do Aansoo* (Two tears, 1952, dir. Anwar Kamal Pasha), *Dupatta* (Scarf, 1952, dir. Sibtain Fazli), *Roohi* (1954, dir. W. Z. Ahmed), and *Qatil* (Murderer, 1955, dir. Anwar Kamal Pasha).[18] The first decade produced few major works in Urdu, but notably many important films began to be released from 1956 onward. From a mere seven films in 1954 in the country in all languages, the number multiplied to no fewer than thirty-two just two years later, in 1956 (figure I.1).[19]

Local production was helped by movements against the showing of Indian films in West Pakistan that came to a head in 1954 in what has been termed the "*Jaal* agitation," as the film in question was the 1952 Bombay production *Jaal*, directed by Guru Dutt.[20] Members of the West Pakistani film industry objected to the showing of this film in West Pakistan, where it was being screened by exploitation of a legal loophole for Indian films intended to be screened only in East Pakistan.[21] As Indian cinema imports came to be more restricted from the midfifties on, local cinema saw an analogous rise in the number of productions and improvement in their quality. New Indian films were banned from being imported in 1962, but films already in the country were allowed to be screened, leading to continued demonstrations by the local industry.[22] Indian films were eventually completely banned in 1965 as a consequence of war between India and Pakistan that year. The restriction on the import of Indian films helped producers and directors to develop local cinema, but as film historian Mushtaq Gazdar underscores, it also enabled plagiarists to work more brazenly.[23]

The *Jaal* issue and the larger question of how to compete against Indian imports divided local filmmakers. Directors W. Z. Ahmed, Sibtain Fazli, and Shaukat Hussain Rizvi led the *Jaal* demonstrations in favor of restricting Indian imports.[24] However, in his reminiscences, the music director Khurshid Anwar, who also began producing films in 1956 and directing in 1962, notes:

> I can assure you that I took absolutely no part in that agitation. It was a conspiracy hatched by the producers and other vested interests to have a free hand to commercially exploit the home markets. With the Indian films out of the way it was left to these ignoramuses to dish out fifth rate plagiarized films to a choiceless audience. Some suffered from an unnecessary inferiority complex and thought that banning of Indian films for a certain period would give a chance to our industry to stand on its own feet. You and I have seen the results of course. The correct thing to do was to have signed a barter agreement with India so that a film could be exchanged for a film.[25]

Mushtaq Gazdar's indispensable survey of cinema in Pakistan is based on periods he identifies by decades since the independence of Pakistan. For Gazdar, the years 1957–66 constitute the "Decade of Reformation," while the website cineplot.com labels 1956–66 "The Golden Era." Production and circulation of commercial cinema began to acquire density and coherence during this period.[26] The chronology followed in this book focuses primarily on Urdu cinema from Lahore from c. 1956 to c. 1969, which I propose as constituting *the long sixties*. A degree of political stability created favorable conditions for cinema to flourish. A set of recognizable stars during this period gained recognition, such that by 1956, eleven films "ran long enough to celebrate silver jubilees."²⁷ The total number of films released in all languages continued to grow during the long sixties and by 1969 was no fewer than 118.²⁸

Technological and infrastructural transformation are important factors in cinema's development in this era. In addition to the overall Ayub-era state-led modernization, and the promotion of capitalist industrialization, the cinema and its audience were facing continuous structural, institutional, and perceptual changes. In Dhaka, the first full-length feature was released in 1956, and good state facilities for film production were set up. In Karachi, Eastern Film Studios was established as a well-equipped studio, and a well-produced English-language film magazine, *Eastern Film*, began to be published regularly from 1959 (figure I.2).

The influential annual Nigar film awards commenced in 1958.²⁹ Industry observers remark that by the late sixties, Lahore films of possessed a quality of swiftness in their narrative unfolding, enacting modernization in the very temporal structure of the film. For example, on the film *Devar Bhabi* (Brother-in-law and sister-in-law, 1967, dir. Hassan Tariq), Yasin Gorija remarks, "The screenplay was written to create a very brisk narrative [*nihāyat chust likhā gayā thā*] and to maintain the pace, much of the interpretation was entrusted to the audience."³⁰

The sense of a more informed audience in 1967 that possessed the ability to understand the cinematic language of the commercial film—with its various genres and techniques such as temporal ellipsis, montage editing, the song-and-dance sequence, and realism shot through with elements of fantasy—is in marked contrast to the comment by another industry observer, Zakhmi Kanpuri, on the early serpent film *Nagin* (Serpent, 1959, dir. Khalil Qaiser), whose theme, Kanpuri notes, was made for the first time in Pakistan: "In those days, people's critical faculties were not fully formed [*logon kā shu'ūr bhī us daur men ziyāda pukhta nahīn thā*], they naively believed what they read or saw on screen."³¹ The ongoing modernization of consciousness and sensibility, the acceleration of temporality, and their manifestation in art, architecture, interiors, fashion, and bodily comportment gathers pace in Pakistan throughout the sixties, and this is both palpable and spearheaded in the cinema.

Color film stock is among the major technological changes that began to be used more widely in films during the sixties. The first movie in full color was an Urdu film from Dhaka, *Sangam* (Confluence, 1964, dir. Zahir Raihan). By the end of the decade, blockbuster films in color such as *Andaleeb* (1969, dir. Farid Ahmad) and *Zerqa* (1969, dir. Riaz Shahid) were

FIG. I.2. Actor Rattan Kumar embracing Neelo on the cover of *Eastern Film* 4, no. 7 (February 1963).

being released. The shift to color is an important facet of the aesthetic and thematic transformations in the post-1971 context during the government of Zulfiqar Ali Bhutto, whose populist rhetoric and relaxation of censorship codes also meant that new themes, regional motifs, and a more kinetic body language began to transform seventies cinema.[32] Post-1971, Punjabi-language productions also overtake Urdu cinema in the number of films produced.³³ The cinema of the seventies thus merits a separate examination, which falls beyond the scope of this study.³⁴

THE FILM SONG AND THE SOCIAL FILM

The centrality of the film song constitutes a distinguishing feature of commercial South Asian cinema between 1940 and 1980. Indeed, songs are so pivotal to movies that the few films made without songs during this period are the exception that prove the rule and are usually ones that aspire to noncommercial values and select audiences. Viewed from an avant-garde perspective, especially by many Western critics, the film song in South Asia is often a puzzling and unwelcome presence, as it disturbs many of the assumptions attached to narrative coherence.³⁵ For many critics, the presence of the film song also places these films unfavorably against experimental and even Third Cinema.

With its intensified affective charge, the romantic and imaginative ethos of the film song has a decisive place in the social melodramatic film from Bombay and Lahore, as it most intensively imbricates realism and fantasy and inseparably weaves together evidentiary history and utopian aspirations. While these films may be characterized as melodrama, or as musicals, these terms do not begin to capture the most distinguishing characteristics of this cinema that departs also from normative Hollywood expectations. The significance of songs in the dramatic traditions of South Asia long predates the arrival of the talkies in India, beginning in 1931. The *Natyashastra*, a Sanskrit aesthetic text on the dramatic arts, includes a discussion of the song as being central to dramatic narrative. Folk theater and oral performing traditions in many parts of South Asia include songs. In the Krishna, Bhakti, and Sufi traditions from the early modern era onward, devotional poetry has been set to music, creating a rich repository that poets and music composers could draw from in cinema.³⁶

Incorporating song into urban theater is a major development in Parsi theater, which flourished in Bombay after the 1860s and was performed in cities across South Asia well into the twentieth century. The first Urdu-language play in Bombay was commissioned in 1871.³⁷ Subsequently, plays in Urdu and Hindi became standard repertoire in Parsi theater, along with those in Gujarati and other languages.³⁸ Another important lineage is the opera *Indar Sabha*, written in Lucknow by Agha Hasan Amanat in 1853 and performed "with special lighting and musical effects" in Bombay in 1873.³⁹ From the mid-nineteenth century onward, Parsi theater included songs as part of dramatic performance.[40] The technological apparatus and various ruses deployed in enhancing the theatricality of Parsi theater would subsequently morph into the magical effects early cinema rendered through editing and special effects. Several Parsi theater plays were made into films, including the *Indar Sabha* in 1931 as an early sound film. The theater scholar Kathryn Hansen notes, "[*Indar Sabha*] returned to its viewers a spectacular, romanticized vision of its collective past, it facilitated the very production of spectatorship within the new environment of the public commercial theatre. Even in the modern trappings of the proscenium arch, the figure of Indar surrounded by his court of admiring beauties constructed a visual icon that synthesized religious, erotic, and political modes of self-identification.... The implantation of performative song and dance sequences before a pictorialized audience remained a defining feature of the narrative structure of Indian cinema."[41]

Many other plays written in Urdu for the Parsi theater were also realized later as films. These include several plays by the celebrated playwright Agha Hashr Kashmiri, who also wrote screenplays for films.[42] Even though Parsi theater started with Gujarati and English-language productions, after the 1870s, a significant number of plays were performed in Hindi and Urdu. The turn to Urdu expanded the appeal of Parsi theater to other communities and allowed for Parsi theater to travel to other cities. The language also enabled playwrights to draw upon Urdu's vast repertoire of poetic and rhetorical resources in writing dialogue and songs. "Urdu poetic art and public speech were highly esteemed," notes Hansen, adding, "By adopting Urdu, the Parsi theater embraced more than a language or community. It gained an entire vocabulary of pleasure, and one that had the advantage of lacking a territorial boundary."[43]

Silent film had a benefit in addressing the vast linguistic diversity of the audience, although this was by no means a straightforward issue even during that era.[44] With the coming of sound in 1931, the question of language became absolutely central, because audiences whose primary familiarity was with Bengali, Marathi, or Tamil, for example, could not be expected to fully understand a film not made in these languages. Arguably, the song, with its musical and lyric character, helped overcome these linguistic divisions, despite being rendered in North Indian language registers. Until today, audiences from across South Asia and even internationally, who may not understand much Hindi or Urdu, nevertheless fondly recall film song lyrics and tunes. This also helps to explain why Bombay—despite its lack of a native community whose members speak these languages as their mother tongue, but being a capitalist city full of migrants from across India—became the most important center for the production of Hindi and Urdu cinema.

Early sound films typically included dozens of songs. For example, the first talkie, *Alam Ara* (1931) had no fewer than thirty songs. In these early sound films, the songs were recorded live, and therefore actors performing in the film also had to be good singers and musicians. Improving technology made possible the transition to playback singing.[45] Cinematic mise-en-scène also suggested to the filmmakers creative possibilities for expanding the spatial domain of sound during the song sequence, far beyond the immediate environs of the actors singing the songs. In an insightful essay on the actress and singer Noor Jehan, Ashraf Aziz has observed that her vocal collaboration with music director Master Ghulam Haider during the forties created a kind of a soundtrack for the accelerating modernity in urban South Asia: "Whereas earlier songs were constructed around melody, Ghulam Haider based his songs on rhythm and percussion."[46] Haider deployed the "dholak, the Punjabi folk drum . . . often played at a brisk pace, brought a sparkling fluidity to the song," and "the dholak-driven, bubbly popular song documented the gathering pace of Indian history better."[47]

Gregory Booth has analyzed how the film industry addressed challenges and possibilities during the first fifteen years since the coming of sound, paving the way for creating a position of centrality of the song to the film. According to Booth, while the Bombay film song witnessed a number of significant aesthetic and professional transitions between 1931 and 1946, its place in the golden-age music of the fifties and sixties was consolidated right after independence: "From roughly 1948 through 1952, many of these incremental changes and other, still more recent developments coalesced into a set of sonic, stylistic, industrial, and cinematic norms that came to define the music of the Hindi cinema over the subsequent 20 or more years."[48] Khurshid Anwar began his career in films as a Bombay-based music director in 1940 and continued working there till 1952, which means that he would have been intimately familiar with the way music and song was becoming integral to melodramatic cinema in this formative period. While earlier scholarship had claimed that the film song had a contingent and modular relationship to the film narrative, recent scholarship has stressed its inextricable centrality to the films of the forties through the seventies.[49] Anna Morcom elaborates:

> Hindi films have a narrative style and structure that is designed for songs, and similarly, film songs are able to fit around cinematic scenes. The

Hindi film narrative has a number of devices for incorporating songs. It is non-linear and the story usually pauses, though not always completely, whilst song sequences take place. The stories themselves assimilate songs by having scenes which take place in musical surroundings . . . film songs incorporate Hindi films in a parallel way to how Hindi films incorporate songs. They contain interludes during which movement and action can take place, they are often "gapped" or have "add-ons" in their musical idiom that negotiate changes of point of view, location, emotion and action, Furthermore, they employ conventions for the musical expression of character, location, emotion, action, and for the perceived grandeur of the cinematic medium itself.[50]

In terms of circulation, marketing, aura, and afterlife, the song has far wider effects than only its being viewed on the screen inside a theater. As much as the film song occupies a central place in the movie, it also constitutes the dominant aspects of popular music when it is detached from the film and saturated across public and private domains. "Popular music in the Indian subcontinent is unique because it consists almost completely of *filmigit*, that is, songs originally featured in the movies," notes Biswarup Sen.[51] Thus songs made for the cinema also achieved the status of becoming the dominant popular music in South Asia. Constantly heard in humble cafés, markets, the workplace, and the domestic sphere, as well as in buses and rickshaws, it overflowed national borders, class divisions, and linguistic, ethnic, and gender divides. The widespread circulation of the film song on radio, vinyl, and cassette tapes from the forties through the seventies meant that the film song assumed an importance that constituted no less than the soundtrack of modern life in much of South Asia.

CULTURAL POLITICS OF THE AYUB KHAN ERA

The long sixties (1956–69) in Pakistan incorporates the era of the regime of President Ayub Khan, beginning in 1958 and continuing until his abdication from rule in 1969. The period from the early fifties already established trends in political economy and culture that the Ayub Khan government would build upon. Pakistan was under authoritarian rule from its very beginning in 1947 and soon after independence became closely aligned with the United States during the Cold War. The nation was saddled with antipopulist and fundamentally antidemocratic regimes that continued under Ayub Khan's rule. The decade of the sixties ended with a period of great political instability: the disturbances of the late sixties led to the overthrow of the Ayub Khan government and soon after that, in 1971, war with India and the breakup of the country with the loss of half of the population. Bangladesh's founding in 1971 was preceded by atrocities on a massive scale by the Pakistan army against the residents of East Pakistan. The independence of Bangladesh radically truncated Pakistan, which had been composed of an East and a West wing since 1947.

Mostly, the Ayub Khan era was primarily a time of centralized political stability and governance, rapid development of institutions, and generally bourgeois liberal values.[52] The fissures and contradictions of this period of authoritarian rule need to be underscored, as filmmakers had to negotiate this matrix of constraints and possibilities. Gazdar's assessment on the ethos of the period is apposite: "The way in which Ayub Khan manoeuvred to assume total political control over the country is questionable, but his outlook towards economic and social reforms undoubtedly was modern and progressive. He was a tolerant person with a secular outlook. The Censor Board during his reign reflected the President's attitude when films like A. J. Kardar's *Jago Hua Savera*, Saifuddin Saif's *Kartar Singh*, Hassan Tariq's *Neend*, Zia Sarhadi's *Rahguzar*, Khalil Qaiser's *Clerk*, Danish Dervi's *Aur Bhi Gham Hein*, and Raza Mir's *Lakhon Mein Aik* were allowed general release in the country."[53]

The elite liberal values that characterized the Ayub Khan era must be contextualized with Pakistan's close alliance with the United States in the Cold War, in which direct production and control of culture by state apparatchiks would have been seen to be closer to the opposed Soviet paradigm. This is evident in the *Report of the Film Fact Finding Committee, Govt. of Pakistan, Ministry of Industries, April 1960–April 1961*, which stressed that it is "problematic whether aesthetic values can be induced into any form of artistic expression by precept or regulation alone."[54] Published in 1962, this 410-page document is, to my knowledge, by far the most comprehensive report on the state of the industry undertaken by any Pakistani government, and an important resource for understanding infrastructural conditions of the era. Its approach to the desired relationship between the government and the private sector is summarized as follows:

> The film industry has so far been subjected to, little or no control by Government on its production side and having operated as a free enterprise it has achieved a production rate of approximately 35 films a year at Lahore and Karachi and 5 to 7 films a year at Dacca where the East

> Pakistan Film Development Corporation has been instrumental in initiating film production. While free enterprise must have its full play in its field, Pakistan cannot ignore the demands of higher national interest. We have, after carefully considering the evidence placed before us and the example of the film industry of other countries, concluded that the stage has now reached where Government must play its part in helping the development of the industry and bringing to it an atmosphere of security and reasonable prospects of commercial success.[55]

Its considered policy recommendations included regulation reform, better tax incentives, infrastructural support, and multiple other ways for the government to support private sector filmmaking. This included availability of financing, access to better technology, training of cinema personnel, and improvement of public taste by creating institutions modeled on the British Film Institute.[56] These recommendations, however, were not implemented, due to a shift in focus by the government after the 1965 India-Pakistan war, according to Mushtaq Gazdar.[57]

While the Ayub Khan regime was unable to intervene much in the commercial film arena, the Department of Film and Publications became very active, producing short films, newsreels, and propaganda.[58] The News Pictorial was a newsreel showcasing the regime's achievements. It was required to be screened in all theaters before a commercial film, but eventually, "the audience became disgusted with the conscious manipulation of events... [and] would enter cinema halls after the end of government newsreels and documentaries."[59] A notorious work was the feature-length "documentary" glorifying Ayub Khan as the enlightened new savior at the beginning of his rule. *Nai Kiran* (A new ray of light, 1960) was made in five languages, and leading actors such as Noor Jehan were coerced into participating. Gazdar has provocatively compared *Nai Kiran* to nothing less than *Triumph of the Will* (1935, dir. Leni Riefenstahl).[60]

Nai Kiran was based on a short story by Qudratullah Shahab, who became a powerful bureaucrat in the Ayub Khan regime. The contrast between the government's approach to literature and cinema is instructive, as unlike literature, commercial cinema never fully came under the state's ambit. Shahab was himself a writer of some distinction, and his autobiography *Shahabnama* provides much insight into the cultural politics of the era.[61] *Shahabnama* is written in elegant and accessible Urdu prose and makes for compelling reading. His account of the Ayub Khan era is fashioned to portray Shahab himself as endowed with integrity, even as he led or was a front-row participant in consequential actions by the government to control the press and organize literary writers.⁶² The press was muzzled by the takeover in 1959 of the Progressive Papers, which published major newspapers in English and Urdu, and with the formation of the National Press Trust.⁶³ And Shahab himself led and organized literary writers in the government-supported Pakistan Writers' Guild (PWG), founded in 1959, with annual literary prizes underwritten by major private business groups.⁶⁴ Shahab justifies forming the PWG as a way to support struggling writers irrespective of their ideology. He narrates his own role as being a sole voice against other senior bureaucrats who "repeatedly tried to influence Ayub with the idea that under the government's patronage, the PWG is cultivating undesirable and dangerous persons, leading with Faiz Ahmed Faiz, Ahmad Nadeem Qasmi, Shahidullah Kaiser [brother of director Zahir Raihan], Shaukat Siddiqui, Abdullah Husain and others." By contrast, Shahab notes, "Opposing this view, I was the only one close to the President who stressed that among the 1,200 members of the Guild were loyal and capable members."⁶⁵ In Shahab's recollection, he even heroically resisted US pressure exerted on Pakistan in this regard, despite the country's being an impoverished and dependent American ally in a charged Cold War context: "We had made a rule not to accept foreign funding [for the PWG], because at that time our country was in the shackles of American aid. . . . [Because of this refusal] the Americans became suspicious that we are troublemakers and may be accepting Russian support, as our bureaucracy was signaling that the PWG is protecting reds."⁶⁶

Needless to say, Shahab's critics have a less rosy assessment of the objectives behind the formation of the PWG and the role it played during the sixties.⁶⁷ The PWG was clearly an influential institution promoting and shaping the course of literary production during the sixties. Such institutional initiatives need not be understood as being solely repressive, however. Rather, as Foucault might remind us, they are productive and have to reckon with new social and aesthetic trajectories that inevitably arise as a consequence of rapid modernization. Possibly for this reason as well, many leftist writers had become affiliated with the PWG, despite its compromised status.

By contrast, the "people's poet" Habib Jalib emerges as an exemplary resistant figure during the long sixties and beyond.⁶⁸ Jalib has characterized the Ayub Khan era as a terrifying period because he trampled over human rights and deployed all manner of antidemocratic measures to extend his rule.⁶⁹ On the collaboration of many writers with the establishment, he notes, "My fellow poets, from whom I expected support, had instead become self-serving and pro-dictatorship to an alarming degree, and had become merely *careerists* [the English word transcribed in Urdu]."[70] Jalib was a key participant in the film industry, writing lyrics for numerous films, and many of the songs based on his verse have become wildly popular.[71] He perhaps achieved even greater renown as an uncompromising political dissident, repeatedly jailed by the Ayub Khan regime and subsequent governments for publicly reciting poetry critical of official policies.[72] His poem "Dastoor" (Constitution) from 1962 against the Ayub Khan regime remains among his most powerful and influential political poems.[73] Its fame has crossed borders, and it was recited in protests against the government in India in 2019 and 2020, some six decades after its original public recitation.[74] Writer and filmmaker Ahmad Bashir underscores the public appeal of Jalib's dissident verse during the sixties: "During Ayub Khan election campaign [in 1962], when Jalib's movement was restricted, tape recordings of his poetry were nevertheless heard by groups of people numbering in the *lakhs* [hundreds of thousands]. Among writers and poets who took upon themselves to raise public consciousness, hardly anyone can be compared to Jalib who achieved such a thorough and embracing effect in such a short time."[75] Jalib himself explained the wide appeal of his political verse as due to them being suffused with *lyric-ism* (the English word transliterated in Urdu): "Why are my poems so popular? One reason is that I deploy lyric-ism in them. I learnt this from earlier public political rhetoric ... at Mochi Gate [in Lahore]. So, I resolved that I would write poems on important public issues, and subsequently my poems assumed greater public significance than merely making speeches in prose."[76]

The literary domain was consequently a charged field during the long sixties, crosshatched by the political tensions of the era. However, as seen above in the failure of the film report's recommendations to be implemented, commercial cinema largely escaped coming under the purview of Ayub Khan's bureaucrats, but equally, it "involuntarily" has "always remained apolitical in its response to the country's internal state of affairs."[77] Apart from cinema being subject to the Censor Board, a colonial-era arrangement that long predates the Ayub years, it continued to flourish as popular entertainment in a bazaar mode. And for the entire twentieth century, commercial cinema in South Asia has been associated with shadowy and informal financing and has been disparaged for being lowbrow and melodramatic, which does not accord well with attempts at top-down manipulation.[78] Unlike literature, commercial cinema was essentially considered as being too trashy to come under the oversight of state institutions.⁷⁹ That may well be another factor inhibiting implementation of the film report's recommendations.

Although primarily the cinema remained overtly apolitical, critique of the Ayub era did develop in some films, especially by East Pakistani filmmakers, who were also opposed to West Pakistan's domination.⁸⁰ This finds a most significant realization in the Zahir Raihan–directed *Jibon Theke Neya* (Glimpses of life, 1970), ostensibly a melodrama of family dynamics but also a powerful and formally innovative allegory of dictatorial oppression.⁸¹ In Lahore, Riaz Shahid's *Zerqa* (1969), discussed in chapter 3, has been understood as critical reflection on Pakistan's internal power dynamics of the era.⁸² In an interview, Jalib himself characterizes his work for the cinema insightfully: "When I entered the film industry, the environment was very favorable.... There was not much remuneration in writing poetry for films, but it fulfilled me in other ways. My ideas received publicity and reached millions of people. In my poetry, I would include verses on anti-imperialism and anti-feudalism. Often, producers couldn't comprehend what I was doing. But I worked with good producers also, such as my friend Riaz Shahid, who would urge me on saying, 'I'll picturize the biggest insult you can level against existing society.'"⁸³

Overall, the sense of stability through the majority of the Ayub years, even if ultimately illusory and ending very badly, has arguably never been repeated in Pakistan's history. It also means that this period of about a dozen years is marked by a sense of coherence of institutions within a relatively stable political order, which allowed commercial filmmakers and other cultural workers to position themselves in relation to it.

REVERBERATIONS IN BOMBAY AND LAHORE

The intimate and shared aesthetic tropes between Bombay films and the Lahore productions rendered it easy for Lahore-based filmmakers to simply lift stories from Bombay productions. On occasion, even dialogue, song lyrics, and shot compositions were borrowed almost verbatim. Industry observers in Pakistan from the very beginning have drawn considerable attention to this charged and controversial issue. Films that were manifestly copied or plagiarized were termed as *sarqa* or *charba*.⁸⁴ The issue divided the film community between those who saw this as a viable way to make local films based on commercially successful predecessors and others who decried the reliance on piracy and emphasized instead the need to develop original stories and films.⁸⁵ During the fifties, Indian films were also available to Pakistani audiences. Their circulation had divided the film community between distributors who benefitted financially and local producers and directors who felt that their own productions were at a considerable disadvantage against this formidable competition.⁸⁶

Plagiarism, even in commercial cultural forms, is a serious concern, and it is not my intention to justify the work of those who resorted to copying. And it must be underscored that since the early fifties, a number of thoughtful Pakistani filmmakers persisted in developing original work.⁸⁷ The *charba* can however be diagnosed as a symptom and manifestation of shared lineages as much as being an ethically questionable shortcut to commercial success. The question of similarity and even of direct drawing of stories, themes, dialogue, and lyrics from Bombay productions by the Lahore industry is a deeper issue whose ramifications go beyond the question of mimetic plagiarism or even imaginative borrowing.

Filmmakers who had previously worked in Bombay and had now moved to Lahore would remake a film in Lahore that they had made or contributed to in Bombay earlier.⁸⁸ And apart from the many direct instances of *charba* in Lahore productions, it is the case that Bombay itself had drawn many of its stories and themes from Hollywood, as well as from the Parsi theater, in which Urdu playwrights have played an important role, including the celebrated work of Agha Hashr Kashmiri and Imtiaz Ali Taj, who were associated with Lahore for part or most of their careers, for example. Urdu writers such as Manto wrote for Bombay cinema, and Urdu poets provided lyrics for its songs before and after 1947. Indeed, the leading Indian film scholar Ashish Rajadhyaksha has provocatively characterized much of Bombay cinema of the forties and thereafter itself as being "diasporic": "The resettlement in Bombay of a seminal tradition, the 'Lahore school' of Hindi filmmaking... also draws our attention to the profoundly diasporic nature of the Bombay-based Hindi cinema. The Bombay cinema, articulating a Sindhi–Punjabi–Pathan diaspora, is a cinema with no state. Its tremendous impact upon modern Indian culture forces us to speculate on the considerably wider domain of the deployment of minority history as a displaced popular culture."⁸⁹ These correspondences between Bombay cinema and Lahore cinema form the bedrock for expression in new cinematic works, as they both draw from and elaborate on a vast and shared reservoir of cultural legacies even as they create new works addressing their present. This is especially the case for Lahore cinema during the long sixties.

The Partition engendered an affect of truncation in the psyche of the generation of filmmakers who traversed it. Was the partial loss of the self compensated for by a compulsive recourse to repetition not only via rampant and open plagiarism but also in original works? This observation becomes more salient when one notes that it is precisely a "symptomatic" film blatantly propagandizing Pakistani nationalism that is guilty of the greatest degree of plagiarism. This is *Bedari* (1957), which Gazdar terms a "carbon copy" of *Jagriti* (1954), and both even starred the same child actor in an identical role, namely Rattan Kumar, who had migrated to Pakistan in 1956 (see figure I.2).[90] Even at the other end of the spectrum, in works that are original, such as in the films of Khurshid Anwar examined in chapter 2, uncanny doubling is a persistent leitmotif. Anwar's films can be understood as Partition allegories, in which characters often play a double role and are often mistaken for each other, as in *Intezar* (1956), or a present fraught relationship between a husband and a wife is haunted by the specter of previous Hindu lovers, in *Ghoonghat* (1962).[91]

Pakistani audiences were already habituated to the marked use of Urdu diction and rhetoric in Bombay films of the 1940s–70s, and familial associations of key Bombay personnel with the territories of West Pakistan also kept these imaginative linkages alive: these include the families of the Raj Kapoor dynasty and actor Dilip Kumar's family, which were both from Peshawar; poet Gulzar, who hails from the Jhelum District in the Punjab; Dilip Kumar's brother Nasir Khan, who acted in Lahore cinema in the early years after 1947; the distributor J. C. Anand, who is related to Indian actress Juhi Chawla; and so on.[92] Indeed, the scale of interconnections between Lahore and Bombay before 1947 defies summarization. And after 1947, many film personnel from India who had a background either in Lahore or in the Punjab made a move to Lahore and settled there. Significantly, this phenomenon did not simply occur only during 1947, but the migration of field personnel to Lahore, and sometimes the reverse migration from Lahore to Bombay, continued throughout the fifties, and even into the early sixties. Later migrants from Bombay to Lahore include the directors Zia Sarhadi and S. M. Yusuf, for example.

The relation between Lahore and Bombay cinema is not confined to the film itself but extends into a wider field of meaning and signification through the production and circulation of charged extrafilmic domains. These include star texts, the widespread leakage of the song into everyday life, and interfilmic and intermedial citations, as well as the political connotations of cinema. None of these are confined to national borders. Rajadhyaksha consequently suggests the need to rethink the cinema of South Asia as participating in this immense realm of signification, which he terms "cinema-effects."[93] Cinema-effects reverberate across many domains. In theme, they echo cultural forms from the past and prefigure future productions. They are inherently interfilmic in this regard, across a *longue durée*, sometimes venturing far back to oral and mythological tropes, Parsi theater, folk forms, novels, Hollywood, Victorian Gothic literature, and most importantly, other South Asian film productions. This is the case, for example, in the serpent film genre, which draws from Hindu and Buddhist mythology and folk motifs and has also been made in Lahore a number of times post-1947, even when the vast majority of Pakistan has been Muslim.[94] In characterization and typage, films in various genres draw upon sedimented figurations and unsettle them toward new ends. Through legal and informal distribution, they constantly spill across geographic bounds and medias. For example, cinema stars from both India and Pakistan find themselves on calendars, posters, and postcards and in magazine images that have very wide circulation in Pakistan, as decor in people's homes, in *pān* (betel leaf) shops, and on vehicles and in restaurants.

The audio of song-and-dance sequences travels exceedingly well, creating ubiquitous sonic and aural fields in public and private spaces across South Asia. Its appeal was used to great effect by Radio Ceylon, for example, which broadcast Hindi film songs regularly when these songs were banned at All India Radio in the early 1950s for about half a decade; these songs found eager listeners in Pakistan as well.[95] Apart from radio audiences, Bombay film songs circulated in Pakistan on vinyl, and with the coming of the cassette, which enabled inexpensive reproduction of music, films songs arranged in various collections by individuals and small-scale entrepreneurs became a ubiquitous feature of Pakistan's urban sonic fabric, being played constantly in homes, buses, restaurants, and other private and public spaces.[96]

THE LAHORE EFFECT

The polysemic correspondences and resonances between Bombay and Lahore has led Rajadhyaksha to further propose that a "Lahore effect" characterized major Bombay films during the forties, both before and after the Partition of 1947. In his essay titled "The Lahore Effect," based on a presentation delivered in Lahore for the Lahore Biennale 01 in 2018, Rajadhyaksha takes as his focus the theme of Anarkali, the mythical story set in the early seventeenth century of the dancing girl who fell in love with the Mughal prince Salim (who later reigned as Emperor Jahangir between 1605 and 1627) but who was finally immured alive in a wall by Emperor Akbar as a punishment for the transgression of daring to desire his son. This romantic and tragic tale was first written up as a theater play by the Lahore-based playwright Imtiaz Ali Taj in 1922. It was then made into cinema repeatedly in Bombay and in Lahore, culminating in the film *Mughal-e-Azam* (1960, dir. K. Asif), which is among Bombay cinema's most lavish and extravagant productions to this day.[97] The recursive draw of this cinematic story for filmmakers in India and Pakistan is only one influential example of the Lahore effect. What this modality accomplishes is the extension of affiliation of memory across time and space, without regard to genre fidelity or even thematic or narrative coherence: "We may be able to track a specific history, with a backstory and an afterlife, that may turn out to be nothing less than the history of subcontinental cinema itself, now viewed as a particular kind of production machine. We would see this cinematic machine as an apparatus that had been anticipated in literature and theatre, incarnated in its most famous version in celluloid film, continuing into a multimedia and multi-industrial post-celluloid afterlife."[98]

Rajadhyaksha further suggests that the Lahore effect instantiates the survival of "cultural memory ... links to several strands that return in film after film: often in the placement and framing of characters, notably the dense close-ups, flaring light-effects, casting, cinematography and sound, and perhaps above all of set design."[99] What this mode accomplishes, in my understanding, is the reproduction and inhabitation of a cultural fabric, a texture that is striated and palpable to the senses and is shaped rather like a Möbius strip, on which one can traverse endlessly, sometimes oriented upright and at other times upside-down. Multiple reverberations emerge from this journey across temporal gaps, and from both the formal and narrative resonances of this circuit. Rajadhyaksha puts it this way: "On this level, it is as though the *making of a film is itself the anthropology of cinema* as films quote one other, fold inside each other, or hover over each other. Every film, thus seen, becomes a history of the cinema. Remakes, along with other forms of a haunting cultural survival, e.g., in the music or in other forms of the cinema-effect, become crucial here."[100]

This mode prevents cinema from being assimilated as *national* cinema, in both India and Pakistan, because each individual film recalls its predecessors not just in cinema, but as artifacts, memories, and mise-en-scène from theater, orality, and even architecture. Its hauntings reverberate far beyond national space and its disciplinary concerns.[101] The Anarkali mythos is exemplary in this regard, as in Lahore there is a Mughal-era tomb named after Anarkali, but the identity of who is immured there has never been ascertained. Moreover, the tomb houses official archives of the Indian Mutiny of 1857 and records of Bhagat Singh's trial (see chapter 2), conflating and imbricating the myth of Anarkali's revolt for the sake of romantic love with the actual revolutionary history of colonial South Asia. Realism and fable, history and myth, narrative and lyric, and past and present, all are inextricably entangled across resonating aesthetic and political sensibilities.

NATIONALISM, PARTITION, AND THE SOCIAL FILM

The social film of midcentury South Asia was thus never comfortably associated with elite respectability and with the nation-state project. The populist bazaar mode of commercial cinema created additional impediments for it to be aligned with nationalism. Manishita Dass has argued that the role of cinema in late colonial India marks a tension "between the professed desire for a 'national' cinema and elite perceptions of a divided audience... visible in anxious elite discourses about a cinematic public sphere facilitating the circulation of a contagious modernity and the unrefined tastes of the masses through the national body politic."[102] Official discussions on commercial cinema right after Indian independence denigrated its vulgar aesthetics as well as its opaque and personalized financing and production arrangements.[103] In Pakistan during the early years, Gazdar has quoted the federal minister of industries, who asserted, "In principle Muslims should not get involved in filmmaking. Being the work of lust and lure, it should be left to the infidels."[104] Commercial cinema's insidious recourse to degraded values was routinely disparaged in Pakistan and was a perennial subject of much hand-wringing and pearl-clutching, as the substantial official report from 1962 notes:

> The average film has no story worth the name and is made to cater to the entertainment needs of the masses.... The formula of a specific number of cheap songs and dances injected without regard to story or situation into melodramatic episodes of love making is corrupting the taste of our people.... No attempt has been made to reach out to literature or history for good themes and even the music of our films tends to follow set

popular patterns in which cheap melodies blended from oriental and occidental sources sometimes satisfy but never enthuse or inspire the masses.[105]

Thus, in neither country was commercial cinema in its existing form seen as being able to bear the responsibilities of articulating a responsible *national* cultural project.

Social reform, however, was not absent in commercial cinema. In his essay on the Muslim social film of 1935–45 as it developed in Bombay and Lahore cinema, Ravi Vasudevan has argued that this genre arose as a response to increasing communalization in India, and partly as a result by Muslim filmmakers countering the denigration of the Muslim community, which was viewed as being socially retrograde.[106] Before this period, the social film primarily evoked the world of bourgeois Hindus and the dilemmas of reform in their universe. By contrast, Muslims had been depicted in this earlier commercial cinema as living in the past in historical stasis, preoccupied with decadent elite *nawabi* pastimes.[107] Another segment of film production catered to other genres and markets, with films based on Arabian Nights themes, Oriental fantasies, and legendary stories (*qiṣṣa* and *dāstān*) of unfulfilled love: "The world of *paris* (fairies) and evil *amirs* (chieftains), genies, and itinerant adventurers who could traverse worlds . . . such cultural forms were critical to the way Bombay cinema was organized from an early period, and through its links with phenomena, such as Parsi theater, the traditions of Urdu romance narrative and poetry, and to the fabulous worlds derived from Arabian Nights and dastan performances."[108]

Vasudevan makes the important observation that such films depicting and deploying "the Punjab, and the Urdu narrative and performance culture it generated," appealed to audiences of "a larger territory that went beyond the subcontinent to include North Africa, the Middle East, and Southeast Asia, straddling Arabic, Persian, and even Malay and Indonesian cultures."[109] Apart from the business angle of "film trade" and export markets in comments in the influential magazine *Filmindia*, from a nationalist standpoint, these films obviously could also not have served the end of bearing the burden of national cinema. Indeed, the fantasy genre is considered as being even lower than the social film, and it came under persistent criticism for forestalling "the cultivation of a realist aesthetic that would do away with fantastical narrative and miraculous enactments."[110] There were also films in other lower genres being produced in Bombay, such as stunt films. All these B-genres were intended to cater to specific audiences and geographic regions, as comments in *Filmindia* make evident. *Dastanic* films continued to be made during the long sixties in Lahore, but from the elite and official view, they were even more unworthy as national cultural exemplars, even more damning as indictments of the allure of fantasy worlds with a "Muslim" inflection.

Vasudevan argues that in the period 1935–45, the Muslim social film finally emerges and grapples centrally with questions of modernity and reform in Muslim communities. Its films include *Najma* (1943, dir. Mehboob Khan), *Elaan* (Proclamation, 1948 dir. Mehboob Khan), *Qaidi* (Prisoner, 1941, dir. S. F. Hasnain), and *Masoom* (Innocent, 1942 dir. S. F. Hasnain).[111] Among the "most suggestive of all" is *Khandan* (Family, 1942), which was a production by Dalsukh M. Pancholi from Lahore.[112] Vasudevan stresses that "the genre was also crucially representational, inscribing a contemporary Muslim presence (whether modernizing or otherwise) on the screen where it had earlier been absent."[113] Their narrative is set among Muslim characters, but these films also addressed wider publics. Here, it needs to be underscored that the All-India Progressive Writers' Association (PWA) was also organized in 1936, and in this association Muslim and Urdu writers and poets played an important role.[114] The Indian People's Theatre Association (IPTA), which was formed in 1943, brought together key writers, poets, filmmakers, and music directors from across India to create cultural forms such as theater and cinema in a progressive register. Manishita Dass has argued that during the forties and fifties, "several of the figures associated with or influenced by the PWA and the IPTA movement turned toward the Bombay film industry, partly in order to make a living—but also in the hope of both reaching and creating a mass audience through the medium of cinema."[115] These included the writers and directors "K. A. Abbas, Bimal Roy, Chetan Anand, Rajinder Singh Bedi, Zia Sarhadi, Saadat Hasan Manto, Ismat Chughtai, Shaheed Latif" and poets Kaifi Azmi and Sahir Ludhanvi.[116] Without this development, the Muslim social film would have been inconceivable.[117] And because the writings of Lahore-based leftist writers and poets like Habib Jalib and Faiz Ahmed Faiz traverse the registers of high cultural forms as well as writing stories, dialogue, and lyrics for song-and-dance sequences in popular films, the division between elite culture and mass genres is productively troubled also in Lahore cinema of the fifties and sixties. The ethos in Lahore during the long sixties is thus comparable to developments in the fifties in Bombay, where "cinema was still an emergent formation, a site of unprecedented transactions between 'high culture' and 'low culture' and of widespread experimentation."[118]

Vasudevan is interested in seeing how this genre addresses the dilemmas of Indian nationalism at a time when that nationalism is being pulled apart by communal and centripetal forces of the Hindi/Urdu divide, and also how this cinema engages with questions of material and psychological hybridity brought about by modernity.[119] Building on this analysis and expanding its scope to think about larger Bombay cinema of midcentury, Rajadhyaksha observes for the later forties cinema, films that instantiate the Lahore effect emerge as among the biggest hits in India at precisely the time when communal strife and nationalism attendant to the Partition of 1947 was most pronounced:

> The blockbusters of 1946 are Mehboob Khan's *Anmol Ghadi* [Precious watch], A. R. Kardar's *Shah Jehan*, and the Ranjit Studio's *Phulwari*. The top hits list of 1947 lead with Shaukat Hussain Rizvi's *Jugnu* [Firefly], two films by Filmistan (*Do Bhai* [Two brothers], directed by Munshi Dil, and *Shehnai* [Trumpet], directed by P. L. Santoshi), and A. R. Kardar's next hit *Dard* [Pain]. The 1948 list features Filmistan's *Shaheed* [Martyr] at the top, followed by Gemini Studios' *Chandralekha* (S. S. Vasan), Wadia Films' *Mela* [Festival] (S. U. Sunny), *Pyar Ki Jeet* [The triumph of love] produced and directed by O. P. Dutta, and Bombay Talkies' *Ziddi* [Stubborn] directed by Shaheed Latif.[120]

Many film personnel who had worked with A. R. Kardar in Bombay over the years moved to Lahore after 1947, including music director and later film director Khurshid Anwar. It is instructive to compare the quotation above with another film that did very well in the Punjab in 1947, the year of the Partition and terrible large-scale violence. The blog commentator Harjap Singh Aujla narrates his father's memory of living through that era in urban Punjab. Released in 1947, *Parwana* (The moth), whose music director was Khurshid Anwar, was extensively viewed during this period of widespread brutality: "All songs of this movie [*Parwana*] became hit[s]. . . . 1947 was not a good year for the film industry, in spite of that *Parwana* did a roaring business, not only in the Ganges Basin states, but in the most disturbed Province of Punjab. Lahore and Amritsar were witnessing bloodbaths of the worst order, but the film *Parwana* was doing great among the Muslims of Lahore and Sikhs and Hindus of Amritsar. Both cities . . . were drawing packed houses."[121]

When society is confronted with political impasses and violence, and exacerbated divisions by ethnicity and faith, it is the melodramatic social film—with its romantic songs embodying aspiration and fantasy—that affectively addresses publics that were being forged in midcentury South Asia. These films proposed an affective counterinterpellation and sought to constitute new mediatized publics beyond the existing ethnic, regional, and communal divides, and the claims of the consolidating nationalisms of the period. The social film greatly flourished in Pakistan during the long sixties for analogous reasons, informed by its rich lineage, and across the terrain shaped by the forces of political economy and the social fissures of modernity.[122]

ARCHIVE AND MEMORY

The liminal status of Pakistani cinema in official cultural policies is underscored by the absence until today of an archive or repository for the vast body of films produced in multiple languages from Karachi, Lahore, and Dhaka, as well as production and distribution records, scripts, screenplays, lobby cards, posters, booklets, journals, magazines, criticism, et cetera. Unlike India and Bangladesh, which have constituted national archives that enable scholars and researchers to have stable access to such materials, and even to view the original celluloid prints, in Pakistan all of this presents an insurmountable challenge in many respects.[123] This lack has created major gaps in our understanding of the historical development of Pakistani cinema. Timothy Cooper, Salma Siddique, and Vazira Zamindar have stressed the need for thinking about the Pakistani media archive in unconventional ways.[124] They have looked at dealers who sell film memorabilia, private collectors who have amassed materials in informal ways, film enthusiasts and fans who have put up a considerable amount of material on the Internet, and publishers and contents of the film magazine *Nigar*, for example. Cooper's and Siddique's analyses propose that while the archive for Pakistani cinema is not formally constituted institutionally, it is nevertheless assembled in fragments by cinephiles in various quirky and popular formats.[125]

On online platforms such as YouTube and Vimeo, fans and cinephiles have placed digitized copies of many films. Much of this material has been drawn from video formats and converted into digital versions. During the eighties and nineties, the Shalimar Recording Company in Islamabad had transferred many films from celluloid to VHS format. Films were also broadcast on television in Pakistan and in the United Kingdom and recorded by fans. Some films on VHS were exported to the Arab world and other regions and were subtitled in Arabic or French. Most of the films that one now finds online are based on these VHS transfers or recordings from TV reruns by aficionados. Many films of potential critical or artistic importance, but which were commercial flops, are likely lost, unless a copy of them on celluloid can be found, which is unlikely after all these decades. A small number of well-known films have been packaged as branded DVDs and have been available in bookstores, but the majority of these transferred films are available informally in bazaars like the Rainbow Center in Karachi from only a few dealers, who press hand-labeled individual copies by request.

All these platforms have many technical problems, however. There is no certainty whether the film one watches online, or one purchases on DVD either in packaged form or in more informal ways, is complete or has missing footage. Another problem is severe quality degradation. Informal entrepreneurs often encrust the screen with their logos, phone numbers, and advertisements, which block parts of the screen and compete for the viewer's attention. Digital copies made from VHS transfers include blurring, distortion, scratches, tracking and formatting errors, muffled audio, errors in sound synchronization, and generally speaking, a much lower level of resolution, sharpness, and contrast, thus rendering any judgment on the aesthetics of the original film provisional and suspect. Kuhu Tanvir discusses an analogous ecology in India of unofficial archives, small-scale physical and digital exchange of cinema and media, and the degradation of the image in this realm. The modality of media exchange and the assembly of materials by amateurs and aficionados she traces share much with initiatives-from-below of popular archiving of Pakistani cinema. Tanvir's focus, however, is on how this growing realm sidesteps issues of legality and challenges the accuracy and probity of the state's archival initiatives. It needs to be stressed that for Pakistan the latter does not exist, and as for the former, the larger ethos is one of immense neglect rather than copyright concerns.[126]

Of concern here is the larger relationship between the partial and degraded archive that one is forced to work with and the subject of memory and history of this important cultural form. Overwhelmingly, the fans of Pakistani cinema of the fifties through the seventies are individuals who were exposed to this cinema when they were growing up. Because of the decline of Urdu cinema from the early eighties onward, and the attraction of television serials from the seventies onward, younger audiences who came to consciousness during this later era have little or no memories associated with the cinema of the long sixties, notwithstanding that older films continue to be rescreened on private TV channels.[127] Many individuals below the age of forty, for example, may never have watched an Urdu film from the period and may have no awareness whatsoever of its significant milestones. But these same individuals may well have some familiarity with famous Bombay films from the fifties onward by directors such as Raj Kapoor, Mehboob Khan, and Guru Dutt, and would have likely watched the Amitabh Bachchan films of the seventies, not to mention the cinema of Bollywood's globalization from the nineties on, the era of the likes of Shah Rukh Khan's stardom. There is thus a profound generational absence of memory and recollection when it comes to the significant films made in Lahore, Karachi, and Dhaka during the long sixties.

One way to understand the work (or the lack thereof) that this amnesia does is to contextualize it with reference to the Lahore effect, which was manifest in Bombay cinema after the Partition of 1947.[128] While Urdu cinema in Pakistan went into decline from the beginning of the eighties—this has lasted several decades and production has never recovered to the levels seen in the midseventies, for example—Bombay films have remained extremely popular in Pakistan, as they largely used language registers and narrative tropes that resonate with the Pakistani Urdu social film. This is no surprise when one considers that many of the scriptwriters and poets in Bombay cinema through the seventies worked with Urdu rhetoric and diction and deployed it in cinema as a kind of shared linguistic register. In terms of theme, Pakistan's Urdu cinema also is segmented in genres that are analogous to the Hindi film, such as the Oriental fantasy, the social film, and a smaller number of productions of the detective film, the horror film, the serpent film, and so on.

In general, Bombay cinema has always enjoyed a higher working budget and could draw on a much larger and deeper infrastructural ecology with far more experience than its counterpart in Lahore. This meant that when the videocassette recorder (VCR) became commonplace in Pakistan from the late seventies onward, audiences could watch Bombay productions in their homes, to the tremendous disadvantage of support and patronage of the Urdu film. The authoritarian regime of General Zia-ul-Haq, which seized power in 1977, also began implementing policies of overt Islamization in the country, with strictures against exhibitionism and the display of women's appearance in media, which further dampened the appeal of local Urdu films for many audiences.[129] Memory and amnesia are therefore instantiated in the makeshift and partial archives that older fans have constituted but which do not transmit their cinephilia to the next generations.

The question of amnesia is, however, larger than the historical and technical reasons provided above. First of all, one must stress that Pakistan's "New Cinema," which has developed since around 2010, does not offer a continuation of industrial practices from the seventies. Although some older studios are still around, such as Evernew Studios in Lahore, they are reportedly in terrible shape.[130] Many of these studios have not converted to digital technology, for example, which prevents their productions from circulating easily to theaters that now only have digital projection. By contrast, the so-called New Cinema is being developed by a new breed of filmmakers whose lineage is largely not from the commercial cinema or older studios. Instead, many of them have worked for advertising firms, private media houses, NGOs, or corporate patrons, or they have been associated with the growing number of television serials—as the liberalization of the media since 2002 has resulted in the proliferation of dozens of private channels with twenty-four-hour programming. The mediascape is thus far larger than during the twentieth century and requires far more content than the single-channel government-owned television station that broadcast only for a few hours during the seventies. Arguably, cinema no longer assumes the most central place in Pakistan's crowded, mediatized public sphere today.

This presents important quandaries for the present study. As most of the films discussed do not have subtitles, or are not yet easily available in good quality formats, will the analysis offered here remain a hermetic academic exercise? Are the readings presented here merely yet another foray in irrelevance and obsolescence, and will they fail to elicit interest in questions that the films examined here raise, whether from the scholarly community internationally or from wider audiences in South Asia and its diasporas? While any prognosis is a risk in gazing at an imaginary crystal ball, one must stress that this study is not the only project that has encountered these dilemmas. The film *Zinda Bhaag* (Run for life, 2013, dir. Meenu Gaur and Farjad Nabi), discussed in chapter 4, is an ambitious attempt to address precisely such questions through practice, and in doing so, it returns to play with reflexivity of form and the recursiveness of cultural memory. *Zinda Bhaag* draws on the Lahore effect, citing multiple references from orality, theater, and cinema across South Asia, from the golden age of the social film from the forties to the seventies in India and Pakistan as well as the aesthetics and characters of the Punjabi film. Moreover, *Jago Hua Savera* (A new day dawns, 1959, dir. A. J. Kardar), discussed in chapter 1, is also a project that encompasses multiple narratives and marshals themes and personnel from across South Asia.

This book, therefore, traverses an arc that argues, above all, that cinemas of Bombay and Lahore, and indeed of the wider network of Bombay-Calcutta-Dhaka-Karachi-Lahore films, have never existed in hermetic linguistic, thematic, and nationalist bubbles—indeed, the very concept of the Lahore effect instantiates precisely the opposite valences. A proper theoretical recognition of the multiply faceted universes Lahore cinema has inhabited is overdue—it has emerged from premodern orality and moved into the digital realm, and it has drawn promiscuously from Hindu mythology, Bengali performance traditions, Islamicate legends, Punjabi and Sindhi oral narratives, Urdu lyric poetry, Sufi conceptions of the self, progressive writing, and historical, social, and magical realism.[131] It has also drawn freely from Hollywood and world cinema, the psychological and sensorial stimulus of modernity, and much more—to recast these in commercial productions that imbricate realism with imaginative fantasy and address multiple publics far beyond the capacity of other cultural forms.

An understanding of this reverberative cultural field can offer important insights for reconsidering questions of affiliation and belonging during the fraught present, when official relations among many South Asian nations are not in an encouraging state and their internal majoritarian dynamics are increasingly hostile to values of multiplicity and plurality. The question of the adequacy of cultural forms to address these quandaries cannot be limited to avant-garde, experimental cinema or documentary approaches but has been more influentially instantiated in the social feature film. Compared to all other artistic forms and despite all of its shortcomings, it is arguably commercial cinema that played the most influential progressive role in South Asia during the twentieth century. It has done so by constituting publics beyond existing social divides, in forging a shared and expanded experience of modernity that extends beyond regional, ethnic, and sectarian affiliations, and in affectively challenging the selective amnesia of nation-state ideologies.

1 BETWEEN NEOREALISM AND HUMANISM

Jago Hua Savera

JAGO HUA SAVERA (A NEW DAY DAWNS, 1959, DIR. A. J. KARDAR) is the only prominent example of a neorealist Pakistani film from the long sixties. Its aesthetics are comparable to the art and parallel cinema of India, rather than to Pakistan's feature productions from that era, which were primarily commercially oriented melodramas and social films.¹ Despite adhering to the formative Italian conception of neorealism and drawing from contemporary Indian productions, *Jago Hua Savera*'s realism is marked by fractures in form, narrative, and address. Its formal fissures include many visible joints across its aesthetic assemblage: it deploys both color and black-and-white film stock, includes songs in an ostensibly neorealist narrative, and uses multiple linguistic registers that are not close to everyday language but are primarily an artifice. In its narrative, *Jago Hua Savera* shuttles between a humanist vision that envisioned traditional rural life as timeless and perennial and a progressive understanding of exploitation and poverty as having become unsustainable. The film's production team was diverse, and its elements included dialogue and songs drawn from diverse backgrounds. *Jago Hua Savera* makes a gambit or opening toward a larger alternative South Asian cinema after the Partition of 1947. However, its audiences were neither fully envisioned nor actualized, and this contributed to its initially disappointing reception.

Jago Hua Savera was the result of a collaboration of themes and personnel from within and beyond Pakistan. The film was directed by Akhtar Jung Kardar (1926–2002), younger brother of the established Bombay-based director Abdul Rashid Kardar (1904–89), and the lyrics and dialogue were written by leading progressive Urdu poet Faiz Ahmed Faiz (1911–84).² Faiz had loosely adapted the overall story from the famous Bengali realist novel *Padma nadir majhi* (The boatman on the river Padma, 1936) by Indian writer Manik Bandopadhyay (1908–56).³ Zahir Raihan (1935–72), who served as an assistant director, subsequently emerged as a gifted and committed filmmaker who made a number of important Urdu and Bengali films during the sixties and the documentary *Stop Genocide* in 1971.[4] Khan Ataur Rahman (1928–97), who plays the lead character Kasim, had been involved in emerging media and cultural productions in Karachi and in Europe during the 1950s. After *Jago Hua Savera*, he went on to have a significant career as an actor in Zahir Raihan's films and also as a director of Urdu and Bengali cinema.[5]

The team included Walter Lassally (1926–2017), a rising young German-British cinematographer who later became prominent for his work on *Zorba the Greek* (1965) and won an Oscar for it; he also worked on Jamil Dehlavi's *The Blood of Hussain* (1980).[6] Experienced Indian film personnel assumed key roles in the production of *Jago Hua Savera*. Shanti Kumar Chatterji, the other assistant director, had served as assistant director for Satyajit Ray's *Pather Panchali* (Song of the little road, 1955).[7] And Indian Bengali composer Timir Baran (1904–87) had composed the music for *Jago Hua Savera*.[8] Baran was the music composer for the iconic film *Devdas* (1935, dir. P. C. Barua) from India, as well as for the Pakistani Urdu films *Anokhi* (Singular, 1956, dir. Shah Nawaz), *Fankar* (Artist, 1956, dir. Mohammad Hassan), and later the Bengali film *Jog Biyog* (1970).[9] The lead actress of *Jago Hua Savera*, Tripti Mitra (1925–89) was also Indian. She had been involved with the Indian People's Theatre Association (IPTA), which was founded in 1943 as a leftist cultural organization and produced numerous realist plays across South Asia, many of which deployed songs, music, and performance in innovative ways.[10] Mitra had acted in Khwaja Ahmad Abbas's realist film *Dharti Ke Lal* (Children of the earth, 1946), as well as in many Indian Bengali-language films.[11] Participation of experienced international personnel in *Jago Hua Savera*'s production helped alleviate the marked lack of experience by the Pakistanis involved—director A. J. Kardar had never made a film, and the production was also a first for Faiz.[12] In enlisting a broad production team, the makers of *Jago Hua Savera* expanded the scope of progressive cultural production beyond national limits.

This broader context suggests that while *Jago Hua Savera* might be considered a "Pakistani" film, it cannot be understood without developments in India, to which Pakistani filmmakers would have had varying access during the fifties.[13] We can understand *Jago Hua Savera* in a wider South Asian context and as a contribution to and a manifestation toward what has been termed "global neorealism."[14] Realism in South Asian cinema has multiple lineages since the 1930s across diverse cultural forms, with "neorealism" notating a trajectory from 1952 onward that drew from the influential

Italian developments but sought also to develop, refine, incorporate, and partly repudiate popular cinematic codes and narrative tropes associated with the "studio *Social*" film.[15]

Jago Hua Savera was awarded a gold medal at the first Moscow Film Festival in 1959 and was also Pakistan's Oscar submission.[16] For decades, it had been lost and not available either nationally or internationally, yet it had acquired a mythical aura domestically. In his memoir, Walter Lassally observes that "by the time of my second visit to Pakistan in 1976 . . . [the film] had become a sort of *Birth of a Nation* of the Pakistani Film Industry, a film which, even though they hadn't necessarily seen it, was discussed by local film buffs in reverend tones."[17] Since its rediscovery and subsequent restoration, the film has been shown at numerous film festivals, such as the Three Continents Festival 2007, the New York Film Festival 2008, and the Festival de Cannes in 2016.[18] The version available now is apparently the one meant for foreign distribution. The local version included a song-and-dance sequence in color, whose incorporation raises important questions as to how highbrow leftist artistic projects understand their own social appeal in relation to the widespread allure of popular cinema in South Asia.

PLOT SUMMARY

Set in the village of Shaitnol on the banks of the Meghna River some thirty miles from Dhaka, the film focuses on the everyday life of fishermen and their families. Mian is the main character. His family consists of his wife, Fatima, who is in poor health and has recently delivered a baby; their children; and an adopted orphaned young man named Kasim (who accompanies Mian as a fishing partner). Mala is Fatima's sister, a young woman who comes to reside in the Mian household in order to take care of her disabled sister and her new baby. Mala falls in love with Kasim over the course of the film (figure 1.1).

Ganju is another fisherman who lives with his paralyzed mother. Neither Mian nor Ganju own their own boats, and thus much of the earnings of their labor is handed over to the boat owner. They are also compelled to sell their catch to Lal Mian, a middleman of some means who is deeply involved with everyday matters of the village, at prices over which they have little say. In order to purchase their own boats, Mian and Ganju save part of their meager earnings after each expedition—this is also "banked" with the grasping but indispensable Lal Mian. Ganju has saved more but is in very poor health.

FIG. 1.1. Mala and Kasim fall in love. *Jago Hua Savera* (1959). © Anjum Taseer, courtesy of Anjum Taseer.

When a Pakistani government delegation comes to conduct an auction for the renewal of fishing rights, Lal Mian wins by outbidding other middlemen, and he uses this as a pretext to further squeeze the fishermen. Toward the end of the film, when Ganju has finally saved enough, Lal Mian delivers a vessel to him, having it dramatically hauled upland to his hut. But Ganju is now far too ill and collapses in a coughing fit. Lal Mian repossesses the boat, ostensibly to resell it in order to provide for Ganju's mother. Watching this, in desperation, Mian scrounges up the savings of all members of his household to add to his savings already banked with Lal Mian. But when Lal Mian's *munshi* (accountant) tallies up all of Mian's savings, they are tantalizingly close to Lal Mian's asking price but still insufficient and suspiciously lower than Mian's own reckoning of how much he has banked with Lal Mian. Mian and his family's hopes for achieving greater financial independence and taking ownership of the "means of production" are frustrated for now. These emotional events constitute a denouement in the film that is otherwise characterized by subdued drama throughout.

Similar to its beginning, the film ends with a lyrical sequence of boats launching at dusk, initiating another seemingly eternal cycle of events. But the cycle's previous iteration had sharpened social contradictions and created greater consciousness in some characters, suggesting that existing hierarchies are not fated to repeat endlessly. This is most evident in the development of Kasim's character, marked by integrity, independence, and growing consciousness. Kasim accompanies Mian on the boats and is subject to the same forces of exploitation as other fishermen who do not own their own vessels. Unlike others, however, Kasim refuses to bank his savings with Lal Mian, and this quiet assertion of independence unpleasantly surprises the latter when he learns of this. Kasim is also aware of Lal Mian's pursuit of Mala and protects her from his advances. And when one of Mian's children has a broken leg that the faith healer brought in by Lal Mian is unable to fix, Kasim insists on taking the child to Dhaka for treatment in a modern hospital, accompanied by Mala. As an outsider to the family unit, Kasim is perhaps freer to breach social custom. In this interlude, the film depicts the bustling streets of Dhaka and its commercial and public spaces, suggesting that for the next generation, the small rural world of Shaitnol will no longer remain a self-enclosed one.

Remarkably, the film depicts virtually every character engaged in saving money. In addition to the fishermen Ganju, Kasim, and Mian, Mian's wife and their young son all are preoccupied with saving even small coins, in assiduously reckoning their sums, and in resorting to unusual stratagems to accomplish this. This depiction sharply contrasts with the probable reality of midcentury rural Bengal, where debt had long figured as a central problem plaguing its rural poor—the emphasis on saving in the film perhaps charts a fantasy of responsible rural life, an imaginative trajectory toward a transformed future.[19]

Exploitation is depicted as part of daily routine and is not excessively dramatized. Even Lal Mian is involved in acts of welfare, and his accumulative motivations are not depicted as being starkly evil. His actions are deeply intermingled in the everyday life of the community: he constitutes nothing less than "a part" of the village's "fate," according to the opening credits (figure 1.2).

By contrast, the state remains distant—the only event where the Pakistani government intervenes in the village is when its official, wearing a *sola topi*, arrives in a large boat flying the national flag, to auction off annual fishing rights. There is no trace of development activities in the village—no clinic, post office, bank, or school—suggesting that the state remains resolutely colonialist, an absentee landlord, interested primarily in the extraction of revenue via middlemen who are in turn deeply involved in everyday acts of exploitation and maintenance of the poor fisherfolk at a bare subsistence level.

FIG. 1.2. Lal Mian, the village middleman. *Jago Hua Savera* (1959). © Anjum Taseer, courtesy of Anjum Taseer.

STYLE AND RECEPTION

The look or style of *Jago Hua Savera* is lyrically cinematic, deploying strong lighting contrasts and editing sequences that track the narrative, punctuated by strong graphic shots of the countryside and the water (figure 1.3).

The frame compositions are well conceived. The film was shot mostly on location, and the sense of realism of the everyday is heightened as the camera lingers on details of evidence and events.[20] The fisherfolk's desperation is portrayed with restraint. The narrative unfolds slowly but steadily—its pacing aligns with the gentle waves of water that the film's evidentiary focus highlights.

Jago Hua Savera is singular in its stark "realist" portrayal, as film historian Mushtaq Gazdar has noted in his landmark study, *Pakistan Cinema, 1947–1997*.[21] Gazdar equates the values of realism here with experimentalism. And part of its realist value is the "focus on the lives" of ordinary people, rather than on "dramatic events." These attributes set *Jago Hua Savera* against mainstream Pakistani cinema of the fifties, in which social concerns are largely subordinated to, or placed within, a melodramatic narrative. Gazdar is certainly correct in describing *Jago Hua Savera* as offering a new set of aesthetic and moral values to cinema produced in Pakistan. The film was released in two versions; the international release was black-and-white, while the domestic version included a color song-and-dance sequence

FIG. 1.3. Mian with son outdoors. *Jago Hua Savera* (1959). © Anjum Taseer, courtesy of Anjum Taseer.

precisely to broaden the film's popular appeal. The film's publicity booklet claims that it "marks the beginning of the avante guard [sic] movement in this country!"[22] But the film failed to find a receptive domestic audience and "was taken down from Karachi's Jubilee Cinema . . . in just three days."[23]

The political environment in Pakistan was not conducive to a film affiliated with progressive politics. The country had been allied with the United States from the early fifties and hostile to leftist cultural and political projects. The Rawalpindi Conspiracy Case of 1951 is an important landmark, in which members of the Communist Party of Pakistan were tried for conspiring to overthrow the government. Faiz was jailed for four years, between 1951 and 1955.[24] The All Pakistan Progressive Writers' Association and the Communist Party of Pakistan were also banned in 1954. These events had a repressive effect on cultural expression.[25] Ayub Khan's coup in 1958 put an end to political instability between 1951 and 1958, but right after seizing power, Ayub Khan exerted greater authoritarian control over journalism, criticism, and cultural policies, including his notorious takeover in 1959 of Progressive Papers, the publisher of *Pakistan Times*, the largest-circulation English-language daily, which Faiz had edited before his imprisonment in 1951, and *Imroze*, an important Urdu newspaper.[26] Ayub Khan was reportedly unhappy with *Jago Hua Savera* and attempted to thwart its release just three days prior to its screening.[27] The producer's son

Anjum Taseer recalls, "My father financed the entire production from his own resources, and although the project was risky, idealism and passion were two driving forces that he could not resist.... The film was shown in February 1959, but the reception was poor. Firstly, people were not ready for neo-realism, and also, I believe the distributors were pressured to cut short the viewings."[28]

The question of *Jago Hua Savera*'s audience and its reception must be further parsed in terms beyond ideological suppression. Was the film intended to circulate locally, and did the sites of circulation include Shaitnol? Dhaka? Karachi? Or was it intended also for, or perhaps even primarily for, the international film festival circuit, which had recently been very receptive to films from India?[29] This quest for international recognition was no anomaly—as even in India, despite its more cinematically literate public and state support, Satyajit Ray observed that his work was possible only via European film festival support.[30]

Jago Hua Savera's devastating initial failure in the domestic market, coupled with the state's political and aesthetic conservatism of the late fifties, meant that *Jago Hua Savera* has remained largely a singular experiment in Pakistani cinema.[31] But if one extends the scope of analysis across South Asia, one can situate *Jago Hua Savera* in relation to other films being produced at the time. Moreover, its collaborative production process underscores that it also can be viewed as a broader move in South Asia toward an embrace and localization of neorealism during the fifties. *Jago Hua Savera* can be posited as attempting to create a progressive cultural form that had cross-regional address, not unlike earlier Indian People's Theatre Association (IPTA) productions, as well as meetings of the All-India Progressive Writers' Association during the forties that Faiz was intimately familiar with and participated in. Exchange of cinema between India and Pakistan since the midfifties was however in the process of attenuation, with national borders that were becoming increasingly harder to traverse and protests in Lahore in 1954 against the import of Indian cinema.[32]

REALISM IN SOUTH ASIAN CINEMA BEFORE 1952

The move toward realism in the cinematic and performing arts of South Asia began from at least the late thirties. Apart from neorealist works from the midfifties, midcentury Indian cinema contains a variable register of aesthetic values and concerns, across which various manifestations of realism are marshaled. Thus, the social film of the forties is imbued with a kind of

Hollywood realism, and in many Indian productions the focus of themes and motivations relevant to society is coupled with the "heterogeneous attractions" of the commercial Indian film.[33] The embrace of realism in fifties Indian cinema was not simply due to exposure to Italian neorealism, but conditions were being prepared within the trajectories of Indian cinema during the forties for the neorealist turn to unfold in the fifties the way it did—long before the fateful 1952 first International Film Festival, which introduced Italian neorealist cinema widely to Indian filmmakers.[34]

Founded in 1936, the Progressive Writers' Association "sought to extend the progressive, rationalist trends in nationalist culture into a critical and socialist direction. Realism was conceived of as an ethic that could oversee this 'progress.'"[35] The subsequent founding of the IPTA in 1943 was extremely consequential for theater and cinema overall, producing a vibrant "movement that in the next ten years or so would directly or indirectly influence almost every important artist in the country."[36] In cinema, developments in realism that Moinak Biswas terms the "studio *Social*" had begun in 1940 with films such as *Aurat* (Woman), directed by Mehboob Khan. Furthermore, the Bengal Famine of 1943 created new artistic, photographic, and theatrical depictions of its grim reality.[37] Rustom Bharucha has stressed how audiences "discovered for the first time" in Bijon Bhattacharya's play *Nabanna* (New harvest), first performed in 1944, "the extraordinary impact of realism in the dialects and street cries of the actors, the minutiae of their gestures, movements, and responses, and the stark simplicity of the set and the costumes."[38] Notably, these influences were relayed into subsequent cinema.[39] Khwaja Ahmad Abbas's *Dharti Ke Lal* (Children of the earth, 1946) serves as a landmark realist film.[40] This was followed by another key film, the 1950 Bengali-language *Chinnamul* (The uprooted), directed by Nemai Ghosh. Both films were supported by IPTA and embraced codes of realism yet in many ways also remained tied to values associated with the "studio *Social*."[41]

Two international films also have relevance for the development of realism in South Asian cinema, and especially for understanding *Jago Hua Savera*. *La Terra Trema* (The earth trembles, 1948), directed by Luchino Visconti, focused on the exploited lives of a fishing village in Sicily.[42] *The River* (1951), directed by Jean Renoir and shot in India, has been widely recognized for its technical and artistic quality, with its "innovative use of technology, documentary sequences, and realist aesthetics."[43] It forms another significant reference, more so as the young Satyajit Ray, who had not yet ventured into filmmaking, assisted in its production. *The River*'s emphasis on the cyclical nature of time marked by the river's flow serves to foreground the temporal dramas of the protagonists, with a "combination of smoothness and disruption" that is emphasized by its sophisticated and limpid cinematography and editing.[44] Renoir spliced the drama of the largely European characters together with documentary ethnographic vignettes, creating a kind of realist epic in which everyday events in the characters' lives were placed adjacent to the eternal cycle of life epitomized by the steady flow of the river and the performance of timeless Hindu rituals that acknowledge that birth and death are cyclical.[45] Film historian Sarah Cooper stresses that Renoir accomplishes this by "the use of dissolves, hastening the pace of time but in a languorous manner, suggesting connections rather than cuts from one moment to the next, and thus a form of continuity across the boundaries of difference."[46] And while *The River* has been criticized for its expatriate orientalist and rose-tinted view of India, which disregards social exploitation and risks trafficking in colonialist clichés, for our purposes, what is significant is how subtly it modulates the relationship between epic time and everyday actions and decisions of human actors.[47] *Jago Hua Savera* also calibrates cyclical time with everyday life, but unlike *The River*, it gestures instead toward the impossibility of the cycle of seasons playing out endlessly in the social life of its protagonists.

NEOREALISM AFTER 1952

The most consequential context for experimental Indian cinema of the midfifties onward was its encounter with Italian neorealism. The embrace of an intensified realism more in keeping with Italian neorealist principles accelerated after 1952 even in mainstream cinema.[48] *Pather Panchali* was released in 1955, the first of the celebrated Apu Trilogy by Satyajit Ray, who acknowledged the decisive impact of this aesthetic after his viewing of Vittorio De Sica's *The Bicycle Thief* (1948): "I knew immediately that if I ever made *Pather Panchali*—and the idea had been at the back of my mind for some time—I would make it in the same way, using natural location and unknown actors."[49] The mid- to late 1950s thus emerged as a key period for the embrace of Indian cinema of a restrained realism. Biswas stresses that the film directors and writers—Bimal Roy, Prakash Arora, Zia Sarhadi, Amar Kumar, Raj Kapoor, and Khwaja Ahmad Abbas—focused on poverty and marginalization and that their aesthetic values embraced urban sites and dramatic lighting.[50] But if Hollywood productions and aspects of the earlier "studio *Social*" can also be labeled as realist, the question arises: What characterizes a neorealist film in South Asia? And how do we situate films like *Pather Panchali* and *Jago Hua Savera* specifically as neorealist rather than broadly realist?[51] For Biswas, it is the crystallizing impact of Ray's contribution in finally equating serious realism firmly with neorealism: "*Pather Panchali* established as a fully formed aesthetic what was only partially operative in earlier Indian cinema, that is, the realist textual principle. The success of this aesthetic was measured in terms of its ability to free itself of impulses characteristic of traditional Indian cinema—textual heterogeneity, lack of individuation, non-secular narrative logic, and the predominance of spectacle over narrative. After *Pather Panchali*, these same impulses were associated with popular cinema."[52] The problem of what constituted serious realism was thus not simply cinematic but also literary, and, indeed, the neorealist turn was premised on imaginatively adapting literary forms into film.[53]

The bifurcation of Indian cinema into serious and commercial trajectories begins at this juncture. But while serious Indian cinema is often viewed in national terms, it was shot through with diverse subnational and transnational vectors. For Neepa Majumdar, the question of nationalism in realist cinema hinges on issues of state patronage and formal and technological constraints, set against a commercial industry that did not receive analogous legal and financial recognition by the government: "In its negotiations and compromises in grafting Italian neorealist aesthetics to an Indian studio-based realism, mainstream cinema lost the historical battle of neorealist status to state-supported filmmakers such as Ray."[54] Biswas has argued that while realism in Indian cinema is partly associated with Nehruvian nationalism, its full scope and diversity cannot be captured via a nationalist framework.[55] This "serious" aesthetic crucially also received legitimacy from recognition in international film festival circuits.[56] Satyajit Ray himself stressed the importance of foreign patronage in making his cinematic experiments possible.[57]

Moreover, in Indian cinema, realism was foregrounded as a facet of mainstream commercial cinema itself even after the genre division. Biswas notes, "A new popular film emerged around the same time that the new realist cinema arrived. It incorporated neorealist elements even as it launched an advanced dialogue with Hollywood—the 1950s films of Raj Kapoor and Guru Dutt are good examples."[58] And Manishita Dass observes that IPTA filmmakers, upon moving to work in Bombay cinema in the forties and fifties, "drew on the IPTA experiment to ... fashion a mass cultural critique of the postcolonial nation-state's failure to extend the rights of social citizenship to the vast majority of Indians."⁵⁹ This is also the case for West Pakistani cinema in Urdu of the fifties and sixties, where realist tropes and social critique of nationalism in commercial cinema include films directed by W. Z. Ahmed, Luqman, Hassan Tariq, Khalil Qaiser, and Riaz Shahid. Midcentury realism in South Asia thus cut across subnational (Bengali), national, and transnational orbits.

In sum, it is worth stressing not simply the divergent values of "serious" neorealist cinema from the commercially oriented social film but also their resonances—themes drawn from literary narratives and a shared focus on social issues. Nevertheless, the neorealist juncture of the fifties also created a dividing framework of production and reception that placed "serious" and "artistic" films *against* the mainstream popular cinema, even as the latter was partially realist as early as in 1940. This emergence of postwar realist cinema must also be seen in relation to the wider context of Cold War humanism globally.

FORM AND STYLE IN ITALIAN NEOREALISM

The Italian background for the emergence of neorealism during and after the 1940s is that of a nation emerging from under fascist rule, with limited equipment and resources available to filmmakers after the end of the Second World War, and with continued extreme uneven development between the industrialized North and the impoverished South. For filmmakers working in South Asia in a context of linguistic and social heterogeneity and unevenness, also with limited technical and financial resources, but wanting to address serious topics such as poverty and exploitation, the ideas and aesthetics associated with Italian neorealism understandably had tremendous resonance.

Among the foundational theorizations of neorealism by Italian filmmakers and critics that remain salient to the South Asian context are key ideas of screenwriter and theorist Cesare Zavattini (1902–89), who, among his numerous contributions, wrote the screenplay for Vittorio De Sica's hugely influential film *The Bicycle Thief*.⁶⁰ In a manifesto published in English translation in 1953, Zavattini exhorts neorealism to avoid illusory narrative plots and stories in order to focus on the truth of everyday life. Since reality itself is "hugely rich," the filmmaker can create a film that will encourage people to "reflect... on the real things, exactly as they are." Zavattini marks a sharp distinction between Italian neorealism and American cinema, as in the latter, "reality is unnaturally filtered... lack of subjects for films causes a crisis, but with us such a crisis is impossible. One cannot be short of themes while there is still plenty of reality."[61] He thus situates poverty itself as a plentiful resource for filmmakers, rather than rendering technical impediments as lacking. Zavattini accordingly repudiates congealed expectations of apparatus and infrastructure that attend to filmmaking as a capitalist artifact.[62]

This everyday reality can be apprehended by the neorealist filmmaker through "a minute, unrelenting, and patient search," which "must sustain the moral impulse . . . in an analytical documentary way."[63] The materials for the film must be brought together by exercising one's "poetic talents on location, we must leave our rooms and go, in body and mind, out to meet other people, to see and understand them."[64] This moral imperative has a technical and aesthetic dimension, in terms of the filmmaker's sensitivity and focus on seemingly minor sites, events, and characters, so that "when we have thought out a scene, we feel the need to 'remain' in it, because the single scene itself can contain so many echoes and reverberations, can even contain all the situations we may need."[65] He urges a turn away from a focus on individual heroism of characters and exhorts filmmakers to be sensitive to local linguistic expressions: "The best dialogue in films is always in dialect. Dialect is nearer to reality. In our literary and spoken language, the synthetic constructions and the words themselves are always a little false."[66] However, this focus on authentic and local linguistic expression will become a fraught issue for Visconti's *La Terra Trema* and also for *Jago Hua Savera*, as both films attempt to straddle fidelity to local authenticity with the problem of the film's implied audience and actual reception in metropolitan and global cine circuits.

JAGO HUA SAVERA AND *LA TERRA TREMA*

La Terra Trema (The earth trembles, 1948) is an Italian neorealist film directed by Luchino Visconti. Although the film has been criticized for being didactic and stylistically unresolved,[67] it nevertheless remains a key milestone in the development of Italian neorealism and the subject of analysis by major film critics and theorists, such as André Bazin and Gilles Deleuze. A comparison between *La Terra Trema* and *Jago Hua Savera* elucidates the character of the latter. *La Terra Trema* focuses on the exploitation of fishermen in the Sicilian coastal village of Aci Trezza, considered remote, underdeveloped, and exotic to the inhabitants of cosmopolitan Rome. The film was sponsored by the Italian Communist Party and was initially intended to be a documentary on the exploitation of the fisherfolk community. Visconti instead created a lengthy poetic and cinematic epic by adapting a late nineteenth-century novel by Giovanni Verga and using local, unprofessional actors. Bazin has observed that Visconti's camera deployed a deep depth of field both indoors and outdoors, so that all of the reality of Aci Trezza that came into the frame of the camera was always in-focus.[68] The mise-en-scène throughout the film remains resolutely situated in the inner and outdoor spaces of Aci Trezza, which produces the effect of oppression and claustrophobia in the viewer, in sympathy with the perceived worldview of the suffering villagers.[69]

One of the fascinations for Visconti in the site of Aci Trezza was that it had scarcely changed at all since Verga described it in his novel, sixty years earlier. The location has powerful mythical associations with the Homeric epics and with Ovid's *Metamorphosis* that are evoked in both the novel and in Visconti's film. In a detailed study of the site in Verga's novel and earlier photography that informed the making of *La Terra Trema*, Noa Steimatsky has noted that "Visconti's prospects for a Marxist" series of films that might suggest "an impending revolution" is "disrupted already in Verga by an enclosed, cyclical, rhythmic sense of time, a mythical order of fate."[70] Visconti departs from other neorealist film in that rather than repudiating myth, *La Terra Trema* instead embraces the epic mythical aura of the site and situates its natural setting and built form as a theatrical set for the ensuing drama enacted by the actors—who are not only individual and encompass the life of the village itself as a totality.[71]

By contrast, the fishing village of Shaitnol on the banks of the Meghna River is endowed with no such archaic myth but is instead imagined in *Jago Hua Savera* in the context of postwar humanism, which I discuss later in this chapter. Film critic Alamgir Kabir has compared the extended opening scene of *Jago Hua Savera* to that of *La Terra Trema*.[72] Both open with an extended lyrical take several minutes long, in which humble fishing boats slowly return back to the shore at twilight. In both films, this creates a mood of immersion in the lifeworlds of the locations, echoing Zavattini's call for "cinema's original and innate capacity for showing things that we believe worth showing, as they happen day by day—in . . . their longest and truest duration."[73] *Jago Hua Savera* maintains this mood of immersion in everyday life throughout the film, an aesthetic that was brilliantly deployed earlier by Satyajit Ray in *Pather Panchali*. In *Jago Hua Savera*, certain visual tropes are effectively repeated: the face of Ganju's paralyzed mother, the emphasis

FIG. 1.4. Fishing boats at Shaitnol. *Jago Hua Savera* (1959). © Anjum Taseer, courtesy of Anjum Taseer.

on the structure, silhouette, and architectonics of the boats, the preparation and eating of rice, the torn vests of the fishermen, and the lyrical riverine landscape (figure 1.4).

The picturesque rendering of the landscape in *Jago Hua Savera*, aspects of which one might also find in a documentary promoting tourism, is an aesthetic issue that neorealism faces at large. Torunn Haaland notes that for Zavattini, the neorealism film is a "lingering in the intersection between anthropological study and a poetic discovery," premised upon "the director's artistic autonomy and presence in the reality encountered." This vantage provides "subjectivity of selection and perspective," which are "decisively . . . creative acts. This essentially is what distinguishes the [neorealist] social documents from documentaries."[74] Bazin also stressed these ideas—for both thinkers, "realism appears to be a question of integral representation, to be achieved through uninterrupted long takes."[75] The experience of the viewer then becomes an immersive phenomenological encounter with the filmed event or object: "Zavattini defines [this] as *pedinamento* or the act of shadowing . . . that reveals the multifarious aspects and dimensions of the studied object, decidedly emancipating the spectator from all *a priori* interpretations."[76] The lengthy opening shots of both *La Terra Trema* and *Jago Hua Savera* can thus be understood as orienting the viewer into an immersive experiential perception of the mise-en-scène, in order to prepare for the encounter with lifeworlds starkly different from those of the films' audiences. The long takes and depth of field in the films' cinematography immerse the viewer in-location, which is animated by actors whose characters are drawn from everyday life.

Both films primarily subject everyday life to their scrutiny and conclude on an expectation of the future horizon that is freighted with the possibility of change. While exploitation is present throughout social and temporal incidences and cannot be dislodged in a single transformative event, and while the cycle of time still retains its hold, there is the suggestion of "the unsustainable nature of these hitherto unchanging realities" in *La Terra Trema*, as well as in *Jago Hua Savera*.[77] In the latter, the film closes with Kasim being engaged to Mala, and with Mian and his family more united than ever. The family has been exposed to the healing power of modern medicine, which means that the future generation will not be afflicted by being disabled, unlike Mian's wife, who suffers daily. And they are now aware that their savings aggregated together is already close to meeting Lal Mian's asking price for a boat. The endless cycle of unremitting stasis and exploitation is thus not fated to continue forever. This sensibility is brought out subtly but powerfully in *Jago Hua Savera*.

HUMANISM AND PROGRESSIVE CINEMA

The difference in worldviews between the lives of the characters and the lives of filmgoers is central to both films in their concern with authentic and exotic locale. While *La Terra Trema*'s site of Aci Trezza becomes resonant via Visconti's epic archaism, *Jago Hua Savera* draws on the trope of timeless continuity-in-adversity of Bengali riverine life, which was not only resorted to in Renoir's *The River* but also had a hold on West Pakistani conceptions of East Pakistan. Consider, for example, a photo essay titled "River Life in East Pakistan" by A. B. Rajput, published in the journal *Pakistan Quarterly* in 1964. In keeping with the journal's national developmentalist agenda and its celebration of diverse facets of Pakistani cultural life, the essay weaves statistical details about commerce on East Pakistani rivers with touristic observations. All the photographs accompanying the text are picturesque. The essay characteristically concludes on a lyrical note that acknowledges hardship but subsumes it within aesthetic pleasure of human accommodation to the cycles of the natural order:

> The rivers of East Pakistan, thus, hum with unceasing activity, day and night, with boats carrying passengers and cargo, with men and womenfolk bathing, washing, fishing and filling the air with soft melodious music of flutes and sentimental songs. The day dawns with a beautiful breeze and the rays of the sun gradually turn the silvery water into liquid gold. The entire area around is full of green glory, providing a romantic background to the golden-brown hamlets. . . . Life goes on unabated, full of adventure and supreme satisfaction in these highly romantic yet extremely precarious conditions, and this has been going on since time immemorial.[78]

It bears stressing that this is not simply the specific colonialist view held by urbane West Pakistanis.[79] Zakir Hossain Raju has argued that two early Bengali-language films released from Dhaka in 1956 and 1960 portray the region as "a rural idyll . . . depicting the riverine landscape of the delta and its beauty."[80] Cyclical time had been arrayed earlier in *The River*. And in the post–Second World War context of the Cold War, human experience in traditional societies and its place in eternal cycles was widely disseminated by influential magazines such as *Life*, whose photo essays depicted life in traditional and rural locales around the world with precisely such tropes.[81] The celebrated exhibition *The Family of Man* (1955–ongoing), curated by Edward Steichen, which traveled globally over decades, also reiterated this sense of humanist realism; its mythological presumptions Roland Barthes has incisively critiqued.[82] The prominence of this midcentury Western documentary aesthetic must be viewed in the modernization theory context of the Cold War—in which social transformation would be achieved primarily by modernization directed from above, rather than by leftist, collective, or community mobilization from below. Unlike revolutionary or leftist depictions of workers, strikers, or peasants engaged in struggle against exploitation and transformation, Western postwar midcentury humanist realism also works as a prophylactic against the more radical claims that visual and performative realism could marshal via Marxist and leftist initiatives, some of which were prevalent in Bengal of the 1940s with the activities of IPTA and the work of artists like Chittoprasad (1915–78), who executed his politically charged expressionist figurative works in inexpensive prints in order to reach broad audiences.[83] Pakistan's alliance with the United States from the very beginning meant that in establishment publications such as

Pakistan Quarterly, traditional society was viewed in humanist terms as eternal and passive, with transformation to be bestowed upon it from statist, institutional, and capitalist developments.

Against this cultural and ideational landscape, *Jago Hua Savera* can be seen as a project caught between eternal humanism and a recognition of the need for change to arise from below. A clue is provided by the rhetoric employed in the film booklet: "East Pakistan is a land of rivers.... In such a land, there live many communities remote from the hubub [sic] of modern civilization.... This is a story of the people of the river: of those who spend their life, in dazzling sun and blinding rain, to hunt for fish that swarm the surrounding waters... of their little human weakness and strength... and deep down of their undaunted, undefeatable spirit."

As is evident, these tropes of ethnographic fascination with remote people whose lives are synchronized with natural cycles are no departure from those deployed by A. B. Rajput above and with Cold War humanism in general. One can, however, posit that *Jago Hua Savera* is both complicit in and critical of this view. In lyrically celebrating the unchanging rhythms of Bengal's riverine village life, *Jago Hua Savera* partakes in West Pakistani exoticism.[84] However, as a neorealist film, it also poetically dwells on the sensory and material character of the environment and attempts to inhabit the lifeworld of the protagonists. It proffers both continuity and change—the cycle will repeat again, but the present traversing of it has introduced a consciousness of exploitation and the promise of modernity in many of its characters. This is not a strongly revolutionary stance that proffers that conditions for dramatic transformation are immanent, but it's not fully a humanist one either.

The booklet's excited description of *Jago Hua Savera*'s pioneering cinematic accomplishment as a kind of conquest is therefore also in character with the tropes of exoticism.[85] The unsettling militarist metaphors in it notwithstanding, it is the case that conditions for filming were difficult and the infrastructure lacking—this is confirmed by the anecdotes narrated by cinematographer Walter Lassally in his memoir.[86] However, the booklet's claim of the pioneering inexperience of the filmmakers must be tempered with the proficiency and perspective the international team members brought to the project. Still, given the inexperience of the director and many of the key personnel involved and, far more significantly, the absence of critical discourse in Pakistan on cinema, we must evaluate *Jago Hua Savera* as a pioneering experiment, rather than the product of a thriving environment in which such a film project would have emerged within established local precedents in critique and praxis.[87]

ANALYSIS OF SONGS

Songs in *Jago Hua Savera* condense many of the issues discussed above and merit closer examination. The opening and closing sequences of the film with lyrical long takes are attended by the incantation of the poem "Bhor hū'ī ghar āo manjhī" (It's dawn, return home boatman), alongside plaintive melodious notes from a single flute, evoking a sense of extended temporality and relationship of human presence within the sensory materiality of nature.[88] The film opens with a long take, an extreme wide-angle shot that divides the screen in half, with the open sky above and water below, over which the titles and credits appear. In the distance, some twenty boats with fluttering white sails are visible. Swaying gently, the camera traverses the space, immersing the viewer in the journey across the water. The song bridges the journey's crepuscular atmosphere into a stilled darkness in which stationary boats with lowered sails and the fishermen are etched by strongly directional lantern light, a realm marked by extended waiting and sudden exertion. After hauling fish, as the fish gasp for air, Kasim and Mian struggle to catch their breath, presenting themselves as precarious and vulnerable beings also.

The next song, "Ab kyā dekhen rāh tumhārī" (Still waiting for your return), also plays extradiegetically, this time attending the sequence when Kasim first goes to fetch Mala. He stands up alone in a boat and maneuvers the vessel in waterways with a bamboo staff. The sequence is a combination of long shots and medium close-ups of the upper half of Kasim's laboring body and of his legs planted on the deck of the boat. Faiz's diction is simple in both poems and draws on Bhojpuri and registers of North Indian languages with folk associations. In both songs, lyrics are set to compositions that recall folk music. Lotte Hoek and Sanjukta Sunderason have noted that these songs are modeled after *bhatiali*, a folk form sung by boatmen especially in East Bengal—these were also deployed "in the Left's national-popular rhetoric in the 1940s."[89]

In her detailed study of music in IPTA productions, Sumangala Damodaran observes, "The use of the 'folk' idiom and the need to focus on it ... was the subject of much discussion within the IPTA tradition ... particularly in terms of its identification as 'truly people's music.'"[90] Indeed, IPTA's

1946 Annual Report accorded a special and elevated status to folk traditions in the Bengal, in relation to other regions of South Asia: "Where classical influence is least felt, folk art has its richest traditions. Having no big temples as in the South or big royal courts like those of the Mughals and Rajput princes as in the North, before the coming of the British, where classical dance and music grew to its full stature under the patronage of princes and priests, Bengal developed its folk forms of art almost to a perfection. Today among all the provinces it is perhaps the richest in folk music, dance and drama."[91] Damodaran notes that when artists use folk songs, usually the songs would be presented "as they were," in order to introduce them to urbanized audiences.[92] However, in IPTA, the fidelity of folk music motifs to their original form was also a subject of contentious debate, as Anuradha Roy points out.[93] It may be recalled that Tripti Mitra and Timir Baran had been associated with IPTA and would have been deeply familiar with this debate.[94]

A *bhatiali* song is included in the Smithsonian collection *Folk Music of Pakistan* (1951), which was compiled with the assistance of the Pakistani government.[95] Willem van Schendel observes that radio broadcasts in rural areas had popularized such folk songs across East Bengal.[96] A translation of a poem mentioning *bhatiali* was published in *Pakistan Quarterly* in 1954. The poet Jasimuddin published a six-page article in *Pakistan Quarterly* in 1956, explaining various styles of folk music in East Bengal that included *bhatiali*.[97] Kardar and Faiz's exposure to *bhatiali* is thus also no mystery. But in *Jago Hua Savera*, the songs have been rendered into a North Indian linguistic register. Can we posit that the two songs are transcreations when rendered in the linguistic registers of Bhojpuri and Purbi? And if so, can this move be situated with reference to the IPTA debates regarding how closely to adhere to folk forms when deploying them in a progressive framework?

The third song was markedly different. And as noted above, only the local version of the film included a song-and-dance sequence in color, with a selection of verses from Faiz's poem "Shīshoṇ kā masīḥa ko'ī nahīṇ" (The shattered glass has no savior), and are reproduced in the *Jago Hua Savera* booklet. Here, the diction is closer to Urdu, with more Persianized vocabulary: is this choice of diction an implied critique of West Pakistani linguistic and economic colonialism over East Pakistan?[98] The song was reportedly performed as playback in the film by noted *ghazal* singer Iqbal Bano, "whose melodious voice had a spellbinding effect on the listeners," writes Agha Nasir, former managing director of Pakistan Television. Nasir's

BETWEEN NEOREALISM AND HUMANISM   49

observations are valuable in providing us with a sense of the character of this lost song sequence:

> The film is in black and white, but the scenes with the dancer Rakhshi are in color. They show a large hall in a magnificent mansion, where a spirited party with a dancer is carrying on [maḥfil-i raqs-o surūd barpā hai], with big landlords, industrial tycoons, high government officers, and corrupt politicians in attendance. The door to the hall is closed. Outside the mansion in semi darkness, the poor faithful servants overhear what's transpiring inside. The cameraman shot these scenes with great skill and ingenuity, such that the shift between color and black and white clearly signified the stark difference between the exploiter and the exploited.[99]

In his memoirs, however, Lassally recalls only the difficulties in filming this sequence: "To complicate matters further, A. J. [Kardar] had inserted a short colour sequence in the film, a musical number intended to be included only in the version of the film to be released locally—in fact considered essential for obtaining a local release at all. But the shooting of this musical sequence caused us a lot of headaches, the first being the set—the only one to be built inside the stage—which represented the living room of a smart modern villa."[100]

Nasir's remarks underscore the importance of the song, but Lassally clearly does not accord much significance to it. While in Lassally's recollection, this song was yet another "complication," Nasir's remarks stress how the aesthetics of the song and the cinematography underscore the film's symbolic message. How to understand this sharply contrasting significance of the song? And what to make of the aesthetic disjuncture—between color employed only for this sequence and black-and-white for the entire remaining film? The song sequence has unfortunately not surfaced so far, but we can speculate on its role based on the two remarks above.

In South Asian cinematic lexicon, an "item number" is a sexualized song-and-dance sequence gratuitously inserted in a cinematic narrative in order to increase audiences, often where the female dancer has no other role in the film.[101] Indeed, in *Jago Hua Savera*, Rakhshi's screen presence is limited only to this sequence. Nevertheless, Nasir's remarks suggest that this sequence has importance beyond its "item number" status and greatly contributes to the film's meaning in the South Asian context by distilling the sense of social disparity in a heightened and concentrated affective register. Which audiences are being activated by this song? Does inclusion of this possibly melodramatic picturization of "Shīshoṇ kā masīha ko'ī nahīṇ" only for *local* distribution cause *Jago Hua Savera* to vacillate between the neorealist and the social film genres but remain a "serious" film when seen abroad? Is this an instantiation of the Lahore effect discussed in the introduction, inserted in order to resonate with local audiences? We cannot definitively answer the latter question without viewing the lost song sequence, but Anna Morcom's gloss of the term *filmi* is suggestive: "the larger-than-life, showy, glittery, glamourous and overly dramatic film world, as opposed to the ordinary and mundane real world."[102] Do these breaches of form, between color and black-and-white footage, and the inclusion of a *filmi*, or commercial song and dance for a local audience in an otherwise austerely shot and scored film, suggest that we might understand this film's composition as a kind of pastiche, or an assemblage that flexes the Lahore effect? This quality of artifice is also underscored by the *bhatiali* songs that are not presented here "as they were" and as IPTA practitioners would have done but recast in Bhojpuri and Purbi and composed as extradiegetic aurality in an otherwise neorealist film.

LANGUAGE AND THE LIMITS OF HUMANISM

Jago Hua Savera positions itself between the humanist focus on the observation of difference that is primordial and eternal, and offering a critique of economic and social exploitation and suggesting that existing conditions are unsustainable. The difficulties of this straddling are most evident on the question of linguistic aporia, across which subaltern voices are translated into dominant linguistic registers. In *La Terra Trema*, Visconti had followed a peculiar strategy of deploying Sicilian as the spoken language of the film, rather than Italian. The dialogue was first developed with the actors, "without a pre-established script, allowing the performers to form their characters and formulate the most authentic ways of expressing a given narrative situation or certain sentiments."[103] But once finalized, the dialogue was "endlessly rehearsed to ensure clarity," lending a sense of stilted unnaturalness to the final performance. Haaland stresses that "no other film encapsulates the oral quality of neorealism or its exclusion of standard Italian with such rigour and with such sacrifices."[104] And Ray has observed that the acting is "deliberate and stylized to the point of ballet."[105] The voiceover in Italian interferes with the call for phenomenological immersion that the visuals hearken toward. Haaland notes that this creates a sense of "estrangement" and disturbs the viewing experience, leading to the film's poor reception, but "this anti-realistic effect may forge critical moments of self-awareness Visconti himself would have known in approaching the long-neglected South as a privileged Northerner."[106]

The role of language in *Jago Hua Savera* is in some ways opposite to that of *La Terra Trema*. In *Jago Hua Savera*, the dialogue is spare, and meaning is conveyed primarily by cinematic composition. And rather than rigorously using a local vernacular in its dialogue, *Jago Hua Savera* deploys mostly a kind of pidgin North Indian language register understandable to Hindi and Urdu speakers. At rare moments, female characters do speak very briefly in Bengali, but they do not speak much throughout the film.[107] The eccentric language in the film was "a peculiar mixture" of simplified Urdu and Bengali that was "easily understandable to neither communities," which contributed to its failure, according to Alamgir Kabir.[108] Naeem Mohaiemen has termed the film an "iconic, but ill-fated, hybrid (featuring an invented Urdu patois for East Bengal)."[109] Rather than seeing linguistic difference itself as an issue that the film might have addressed in narrative terms, the film instead posits a kind of synthetic resolution, using a form that emphasizes cinematic and visual compositions and editing, but spare dialogue, to strive toward broader intelligibility. And the larger framing of the project itself brings up issues of how subalternity is viewed from the vantage of gendered privilege—in this case with the additional twist that it was enjoyed by the largely West Pakistani team of filmmakers.

The film was not alone in this striving toward a shared intelligibility between Urdu and Bengali. For example, a 1959 essay in the establishment-oriented *Pakistan Quarterly* argued on the basis of linguistic evidence that dominant regional languages of North India and West Pakistan and including Urdu and Bengali were derived from a common "primitive Prakrit" origin.[110] Rather than evaluating the merits of the essay's argument, here I underscore the choice of the theme itself, which stresses a shared history that spans all the major regional languages of East and West Pakistan and includes Urdu in its capacious ambit. Moreover, the text of the essay is placed in a symbolic graphic layout, framed by letters of the Urdu and Bangla alphabets. The left column is composed of Urdu letters linked together with calligraphic flourishes, while the right column attempts the same with the Bangla alphabet. On the top, the calligraphed English title is comparatively small in size and placed in a dominant field of floating elements composed of the letters of the two alphabets and foliate patterns. The quest for linguistic breadth that would override the difference between Bengali and Urdu is thus enacted here through aesthetic form as well.

But by 1959, the year of *Jago Hua Savera*'s release and the publication of the article discussed above, this project of harmony was already freighted. The question of language differences between East and West Pakistan had emerged in 1948, right after the creation of Pakistan.[111] The 1952 language movement was suppressed violently; it became central to the consciousness of East Pakistanis in subsequent years, and it is commemorated by the Shaheed Minar located at the center of Dhaka, first erected in 1952 in a makeshift guerrilla act during curfew. (In its permanent form, it is perhaps Bangladesh's most iconic monument now.) And *Hamari Zaban* (Our language), a film produced in Karachi whose theme is reported to assert the position of Urdu against Bengali, had been released in 1955.[112] The issue of language would have been quite a central problem, especially for leftist intellectuals, who had already witnessed the traumatic effects of the Partition, in which the Hindi-Urdu divide was central.

The specific linguistic character of Faiz's contribution to the lyrics and the dialogue of *Jago Hua Savera* can perhaps be understood through Aamir Mufti's detailed analysis of a poem by Faiz written in 1965, right after the war between India and Pakistan. Mufti notes that in the poem "Sipāhī kā marṣiyā" (Soldier's elegy), Faiz eschews the Persianate diction of "high" Urdu and instead "turns to an idiom whose resonances are . . . 'Hindavi.'" Mufti further notes, "The poem opens up a window on the vast linguistic-literary vista—Braj, Avadhi, Bhojpuri, Dakhni, Maithli, Rajasthani, to name just a handful of the vernacular language forms that the northern region (and its southern outposts) have produced over the centuries—that has been occluded from view in the standardization of rival 'Hindi' and 'Urdu' registers. . . . [In the poem] the surface of modern language is peeled off to reveal submerged sounds and meanings."[113] One might therefore consider the experiment in the language of *Jago Hua Savera* analogously: as an attempt to bring the intimate stranger into an affective relation with the self. Nevertheless, one notes that Bengali remains absent in the linguistic register Mufti has identified above, falling outside intelligibility even by this expanded North Indian linguistic register. The problem of linguistic incommunicability in *Jago Hua Savera* thus could not be addressed by dialogic incorporation toward a greater synthesis.

On the other hand, it is also the case that progressive writers were concerned to focus on issues of social exploitation that would elicit wider solidarities, rather than focusing on ethnic and linguistic divisions that were fuel to the fires of communal divisions and violence that led to and attended the 1947 Partition. Moreover, an argument can be made that during the late fifties, a film attempting to reach a wider audience in South Asia (including eastern Bengal) might deploy the widely legible and simplified Hindi-Urdu that Bombay cinema had broadly popularized. David Lunn and Madhumita Lahiri have independently argued that "Hindustani" emerged as a spoken composite idiom that developed in the commercial films from Bombay after the arrival of the talkies in 1931.[114] Lahiri notes,

> Unfolding in the Marathi speaking region of western India, with numerous Bengali, Punjabi and Urdu speakers in the mix, Hindustani, in the sense of a mixed, accessible argot becomes the *de facto* and *de jure* language of this commercial sound cinema known as Bollywood, which I use here to refer to a consolidated filmmaking idiom, not simply any film made in Bombay (now Mumbai). The language ... is a flexible, miscible, endlessly expanding collage, using the syntactical structure common to Hindi and Urdu, but throwing in words from other languages at will: Persian, Sanskrit, Punjabi.[115]

Although commercial films' aesthetics have been endlessly disparaged by purists, this is an arena in which serious writers affiliated with the Progressive Writers' Association consciously participated. They had been committed to Hindustani as a language that could overcome regional and religious divides. And in a largely nonliterate South Asia of the mid-twentieth century, they understood film's vast potential to address audiences far beyond the reach of other mediums. It's worth stressing that many Hindi-Urdu films had been produced in Calcutta, including several in the mid-1930s by director Abdul Rashid Kardar (none other than the brother of A. J. Kardar). Bengal was thus no stranger to the production and circulation of Hindi-Urdu cinema. Indeed, the use of an idiom that Bombay and Lahore cinemas had helped forge was also prevalent in cinema in both East and West Pakistan, and Dhaka in the 1960s emerged as an important center for filmmaking in Urdu, with over fifty releases by 1971.[116] Moreover, exchange of film personnel between Lahore and Dhaka was not unusual, and Lotte Hoek has argued, "Between 1958 and 1971, the film industry of Pakistan straddled Lahore, Karachi, and Dhaka in a cross-wing love affair between stars and audiences, producers and profit, directors and fame, which could not always be assigned exclusively to either East or West, Urdu or Bengali."[117]

On the other hand, East Bengal's focus on Bengali-language cultural forms during the mid-twentieth century marked its departure from the multiple porous layers of cultural forms in Calcutta and West Bengal. Willem van Schendel has stressed that emerging developments in East Bengal after 1947 were forging a new national cultural trajectory that diverged from both Calcutta and Lahore, one that was "not bilingual (Bengali–English or Bengali–Urdu)," and in which expression in Bengali language was central.[118] Consequently, the absence of Bengali-language materials or explanation, in *Jago Hua Savera*'s opening credits, as substantive dialogue, as song, as subtitle, or in the booklet, is telling—it marks the unawareness in West Pakistani intelligentsia of the specificity of the emerging public linguistic and cultural sphere in East Pakistan.

Jago Hua Savera is best seen as an experimental project and a kind of opening gambit, rather than a product of a mature ecology of serious, experimental filmmaking accompanied by a robust discursive reception that would subject such ventures to critical scrutiny in Pakistan. It might have been received as a serious film in a wider South Asian context, and as we have seen, its production and its theme emphatically invite such a reception. But political and cultural currents ran in the reverse direction. Growing tensions between India and Pakistan since the fifties led to the banning of new Indian films in Pakistan by 1962. The 1965 war between India and Pakistan put an end to all exchange of films across borders. Widespread racism among West Pakistanis toward the inhabitants of East Pakistan also foreclosed genuine critical possibilities for dialogic understanding across languages, ethnicities, and lifeworlds. In contrast to the parallel cinema that developed in India with government support, in Pakistan conditions of patronage and reception were not conducive to build upon the experiment in a sustained manner.[119] The project of leftist filmmaking in Lahore's cinema, however, continued in a commercial register in the films of Khalil Qaiser and Riaz Shahid of the late fifties and sixties that examine minor and subaltern lives under exploitative circumstances.

The project of *Jago Hua Savera* also had to confront impassable aporias: its relevance for local publics and its legibility in the film festival circuit abroad, its breach of neorealist aesthetics in its songs and dialogue, and the strangeness of its linguistic register as it sought to overcome divides that were to become intractable. Moreover, as primarily the vision of West Pakistanis, *Jago Hua Savera* was caught between a humanism that saw rural life in East Bengal as lyrical and timeless and a progressive stance that viewed these conditions as exploitative and unsustainable. Alamgir Kabir was sharply critical of the film precisely for its awkward language and for its exoticizing of the riverine landscape of East Bengal. Nevertheless, his comment that *Jago Hua Savera* "still remains the only example of efficient film-making in Pakistan," published in his book as late as in 1969, suggests that Kabir also valued its cinematic approach, as well as the questions that it raised, as being important for subsequent serious cinema to grapple with.[120]

Jago Hua Savera moreover asks important questions about the relevance of an artistic form for its historical, social, and aesthetic significance. To what degree is fidelity to a genre like neorealism meaningful in a South Asia, where the commercial film has long reigned supreme? Who are the publics for a socially relevant cinema? How does a narrative artistic form overcome ethnicity, language, and other differences in its address without losing its locational specificity? A group of filmmakers associated with Khurshid Anwar, who addressed many of these questions in a lyric and romantic register, is examined in chapter 2. Their melodramatic films are suffused with pathos and melancholy, as they grapple with the sundering of local lifeworlds by a corrosive capitalist modernity and with the growing consolidation of an amnesiac nationalism in Pakistan in the wake of the Partition of 1947.

2 LYRIC ROMANTICISM

Khurshid Anwar's Music and Films

MUSIC, WRITING, AND DIRECTION IN THE FILMS OF KHURSHID Anwar (1912–84) weave centrally around the conflict between the "East" and the "West."[1] While this is a stock theme in commercial Indian and Pakistani cinema, Anwar renders this tension distinctive by the role music plays in its invitation to heal the unbearable implications of this divide. His films notate tremendous ambiguities in the staging of the East-West rift and create a modality less defined by rigid polarities than by immersion in a fraught process of becoming. In a further twist, the "East" here has a prelapsarian evocation that harks back to a conception of India before its dismemberment by the trauma of the Partition in 1947. In this sense, this elegiac body of work is suffused with a melancholic romanticism and offers an implied address that is sharply at variance with the claims of Pakistani nationalism. Rather, post-1947 realities only amplify the deep psychic damage within the films' sensitive and traumatized characters.

During the 1940s and early 1950s, Anwar had worked as a music director in Bombay and later continued this career in Pakistan. Renowned as a peerless music director in Lahore, he is also considered one of the most sophisticated directors of Pakistani cinema, as well as a writer and producer (figure 2.1). In his Lahore films, he worked closely with major cultural practitioners, including the director Masood Pervaiz (1918–2001), the author and playwright Imtiaz Ali Taj (1900–1970), poets Qateel Shifai (1919–2001) and Tanvir Naqvi (1919–72), the star actress and singer Noor Jehan (1926–2000), and the playback singers Naheed Niazi and Zubeida Khanum (1935–2013). His collaborations with Masood Pervaiz resulted in a small number of significant films—*Intezar* (The awaiting, 1956), *Zehr-e Ishq* (Poison of love, 1958), *Koel* (Nightingale, 1959), and *Heer Ranjha* (1970). Noted Urdu poet Qateel Shifai wrote *Zehr-e Ishq*'s lyrics, and famous playwright Syed Imtiaz Ali Taj provided the dialogue.

Taj has played a key role in the revival of Mughal historicals in Indian cinema—he had originally written the play *Anarkali* (1922), which ignited

FIG. 2.1. Khurshid Anwar (back toward camera) with musicians, c. 1957. Courtesy Khwaja Khurshid Anwar Trust.

the phenomenon of Anarkali revivalism that spanned decades, as discussed in the introduction.[2] As an Urdu playwright, Taj can be viewed as a successor to Agha Hashr Kashmiri (1879–1935), a most important playwright of Parsi theater during the early twentieth century.[3] A significant genre of silent and early sound cinema relayed the presentation of spectacle, frontal orientation, and declamatory Urdu rhetoric characteristic of Parsi theater into cinema as late as the 1950s.[4] Taj was also a key player in the Lahore literary arena.[5] His remarkable career includes his prolific writings, his considerable organizational work in promoting Urdu literature, his deep involvement with theater, and his work with cinema in Bombay and Lahore.[6]

KHURSHID ANWAR'S EARLY YEARS

Khurshid Anwar began his career in cinema as a music director in 1940 and later directed several important films during the 1960s and 1970s. Anwar is a multifaceted persona. Born in 1912 in Mianwali in Punjab, he attended Government College in Lahore, from where he received a master's degree in philosophy in 1935. After working in Delhi at All India Radio for a year, he moved to Bombay in 1940 to begin work in the cinema as a music director. The last

Bombay film he was involved with was *Neelam Pari* (The sapphire fairy, 1952). His career in Lahore cinema commenced with his role as writer and music director for *Intezar* (1956), which is discussed later in this chapter. His involvement with Lahore cinema includes his work as a music director, as a screenplay writer, and as director for a series of important films for over a decade.

Anwar was music director for *Koel* (Nightingale, 1959), *Ayaz* (1960), *Haveli* (Mansion, 1964), *Sarhad* (Border, 1966), *Heer Ranjha* (1970), and *Salam e Mohabbat* (Salutations of love, 1971), among others. In addition, Anwar was music director, screenwriter, and producer for six key films: *Intezar* (The awaiting, 1956), *Zehr-e Ishq* (Poison of love, 1958), *Jhoomer* (The jeweled forehead pendant, 1959), *Ghoonghat* (The veil, 1962), *Chingari* (Spark, 1964), and *Hamraz* (The confidant, 1967). Anwar was also director of three of these: *Ghoonghat* (1962), *Chingari* (1964), and *Hamraz* (1967), while the earlier three—*Intezar* (1956), *Zehr-e Ishq* (1958), and *Jhoomer* (1959)—were directed by Masood Pervaiz. These, along with *Koel* (1959), also directed by Pervaiz, will be the general focus of this chapter, but I focus in depth on *Intezar* and *Ghoonghat*. The close association of Anwar and Pervaiz in writing, composing, producing, and directing this cluster of films offers a reiterative vision for the ambitions of this romanticist project, which unfolds across a decade, and in which they are joined by poets Qateel Shifai and Tanvir Naqvi and by the singer Noor Jehan.

Born in a prominent and well-off family, Anwar was exposed to music and theater from an early age.[7] His father, a barrister by profession, is reported to have possessed a massive library of books and a gigantic collection of gramophone records, and he held regular musical gatherings in his home in which major exponents of Hindustani music would perform.[8] Apart from this broad exposure to literature and music, Anwar mentions his study of music with Ustad Tawakkul Hussain Khan, whom even the renowned Hindustani classical singer Bade Ghulam Ali Khan considered to be a rival.[9] Anwar also mentions writing poetry in his early years, successfully contributing to leading literary journals: "*Nairang-i-Khayal* was the top literary magazine of those days. I got one of my *ghazals* [lyric poems] published in it when I was merely a child studying in the 8th class. In Government College, Faiz and [poet] Noon Meer Rashid were my seniors by one and two years, respectively. We all wrote poetry and got it published here and there. [Poet] Akhtar Sherani once opined in his magazine *Rooman* ... that out of these three, young poets Khurshid Anwar seemed to be the most promising. But that was when we were really young."[10]

Anwar's father was also very keen on theater. Attending theatrical performances at a young age fired Anwar's imagination. "I used to sneak off to the theatre pretty regularly. Upon being caught once I was granted official permission by my father to attend whenever there was theatre around."[11] In memoirs published in the Urdu newspaper *Imroze* as fifteen serialized weekly interviews in 1983, Anwar recounts that from childhood he had an excellent grasp of acting and screenplay writing, which helped him in his later career in the cinema when preparing scripts and directing.[12] Anwar describes his early love for theater while he was still in school in class 6 or 7.[13] He would frequently stay up late at night to attend theater performances to such a degree that he would fall asleep during school the next day.[14] Anwar describes meeting in 1935 the playwright Rafi Peer, who had returned from Germany to Lahore and was living at the home of someone related to Anwar's family. Anwar, who was twenty-three years old, was deeply inspired by Peer's consuming commitment to the theater. Peer would work late hours engaged in solitary writing and in production with the actors. With Peer's encouragement, Anwar wrote his first play, which was broadcast by All India Radio in cities across India. In Lahore, the play was first produced by Rafi Peer and subsequently by Imtiaz Ali Taj.[15]

In 1935, Anwar passed his MA exams in philosophy from Government College. He came in as First Division, the only one to have achieved this distinction in some thirty years, and was awarded a gold medal. Subsequently, upon his father's insistence, he traveled to Delhi to take the Indian Civil Service (ICS) exams in 1936. According to Anwar, while he achieved high evaluations in all his written papers, he did poorly in the oral examinations, as the British authorities did not wish him to succeed due to his prior record and imprisonment for anti-British activity, which is discussed below.[16]

Anwar appears to have become increasingly involved with music after his ICS exams. He joined Lahore's newly formed radio station as a program producer, subsequently moving to Delhi circa 1939 to join All India Radio (AIR).[17] The blog commentator Harjap Singh Aujla notes, "Patras Bukhari was a bigwig at All India Radio Delhi. Khurshid Anwar knew him.... There was no dearth of poets in India at that time. Thus, there was plenty of good poetry to make tunes. Khurshid Anwar loved his tryst in New Delhi with the art of music composition."[18] At AIR Delhi, Anwar introduced a new program titled "Duets with Dialogues," in which a male and a female voice would alternately sing of their desire, in lyrics written by poet Behzad

Lakhnavi. Due to the popularity of this program, Anwar began to receive letters from filmmakers in Bombay, requesting him to compose for the cinema. Around 1940, the Lahore-born Bombay cinema director Abdul Rashid Kardar (brother of A. J. Kardar, director of *Jago Hua Savera*, discussed in chapter 1) finally persuaded him to relocate to Bombay, a move that launched Anwar's career in cinema.[19]

Exposure to this rich cultural background, which Anwar was immersed in since his childhood, has been seen by critics to have provided him with resources for his future work as a music director. His knowledge of music further developed during his stint as a music programmer for radio in Lahore from 1936 and in Delhi circa 1939–40.[20]

KHURSHID ANWAR'S BOMBAY YEARS

Anwar was music director in eleven films made in Bombay between 1941 and 1952. The films whose music was well received by the public included *Pagdandi* (The path) and *Parwana* (The moth), both released in 1947. The latter film was extensively viewed during the Partition violence of 1947, observes Aujla, whose father was witness to developments in the Punjab and North India during the turbulent forties:

> *Parwana* starring brilliant singer actor K. L. Saigal and Suraiya catapulted Khurshid Anwar into the galaxy of all time great music director. All songs of this movie became hit[s]. . . . 1947 was not a good year for the film industry, in spite of that *Parwana* did a roaring business, not only in the Ganges Basin states, but in the most disturbed Province of Punjab. Lahore and Amritsar were witnessing bloodbaths of the worst order, but [the] film *Parwana* was doing great among the Muslims of Lahore and Sikhs and Hindus of Amritsar. Both cities . . . were drawing packed houses.[21]

From this experience, Anwar would have likely become more aware of the role of music in creating an immersive healing sensorium that affectively enacted a romantic mythos beyond the fractures of life in a divided postcolonial modernity.[22] Anwar's last film in Bombay was *Neelam Pari* (1952). He had already moved permanently back to Lahore, but he returned to Bombay for a few weeks to finish this assignment.[23] Anwar's status in the Bombay film industry needs to be contextualized in the broader traffic between Bombay and Lahore after the emergence of the talkies in India in 1931.[24]

The writer Ashraf Aziz has situated the modernity of film music during the 1930s onward as having been impacted by the "rhythmic/percussive assertiveness" drawn from the sonic aesthetics of the Punjab, while film historian Ashish Rajadhyaksha has argued for a broader "Lahore effect" that flexed from the thirties onward in Bombay and Lahore cinema.[25]

Anwar's career in Bombay overlaps with currents that led to the transformation of film music in Bombay. Anwar worked with the important singers Kundan Lal Saigal and Noor Jehan, and his compositions from 1947 onward are held in critical regard.[26] Although musicologist Gregory Booth does not list him as among the six key persons who precipitated the transformations toward the mature film song of the fifties, Anwar worked in Bombay cinema from 1940 till 1952, crucial years for the film song coming to maturity in its aural and narrative significance in the golden-age melodramatic cinema of the fifties and sixties, with which he would have been intimately familiar.[27]

KHURSHID ANWAR'S POLITICAL ACTIVISM

To understand Khurshid Anwar's songs and films from his mature career in the long sixties, it is essential to account for his seemingly unrelated involvement with resistance movements against the British during the late 1920s and early 1930s. This was when Anwar was about seventeen or eighteen years old. There are two facets to his youthful political involvement. First there is his exposure to Bhagat Singh's trial, then there is Anwar's own involvement in a clandestine resistance cell and his subsequent arrest and imprisonment.

One of the most iconic figures in the revolutionary struggles against the British in North India in the late 1920s—a time of the radicalization of young people—was Bhagat Singh (1907–31), who was executed by the British when he was only twenty-three years old. Singh had studied in Lahore and became politically radicalized there in his teens. He was a strategic thinker and a voracious reader, well-informed about historical and political developments internationally, including Marxist thought and radical nationalist movements in Europe.[28] Sometime between 1924 and 1926, Singh had founded the Naujawan Bharat Sabha (NJBS), a youth organization with a socialist and nationalist orientation.[29] He also became a member of the Hindustan Republican Association (HRA), which later became the Hindustan Socialist Republican Association (HSRA) in 1928, partly modeled after the Irish Republican Army (IRA).[30] The HSRA members carried out several spectacular attacks against symbols of British authority. In these actions, they were drawing upon earlier nationalist struggles, as well as on the precedents set by episodes in international anarchism, rather than on the pacifist course adopted in the 1920s by Gandhi and the Indian National Congress, which the HSRA members viewed as being insufficient to address colonialism.

Singh was a highly charismatic leader. He wrote extensively and exploited print media and magic lantern presentations to inspire others to support revolutionary anticolonialism. An avowed atheist, he was resolutely anticommunal, rendering his movement appealing to various publics.[31] In early 1929, Singh and one of his associates were arrested after they threw smoke bombs and leaflets in the Central Legislative Assembly in Delhi. These actions, which were accompanied by the pair proclaiming the revolutionary slogan *"inqilāb zindabād"* (long live revolution), were not intended to kill anyone but meant to rally public opinion toward revolutionary struggle. Consequently, the pair did not attempt to escape the scene after their disruption, inviting arrest.

Singh and B. K. Dutt surrendered themselves to the police on April 8, 1929. Their trial for the bombing was held in Delhi, leading to their sentence to life imprisonment on June 12, 1929. They had embraced the proceedings as an opportunity to proclaim their cause publicly, "to let the imperialist exploiters know that by crushing individuals, they cannot kill ideas."[32] Singh and his associates were subsequently moved to Lahore to undergo another trial, the second Lahore Conspiracy Case, or simply the Lahore Conspiracy Case, whose "charge sheet included thirty-two revolutionaries, comprising the entire Central Committee as well as the HSRA's junior members."[33] The protracted trial at the Magistrate's Court, which started on July 10, 1929, and lasted for more than a year, was marked by the accused theatrically breaching court decorum, their rebellious spirits reverberating in the crowd chanting slogans outside.[34] The imprisonment and trial of HSRA associates on charges of bomb making and prior subversive activities attracted widespread concern across India, forcing the leaders of the Congress to support their cause in public. Despite the defiant spirit of many of the accused, the authorities had turned seven of the thirty-two into approvers, or collaborators with the British, who "would be subject to intimidation and violence inside and outside the court" by the public and one of whom was shot and killed in February 1930.[35] The court announced its verdict against Bhagat Singh on October 7, 1930. He and two others were to be sentenced to death by hanging, and seven others received life sentences.[36]

The three were executed on March 23, 1931, hanged in Lahore Jail, their bodies secretly cremated by jail authorities and their ashes immersed in the Sutlej River in order to forestall their growing status as heroes and martyrs.[37]

The tribulations of Bhagat Singh and his associates, and nationalist revolutionary rhetoric, were amplified among the public in oral and written registers. In addition to posters with images, prose and verse abounding in rhetorical flourish, much of it suffused with poetic tropes from Urdu, was also widely circulating and much discussed. Ram Prasad Bismil (1897–1927), a founding member of the HRA who had been executed in 1927 for the Kakori train robbery in 1925, had composed memorable revolutionary poetry in Hindi and Urdu that had continued to circulate. And in Bhagat Singh's purported last letter, written from jail on March 3, 1931, he wrote down several couplets of Urdu poetry.[38] This rich iconology of martyrdom began to develop during the days of the trial itself. Images of the imprisoned youthful HSRA members began to proliferate in posters and leaflets distributed in markets and meetings.[39] Bhagat Singh and his associates have also been the subject of several hagiographical movies over the years. Of interest here is the imbrication of their revolutionary politics with romantic cultural tropes, expressed in Urdu poetry, iconicity, and the moving image. Even though Khurshid Anwar's films in Lahore during the long sixties never directly address politics, the political realm remains adjacent to seemingly private tribulations when evoked via these mediums and cultural registers.

Recent scholarship on Bhagat Singh and his associates has taken important critical turns, which reformulate the afterlife of the Bhagat Singh phenomenon in ways that do not easily settle into congealed history.[40] J. Daniel Elam has examined the reading practices and political thought of Bhagat Singh, seeing in them a radical and open-ended potential toward the fashioning of new political subjectivities. Elam observes how, in his notes and writings, Singh sought to encourage the reader to "practice self-cultivation without the demand to attain mastery," rather than providing formulaic answers to what constitutes proper revolutionary activity or its ends.[41] It must be stressed that the crisis of "proper politics" was arguably exacerbated in Pakistan during the fifties and sixties, when political horizons had become circumscribed by nationalism on the one hand and leftist cultural politics on the other, and where no coherent opposition could be identified, unlike the case of Bhagat Singh and the British. I argue that Anwar's films from the long sixties also stress the significance of "self-cultivation" in an open-ended way, in order come to terms with the aporias of the present.

Another facet of new research on HSRA is in seeing what modalities for thinking and capacities for acting were available to these young people, given that they lived at a time when revolutionary thinking was inextricably shaped by numerous international resonances. Chris Moffat's study includes an examination of the effects of Bhagat Singh's spectral presence on the living, how it remains a force of "dissensus" that disturbs normative ideas of the political community in postcolonial South Asia: "This vision of a political community that draws together the living and the dead allows us to think differently about the force and effects of anti-colonial histories in a postcolonial present.... To acknowledge the work of the dead is to accept that the living may face the future but can be distracted, deterred or roused by their sense of obligation, duty or debt to the heroes or victims of struggles past."[42]

Significantly, Moffat also examines how activists have invoked Bhagat Singh in contemporary Pakistan during the past three decades.[43] An analogous specter is evident in the films of Khurshid Anwar, of Indic worlds under erasure in Pakistan.

KHURSHID ANWAR'S POLITICAL AWAKENING

During his career and after his death, Khurshid Anwar has enjoyed a reputation as a highly intelligent, educated, and refined professional, whose knowledge of Hindustani music was unrivaled. However, his involvement with political activism during this time was a subject of speculation in later years. For instance, a recollection published in 2011 by Ustad Ghulam Haider Khan observes, "In his personal life, Khawaja Khurshid Anwar was a shy, reserved and unsocial person.... He avoided big gatherings and wasn't fond of sharing his personal affairs with others."[44] In an interview in English with Javed Usman, Anwar underscores that his melancholic outlook is the result of thwarted youthful love: "I can trace the pathos of my music to an early experience of mine which to this day has manifested itself in all that I have created. I fell madly in love with a girl when I was in my teens.... When I turned 16, she suddenly died. I was completely shattered. The scar has remained."[45] As to why Anwar is "shy and introverted," he replies, "There has been a streak in me, since her death, which prevents me from becoming outward and warm. But, definitely, with the passing of years I have increasingly withdrawn into myself because of the deterioration in the quality of the people I have had to face in my professional as well as general life."[46] However, as Ustad Ghulam Haider Khan notes, another factor in the introverted Anwar persona may have been the rumored suspicion that he betrayed Bhagat Singh's cause: "The only stain on his character, as told by some old denizens of Lahore, was that he saved his skin and surrendered information concerning the whereabouts of the anti-imperialist rebel Bhagat Singh, who was later caught by the British and hanged."[47]

Considerable ambiguity still surrounds the historical record of the HSRA and its activities. This is partly because many of their meetings and activities were conducted under the cloak of secrecy, as the British authorities at various levels, including the local police, were continuously involved in planting accomplices among anticolonial groups, turning those arrested into collaborators, and exerting pressure on suspects during trials to turn into an "approver" who "was both an informer and an accuser" and would testify against the others. The suspicion of being a collaborator during revolutionary activities, and of becoming a possible turncoat during trials, also created tensions and suspicions between small groups of members tasked with carrying out bomb making and other clandestine activities. Anyone tainted with being unreliable as a comrade, collaborator, or "approver" would bear this stigma in their future.[48]

This burden of memory and the rumors of his alleged betrayal may well have weighed heavily on Khurshid Anwar: in 1983, shortly before he passed away, he gave an extended series of interviews to a journalist that was serialized over fifteen weeks in the Urdu newspaper *Imroze*'s Sunday edition. The interviews are precise in many details, but some names, events, and organizations remain without specificity. Frail, but still possessed of a sharp memory, Anwar ranges widely in remembering facets and episodes of his life: friendship and rivalry with Faiz Ahmed Faiz, vacationing in Kashmir with Mulk Raj Anand, his early fascination with theater, involvement with All India Radio and later with Radio Pakistan, remembrance of the classical musicians, film music directors he knew and playback singers he had worked with, and the question of sectarian interpretation of music scholarship by Pandit Vishnu Narayan Bhatkhande, a scholar who systematized the modern classification of Hindustani classical music.[49] In these interviews, Anwar discusses his work as a music director in Bombay films only in a single interview and does not discuss his work in Pakistani cinema at all.[50] The topic toward which he devotes the greatest attention is the period of his political involvement between 1929 and 1931, suggesting that this was a deeply formative experience and that suspicions and rumors regarding his role remained unsettling for him, even at the end of his life.

Khurshid Anwar was about seventeen years old in 1929, the year of Bhagat Singh's spectacular bombing in Delhi and his arrest. Bhagat Singh was an "ideal" and "hero" for him.[51] Anwar was involved in demonstrations against the Simon Commission of 1928, along with the organizers from the NJBS.[52] Anwar began attending the trial of Bhagat Singh, which brought him to the attention of other revolutionaries and the authorities: "After I had attended 10 or 12 sessions of the Bhagat Sigh trial, one day a young man approached me at the Oval Grounds of the Government College. He had a briefcase with him. After speaking to me of patriotism and lauding me for being a freedom lover, since I was attending the trial that many others avoided [so as not to be noticed by the British authorities], he mentioned that the leadership of the 'Central Revolutionary Party' of India was impressed by my bravery and commitment."[53]

That day, Anwar was recruited by this man, whose name was Rahim Baksh and who was an MA student of economics at the Government College. At that meeting, he stressed to Anwar that "you will need to risk your life, make bombs, and use firearms." He asked Anwar to select a pistol from the briefcase and suggested that he practice shooting with the firearm. Anwar subsequently met other recruits. The group became involved in bomb making and planned a bank robbery in the city of Gujarat, which they did not carry out.[54] Nevertheless, they were arrested, as one of the bomb makers, who was picked up on other charges, apparently turned state's witness.[55] Moreover, Rahim Baksh himself was later revealed to be a British collaborator.[56]

According to his memoir, Anwar was arrested in 1929, for making bombs and spreading terror. After being jailed for four or five months, he was released, and he continued with his education.[57] During his arrest, he was under tremendous pressure by the police to turn state's witness, or "approver" in British India, someone specifically groomed to assist in prosecuting conspiracy trials during the twentieth century.[58] To shield his associates from this pressure and to avoid becoming an approver, Anwar devised a ruse: he agreed initially to become a witness, but on the condition that he would provide his testimony only the day before the trial.[59] Despite immense pressure applied on him right before the trial, including being shown the collaboration of Rahim Baksh with the police and a dramatic threat by Anwar's father that he would shoot himself if Anwar did not cooperate with the authorities, Anwar emphasizes that he flatly refused to provide testimony against his comrades.[60] Only Anwar was found guilty and given a jail sentence of two years, while all his partners were released.

In the meantime, higher authorities in the British government became aware that the police had manufactured this case. During the appeals process, the British judge himself advised Anwar's father to hire a noted lawyer, who managed to have Anwar acquitted.[61] In total, Anwar had spent four to five months' time in prison. In his *Imroze* interviews, Anwar is especially at pains to clear his name from being called an approver or state witness in the Bhagat Singh trial:

> It is necessary for me to absolutely clarify my involvement with Bhagat Singh. I saw him for the first time only at his trial. At that time, I was only 16 or 17 years old. During the trial, no one could meet Singh or his associates. None of his companions were Muslim, and in any case, I did not know any of them. It is therefore out of the question that I could have become a state witness against him. . . . I have never been a state witness in any trial . . . the case I was sentenced for was unrelated to the Bhagat Singh trial.[62]

Moreover, it's difficult to accept the veracity of the rumors of Anwar becoming an approver, or else why would he have served any jail time if he had indeed been a British collaborator?

Nevertheless, this charged period arguably deeply shaped his later career. Ustad Ghulam Haider Khan observes that "Anwar lived a lonely and quiet life" and adds, "He must have been devastated by Bhagat Singh's death. Perhaps it was such a devastation that he brought to his music, which was full of subtle microtones and bold glides and always pervaded by a heartrending anguish."[63] In his interviews, Anwar clarifies his political leanings in many places. He situates himself against emerging leftist writers and intellectuals such as Faiz Ahmed Faiz, whose years studying at the Government College overlapped with Anwar's and with whom he had become close friends. Anwar repeatedly dissociates himself from Marxism and communism even during college days. For example, recounting a summer vacation to Kashmir with Faiz and two other writers from Lahore, he notes, "We met Mulk Raj Anand, who was a well-known communist. At that time, Faiz was totally unfamiliar with communism. . . . I had completed my MA in Philosophy, had already studied Hegel and Marx, and was very knowledgeable about the strengths and weaknesses of communism. That is why it never influenced me."[64] According to Anwar, Anand saw the world through a narrow Marxist lens, almost to comical effect: "When I would draw Mulk Raj Anand's attention to the colors of the sunset among beautiful mountains and streams, he would remark, 'These colors are reminiscent of the blood of the toiling Russian peasants.'... Despite lengthy discussions, he was unable to influence me. The reason is that communism does not uphold any ultimate values."[65] Anwar also understands Bhagat Singh as someone not primarily influenced by communism. Rather, he suggests that Bhagat Singh's "ideal" was the Irish Republican Army, which was also fighting against the British.[66]

My purpose here is neither to ascertain the young Faiz's awareness of Marxism nor to determine Bhagat Singh's ideological stance.[67] Anwar's insistent retrospective disavowal of Marxism and communism is of interest here because this can help explain why his later film work, despite being deeply engaged with the affective burden of colonialism, is suffused with romantic melancholy, rather than, for example, allegories of political struggle against colonization, such as in the films of his younger contemporaries Khalil Qaiser and Riaz Shahid in the Lahore film world.

Anwar's melancholic outlook is also evident in the reception of the "signature tune" he composed for Radio Pakistan upon independence, in 1947. In an interview, he notes that the tune, with "light rhythm," was intended to evoke an "Oriental" feeling (*mashriqiyyat*): a composition with its main section deploying the clarinet and based on the sound of Qur'anic recitation (*qir'at*). The tune was first played on the radio on August 14, 1947, and continued to be played for the next six months. However, a senior classical musician, probably none other than Bade Ghulam Ali Khan himself, criticized it, claiming that it sounded like a "poetic lament suffused with pain [*kisī marṣiye ke dukh se ubhrī ho*]."[68] It was consequently replaced by a tune composed by Bade Ghulam Ali Khan and Z. A. Bukhari, director of the newly established Radio Pakistan.[69] In addition to having his tune rejected, Anwar recounts that his persistent, ongoing criticism of Radio Pakistan's leadership for their ignorance of music eventually led to his being blacklisted from appearing on the radio.[70] Despite his unpleasant experiences with Radio Pakistan, he continued to tirelessly promote knowledge of classical music. According to some observers, Anwar's greatest contribution to culture, even beyond his work as a renowned film music director and director of films, is his massive project Ahang-e-Khusravi: thirty long-playing albums that document Hindustani classical music. Ten albums demonstrate over ninety ragas, and another twenty albums record the distinctive musical styles of various lineages of hereditary musicians (*gharanas*). It is "a work that was unique in subcontinental music history at the time, and has perhaps no parallel to this date."[71]

Given his avowed repudiation of Marxism, his prior affiliation with Bhagat Singh's anti-imperialist politics, and his deep interest in bridging the legacy of Hindustani classical music in a dialogue with modernity via the film song, Khurshid Anwar emerges as an exemplary figure among the Lahore Romanticists. In his work for Lahore cinema from 1956 onward, he inhabits the capaciousness of the social film to mourn the Partition and to engage with a modernity that is endlessly seductive but dangerously fatal—necessary, yet impossible. He is especially well-placed to do so, with the song-and-dance sequence in the fifties social film having become the most symbolic site for narrative and affective charge. Melodramatic conventions such as missed encounters and emotive identifications are all used repeatedly and effectively in Anwar's films, as is genre crossing.[72] Above all, the Partition's reverberative effects are evoked in Anwar's films of the long sixties, in doubled and misidentified characterization, Gothic specters, Indic "primitivist" myths, and ruined and traumatized lives.[73]

Bhaskar Sarkar's observations in his substantial study of Indian cinema's engagement with the Partition are apposite for Anwar's projects. Sarkar notes that a "traumatic experience need not unfold at a lag: it can generate a temporality all its own, one that runs alongside and yet in out of sync with the present."[74] As in the film *Ghoonghat* (1962), the male lead character lives in a dream world whose thrall persists till the very end of the film. Doubling and misidentification is another trope repeatedly deployed in Anwar's films. In *Intezar* (1956), the lead character and his disreputable brother, played by the same actor, look identical and threaten confusion in the resolution of the love triangle between the brothers and the lead actress and singer, played by Noor Jehan. And in *Ghoonghat*, "figural sublimations and displacements" are central, based on "irrational" Hindu beliefs in reincarnation that the consolidation of Pakistan as a Muslim nation ought to have put to rest.[75] The present-day couple is haunted by the myth of an earlier pair of Hindu lovers, which confounds the male lead character, who becomes "enfeebled, hystericized, queer, and nearly insane," to quote Meheli Sen's characterization of the Gothic film from Bombay.[76] Indeed, doubling and repetition in a larger sense characterize Anwar's cinematic oeuvre itself. *Intezar* and *Koel* (1959) explore a narrative that is uncannily similar. *Jhoomer* (1959) and *Chingari* (1964) ostensibly narrate how westernization leads characters far beyond the bounds of accepted morality, but in doing so, both evoke an unsettling and conflicted affect in the viewer. And the actress Shamim Ara plays a double role as twin sisters in the Gothic mystery film *Hamraz* (1967), similar to the doubling of the male characters in *Intezar* (1956).

INTEZAR (1956)

Anwar's career in the Urdu cinema in Pakistan includes the work he did as music director and writer of dialogue in the films of the later fifties, which include *Intezar* (1956), *Zehr-e Ishq* (1958), *Jhoomer* (1959), and *Koel* (1959). *Intezar* and *Koel* have corresponding plots. Both films revolve around a story with a master classical musician living in an idyllic mountainous rural setting, whose daughter is also becoming a gifted singer under his tutelage. As a child, the daughter develops a deep friendship with a boy living nearby, who moves away, evoking a lasting sense of longing and heartache in both the girl and the boy that persists over years and decades, even after both have reached adulthood. The death or absence of the father figure creates difficult circumstances for the daughter, now a young woman, compelling her to accede to the machinations of unscrupulous men who wish to exploit her unrivaled musical talent as a nightclub singer in the city. Here, the purity of Indian classical music is staged against debased westernized music, which becomes emblematic of the moral quagmire in which the girl finds herself in a modernity that induces not only moral corruption but also psychic trauma in its sensitive characters.

This skeletal summary might convey the sense that both films follow a common narrative in South Asian cinema. Repetition of narrative tropes, however, is not a good indicator of the significance of artifacts of popular culture.[77] Rather, what distinguishes these productions from innumerable other films that stress the same basic divide between the prelapsarian "East" and the fallen "West" is the way Anwar's aural compositions and the film's dialogue work with the camera to stress specific effects. In the case of *Intezar*, intercinematic references pervade its dialogue and songs to create a sense of a knowing, referential, even ironic participation as a film that situates itself within the unfolding history of both South Asian and Hollywood musicals. By contrast, *Koel* conjures a phenomenological aura of being immersed in gyres, circular movements, and orbits that evoke a ceaseless energy that pervades life on screen. Even as both films ostensibly stage the contrast between the purity of Indian classical music and corrosive Western influences, the films' formal elements, dialogue, and the songs themselves are far more complex—conflicted, even duplicitous in how they address this binary.

Intezar was the first major film Anwar worked on in Lahore. Imtiaz Ali Taj contributed to its dialogue. As noted already, Taj's long association with cinema started with his celebrated play *Anarkali* (1922), which was adapted on screen multiple times, and continued to his directing two films during the mid-1930s and *Gulnar* in 1953.[78] The two poets who contributed lyrics to *Gulnar* are Qateel Shifai and Tanvir Naqvi, who both subsequently worked with Anwar on numerous films. *Gulnar*'s music was composed by the legendary composer Master Ghulam Haider—this was Haider's last film.[79] In addition, as a writer, Taj participated in the Lahore-based Pancholi Studios film *Khandan* (Family, 1942, dir. Shaukat Hussain Rizvi), with music directed by Master Ghulam Haider, and the Bombay film *Pagdandi* (The path, 1947, dir. Ram Narayan Dave), with Anwar as the music director. Noor Jehan starred and sang in numerous films in which these individuals has been involved.[80]

Thus, the careers of a group of poets, writers, directors, composers, singers, and actors who had been engaged with both Bombay cinema and Lahore cinema for several decades were already entangled in numerous productions before *Intezar*. In this sense, we need to situate *Intezar* and *Koel* both with reference to continuity with the legacies of Bombay and Lahore cinema but also to mark their distinctiveness in relation to the effects of the Partition, the drive toward modernization in Pakistan that was accelerating from the late fifties onward, and the reformulated ensemble of patronage, infrastructure, and expertise available to a Lahore that could no longer draw upon the much larger and more sophisticated ecology of the Bombay film industry. Despite this lack, "the film's photography and sound are good. For a newcomer, Nabi Ahmad's work behind the camera is commendable. Some of the outdoor shots are especially worth mentioning," the renowned journalist and human rights advocate I. A. Rehman's review of *Intezar* had noted.[81]

PLOT SUMMARY OF *INTEZAR*

Intezar's narrative is centered on the pair Nimmi and Salim. Nimmi resides with her father, a gifted classical musician, in a small house set in a beautiful mountainous region. They are attended to by the unscrupulous Lachoo and his daughter Cheemo, who is the same age as Nimmi. Across the valley is a bungalow in which Salim is staying with his mother. They are originally from Karachi but have been residing in the bungalow for some time. Salim, Nimmi, and Cheemo become fast friends, but due to their respectable upper-class status, Salim's mother dislikes him spending time with the two girls, especially when they sing and dance to accompany Nimmi's father's musical exercises. Nevertheless, Salim and Nimmi have become very close. They signal to each other from across the valley at night, Salim with a flashlight and Nimmi with a lantern. When Salim and his mother depart for Karachi in an automobile, an emotionally overcome Nimmi insists on climbing a hill to see them leave. In anguish, she loses her balance and tumbles downhill, losing her eyesight as a result.

Fifteen years pass. Salim (played as an adult by Santosh Kumar) has become an emotionally disturbed person who cannot sleep at night, wakes up to repeatedly signal with a flashlight from his window in his Karachi home, and compulsively plays the sitar at odd hours. Recognizing the effects of childhood trauma, the doctor advises him to return to the mountain bungalow. We learn that Salim's father was a dissolute character, which is why his mother was insistent on keeping Salim away from performing entertainment in his childhood. However, Salim's brother, Naeem (also acted by Santosh Kumar in a double role), has followed the father's wayward path. Naeem is owner of the Rang Mahal theater, where risqué and tasteless musical and dance performances are held. A gambler and spendthrift, Naeem is constantly sponging on the saintly and troubled Salim, who always indulges him and even transfers half of his fortune to Naeem early in the film.

When the traumatized Salim (accompanied with his loyal elderly attendant) arrives at the mountain bungalow, chimney smoke and lights alert Cheemo that someone has returned. Although Nimmi (played as an adult by Noor Jehan) constantly keeps alive the hope that she will be eventually reunited with Salim, due to her blindness she is unable to see that the bungalow is now inhabited. Cheemo and her father, Lachoo, hatch a conspiracy, in which Cheemo pretends to be Nimmi and begins to meet Salim regularly. A difficulty soon presents itself—Cheemo can dance but cannot sing, yet Salim insists on hearing the soothing balm of Nimmi's singing voice to alleviate his trauma. Cheemo resolves this by forbidding Salim to visit Nimmi's home and requesting that Nimmi sing only at night, so that Salim in his bungalow can hear her soaring and floating voice across the valley but he cannot see the singer. Nimmi is also unable to see his flashlight signals due to her blindness. The pretense of Cheemo as Nimmi is thus maintained for Salim, even as he remains puzzled when meeting Cheemo about whether she could indeed possess such a mesmerizing voice. One night, Nimmi's father, whose health has been poor, passes away dramatically, collapsing on his veena during a swan-song practice session. Before dying, he has asked Nimmi to memorize Salim's Karachi address.

In the meantime, the Rang Mahal theater is facing difficulties. Music director D'Souza, a Goan Christian, is dismissive of Indian classical music

FIG. 2.2. The Latin-themed song orchestrated by D'Souza, "Javānī kī raten javānī ke din" (Days and nights of youthful passion), with Pepita accompanied by male and female performers, on the Rang Mahal stage. *Intezar* (1956).

and is interested only in music derived from Hollywood productions, especially jazz and Cuban-inflected compositions (figure 2.2).

However, Naeem wants the club to attract more customers and is looking at alternatives. Lachoo had written earlier to Naeem's club manager, Ghafoor, of Nimmi's singing talent and Cheemo's dancing abilities. Now Ghafoor also arrives in the mountains in order to recruit both as fresh talent for Rang Mahal. With Nimmi's father now deceased, this becomes possible, just as Lachoo had schemed. Lachoo convinces Nimmi to move to Karachi so that she can search for Salim and have her lost eyesight medically treated. The final song Nimmi sings in the valley before leaving is at night, at one end of a suspended footbridge that connects her side of the mountain to the one across the river, where Salim's bungalow is located. When a transfixed Salim arrives at the other end of the footbridge and begins to walk across, a horrified Cheemo witnesses Lachoo attacking him with an ax and throwing him into the river. Cheemo is a passive accomplice-witness in this dastardly plot.

With the arrival of Nimmi, Cheemo, and Lachoo in Karachi, on meeting Naeem (who looks exactly like Salim), Lachoo is panicked in thinking that it is Salim who survived the attack and will now recognize him as the attacker. Naeem eventually sets aside D'Souza's compositions, musicians,

FIG. 2.3. Naeem (right) selfishly tries to convince his look-alike brother Salim (left) that Naeem should remain misrecognized as Salim, so that Nimmi and Naeem can be together. *Intezar* (1956).

dancers, and singers. Instead, now Nimmi sings and Cheemo dances in new compositions ostensibly based on Indian classical music, creating great audience demand for Rang Mahal. Nimmi continues to seek Salim's whereabouts. One day, Salim, who has survived his attack and fall but lost one of his legs, walks into Rang Mahal on crutches and sees Cheemo dancing, while Nimmi sings from behind a curtain. Cheemo refuses to recognize him, but Nimmi overhears their conversation. As he leaves the empty theater, Nimmi sings the evocative song "O jāne wāle re, ṭhero zarā ruk jā'o" (Pause a bit, don't leave yet). Salim recognizes the familiar voice but remains puzzled and leaves without meeting Nimmi.

Nimmi continues to seek Salim and visits his home on Lytton Road in Karachi. Eventually, she begins living there. Meanwhile, because of Nimmi's beauty, voice, and character, Naeem also begins to fall in love with her. Finally, Nimmi's eyes are operated on, and she is able to see. Salim is overjoyed but now afraid that Nimmi will reject him because he is disabled. Naeem selfishly tries to convince Salim that he should remain unrecognized as Salim, so that Nimmi and Naeem can be together (figure 2.3).

Eventually, this triangle is resolved by Nimmi, who attends to the brothers' contrasting affiliations for music. She confirms this by pretending to lose her eyesight again and seeing that the brothers have sharply

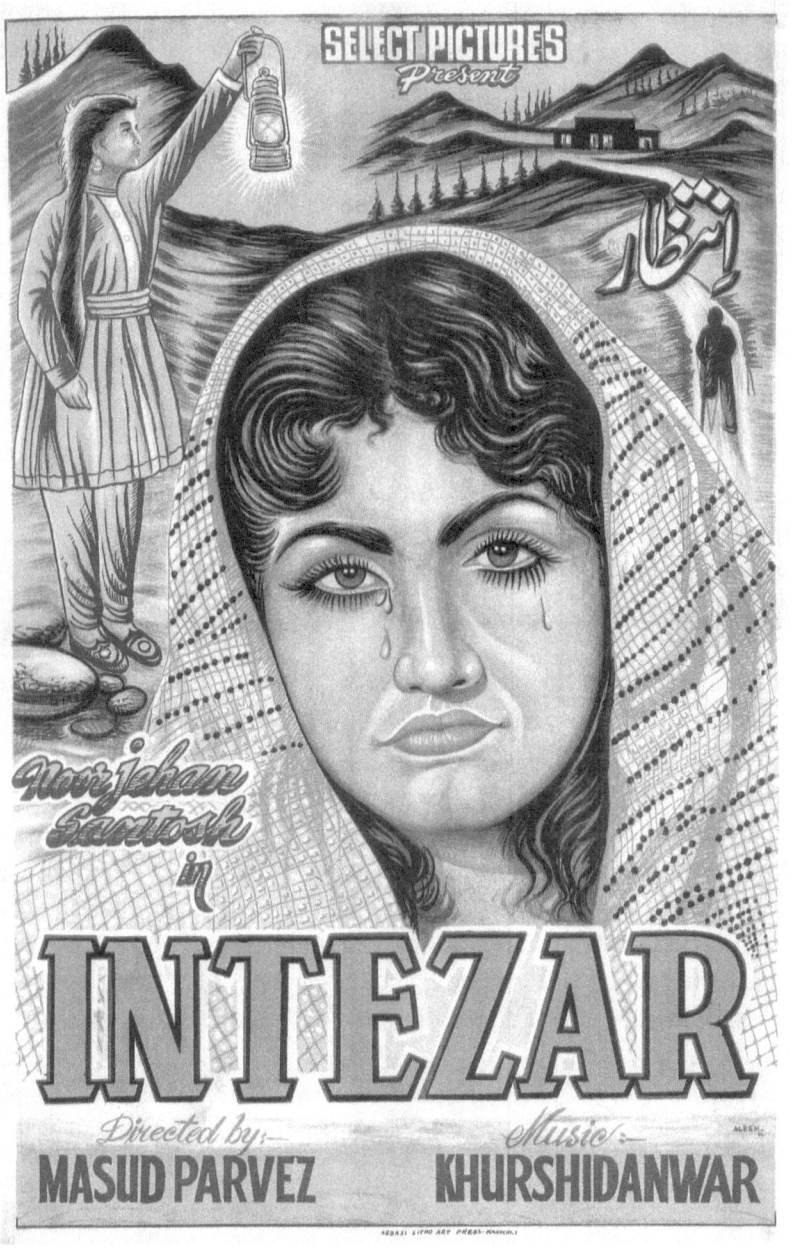

FIG. 2.4. Publicity poster of the film *Intezar* (1956), similar to the image advertising the new live show titled *Intezar* in Rang Mahal within the film.

divergent behavior: Salim is sensitive and generous, while Naeem is profligate and dissolute even as he now wants to reform himself for the sake of her love.

Without Nimmi singing at Rang Mahal every night, the theater founders, as Cheemo's dancing alone is not sufficient to draw big or appreciative audiences. When Nimmi returns in a pathos-laden triumph at the end, the program and publicity material in the lobby changes from the live show called *Aankh ka nasha* to a new live show titled *Intezar*. The latter's publicity image is analogous the actual poster of the film *Intezar* (figure 2.4), collapsing the distinction between the film itself and the theatrical show nested in it.

Lachoo and Cheemo fall out of favor and are thrown out of Rang Mahal. As revenge, they set fire to the theater. In the final and sole moral act of his entire life, Naeem sacrifices his life to help Nimmi escape the burning building so that she can be united with her true love, Salim.

CHARACTER REVELATION THROUGH PERFORMANCE

A romantic mythos of poiesis and musical affiliation, *Intezar*'s music and camerawork is focused and immersive. The East-West opposition is primarily staged as a contest between competing musical universes, which have inner moral and psychic dimensions. Sensitivity, generosity, inner reflection, and moral affiliation are contrasted against carefree dissolution, moral transgression, and destructive behavior. They assume a specific valence that is premised above all on the seeming competition between musical styles.[82] Identity is affiliated with music and taste, which is expressive of psychic damage as well as outward bodily mutilation. However, the connotative stakes of the film are far more unsettling than the starkly binary denotative message.

Firstly, *Intezar* presents itself as a fabrication that emerges from the world of acting and performance. The film is laced throughout with knowing or "winking" references to the history of theater and cinema.[83] D'Souza, for example, typifies the presence of Goans in westernized South Asian cinema music: "In the film industry, the Indian-Western dichotomy had the potential to be enacted as a divide between Goan musicians (Western) and 'Indian' (that is, non-Goan) musicians," notes Booth on music in Bombay cinema.[84] Rang Mahal is located in Karachi, a port city that was part of the Bombay Presidency during the British colonial era and had a small yet significant population of Goan Christians who had been involved in performing Western music in hotels and clubs.[85] In yet another interfilmic reference, *Intezar*'s D'Souza may refer to the "legendary Goanese music arranger Sebastian D'Souza" in Bombay.[86] "Sebastian D'Souza had been working in Lahore . . . playing in nightclubs and doing some work for music directors in that city; but in 1947, when Lahore became part of the new nation of Pakistan, many musicians, D'Souza among them, returned to India," notes Booth.[87] The memory of the actual Sebastian D'Souza's presence in Lahore might well have lingered in the city when *Intezar* was being conceived.

When Nimmi stops singing the forlorn "Chānd hanse duniyā base royay merā piyār" (The moon smiles, the world flourishes, but only my love weeps) outside her home, pacing slowly against a night sky illuminated by a full moon, her agitated father, in front of a small fireplace inside, begins playing the veena. The sounds of his frenzied playing float outside, and Nimmi, listening, moves toward the door. The sequence is composed of cross-cut editing of medium close-ups of Nimmi and her father, their music creating a sound bridge that ends with a single loud note of the veena that Nimmi hears. In the next shot, her father's body is collapsed on the top of the instrument, and the camera pans from right to left, accompanied by a sustained piano note, to frame the father and then the doorway where Nimmi enters. The camera tracks back, exits the front door, and focuses on the dark wall outside the house as Nimmi slowly crosses the threshold. The blankness of the screen and the short silence after the dying piano note are sharply punctuated by Nimmi's horrified scream as she sees her father's slumped figure. The temporal dilation of Nimmi's entry is thus bracketed by two musical notes, one "Indian" and the other "Western."[88]

The death of the father, emblematized by the last note of the veena and immediately replaced by the piano exclamation, also marks the efforts of D'Souza to replace Indian with Western music. Thus, the very next establishing scene shows the interior of Rang Mahal, where D'Souza's band, with trumpets and maracas, bass, drums, and dancers dressed in striped Latin skirts, is practicing a jazzy composition, with D'Souza on the piano to the right. This is framed in a medium-long shot with Naeem in the foreground, quickly throwing up his hand and moving across the frame toward D'Souza. The next sequence is a shot/reverse shot composition of a face-to-face conversation between Naeem and D'Souza. Naeem exclaims in exasperation: "D'Souza, kuch jamā nahīṇ tumhārā music" (Your music has not come together). Replies D'Souza jauntily in Bombay-inflected diction, "Hamārā music ẓarūr jame gā" (My music will surely come together). He goes on to state that he composed music for the film *Banjara* ("Ek dam [fully a] smash hit") and also the film *Navela* ("Aay-one!"). When Naeem objects that the first film had music composed by a Mahinder Kishan, the latter by a Bashir Zaidi, D'Souza counters him by saying that although their names are associated with the films, the work in both films was actually done by him. D'Souza's comment on the misattribution of music compositions in these two fictitious films may simply be the excuse of an incompetent music arranger like *Intezar*'s D'Souza. However, Booth has written on the *real* D'Souza, the arranger Sebastian D'Souza in Bombay films who "worked with a wide range of film composers ... but because arrangers and assistants have been inconsistently listed in film credits, there is no way to know with certainty the actual number of film scores with which he was involved."[89] The unattributed labor and the exploitation in the South Asian cinema industry of assistants is also an ironic reference in *Intezar*.

Intezar's D'Souza's playful insistence on the value of his Western-oriented compositions, and the residue of Indian musical memory that the dancers still embody, marks a central paradox of the film and indeed of many of Anwar's other films. What popular musical form possesses the capacity to address the phenomenological and bodily capacities of an accelerating modernity? What is lost in this process? This is staged in Anwar's films above all on the plane of music. Despite Anwar's classicizing emphasis, the cultural logic of the commercial film industry requires a translation of both classical and folk forms into hybrid and experimental arrangements. The purity of form and the extended duration of classical compositions does not favor their mass reception in a mediatized form that he is working in. On the peripheral role of pure folk and local music in modernity, Biswarup Sen's observations are apposite: "Popular culture cannot, it seems, arise out of local forms; it requires the universalizing import of Hindi film songs. And though, according to some detractors, that music is 'a curious and somewhat bizarre blend of East and West,' which 'is not so much Indian as a form of commercial hybridization from various sources,' it is to *filmigit* [film song] we must turn to in order to understand the role of music in modern India."[90]

Despite *Intezar*'s portrayal of D'Souza as a somewhat cartoonish and incapable musician unable to salvage anything worthwhile in Indian music for today, it is precisely in relation to the problem of "commercial hybridization" where D'Souza's insistence on Western instrumentation might be understood, in a manner that differs in degree but not in essence from Anwar's position. This is despite the preference in official circles and among respectable classes in India and Pakistan for locally grounded musical development, which the Goan musicians were perceived as not adhering to.[91] Film music foregrounds combination, translation, and adaptation over purity and authenticity for it to appeal to a wide audience. Anna Morcom, who has examined the role of Western music in Indian cinema at length, notes that "eclecticism was successful in Hindi film music [because] ... it helped transcend regional/class/caste/ethnic/religious boundaries."[92] Moreover, Western music as score has been adopted as a widely accepted convention in Bombay (and Lahore) cinema. It accompanies cinematic narrative modes associated with dynamism, action, and disturbances and is thus deployed to evoke these specific moods and effects: "Sections of action and plot progression usually involve Western techniques such as harmonic sequences and juxtaposition of orchestral timbre or style."[93] These situations are almost never accompanied by a raga-based composition.

D'Souza makes snide and disparaging remarks on Indian classical performing traditions throughout the film. He states that he has instructed the dancers to forget "Master Ghafoor's *taa thai taa thai*" (beats associated with Indian music), but the dancers were not able to do so. When meeting her for the first time, he quizzes Cheemo, Can you perform dances such as rumba, samba, and tango? In the next sequence, Ghafoor, dressed in a Nehru jacket and jodhpur trousers, with Cheemo and Lachoo on his left and Naeem on his right, describes Nimmi's dancing abilities, claiming that she can re-create the aura of *Indar Sabha*'s legendary atelier: "Indar ke ahkāṛe kā samā' bāndh detī hai."[94] But her dance is "*ṣaqīl*" (difficult), which D'Souza, who enters the frame on the right, immediately understands as being classical and thus undesirable. Next, in a medium-length close-up, Ghafoor parodies dance moves, uttering the names of various styles of classical dance: "Kathakali, Manipuri, Bharatnatyam." At each utterance, the camera cuts to show D'Souza's mock-horrified gestures. In the next sequence, Naeem admonishes Ghafoor, saying he has no use for such dance in his theater: "Tell her to get an Indian passport instead!" suggesting that the Partition had led even commercial forms of entertainment to have become freighted with anxieties regarding cultural separatism. Consequently, in Pakistan's film and theater, Indian classical forms should no longer have any place.[95] Nevertheless, Ghafoor proclaims that the blind Nimmi has the voice of a *koel* (nightingale), and he convinces Naeem of his scheme of playback singing in the theater modeled on the film song.

Nimmi's voice will pervade the stage, while Cheemo will lip-synch and dance in front of the audience.[96]

This "discovery" of the effectivity of playback singing in theater performance in *Intezar* is possibly also an intercinematic reference to the accidental "discovery" of playback singing and dialogue in the celebrated Hollywood musical comedy *Singin' in the Rain* (1952), a film set in 1927 that depicts the technical, aesthetic, and ethical issues that the arrival of the talkies that year posed for Hollywood studios and actors.[97] Lina Lamont (played by Jean Hagen) is a leading character in stock adventure and romance films of the silent era, but her shrill and heavily accented voice is completely unsuitable for the talkies. This problem is overcome by the accidental discovery by the hero's sidekick that the voice of Kathy Selden (Debbie Reynolds) can become the playback substitute for Lamont's. In the film, the falseness of Lamont's voice on screen indexes her fraudulent and manipulative character—voice thus becomes a marker indicating the state of inner morality.[98] The denouement of her base character happens not on celluloid but in a theatrical setting in front of a live audience when she insists on lip-synching and moving her body with the song—with Selden singing behind her, concealed by the stage curtain. During the performance, the curtain lifts to reveal the ruse of Lamont's false voice and her duplicitous character. It is thus the theater stage where aesthetic and moral truth become simultaneously audible and visible in *Singin' in the Rain*, *Intezar*, and *Koel*.

In *Intezar*, there is a medium master shot of a rehearsal, with musicians and dancers and Ghafoor belting out a coarse tune, seated on the left next to a seated and withdrawn Nimmi. When D'Souza objects to the singing, Ghafoor retorts with parodic moves and lyrics. D'Souza addresses Nimmi (played by Noor Jehan herself), "Yeh chokrī samajhtī kai hai apne āp ko? Lata Mangeshkar yā Noor Jehan?" (Who does this girl think she is? Lata Mangeshkar or Noor Jehan?), prompting a twitter of laughter from the dancers in the background.[99] Whether the laughter mocks the pretensions of Nimmi within the cinematic diegesis, or "winks" at the audience in a widely shared recognition of the star text of Noor Jehan, remains unresolved. The pretense is of Nimmi–Noor Jehan as a theater persona not being recognized as Noor Jehan, the leading film actor and singer—yet *everyone outside the film, and possibly even inside, knows otherwise*. The offhand "inside joke" of mentioning Noor Jehan and Lata Mangeshkar together also cites the importance of the overlapping trajectory of the two celebrated singers in Bombay cinema. Noor Jehan preceded Mangeshkar in achieving stardom in the 1940s in Bombay. She was both a star actor and a singer. Mangeshkar remained solely a playback singer for more than five decades. Indeed, she is the foremost exemplar of a shift in the industry, in which playback singers became recognized as stars in their own right.[100] Noor Jehan's star text emerged at a time when the singing and the acting body was ideally invested in the same body.[101] Mangeshkar's rise to being the most important playback singer came right after Noor Jehan's departure from Bombay to Lahore in 1947 due to the Partition.[102] In Lahore, Noor Jehan continued to act and sing for films until *Baji* (Sister, 1963), after which she continued as a playback singer for dozens of Urdu and Punjabi films until 1996. In *Intezar*, these playful, parodic scenarios are thus instructive in situating the relation between theater and cinema and between the film's internal narrative and numerous outside references. *Intezar* is a film whose narrative follows the destiny of the hero (Salim) and heroine (Nimmi), but equally, the theater of Rang Mahal can be considered as an "industrial" actor in the narrative, whose tragic but morally satisfying end is death by immolation.

Throughout the film, D'Souza advocates for Western music with a kind of missionary zeal. Toward the end, as Naeem falls in love in Nimmi and poses in front of her as Salim, it is the character of music that reveals to Nimmi the true inner self of Naeem. Nimmi convinces Naeem that Rang Mahal should feature Indian music, reminding Naeem (posing as Salim) that when Salim had played the *malhār* raga on the sitar for her, it had evoked *sāvan* (the rainy season in North India) with its rich romantic associations and symbols—birds singing, clouds, breezes, rain, and yearning lovers.[103] The theater gets ready to put on a new program based on Nimmi's inspiration, but characteristically, D'Souza misinterprets Nimmi's wishes due to his cluelessness of the relevance of local traditions. Naeem telephones D'Souza and instructs him to prepare a new performance titled *Intezar*, to replace *Aankh ka nasha*. D'Souza remains unable to interpret such a fertile reference to Indian aesthetic lineages but understands it only as a prompt for a Hollywood-style musical that he conflates with *Singin' in the Rain* (1952): "*Intezar* . . . A-one idea! . . . Wonderful! Waiting . . . waiting in the rain . . . ek dam music jamā'e gā [I'll compose the music for it right away]," and he proceeds to compose a jazzy tune on the piano. The alacrity with which *Intezar*'s D'Souza works is reminiscent of the real Sebastian D'Souza, who reportedly worked with legendary speed.[104]

This exchange is revelatory also for the links between theater and cinema. *Aankh ka nasha* (Intoxication for the eyes) was the title of a well-known play published in 1924 by the celebrated playwright Agha Hashr Kashmiri, the predecessor of the playwright who is considered to be his successor, Imtiaz Ali Taj (who wrote *Intezar*'s dialogue). It was also the title of several Bombay films (1928, 1933, and 1956) and a 1957 Lahore film.[105] Given that *Intezar* was released in 1956, the play and its theme in cinema would have resonated with many viewers. Moreover, the new theatrical performance within the film is also called *Intezar*, conflating it with the film's title and, by extension, its cinematic narrative. Summarizing Agha Hashr Kashmiri's career with reference to the relation between theater and film, Kathryn Hansen notes:

> The social had a long historical arc. In western and northern India, commercial theater in Gujarati, Urdu, and Hindi flourished even as a new industry—cinema—took birth. Social dramas were written anew, addressing changing conditions and an emerging national consciousness, and old material was reworked for its perennial appeal. . . . Above all, Urdu playwright Agha Hashr made a lasting impact. . . . He often turned his socials into screenplays: *Ankh ka Nasha* [Intoxication for the eyes] (1928), *Asir-e Hirs* [Prisoner of desire] (1931), *Khubsurat Bala* [Beautiful affliction] (1927). Through setting, costume, and language, especially use of the Urdu *ghazal* and Hindustani music, Hashr's distinctive approach anticipated Muslim social films of the 1940s and 1950s.[106]

From another facet, this default dependence by D'Souza on the Hollywood musical demonstrates how Hollywood exerted its magnetic influence on Urdu and Hindi cinema during this era. One of the objectives of Anwar, Taj, and others in *Intezar*, *Koel*, and other films of the era is thus to ostensibly offer an alternative to the seductions of Hollywood film and music. However, by working within a commercial logic of cinema in Bombay and Lahore, which encourages the film of the era to include several songs in varied styles, moods, and orchestrations, what *Intezar* and similar films proffer instead is an ensemble of composite sonic and visual objects, whose attractions and charms are not premised on their being solely "Indian" or purely "Western." Rather, these diverse and hybrid compositions amplify sensorial modernity even while overtly decrying its corrosive effects.

In the next sequence, D'Souza comically misinterprets Nimmi's desire. A medium shot frames Naeem's back and three dancers dressed in slick raincoats twirl floral umbrellas as they perform dance steps that Naeem is orchestrating, accompanied by a swinging jazz tune. This composition is

LYRIC ROMANTICISM 83

FIG. 2.5. Nimmi addresses Naeem (who is posing as Salim), looking directly at the camera to exclaim, "Do you consider this a song? You call this a song? Salim, *you*?" *Intezar* (1956).

indebted to *Singin' in the Rain*'s opening scene and its publicity materials, and it emphasizes D'Souza being slavishly in thrall to the Western culture industries. The camera pans sharply left to frame Nimmi (whose eyesight is restored), dressed in a handsome black sari, sitting in an armchair in a resigned posture. As the camera moves closer to Nimmi, the next scene cuts to show Naeem at an angle in a medium close-up, gleefully moving his limbs in repetitive movements to orchestrate the music. The camera returns to Nimmi in a medium close-up, as she covers her ears and rises in disgust. A rapid sequence of edits flashes an image of Naeem, followed by D'Souza rising from the piano and moving toward the camera, while Nimmi exclaims, "For God's sake, stop this racket!" The camera pans to follow Nimmi as she walks quickly across the frame to address Naeem. She turns to face him, now looking directly at the camera to exclaim, "Do you consider this a song? You call this a song? Salim, *you*?" (figure 2.5).

The reverse shot shows a close-up of the bewildered Naeem. However, because Nimmi has addressed the camera with her direct gaze, the viewer is interpellated to assume the place of the befuddled Naeem. *Intezar* breaches the cinematic diegesis yet again, this time to address the external world via the gaze. As Nimmi departs and a dejected D'Souza finally gives up, he utters wistfully to Naeem as he leaves Rang Mahal forever, "Hamārā music

FIG. 2.6. Nimmi sings and leads dancers in the final song on Rang Mahal's stage, "Sāvan kī ghanghor ghatā'en" (Cloudy breezes of the rainy season). *Intezar* (1956).

jame gā . . . Spain meṇ jame gā, America meṇ jame gā, England meṇ jame gā . . . par idhar kabhī nahīṇ jame gā" (My music will surely flourish . . . in Spain, America, England, but never here).

This episode signals the supposed triumph of Hindustani classical legacies, which are shown to be ostensibly realized in the final song on Rang Mahal's stage, titled "Sāvan kī ghanghor ghatā'eṇ" (Cloudy breezes of the rainy season), but the composition of the song is more complex and ambitious. The conceit here is that the truth of the sincere and morally upright character of Indian music cannot remain a private secret between Nimmi and Salim but must be performed publicly and theatrically for it to establish itself against morally and aesthetically corrupting Western music (figure 2.6).

Nimmi, who has suspected since the recovery of her eyesight that something is not right with Naeem posing as Salim, returns to Salim's house dejected, but is revived by hearing the sitar that is played by the real Salim in another room. Next, a crucial long take of Nimmi bears central meaning in *Intezar*'s denouement. Swaying and moving across the room joyfully with the sitar sound, Nimmi's figure dissolves into a superimposed sequence of shots—the close-up of her face is overlaid with Salim playing the sitar, accompanied by its sound, and in the next scene the overlaid image cuts to Naeem moving like a wound-up mechanical toy as he orchestrates music in Rang Mahal. The extended take continues with a lingering framed close-up of Nimmi's face superimposed with various images of her encounters with Salim, Naeem, and objects that exemplify their personas. An awareness of the deeper reality of the two characters slowly filters into Nimmi's consciousness. Crucially, it is not through sight, but through music, that the truth of the duplicitous scenario is revealed to Nimmi. It is later simply confirmed by actual vision, when Nimmi feigns blindness again to stealthily observe the contrasting behavior of the two brothers.

FABLING IN *INTEZAR*

In *Intezar*, the unstable shuttling of references through knowing jokes and intercinematic correspondences suggests that although ostensibly providing a moral lesson, the film itself is a fable whose relation to the social reality outside can be extricated neither from the world of cinema and theater nor from Bombay cinema and Hollywood. Another cluster of references for the latter in *Intezar* focuses on the role of jazz, Latin, and Cuban music in South Asian cinema, whose champion is the redoubtable D'Souza. A key film that consolidated Latin influences in Bombay cinema is *Albela* (Stylish, 1951), whose breakthrough music was composed by the C. Ramchandra (1918–82), and which has been analyzed by Bradley Shope in his essay on jazz and Latin influences in midcentury Bombay cinema.[107] *Albela* clearly was on the mind of *Intezar*'s writers. In *Intezar*, D'Souza jauntily hums the 1951 *Albela* song "Meray dil ki ghadi kare tick tick tick" (The clock of my heart beats tick tick tick) in a scene with Pepita, the lead dancer. Shope notes that the song in *Albela* has an "implied three + two clave ... emphasized by a rolling piano, which gives a Latin American feel, and is a technique prominently featured in some musical segments of [Carmen] Miranda's films *Copacabana* and *That Night in Rio*." Pepita is keen on Naeem, although the latter disparages her by calling her "Carmen Miranda," even as Pepita insists that her dance moves are so compelling that they are copied by the film industry.

The Latin-themed song in the film, "Javānī kī raten javānī ke din" (Days and nights of youthful passion), with Pepita accompanied by male and female performers, is performed early in *Intezar* on the Rang Mahal stage, before Nimmi arrives to level her critique of Western music and bring her Indian classical singing abilities to Rang Mahal. But even after her arrival, Nimmi herself does playback singing for a "*behūda gānā*" (lewd song), "Ānkh se ānkh milā le" (Let your eyes meet mine), an inebriated club song in which Cheemo is the lead dancer, in a mise-en-scène of a bar setting, accompanied by dancers in long, striped skirts, whose outfits can be compared with the outfits in the "Deewana yeh parwana" (This intoxicated moth) song in *Albela*.[108] The seated audiences' heads sway with "Ānkh se ānkh milā le," suggesting the powerful aesthetic force of this "Western" song on Rang Mahal's audience. The role of the female stars in the film and especially in this sequence recalls Manishita Dass's observation on the fraught negotiation of modernity by the female body in late colonial-era cinema: "The cinema as a form of mass culture thus came to be seen as a strange Circe-like creature, seductive yet vulnerable, posing a threat to both the authority of the lettered city and the welfare of the mass public by exposing the latter to images of modernity, yet in thrall to the dangerous desires and crude tastes of the very mass public that it enthralled. Not surprisingly, the female film star often came to function as a metonymic figure representing the cinema in its duality, at once inviting the gaze of the mass public and being objectified by it."[109]

Intezar's conception of the public and its receptive and critical abilities is accordingly circumscribed but suggestive, nevertheless. The audience can evidently consume only whatever they are presented with onstage in a straightforward manner. But even here, the film tries to have it both ways. Even before Nimmi and Cheemo's arrival at Rang Mahal, the songs and dances orchestrated by D'Souza and led by Pepita appeared to draw full audiences. "Both schools of music and music-lovers have ample opportunity for showing their art," noted I. A. Rehman in his review.[110] Why then is there need for the "Hindustani" musical revolution that Nimmi will eventually enact there (see figure 2.6)?

These seeming crossings are a clue to the subtlety of Taj and Anwar's conception of the work done in the aesthetic realm: they are deeply aware that the seeming binaries of indigenous and foreign, and representation and reality are above all tropes that possess plasticity and require a process of engagement both by filmmakers and audiences to yield a way forward. This is the wisdom behind the sleight of hand that *Intezar* and *Koel* proffer in their diegesis, where the audience can indeed have it both ways, valuing local music and performance practices while partaking of the new developments of modernity. Moreover, *Intezar* is a sustained meditation on the loss of memory and the destruction of the sensorial inhabitation enacted in Pakistan in the wake of the Partition of 1947, a theme that *Ghoonghat* revisits and tackles more centrally.

GHOONGHAT (1962)

In the main narrative of *Intezar* and *Koel*, Khurshid Anwar shows abiding concern for the loss of Indian music from the consciousness of audiences. In *Ghoonghat* (The veil), Indian music itself becomes associated with a specter, subsumed under for the loss of the larger South Asian cosmos, whose sundering due to modernity was most brutally experienced and magnified in the wake of the Partition of 1947. An earlier film, *Zehr-e Ishq* (1958), also cowritten by Imtiaz Ali Taj and Anwar, with music by Anwar, and directed by Masood Pervaiz, marks the loss of a richly sensorial, primitivist Indic lifeworld by a rationalized bourgeois Pakistani modernity.[111] *Ghoonghat* recasts this trope by situating this tension between the past and the present as a spectral presence whose hold is powerful and pervasive, which a contemporary reviewer also stressed: "The substantial part of the picture . . . is the world of spirits, which appears to be more realistic than the matter-of-fact scenes of everyday life, which only serve as a backdrop, against which the main emotional experience is projected. This world of spirits is a dream world conjured up by the artistic genius of Khurshid Anwar by an exquisitely sensitive blending of ethereal patterns of melody with suggestive pictorial imagery."[112]

Anwar composed the music, wrote the story and screenplay, and directed and produced the film.[113] Dialogue is by a Naseer Anwar. The playback singers included Noor Jehan, Naheed Niazi, Naseem Begum, and the emerging *ghazal* singer Mehdi Hassan. The film is a significant achievement in the history of Pakistani cinema, for its sustained mood of Gothic suspense, its shimmering and fluid camerawork, its cogent editing, and the immersive picturization of its haunting songs. The film deploys narrative tropes characteristic of much of Khurshid Anwar's work during the late fifties till the midsixties—a weak and indecisive male hero suffering from traumatic loss, and the capacity of indigenous music to conjure and transform the affective universe of the protagonists. *Ghoonghat* was a submission for the thirty-sixth Academy Awards for Best Foreign Language Film in 1963 but was not nominated. For Pakistani cinema, this was nevertheless a milestone: the previous Oscar submission was for *Jago Hua Savera* in 1959, but the next submission was after a long five decades, in 2013 for *Zinda Bhaag* (Run for life, 2013).

Ghoonghat is primarily a Gothic suspense in which Shahid (played by Santosh Kumar), a writer of fiction and a man disconnected from reality, becomes enamored of the spectral female figure of Usha Rani (played by Nayyar Sultana). There are four main sections of the film. The opening sequence on the train is marked by claustrophobia and dissonance; the second section plays out inside a bourgeois bungalow in Lahore haunted by uncanny revelations. The third section is the longest, set in the wooded hills of Purban and characterized by languorous atmospheric effects in which Shahid repeatedly encounters the Rani in a dreamlike state. Finally, the film's denouement, the resolution of a whodunit, is placed in compressed form at the end in the Dak Bungalow in Purban.

GHOONGHAT'S OPENING SEQUENCE

The opening sequence of the film, which lasts over seven minutes, is a consequential train journey, filmed and edited to enhance claustrophobia and unease. Interior and exterior scenes from the train are overlaid with the title images, written in elegant and bold Lahori *nastaʿlīq* calligraphic script, which periodically appear throughout the opening sequence. The tension between the newlywed bride, Naheed, who has not yet unveiled her face (or lifted the *ghūnghaṭ*) for Shahid is set up right at the onset of the sequence.

The film opens with a soundtrack of a traveling train. The screen is pitch-black except for a small and blinding headlight of the train's engine moving forward and the faint glint of reflected light from the two train tracks. The establishing sequence ends with a dissonant sonic note. The next scene is inside the carriage. Attended with *shehnai* music, the camera pans from a *sehra* (floral headdress and veil) hanging on the wall to a medium close-up shot of the seated bride's back. Naheed's elaborate gilt dress, the *sehra*, and the *shehnai* (wind instrument associated with Muslim weddings) telegraph her status as a newlywed. The next shot shows her from the front, her face completely veiled by an elaborately embroidered fabric. As the wind ruffles her dress, a reverse shoulder shot frames Shahid in medium close-up from low angle, dressed in a white kurta (loose shirt), fondling a necklace of white flowers. Her dark dress and seated profile contrast with his white standing form. "Ham do ajnabī ek ho gaʾe, apnī manzil kī jānib jā rahe haiṉ" (We are two strangers who have become one, heading toward our destination), he says softly. Naheed uncomfortably huddles as Shahid leans over her: "You must have read my stories." A reverse medium shot shows her swaying in assent, as he continues, "One day, when I asked my mother about my bride, she laughed and replied, 'Remember the story you wrote, *Purban kī Rānī* [The Rani of Purban]? Now imagine that I am bringing you *Purban kī Rānī* herself!'" Hearing this, the veiled Naheed is visibly agitated. The next shot frames both figures—Shahid looking in the distance, saying wistfully, "The Rani of Purban . . . I had seen her in my childhood, a faint and unfocused image [*dhundlī taṣvīr*], dressed in a white sari with a jasmine [*motia*] necklace, wafting fragrance and disappearing in the mist." Shahid looks away and moves out of the frame as the camera swings right for a medium close-up of Naheed on her train berth, as loud, intrusive *shehnai* notes evoke a dissonant aura.

The camera returns to symmetrically frame Shahid frontally between two *sehras* hanging in the back, as he says, "It's my lifelong dream to see her." The camera frames Naheed's back for a shoulder angle shot of Shahid as he comes closer, leaning over her head as he says, "Today I want to see my dream realized" (Āj main us khvāb kī ta'bīr dekhnā chāhtā hūn). He sits next to her, holding a jasmine necklace he says is "similar to one that she wore," and asks her, "Lift your veil so that I can place this around your neck" (Ghūnghaṭ uṭhā'iye, use main āp ke gale men ḍāl dun). She reaches out her hand to stop his hand, a close-up shot of two hands embracing with the garland, attended by the sound of clashing cymbals. "Mu'āf kījiye gā" (Please excuse me), he says, as a medium close-up shoulder shot depicts Shahid attempting to gently embrace Naheed, but her hennaed hand on his chest prevents this. He kisses her hand, and she waves her sari border uneasily, perhaps to circulate air in the stifling carriage. Cognizing that she is overheated, he states that he will return to his seat across from her but does not offer her any water to quench her thirst or to ease her journey. Oblivious to her needs, he instead pursues his obsession: "Lift your veil, aren't you overheated? . . . in any case, when you reach home, you will have to lift it." And as he reclines, he casually drops the bombshell, "The veil must reveal Usha Rani behind it . . . the Rani of Purban," startling Naheed, whose profiled body jerks upward like a horror film character, attended by an ensemble of dissonant notes (figure 2.7).

This uncomfortable and claustrophobic encounter between two strangers has already been freighted with Shahid's impossible desire to have his bride conform to a specter. In the next scene, the camera moves toward an earthenware water pot, and the scene dissolves in a graphic match to the train's headlight hurtling through the night. The inside and outside train scenes continue to build on an uncanny aura, by focusing on isolated details of the train carriage, discordant diegetic sounds of banging doors and

FIG. 2.7. Opening train sequence in *Ghoonghat* (1962). Oblivious to Naheed's needs, Shahid pursues his obsession: "Lift your veil ... it must reveal ... the Rani of Purban."

rattle of the train tracks and the whistle, loud, dissonant extradiegetic notes, and unsettling strobe lighting from the windows of the moving train. Shahid wakes up to find Naheed missing, with only her jasmine necklace lying on her berth. He pulls the emergency chain to stop the moving train. Shahid's father, who has been in another carriage, comes to find out what is happening and suffers a fatal heart attack when he learns that Naheed has gone missing. A smashed water pot, a banging door, abandoned shoes, broken bangles, and the veil on the floor are all that are left of Naheed's former presence. The sequence ends in a fade to black of an aerial wide-angle shot of the train moving away from the camera into the dark night.

BOURGEOIS DOMESTICITY AND SHAHID'S TRAUMA

The opening sequence effectively sets up the premise and the mood of the film. Shahid, an impractical man half living in a dream world of his childhood that seeps into his fiction writing, is completely disconnected from his bride, whose face he has never seen. Her mysterious departure propels the plot forward, now to Lahore. In the next episode, set in Lahore, the establishing shot pans from a wide-angle shot of a luxurious Art Deco bungalow's manicured lawn, with children playing and laughing, to the outside of Shahid's bungalow next door. Inside, Shahid's home is in crisis, in contrast to the happy familial life next door. Shahid, alone in his study, has retreated into the hermetic inner world of his room, where he drinks alcohol, plays the sitar, and stares into space. His mother, his elderly nanny, and his boisterous friend Jameel (played by Agha Talish) visit him there but cannot draw him out of his stupor.

Next, we see Naheed's father, a frail man elegantly dressed in a black *achkan* (Nehru jacket) and *qarāqul* (wool) cap, waiting inside the front door. He pleads with Shahid's mother to allow Naheed to become united with Shahid, but the mother will have none of it. She drives Naheed's father away with an impassioned dialogue in which she accuses Naheed of having not only caused the death of her husband but also propelled Shahid toward infantilism, and this is attended by a sonic field of Shahid's singing voice wafting through the bourgeois domestic space.

"Your friend Jameel says that you are no longer Shahid but have become Devdas," Shahid's mother slowly explains to Shahid after entering his room, evoking an interfilmic reference to the most famous tragic hero of Bombay cinema.[114] Jameel enters next, with the greeting "Hello, Devdas the Great!" and is startled to see Shahid's mother in his room. "Is this a milk whiskey or whiskey milk?" he jokes, examining Shahid's glass. "Devdas became a drunkard, and finally died, but our Devdas will live!" he grandly declares, referring to the hero's tragic fate in the *Devdas* films. Apart from his alcohol addiction, Shahid has also been secretly purchasing toys and hiding them behind his books. With a flourish, Jameel dramatically rotates the bookshelf to reveal the giant stash of toys arranged as a collection, an amassing of multiple fetishes that nevertheless cannot compensate for Shahid's lost object of desire.

The next sequence shows the outside of a toy store. Shahid enters, attended by percussion music, buys two dolls, brings them home, but is startled to see his mother and nanny already in his room. In a shot/reverse shot sequence, the two women stand in front of his toy cabinet, while he holds the newly purchased dolls in both hands, with a woman's portrait by artist Abdur Rahman Chughtai (1894–1975) on the wall at his left.[115] The Lahore-based Chughtai had developed a painting style drawn from Mughal art, Art Nouveau, and wash techniques from the Bengal School of Art in Calcutta.[116] A key subject for the artist are portraits of women who are idealized toward unreality. As the poet Faiz has noted, Chughtai rendered the beloved in line and color in a more ravishing actualization (*'ālam-i vujūd*) than that of the *ghazal*'s imagined beloved (*'ālam-i taṣavvur*).[117] Chughtai himself claimed that his impossibly idealized portraits nevertheless exerted vital influence over women's sense of self-presentation: "My pictures have influenced women to become more refined in their dress, makeup, and grooming. When a woman attends a gathering dressed and adorned in a manner reminiscent of my paintings, observers associate her with 'Chughtai Art.'"[118] The mise-en-scène of this shot/reverse shot sequence, which places the characters in a space dense with visual references to idealized female fetish figures, evokes Shahid's consciousness, which is already suspended between the worlds of reality and imagination, and which subsequent events in the film's narrative will serve to deepen and propel toward crisis.

THE GHOST AT PURBAN

In an effort to break out of the limbo at home, Shahid's mother informs him that it is the season when timber is being harvested for the family business, and that he needs to go to Purban to attend to it. The film's location now moves to the forested mountainous region where Purban is located and remains there for the rest of the film. In a clearing among the trees is a small, abandoned Hindu temple, which will play a crucial role in the subsequent narrative. Several activities are transpiring in Purban. The local residents are involved in subsistence livelihoods and work for Shahid's family business of timber harvesting. When Shahid arrives in Purban with Jameel, they unexpectedly find that they are not able to reside in his family home, Sunder Nivas, because it is temporarily occupied by a group of young college-educated women who are vacationing there. Instead, Shahid and Jameel stay at the Dak Bungalow, where they encounter a mysterious young woman who is also residing there. Farzana (played by Neelo; see figure I.2) often dresses in form-fitting Western clothes and is bold in her manners with strangers. She playfully brandishes a pistol. Although mistaken for a police officer by Jameel, she is later revealed to be a notorious smuggler who is on the run from the police and finds the area of Purban convenient, because it is situated near the border and there are caves in a hill nearby where she can stash smuggled shipments brought by convoys at night. Because the haunted temple is near the caves, no one ventures there, making it an ideal deposit. Farzana is a hard-boiled femme fatale who falls for Shahid. "Āp ke Devdas ne mere dil kī gahrā'iyoṇ meṇ so'ī hū'ī 'aurat ko bedār kar diyā hai" (Your Devdas has awakened the woman asleep in the recesses of my heart), she confesses to Jameel. But Shahid does not reciprocate her advances, as he is totally in thrall to the ghost of Usha Rani.

The local residents remember the haunting legend of Usha Rani from before the time of the Partition. According to this harrowing story, Usha Rani was the daughter of the temple priest who fell in love with Shyam, the son of a wealthy businessman from Lahore who was visiting from the city. Forbidden by his father to marry into Usha Rani's poverty-stricken family, Shyam was forced to return to the city and was coercively betrothed to another woman from a more suitable class background, whom he had never seen. In despair, Shyam committed suicide by drinking poison on his wedding night, before lifting the veil from his new bride. Usha Rani drowned herself in the lake in Purban, but her spirit continues to haunt the valley even today, in search of her lost beloved.

In character with Anwar's other films, songs play a central symbolic role in the film's narrative arc. *Ghoonghat*'s songs were written by Tanvir Naqvi, prolific writer of film lyrics who specialized in writing the *gīt* rather than the *ghazal*.[119] The songs are notable for their diction; many of them avoid a heavy use of Persianate vocabulary and high Urdu phrasing and instead deploy North Indian language registers of closer to Hindavi, Purbi, and Bhojpuri. One of the songs has the opening lyrics "Rāhoṇ meṇ ṭhārī maiṇ naẓareṇ jamā'e / janam janam ke ās lagā'e / ko'ī ā'e?" (With my gaze affixed on the road / overflowing with the desire of many past incarnated lives / when will he come?). This song comes right after a villager in Purban has narrated the haunted tale of Usha Rani to one of the college women. The song begins with a long shot of Sunder Nivas in mist, in front of which the four college women walk forward slowly. The camera then frames the temple in long shot, a landscape of hills, trees, and mist, lit by the raking light of early morning or before sunset, which creates a dramatic play of light and shade on the temple facade and the foreground. Bells ring, a chorus begins singing, and Usha Rani emerges from the temple swaying and dancing, a striking, statuesque figure in a white sari against the darker landscape. Her "hand and body movements on the line '*Kab 'āenge*' [When will you arrive?] add to the mystery of the sinister atmosphere," notes Amjad Parvez.[120] The theme of reincarnation and extended temporality is a leitmotif in the haunting lyrics and Usha Rani's movements: "Kitne zamāne bīte akhiyāṇ bichā'e" (How many eras have passed in front of my awaiting eyes). The song is effective in its narrative force—as soon as it ends, the car carrying Jameel and Shahid appears on the road.

In her analysis of midcentury Gothic cinema from Bombay, Meheli Sen has highlighted the narrative imperative for the specter to be gendered, which alone has the enthralling power exerted by the song: "The affective terrain of partnership and mutuality demanded by love duets [in other social films] is never animated in these songs; the power to enthrall, seduce, and render silent remains with the woman/ghost."[121] This is also the case in *Ghoonghat*. Shahid's abject inability to sing back or sing along is therefore in keeping with this convention of the cinematic Gothic in South Asia, in which it is the female specter and voice that constantly haunts the male bourgeois character toward irrationality and a temporality that transcends modernity.

Given his infantile mental state, when Shahid returns to Purban, where he had gone in his childhood, he becomes completely enthralled with Usha Rani from the very beginning. Even as they drive to Purban, Jameel and Shahid encounter what appears to be the ghost of Usha Rani. She emerges in front of the car, a waltzing and bewitching presence in a white sari, waist-length hair, a *bindi* on her forehead, and adorned with a garland of white flowers. She asks for a ride from Shahid and Jameel in their car and is seated in the back. But when the car arrives at the Dak Bungalow in Purban, she has mysteriously vanished from the car, leaving behind only her garland.

Shahid becomes more and more enthralled with the spectral figure, whose presence is palpable across the sensorial realm, in sound, scent, and sight, but not through touch. Characteristically, when the abandoned temple's bells mysteriously swing and ring without anyone present at the temple, they signal that Usha Rani will make her appearance. She meets Shahid among the trees, shrouded in a foggy and misty aura, a graceful figure moving effortlessly in the forest. The song "Chan chan chan merī pāyal kī dhun" (My ankle bracelets sing chan chan chan) is filmed on a meeting between Shahid and Usha Rani in the mist-laden woods. Its unusual musical composition pauses between verses when Usha Rani disappears in the woods, only to appear playfully and mysteriously in another spot behind him as he wanders among the trees looking for her. The pauses are punctuated by the sound of *ghungroo* (ankle bells) and birdsong. The song's diction is in Hindi, and Usha Rani dances in a classical style and strews flowers in his path. At the end of the song, she appears as an apparition in the sky, framed centrally behind by the canopy of the trees, from which rays of vibrating light animate the surrounding mist, rendering her as a figure reminiscent of a goddess in a Hindu mythological film imparting *darshan* (beholding the deity) (figure 2.8).[122]

FIG. 2.8. Usha Rani appears at the end of the song "Chan chan chan merī pāyal kī dhun" (My ankle bracelets sing chan chan chan) as an apparition, reminiscent of a Hindu goddess in a mythological film imparting *darshan* (beholding the deity). *Ghoonghat* (1962).

Usha Rani has forbidden Shahid to touch her, because she warns him that she is a cold specter that needs a body to become fully human again. She sings haunting songs and points out places in the forest where she and Shyam used to meet in their previous lives. She urges Shahid to remember his past life as Shyam, and she shows him two places where the names of Usha and Shyam have been inscribed on tree trunks in Hindi (Devanagari) script (figure 2.9).

Although he is unable to read Hindi or remember his supposed previous incarnation, nevertheless he is more and more infatuated with Usha Rani. The only way for them to be together, she eventually counsels him, is for him to bring his wife Naheed to Purban and to drown her in the lake. After her drowning, Usha Rani's ghost will inhabit Naheed's body, and they will finally be together in the present incarnation of their lives, a union they were unable to achieve in their previous lives. *Ghoonghat*'s characters doubled across time with a promise of union based on a reincarnation theme recalls the celebrated Bombay Gothic film *Mahal* (The mansion, 1949, dir. Kamal Amrohi). Sarah Waheed's analysis of *Mahal* foregrounds the centrality of Partition's trauma as its context: "*Mahal* asks questions that are working through the traumatic underpinnings of their moment, and take on an ethical hue: can one continue to love a woman who is dead? If not,

FIG. 2.9. Usha Rani shows Shahid the names of Usha and Shyam inscribed on tree trunks in Hindi (Devanagari) script. *Ghoonghat* (1962).

then what are the means one must pursue in order to forget? What happens if one discovers that the dead is not really dead after all?"[123] Analogous questions can be posed for *Ghoonghat*'s main characters.

The guileless Shahid is so deeply enthralled that he goes along with this macabre scheme in a half stupor. He arranges for Naheed—whom he has not met since she disappeared from the train—to come to Purban ostensibly for their long-delayed honeymoon. She arrives on a haunting night graced with a full moon. Bent forward with her head covered with her veil and her face not visible, Naheed follows him to the lake, and they ride on a small boat. The still water of the lake and the misty environment lit by moonlight evoke an otherworldly Gothic aura. In the boat, Naheed is seated in the same position as she was at the beginning of the film in the train carriage, dressed in the same embroidered bridal wear, with the veil covering her head. After Shahid rows the boat to the middle of the lake, he asks Naheed whether she is willing to make any sacrifice for her husband. "Can you give up your life for me?" he asks her, to which she replies, "My life is yours." She then gently asks him to throw her overboard with his own hands. Nevertheless, the indecisive Shahid hesitates to carry out Usha Rani's instructions, as conflicting voices are ringing inside his head—Usha Rani's urgings to drown Naheed and his own conscience about becoming a murderer—attended by tortured, dissonant music. A long shot frames both figures standing on the opposite sides of the boat, a scream is heard, and Naheed falls in the still water unassisted by Shahid. The stunned Shahid rows the boat back to shore, passing silently by Naheed's veil floating on the lake. The police are waiting on the shore and promptly arrest Shahid for Naheed's murder.

DENOUEMENT AT SUNDER NIVAS

The film changes gear again and now moves toward the finale, which is akin to a denouement scene in a detective film.[124] Shahid is brought to the bungalow of Sunder Nivas, where a group is already assembled, consisting of the college-educated women, Shahid's mother and nanny, and Naheed's father. Shahid is lectured to, first by the genial police chief. The police chief tells the assembly that Naheed is indeed alive and was with his wife this morning, reading together the famous short story "The Rani of Purban" by the acclaimed writer Shahid. He berates Shahid for not living in the modern era: "Javāb nahīṉ hai āp kā. Bīsvīṉ ṣadī meṉ raihte haiṉ aur kahāniyāṉ āp Laila ke zamāne kī likhte haiṉ!" (You are really something. You live in the twentieth century but write stories from the time of Laila [Majnun])!). He informs Naheed's father that his daughter is "one in a million" (lākhoṉ meṉ ek), a common phrase in Urdu. "You are a strange one, chasing after a shadow despite having been married to such a singular wife" (Aur āp bhī lākhoṉ meṉ ek, keh aisī bīvī pā kar bhī sā'e ke pīche mare mare phirte rahe), he tells Shahid (figure 2.10).

Next, one of the assembled women grills Shahid for believing in wild fantasies about women. She accuses him of denying material needs and desires of real women, preferring instead to live in his otherworldly stories, where women are impossibly idealized. Pacing in front of and around the seated Shahid, she declaims, "Writers like you have elevated women on a pedestal, making them into goddesses and comparing them to the song of spring, starlight, the scent of flowers, birdsongs, and other such nonsense. You forget that she is human like you; her lips can smile, her eyes can shed tears, her steps can stumble, and she can have flaws. Then why do you still consider her as a goddess?"[125]

She then gently counsels the seated Shahid that it's not too late, and that he needs to forget the imaginary goddess and embrace the actual woman who has become his partner in life. A medium close-up shows her waving a bottle of jasmine perfume behind him, as temple bells begin to ring in the distance. The camera cuts to show a full-size percussion pipe organ that

FIG. 2.10. Denouement at the Dak Bungalow. *Ghoonghat* (1962).

one of the college women is jauntily striking with a hammer, revealing the artifice behind the sonic and sensorial associations evoked by Usha Rani. Next, the front door opens to a cloudy horizon animated by a central visionary and vibrating light emanating from behind the moving clouds—Usha Rani is framed from a low angle entering through the doorway, very suggestive of the appearance of divinities in Hindu mythological films and similar to her previous appearance at the end of the "Chan chan chan merī pāyal kī dhun" song. Shahid exclaims, "Usha! My Usha!" while Naheed's father calls out, "My daughter!" It turns out that the ghost of Usha Rani is indeed Naheed. At this precise moment, however, the figure of Usha Rani is fully interpellated with Naheed and is now doubled forever in Shahid's imagination. The ghost has been corporealized into a living figure in an inextricable manner, suggesting that even the whodunit ending that is meant to create a bourgeois rational resolution remains fundamentally unstable and haunted. The lifeworlds prior to the Partition cannot be banished from the consciousness of modernity.

In a flashback, Naheed explains the events that transpired in the train carriage. After Shahid had freighted Naheed with the fantastic expectation that she ought to look just like the spectral Usha Rani after her veil was lifted, Naheed became apprehensive that this would be impossible. She also felt suffocated in the train carriage due to heat and thirst. As she recalls in a voiceover during the flashback, she desperately moved about in the carriage to try to pour water from the empty pot to quench her thirst and to open the window shutters for air: "My veil had become my shroud. I felt that my life was ebbing from my body. My throat was parched. I needed a sip of water to survive. The train carriage had become overpoweringly claustrophobic and had become a grave.... This first night after the wedding ceremony... so frightening, so poisonous.... Better for me to die than to find out that my husband prefers to see someone else rather than me." In desperation, she spied a water stand at the next stop on the train platform and got off to have a drink but was unable to get back on the train in time. In order to save her marriage, Naheed, with the help of her college friends, planned out the elaborate ruse of playing Usha Rani, in order for her to enact Shahid's idealized fantasy and then to bring him back to reality. The film ends with the reconciliation of Shahid and Naheed, with a closing wide pan shot of the misty landscape of Purban that ends at the temple, attended by the sound of a chorus and the insistent ringing of the temple bells.

ANALYSIS OF *GHOONGHAT*

The film is rich and multilayered, carefully assembled from several genres, including the Gothic film, the detective film, the social film, and the musical, with elements drawn from the Hindu mythological film and horror cinema. Rather than fragmenting the audience's expectations, these elements create unexpected turns and compel the audience to remain enthralled by the mystery of Usha Rani—is she really a ghost, or is this all an elaborate ruse? There are, however, a few loose threads in the film that remain unresolved.[126] The plot hangs together by improbable coincidences, such as the return of Shahid to Purban, although this is not dissimilar to a film such as *Vertigo* (1958) by Alfred Hitchcock, which also deals with returning to the traumatic site with doubled and mistaken identifications. Although the appearance of the ghost of Usha Rani is finally revealed to be an elaborate subterfuge, the ghost is not yet laid to rest. Who did the young Shahid actually see at Purban years ago, or was it all a figment of his overstimulated imagination to begin with? In case of the latter, how to explain the long-standing local legend of Usha Rani? "*Ghoonghat* was an imaginative film, which the general public could not understand when they first viewed it. Gradually, however, the public began to comprehend it," notes Yasin Gorija.[127] Perhaps the initial difficulty in general understanding was due to *Ghoonghat*'s unexpected genre crossing, as well as unresolved issues in its narrative.

The role of women in *Ghoonghat*'s social world is paradoxical. On the one hand, women are expected to make any sacrifice—even to embrace death—to fulfill their traditional roles in a marriage by conforming completely to their husbands' desires and suppressing their own. But we learn at the denouement that Naheed is highly accomplished in many fields. Not only was she a champion swimmer, but she also won first prize in college with her singing and dancing—abilities that enable her to play the ruse of Usha Rani with aplomb. Her friends from college also appear very capable and flawlessly execute the support Naheed needs to convincingly assume the role of Usha Rani. And Farzana, the head of an international smuggling operation and living alone in the Dak Bungalow, is clearly possessed of considerable agency and independence. By contrast, the male characters are largely duds. Jameel is amusing as a bon vivant, but the narrative does not reveal anything else about his abilities or character. Naheed's father has a marginal role, a figure of pathos eliciting compassion as he is unable to resolve the marital divide. Above all, apart from Shahid's status as a fiction writer—whose writing is ridiculed at the end of the film for being out of sync with the times—he is indecisive throughout the film, enthralled only by the vision of Usha Rani and the influence she (played by Naheed) exerts on him at Purban. How will a capable and strong-willed Naheed deal with a flunky dreamer like Shahid, after they are reconciled? A conservative and patriarchal view of women here is at odds with the persistent crisis of masculinity and the gender-liberating potential of modernization, and this is a highly productive tension throughout the film.[128] Anwar himself spoke about his film firmly in the context of Bombay cinema, underscoring its exploration of the crisis of masculinity in modernity. Javed Usman's interview question and Anwar's response merits quoting at length:

> JAVED USMAN: "It appears to me that a number of . . . [your films] had stories of the type which contained mist engulfed hills and valleys, haunted villas, spirits, echoes and strange sounds and tinkling of far-off bells, and amidst all this otherworldly atmosphere was placed slightly deranged heroes talking of eternal love and so on. There was beauty in the music and the scenery, but the attitude behind all this heavy romantic imagery seems one of escapism to me. Would you care to comment?"
>
> KHURSHID ANWAR: "[P. C.] Barua was one of our great pioneers. An incomparable scriptwriter, good director, and Leftist. His *Jawab* [Question, 1942] revolved round the character of an indecisive, weak,

and utterly wasteful young man. When the young man rises for breakfast, there has to be *sitar* playing before he can get into the right mood, for example. Two girls love him, but he is incapable of choosing between them. In the end they decide the issue among themselves. That is a rough idea of the plot. Baburao Patel in those days considered himself to be the leading film critic of India and he also owned a top magazine *Filmindia*. He too, by the way, was a Leftist. Patel tore Barua to pieces and criticized him for having made a film on an incredibly ridiculous situation. Patel thought the character was too unnatural to make any sense. Barua in his rejoinder destroyed Patel's criticism by simply pointing out that the young man in fact was a symbol of the contemporary middle class which, in his opinion, was devoid of all will to make decisions for itself and . . . others decided its fate while it sat smug in its petty comforts. In the same way my approach toward *Ghoonghat*'s main character was extremely critical, one who is shown to be living in a world which is a figment of his imagination. He wanders in the valleys in search of her [sic] dead beloved. His wife poses as a spirit to win him back and jolt him into realizing that he has been acting stupidly."[129]

Ability and decisiveness as normatively being in the possession of men is a leitmotif in a whole ensemble of films from the early days of Indian cinema. Its crisis is also a central motif in several others, the most celebrated manifestation being *Devdas*, originally a novel in Bengali by Sarat Chandra Chatterjee published in 1917, which was repeatedly made into film in multiple languages, including in 1928 in the silent era (directed by Naresh Mitra), in Hindi in 1935 (directed by P. C. Barua) and again in 1955 (directed by Bimal Roy). Recall that Jameel jokingly refers to Shahid in his infantile state as a Devdas. *Ghoonghat* partakes of this "Devdasian" crisis of masculinity, in Shahid's inability to distinguish between material needs and fantasy and his incapacity to inhabit the chronotope of modernity. But *Ghoonghat* goes further.

ALLEGORY OF THE PARTITION

Above all, *Ghoonghat* is a deeply reflective film about the latent and delayed consequences of the Partition of 1947 on memory and subjectivity. The hauntings it evokes all draws from a past that shared with Hindu life and that has been in a process of being irrevocably lost with the consolidation of Pakistan as a Muslim-majority nation. Usha Rani urges Shahid to remember his previous incarnation as Shyam, which he is of course unable to do, but the force of the exhortation needs to be underscored. Similarly, Shahid cannot read the Hindi names on the trees, as the Devanagari script was no longer in common use in Pakistan after 1947. The graffiti-like Hindi writing can also be compared with the beautifully calligraphed film titles in *nastaʿlīq* script, suggesting aesthetic tension in an effort of affective overcoming of an unwelcome past. The Hindu temple is abandoned and forlorn, appearing as an archaeological relic from a distant past rather than a devotional space in active use as recently as 1947.

And yet the ghosts remain revenant. Usha Rani's legend is narrated by the local residents, the temple bells insistently ring, and the incomprehensible Devanagari script returns. But these returns are discrepant, at an angle. Usha Rani cannot be touched, the heart accompanying the Hindi graffiti is upside down in one of the inscriptions, and the names are also slightly misspelled.[130] Above all, it is the non-Islamic, "irrational" Hindu conception of reincarnation that is central to the film's narrative and propels it forward. "No universal modernity can fully subsume the desires and fantasies driving Indian subjectivities, or supplant the granular nature of local lifeworlds," Bhaskar Sarkar has noted in his study of Indian cinema's relation to the Partition.[131] The loss of the past has psychic effects that cannot be fully redeemed or overcome by rationality, despite the exhortations of the police chief and Naheed's friend at the end of the movie.

The romantic reckoning with the Partition that is imbricated with the corrosive effects of modernity is a central theme of many of Anwar's films from the midfifties to the midsixties, including *Intezar* and *Ghoonghat* as discussed above, but also in *Zehr-e Ishq* (1958), for which he wrote the screenplay, as well as *Chingari* (1964), which he directed in addition to writing the screenplay and story.[132] Indeed, linking modernity with the irrevocable loss of a sense of a wholeness of being, separation from Indic and local lifeworlds, and the resulting trauma evokes a crisis of nationalism and patriarchy that cannot be overcome, despite endings in these films that attempt to rehabilitate bourgeois domesticity but, as we have discussed, do so in a highly implausible register. Bhaskar Sarkar's important study on the Partition has focused on Indian cinema.[133] By understanding how Lahore-based filmmakers responded to the Partition, a fuller and more nuanced picture emerges of the reverberative effects of the destructive emergence of modern nationalism, a most consequential development in modern South Asian history.

The spectral and uncanny return of ghosts of the past in Anwar's films can be thought alongside Chris Moffat's reflections on the afterlife of Bhagat Singh and the obligations owed by the living toward the memory of exemplary figures. As Moffat notes, "My aim is not to attribute a ghostly agency to the dead but rather to question the presumption that the living stand confidently in an emancipated present, able to draw selectively from the past but remaining in no way bound to it."[134] Rather, the past makes insistent and affective claims that cannot be neatly compartmentalized. While Moffat's study focuses on the work of activist cultural politics, Anwar's cinema remembers the past in a melancholy register. Does this also evoke an engagement with Bhagat Singh's memory, especially since Singh's steadfast call toward liberation beyond communal divisions was such a formative experience for the young Khurshid Anwar and since Anwar continued to hold him in the greatest esteem until the end of his life? Anwar's cinema insistently urges its audience to remember a recent past not defined by the selective amnesia of the nation-state and suggests affective potentialities of cultural forms that might heal colonial modernity's fractures of the self. Anwar's cinema moves away from overt cultural politics to offer a profound reflection on the divided ego, inhabiting these fissures in an affective and open-ended manner.

3   CINEMA AND POLITICS

Khalil Qaiser and Riaz Shahid

SINCE THE LATE THIRTIES AND ACROSS THE PARTITION, PROMInent writers and poets made influential contributions to the cultural left in Lahore. A broadly leftist orientation continued to characterize much of Lahore's cultural universe during the long sixties. This culture was sustained by intellectuals contributing creative and critical writing in journals, participating in literary circles, and writing screenplays, dialogue, and lyrics for the cinema. The commercial film remained an important platform for the exploration of socially conscious themes. The films that emerged from this crucible revisit many of the concerns of *Jago Hua Savera* in the context of alternative cinema made by personnel involved in the midcentury Marxist and leftist cultural scene of South Asia. Broadly speaking, in Bombay and Lahore cinema, the commercial cinema of the fifties through the later sixties embedded leftist ideas about social inequality, the examination of hierarchies between the bourgeoisie and the poor, and the gap between the rural and the urban, cast in narratives that picturized their appeal to larger and multiple publics. Many commercial films were based on formulaic plots, stock characters, and typage, and they included a variety of song modalities as well as villains and comic sidekicks. Nevertheless, they offered strong and appealing narratives on social justice, equality, and the possibility of love transcending entrenched social hierarchies.[1] These productions imbricated realism and fiction in a romantic register. They foregrounded a recursive theatrical modality that layered and collapsed history and fable, allied with specific production values, which included "dense close-ups, flaring light-effects, casting, cinematography and sound, and . . . set design," characteristics that Ashish Rajadhyaksha identifies with the Lahore effect.[2] As we have seen in chapter 1, even *Jago Hua Savera*, which strove to follow neorealist principles and was shot in black-and-white, nevertheless included a commercial segment, in the inclusion of a dance song in color for local distribution. As the long sixties progressed, Lahore became a major center of film production in the Global South, when measured by the number of films released every year.[3]

Khalil Qaiser and Riaz Shahid have been widely seen as forming a team, with commitments to leftist and "revolutionary" filmmaking.[4] Other directors affiliated with many of the projects of Khalil Qaiser and Riaz Shahid are Iqbal Shehzad, Jamil Akhtar, and Hassan Tariq.[5] Writers who contributed the story, the screenplay, and the dialogue to these projects included Riaz Shahid and Ali Sufyan Afaqi. Lyricists, many of whom were leading figures in Urdu literature, included the poets Tanvir Naqvi, Qateel Shifai, Faiz Ahmed Faiz, Saifuddin Saif, and Himayat Ali Shair.[6]

These and many others were involved in dozens of projects in this era. The genres they worked in are surprisingly diverse, such as the detective film *Raz* (The secret, 1959, dir. Humayun Mirza); *dastanic* and serpent films *Dosheeza* (Damsel, 1962, dir. Khalil Qaiser) and *Nagin* (Serpent, 1959, dir. Khalil Qaiser); the social films *Shikwa* (Complaint, 1963, dir. Hassan Tariq), *Sawaal* (The question, 1966, dir. Hassan Tariq), and *Maa Baap* (Mother and father, 1967, dir. Khalil Qaiser); historical films on resistance against colonialism, such as the Khalil Qaiser–directed *Ajab Khan* (1961), *Shaheed* (Martyr, 1962), and *Farangi* (The European, 1964) and the Riaz Shahid–directed *Zerqa* (1969); and films on sexual exploitation and class divides, like *Neend* (Sleep, 1959, dir. Hassan Tariq), *Clerk* (1960, dir. Khalil Qaiser), *Khamosh Raho* (Remain silent, 1964, dir. Jamil Akhtar), and *Badnam* (Disgraced, 1966, dir. Iqbal Shehzad). From this extensive corpus, the focus here is on a small subset of this oeuvre that foregrounds exploitation in modern everyday life. These are social films that examine the dilemmas of individuals and families through melodramatic and realist narrative tropes, songs, and typage.

Khalil Qaiser began his career as assistant, along with Hassan Tariq, to the film director Anwar Kamal Pasha during the early and midfifties.[7] Qaiser emerged as an independent director by the later fifties. He wrote the story for the film *Qismat* (Fate, 1956, dir. Nazir Ajmeri) and directed *Nagin* (1959), a fantasy film in the genre of the "serpent" film of South Asia, in which characters shape-shift between the human and the reptile.[8] His first leftist film is *Clerk* in 1960, in which he was lead actor and director, and to which Riaz Shahid contributed the dialogue.[9] Khalil Qaiser and Riaz Shahid's collaborative work included *Clerk* (1960), *Dosheeza* (1960), *Shaheed* (1962), *Farangi* (1964), and *Maa Baap* (1967), the latter released after the death of Qaiser, whose life was tragically cut short when he was inexplicably murdered by unknown assailants in his home at night in 1966. Riaz Shahid also passed away early, from cancer in 1972. Nevertheless, Riaz Shahid's stories, screenplays, and dialogue were used in films made as late as 1978, such as *Haider Ali*, directed by Masood Pervaiz.

Khalil Qaiser is best known today for directing a series of popular films on colonialism and imperialism. *Shaheed* (1962) is a historical story about a heroic resistance figure fighting against British colonialism, and in *Farangi* (1964), a figure loosely modeled on Lawrence of Arabia schemes to extend imperialism to profit from the discovery of oil in an unnamed Arabian locale. The trajectory of anti-imperialist filmmaking was carried forward after Qaiser's death in 1966 by Riaz Shahid when he directed the blockbuster film *Zerqa* (1969), to which he contributed the story and dialogue as well. *Zerqa* is reportedly inspired by the life of the charismatic Palestinian resistance fighter Leila Khalid.[10] Its songs, written by noted leftist poet Habib Jalib and performed by the *ghazal* singer Mehdi Hassan, have become celebrated for their stirring lyrics, and for their coded resistance toward Ayub Khan's faltering government of the later 1960s.[11]

Riaz Shahid, whose original name was Shaikh Riaz Ahmad, started his career as a journalist and writer, writing for newspapers and journals in the early and midfifties.[12] He published a novel, *Hazar dastan*, in 1955.[13] By the later fifties, he was deeply involved in the cinema, apparently by the encouragement of poet Faiz Ahmed Faiz. Shahid was a multifaceted persona and a highly prolific writer, renowned for writing captivating stories and stirring dialogue.[14] He reportedly started his film career by writing the story for the film *Bharosa* (Trust, 1958), by convincing the director, Jafar Bukhari, to accept him as a writer upon their very first meeting.[15] He wrote the story, screenplay, and dialogue of the commercially successful and critically lauded film *Neend* (1959, dir. Hassan Tariq), a social film that examined sexual exploitation of a female employee by the owner of a coal firm.[16] The film *Susraal* (The in-laws' home, 1962), which Shahid directed and for which he wrote the story and dialogue, perhaps his least programmatic film, is an affectionate look at the minor and flawed characters living in the Walled City in Lahore. And *Khamosh Raho* (1964), for which Shahid wrote the story, screenplay, and dialogue, and which is directed by Jamil Akhtar, is on the kidnapping of poor rural women and their prostitution in the city. The film *Badnam* (1966), directed by Iqbal Shehzad and based on a short story by the writer Saadat Hasan Manto, for which Riaz developed the screenplay and dialogue, also examines the nexus between class and sexual exploitation.

Riaz Shahid has become legendary for the speed and ease with which he wrote film dialogue, and the rhetorical force of his language, which cut across genres.[17] His writing consistently deploys idioms and metaphors that abound in Urdu, and it creates dynamic scenarios by the use of allusion, double entendre, and the mot juste. Mushtaq Gazdar notes, "Riaz Shahid had an uncanny talent for writing dialogues in rhythmic form. Perhaps he was influenced by Khalil Gibran's diction and could enforce his argument through a jigsaw of vocabulary that would captivate the audience completely. He was the first screenwriter whose name was advertised on cinema billboards, posters, and newspaper advertisements."[18] In his writing and his later direction, Riaz Shahid represents an important attribute of Lahore cinema overall, in its emphasis on rhetorical flourishes and exclamatory force.

In this respect, Lahore's films differ from the cinema that was emerging in Dhaka during the sixties, which is arguably more cinematic in its drawing from folk aesthetics, a more fluid use of camera movement, montage editing, and lyric picturization of songs. In his book on Pakistani cinema, published in 1969, the film critic Alamgir Kabir accordingly noted, "Melodrama and 'stagey' production are the two prominent characteristics of Pakistani productions in general. The trends are stronger in Urdu or Punjabi films than in Bengali productions."[19] Most damningly, he notes that Lahore and Karachi productions fail as *cinematic* artifacts, as they rely instead on theatrical frontality: "Most of the West Pakistani productions force one to suspect that their directors would probably have been the happiest people on earth if such techniques as montage, editing, etc. did not exist. They like to concentrate only on getting clear, well-lit pictures keeping the actors as far as possible within focus. Shot compositions are the simplest practiced these days with the characters lined-up horizontally across the 'frame' in a way that is known as 'frontoriented.' For most part of the film, the camera photographs from chest level and unusual angles are avoided painstakingly."[20]

However, Riaz Shahid's early film *Susraal* (1962), which he wrote and directed, emphasizes dialogue between characters but also pays close attention to cinematic style, with consistency in lighting and mise-en-scène, sophisticated match cut editing, and effective deployment of camera angles, pans, and choice of background music and sound. This film avoids typage and foregrounds the discrepant lives of minor and flawed subaltern characters. Unfortunately, the film was not commercially successful—and these qualities largely disappeared in his next major directorial venture, *Zerqa* (1969), which adheres more closely to Alamgir Kabir's depiction, but which did extremely well at the box office.

However, the larger question Kabir poses with regard to the aesthetic modalities of commercial cinema in Lahore is important to address.

Barring a few films, most notably *Jago Hua Savera*, Kabir is extremely critical throughout his book of the multiple failures of West Pakistani cinema—for its slavish adherence to the formulaic codes of Bombay cinema, its lack of cultural awareness, its gross plagiarism of Indian themes, its reliance on stereotypical characters and typage, the absence of realism, and the display of gratuitous and vulgar sexuality.[21] Kabir understands good cinema as being technically innovative and raising critical and unsettling questions regarding social dilemmas. He notes that even the conventional love triangle in commercial cinema that formulaically negotiates class divides has the potential to evoke larger questions of social inequality in the audience, provided it's framed in such a manner: "The filmic portrayal of those simplified ideals of life if presented with genuine social consciousness could still contribute substantially toward the content. But few efforts are ever intended to be so. A poor girl's moral right to love a rich, handsome young man is never presented as a social protest. The inhumanity of economic and social inequality is never brought to the fore. This is a serious deficiency and it reduces the love that is portrayed to a mere outpouring adolescence."[22] Kabir stresses that good cinema requires audiences that possess cultivated critical capacities. In contrast, "in West Pakistani cities, where a middle-class with refined taste is a comparatively recent phenomenon in the social scene and too insignificant to make its presence felt, these [vulgar] films do very well."[23]

Kabir believed in the capacity of cinema to develop a critical consciousness among its viewers. As a critic, Kabir was a fellow traveler with the filmmakers of the long sixties whose work he writes on. A critic is expected to evaluate the work of contemporaries with high expectations, and to be sharply critical and dismayed by the persistent reiteration of stereotypical and compromised works. But when the cinema of the past is under scholarly scrutiny, the critical task is not to lament what could have been and which now cannot be altered by critique but to explain actual concrete developments in infrastructural, social, and aesthetic terms and to analyze how cinema intervened in and intersected with the cultural politics of that historical conjuncture.

What work does commercial film do in a rapidly modernizing society? The long sixties were governed by politically authoritarian but socially liberal regimes that repressed overt leftist political and cultural forms, where social and economic divides were becoming sharper, and where an uneven but influential top-down effort was underway to manage the cultural life of both West Pakistan and East Pakistan. Gazdar notes that by 1969, the decade-long rule of Ayub Khan "had created feelings of provincialism amongst the middle classes and socialistic tendencies among peasants and laborers."[24] Popular commercial cinema does makes important interventions in this era in articulating new conceptions of self and community. This transformation of consciousness across the sixties is a response to intertwined and conflictual forces, in which the work that cultural forms do is never marginal or incidental. Kamran Asdar Ali has analyzed at length the imbrication of leftist political movements with literary developments in Pakistan from the fifties through the early seventies.[25] Cinema was very much a fellow traveler in this journey. Leading filmmakers were affiliated with or influenced by progressive writers. However, their films had to submit to the ideological and ham-fisted decisions of the government-appointed Censor Board before they could be released, meaning that even the most socially committed filmmakers had to work under significant constraints.[26] The reportedly heavy-handed censoring of *Yeh Aman* (1971), directed by Riaz Shahid, is seen to have contributed to his disillusionment and subsequent death in 1972. This example is but one of numerous structural impediments and diminished possibilities for realizing bold, socially meaningful cultural projects.[27]

Kabir published his book in 1969. The emergence of cultural studies as a discipline since has reformulated questions that one can ask of the critical capacities of popular and mass cultural forms that rely on repetition, seeming accessibility, and apparent lack of dissonant criticality. For example, Fredric Jameson notes that expectations of sedimentation and repetition are crucial for the audience when they encounter popular cultural forms.[28] Jameson argues for the imbricated yet seemingly disjunctive interrelationship between elite cultural forms and popular genres, and he stresses that neither elite avant-gardist forms nor popular artifacts uniquely or solely possess critical potency: "You do not reinvent an access onto political art and authentic cultural production by studding your individual artistic discourse with class and political signals."[29] Rather, popular forms, in their genre repetition and typage, do "transformational work on social and political anxieties and fantasies," by managing them or by repressing them, "gratifying intolerable, unrealizable, properly imperishable desires."[30] And for midcentury Bombay cinema, Aarti Wani has argued that individualized romantic love in melodramas of the fifties constituted "a fantasy of modernity," in which individuals were no longer bound by traditional kinship or national obligation but where "the modern couple ... freed from family structures and at liberty to love and desire helped envision a fantastically free zone of romance with intimations of an alternative community."³¹ Can a "mere outpouring adolescence" on screen nevertheless still manage to evoke aesthetic and political concerns, in which the implied addressee becomes freer to imagine possibilities beyond customary affiliations, no matter how far-fetched or unrealistic these may appear?

Popular culture is a field of ongoing contestation. The landscape of practitioners from the midfifties to the later sixties was undoubtedly deeply shaped by official forces and elite expectations, but it was not fully delimited by these. Writing on popular culture, Stuart Hall underscores a "double-stake," or the "double movement of containment and resistance, which is always inside it."³² For Hall, all modern cultural forms are "contradictory . . . composed of antagonistic and unstable elements," and the analysis of popular cultural forms consequently needs to view them as a field of relations crosshatched by tension and a struggle over hegemony.³³ In examining the films of Khalil Qaiser and Riaz Shahid, this chapter correspondingly sees how their works excavate multiple fault lines across a dynamic and processual social formation marked by antagonisms and fractures.

While our emphasis here is on the films that focus on contemporary life and issues of sexual exploitation and class divides rather than their more famous anti-imperialist films, a well-known anecdote associated with the film *Zerqa* (1969) exemplifies how popular imagination sutures a sensibility of political resistance with popular aesthetics. *Zerqa* focuses on Palestinian resistance. A very well-circulated song in the film, "Raqṣ zanjīr pahan kar bhī kiyā jātā hai" (You can dance even in fetters), was written by noted poet Habib Jalib and memorably rendered as a film song by leading *ghazal* singer Mehdi Hassan. Jalib's reminiscences on the process of composing poetry for Riaz Shahid's films are noteworthy for the close relationship and common horizon they both shared:

> I worked with good producers also, such as my friend Riaz Shahid, who would urge me on saying, "I'll picturize the biggest insult you can level against existing society." He used to lock us up in a room for four or five days, the music director, him, and myself. We would be very casual and informal with one another. I would write verse and Riaz Shahid would retort, "what rubbish have you written, don't you know what good poetry is?" We would eventually settle the matter. He would then ask [the singer] Mehdi Hassan to come, and all four of us would sit together and compose the film song.³⁴

"Raqṣ zanjīr pahan kar bhī kiyā jātā hai" is picturized on the Palestinian heroine, who is forced to dance in chains by the Israeli general. The heroine is played by the actress Neelo, who had become Riaz Shahid's wife in real life (see figure I.2). Neelo had evidently been forced to dance for the Shah of Iran during his visit to Pakistan in 1965, and accounts of this incident were in wide circulation.[35] Jalib himself viewed this incident in geopolitical terms, stating to Riaz Shahid that "Neelo *begum* has performed a major anti imperialist role, by refusing to dance for the Shah of Iran, who is US imperialism's biggest police chief in this region."[36] Characteristically, this comment sutures melodramatic aesthetics with social critique. The poem that Jalib contributed to the film was a slightly modified version of the one he first wrote to mark Neelo's coercion by the state.[37] Jalib's original lyrics included

> Tū keh nāvāqif-i-ādāb-i-shahanshāhi thī
> Raqṣ zanjīr pahan kar bhī kiyā jātā hai
>
> You are unaware of the tenets of imperialism
> You can also dance in fetters

Jalib modified these lyrics for the film as follows:

> Tū keh nāvāqif-i-ādāb-i-ghulāmī hai abhī
> Raqṣ zanjīr pahan kar bhī kiyā jātā hai
>
> You are unaware of the tenets of slavery
> You can also dance in fetters[38]

The film song has become very famous, further lending this incident a rich afterlife far beyond the film itself.[39] Indeed, today, the mention of Riaz Shahid's name evokes this incident prominently and repeatedly in popular discourse, while even a short description of his more "artistic" film *Susraal* (1962) is now hard to find in contemporary discussions, even though it was awarded first place at Pakistan's twenty-fifth anniversary program by the Pakistan Television Corporation.[40]

Can we understand the film *Zerqa*, and specifically the song "Raqṣ zanjīr pahan kar bhī kiyā jātā hai," as an exemplary popular form possessing the affective capacity for political awareness under authoritarianism? The film deploys the commercially oriented song-and-dance sequence to suggest a link between repression within Pakistan and resistance in Palestine. Here, the Palestinian context is narrated by blending realism and fantasy, and it serves as a political allegory of Pakistani society during the sixties. A commercial film drawing from repetitive tropes and emphasizing declamatory prose and the rhetorical tropes of Urdu poetry rather than fluid camera movement may not conform to expectations of critical and avant-gardist cinema, but its potentialities for evoking "unrealizable, properly imperishable desires" need be to situated in the specific historical and social contexts of its production and reception.[41]

The constant imbrication of realism and fable, narrative and lyric, event and literary trope, is also characteristic of the Lahore effect, as film historian Ashish Rajadhyaksha has argued.[42] Because the songs of *ghazal* singers like Mehdi Hassan and writings of leftist writers and poets like Habib Jalib and Faiz Ahmed Faiz traverse the registers of high cultural forms—as the latter wrote stories, dialogue, and lyrics for song-and-dance sequences in popular films—the division between elite culture and popular genres is also productively breached. Habib Jalib wrote profusely for the cinema, but he is legendary as the author of highly influential poems that questioned authoritarian decisions by the Ayub regime and later governments, as well as for his outspoken public activism, for which he was jailed multiple times in his life.[43] In the verses above, for example, the trope of the dance in chains cuts across the levels of popular and high-cultural forms. This is evident in the use of the same trope in the prominent poem by Faiz Ahmed Faiz, whose diction is considered more elevated and refined that Jalib's:

āj bāzār meṇ pā-ba-jaulāṇ chalo
dast-afshāṇ chalo mast-o-raqṣāṇ chalo

Walk through the bazaar in your shackles
With open arms, in a trance, dancing![44]

As a trope in Urdu poetry, the bazaar can be understood as an instantiation of the public sphere, in which dissent might be expressed in an affective register, rather than a space for making civic demands rationally and discursively. Significantly, the bazaar is also a commercial space, an arena of transactions between strangers and across commodities and ideas. In Urdu, the term *bāzārī* has the connotations of being lowbrow, ordinary, or common, as opposed to the sense of elitism and exclusion. A *bāzārī ʿaurat* (a woman of the bazaar) is a courtesan or prostitute. Rather than a rational public sphere, the bazaar public sphere can be posited as both a discursive and an affective realm, in which ideas and bodies transact in mutually imbricated ways with charged affect.[45] Keep in mind that early cinema in South Asia emerged from the bazaar matrix, rather than from the salon or the elite realm of art, as Kaushik Bhaumik has shown.[46] Thus the politics of cinema in South Asia historically was not confined only to art and alternative cinema but cuts across genres and the hierarchy of cultural forms, which encompasses the commercial film.

As Stuart Hall has theorized, the terrain of affective popular politics is crosshatched with multiple fault lines.[47] Neelo is the screen name of Cynthia Alexander Fernandez, who was born in a Catholic family and adopted Islam only later, after her marriage to Riaz Shahid.[48] The place of religious minorities in Pakistan has never been secure, yet here the travails of an actress of a Christian background becomes a synecdoche for wider oppression under authoritarian rule.[49] The year of *Zerqa*'s release, 1969, also marks Ayub Khan's abdication and Yahya Khan's assuming power among growing disturbances in both wings of the country, but especially in East Pakistan, which eventually led to the liberation of Bangladesh in 1971 after a bloody struggle. Many factors contributed to the breakup of Pakistan, including economic and power imbalances between both wings, but cultural and affective elements were also central and included widespread everyday expression of racial and cultural superiority by West Pakistanis against the inhabitants of East Bengal. The imposition of Urdu and the denigration of Bengali language was a key facet of this domination.[50] Emphasis on Urdu rhetoric in Lahore cinema by filmmakers may also have unwittingly contributed to shoring up the widespread West Pakistani assumption of the superiority of Urdu.[51] As cultural studies has demonstrated, popular cultural affectivities are thus not singular or uniformly progressive in their political valence but inhabit and project the riven and divided character of the social formation they inhabit.

The relation between popular cultural forms and leftist activism was already in place well before the long sixties. The impact of the leftist cultural movements in India since the midthirties, including the All-India Progressive Writers' Association and the Indian People's Theatre Association (IPTA), as well as the impact of neorealism during the fifties on commercial cinema, has been discussed in chapter 1. The engagement by the IPTA-affiliated filmmakers in the fifties commercial Bombay cinema was not purely realist but rather melodramatic and social. According to Manishita Dass, this cinema was "characterized by a populist approach to the experiences of the urban poor; broad strokes and emotive flourishes; an accessible lyricism; a combination of naturalistic acting styles, expressionist modes of performance, and agitprop techniques borrowed from leftist street theatre; and ... extensive use of songs and dances as narrative devices, means of emotional expression, vehicles of social critique, and tools of urban exploration." [52] These approaches continue in the projects of the Lahore-based filmmakers examined in this chapter across the long sixties. The subsequent discussion focuses on projects that Khalil Qaiser and Riaz Shahid worked on together or with others, specifically their films that tackle everyday exploitation, rather than their historical or anti-imperialist films.

CLERK (1960)

Clerk is an early collaboration between Khalil Qaiser and Riaz Shahid. Qaiser directed the film and also played the lead role as Anwar, a clerk working along with a handful of other employees in a grim office belonging to the wealthy, lecherous, and cruel Seth Abdullah. Riaz Shahid contributed the dialogue to the film, whose story was penned by Younus Rahi. The spare and grim low-budget aesthetics of the film accord with the theme, which focuses on the monotonous lives of petty office employees, who barely earn enough to make ends meet, are often in debt for petty sums, and are unable to cover medical bills and education expenses of their family members. The delivery of dialogue also evokes the gray flatness of their existence. Although the dialogue is rhetorically powerful and is composed of phrases of irony, metaphor, and double entendre, its enunciation by the characters is rarely declamatory or flamboyant. As a lead actor, Khalil Qaiser does not cut a dashingly handsome and charismatic figure but presents a dour man weighed down by the responsibilities he has to bear. The film was not commercially successful due to its grim theme and the gray aura it evokes, as well as the absence of star power, despite Musarrat Nazir's lead role as Najma (figure 3.1).[53]

The film opens with Anwar working alone at his desk on the office floor, with only the *chaprāsī* (office boy) in attendance. The clock on the wall confirms that it's past 9 p.m. Anwar eventually asks the office boy to take a bundle of files that he still needs to work on and tie them on his bicycle rack. At Anwar's home, the camera pans from a shot of his mother sitting on the floor preparing dinner for Anwar, who enters through the door with his

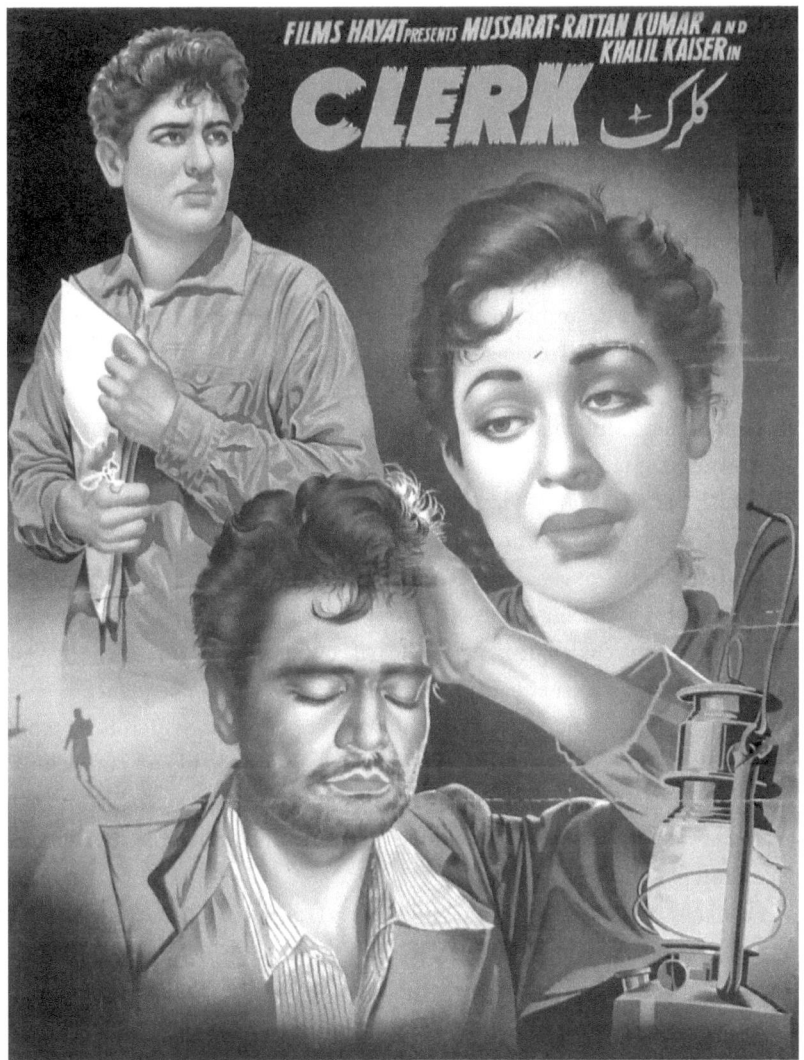

FIG. 3.1. Publicity poster of *Clerk* (1960), with Rattan Kumar (top left), Musarrat Nazir (right), and Khalil Qaiser (bottom).

bicycle. She urges him to eat dinner as he sits down, but he is immersed again in the files. In anger, she dramatically flings a file into the air. Its papers become detached and fly across the camera, leading to the opening credits, which appear on suspended sheets of paper that successively flit by the camera, pausing momentarily to reveal the credits in simple English calligraphy. The animated character the paper sheets possess contrasts with the manner in which life itself is sucked out of the clerks, by a job that requires them to work long hours in tedium and poverty. Over the course of film, we get glimpses of the other lives on the office floor. Every character faces financial challenges or the inability to find time or resources to attend to family emergencies. The *qawwali* song-and-dance sequence on the office floor, "Ghar se chiṭṭhī ā'ī" (A letter from home has arrived), humorously laments their thwarted lives. The sole exception is the Anglo-Indian secretary, the steno, the only female employee, whose desk is also on the office floor, and whom the other employees attempt to court with flirtatious body signals and innuendo-laden dialogue that goes nowhere. As it turns out, the steno is cozy with the boss when they are alone in his office. For women, therefore, to work outside the home is to risk such dishonorable encounters and liaisons.

Anwar is romantically involved with Shamim, a poor young woman who lives with her sister. On the prowl for young flesh, Seth Abdullah asks his madam to procure someone new for him. The madam convinces Shamim's sister to have her married to Seth Abdullah against her wishes. Shamim loves Anwar, and she grieves with his photo when she realizes that she no longer has a future with him. Anwar learns of Shamim's plans when he visits her one day with an engagement ring. Their encounter sequence is shot through a window that opens into Shamim's bedroom, which is covered with newspapers in place of wallpaper, foregrounding her grim conditions. The window has steel bars reminiscent of jail cells, suggesting how both characters are imprisoned in their miserable lives and are destined to remain separated from each other.

Earlier, in the streets, an adolescent Amjad (played by Rattan Kumar, see figure 3.1) robs Anwar. Amjad is dressed in a striped shirt and a bandana, like a street-smart pickpocket from the films of the fifties, following Kumar's own roles as a child star playing a street kid in Bombay films such as *Boot Polish* (1954, dir. Prakash Arora).[54] Anwar chases Amjad to his home, a dark and run-down interior whose only decor is film posters pasted on the shabby walls. Here, Anwar encounters Najma, Amjad's elder sister. It turns out that Amjad has been unable to find a job and has resorted to crime in order to provide for his sister. Anwar convinces Amjad to become the new office boy, and Amjad abandons the life of street crime in exchange for petty but honorable employment in Seth Abdullah's office. Eventually Anwar agrees to marry Najma, as Shamim is no longer a possibility for him. By marrying Najma, he would rescue a young woman whose poverty barred her from marriage to a well-to-do groom.

After a simple wedding ceremony attended by very few people, Najma comes to live with Anwar and his mother. While Anwar's ailing mother is joyful in welcoming Najma, Anwar is initially distraught at having assumed another responsibility that he cannot fulfill and avoids coming home, staying late hours in the office. Anwar's mother, however, convinces him that by ignoring Najma, he is doing injustice to both himself and Najma, who has become deeply depressed. Their marriage is consummated only then, after a day of riding on his bicycle together, walking in a park, jauntily riding a tonga, going to a film theater, and finally moving to their bedroom, accompanied by an intimate song by Najma. But unlike the usual scenario in social films where extended meetings in public places accompanied with songs eventually leads to marriage and union later, here these rituals of courtship are reversed, come well after the marriage, and are kept very brief in the whole film. In the song sequence "Kyūṇ jagāte ho mere sīne meṇ armānoṇ ko" (Why do you awaken desires in my breast?), sung by Najma, Anwar and Najma are framed in a close-up with their backs against each other, but they turn slowly in sync with the camera to be framed in profile, and eventually face-to-face, suggesting their reconciliation and intimacy.

Najma gives birth to two children. As they grow up to the age when they need to attend school, Anwar feels more and more incapable of providing for them and paying their school fees. One day, after being denied entry into school due to nonpayment of fees, Anwar's sons show up to his office when he is with Seth Abdullah, who, instead of expressing sympathy, accuses Anwar of orchestrating this drama. Amjad decides to help by becoming a pickpocket again, but he is arrested at his very first aborted attempt and put in jail. Next, the desperate Anwar steals money when counting a wad of notes in Seth Abdullah's office, but he is caught and also placed in jail in the same cell as Amjad. Najma, dressed in black, mourns his absence in the song "So jā so jā dard bhare dil ab to so jā" (O mournful heart, sleep at last!) as the camera frames her in close-up and alternately pans across the dilapidated home, now with almost no furnishings except for the reed mats the children are asleep on with their schoolbooks and *takhtī* (writing slate). Anwar's bicycle serves as a substitute for his actual presence, the camera's framing of the spokes of the bicycle wheel reminiscent of the bars of the jail cell in a match cut. Najma and the children are now without any means of livelihood. The children first sell off their prized school textbooks then resort to begging in the streets, as they adamantly refuse to let Najma go to work as a domestic servant. Recall that the audience has already encountered the steno's flexible morality and has accordingly been primed to the dangers that working women face.

Subsequently, the camera tilts from a close-up shot of a large signboard placed on top of the entrance of the People's Orphanage, whose patron is none other than Seth Abdullah, to the ceremony inside. Seth Abdullah is presiding and is being lauded as the patron behind this noble venture. Najma arrives outside with her children and requests the organizers admit them even though they are not strictly orphans. Seth Abdullah agrees, as he is now smitten with lust for Najma, having already tired of Shamim and having sent her back to her sister's home. Seth Abdullah suggests that Najma come to his home as he has a job for her sewing clothes. When Najma arrives the next day, an intoxicated Seth Abdullah traps her inside and attempts to rape her. Meanwhile, Amjad, who has been released from prison, manages to track down Najma, arrives just in time to prevent Seth Abdullah's assault on her, and murders him in a fit of rage.

Shamim visits Najma and informs her that while she had been informally engaged to Anwar earlier, things have moved way past their earlier attachment. Shamim has inherited Seth Abdullah's considerable fortune, and she is interested now in helping Najma and the children. Anwar is released from prison, but by now he has been driven to lunacy by the mental anguish he suffered as a victim of circumstances. He wanders into the orphanage behaving like a deranged man. The children heckle him, bringing him to the attention of Najma and Shamim, who are visiting the orphanage that day. Najma recognizes Anwar, they reconcile, and soon he is fully rehabilitated.

Najma, Shamim, and Anwar now embark on an ambitious plan to provide shelter and education to orphaned children, expanding the orphanage and a school in a tall new building planned for this purpose. Shamim agrees to taking care of the two children while Najma and Anwar plan to visit other towns and villages, driving there in a large convertible automobile, to bring deserving children to the new school. The ending of the film proposes a happy resolution and offers a didactic social message of the importance of education among the poor and the disadvantaged. However, these are all schemas for the future. The new school building is mentioned as being ready but never shown on screen, and the plans for the orphanage and the school are not depicted at any stage of realization.

The closing shot frames the large convertible at the entrance of the orphanage. The car is framed on the wall and the bottom with banners with Urdu text, foregrounding the importance of writing in this film. Recall that the opening credits of the film begin with loose papers from an office file that become animated in space and provide the mise-en-scène of the credits sequence. The large bundles of files containing office papers that Anwar works on for interminable hours are now replaced by another kind of writing that emphasizes education. The struggle of Anwar's children to continue to go to school, their attachment to their homework and on learning while at home, and the profound dismay they feel when selling their textbooks serve to reinforce the shift from bureaucratic and soulless writing to one that cultivates human potential. Nevertheless, the happy ending scenes are almost an appendage, in a film whose overall thrust is on the crushing force of the iron cage of exploitative low-end office employment on the lives of its workers and their kin.

SUSRAAL (1962)

Susraal is a remarkable film on many levels, and yet there is virtually no mention of it in the popular press or summary briefs prepared by veteran observers of the film industry. *Susraal* is listed in neither in Yasin Gorija's compendium of the one hundred best films from Pakistan nor in the larger compendium by Zakhmi Kanpuri, which has over two hundred films listed in it.[55] Aijaz Gul, in an overview essay on Pakistani cinema, mentions its title, along with *Jago Hua Savera*, the Masood Pervaiz–directed *Sukh Ka Sapna* (1962), and *Dhoop Aur Saey* (1968), directed by Ashfaq Ahmad, as "alternate cinema" and notes that these were all commercial failures. Contemporary playwright Faseeh Bari Khan, who has written well-received plays for television, lists *Susraal* among films he finds to be important.[56] Apart from these fleeting references, one searches in vain to find even a brief descriptive account of the film. However, for the country's twenty-fifth anniversary program in 1972 by Pakistan Television Corporation, six landmark films were shown, one every weekend. These films were selected by the Pakistan Film Producers Association—*Qismat, Susraal, Ishq Par Zor Nahin* (Love cannot be coerced, 1963, dir. Sharif Nayyar), *Riwaaj* (Custom, 1965, dir. Diljeet Mirza), *Badnam*, and *Hamraz* (The confidant, 1967, dir. Khurshid Anwar). A small jury was appointed to select the leading films among these. *Susraal*, written and directed by Riaz Shahid, was awarded the best film, while *Badnam*, whose screenplay and dialogue were also written by Riaz Shahid, was accorded the second place. Faiz Ahmed Faiz, who was a member of the jury, recalled that the jury was unanimous in agreeing on these as the two best films. The main debate that ensued was about the relative merits of the two and which one should be accorded the first place.[57]

As we have seen in *Clerk*, many of Khalil Qaiser and Riaz Shahid's films bear a didactic message, frequently delivered toward the end of the film with a rhetorical flourish.[58] *Susraal* also falls prey to this subsumption of the film's narrative—with its multiple significations and discrepant affects—into a moralistic envelope at the end of the film. But if one disregards this, the rest of the film is a remarkably fluid and subtle work that has several qualities— including sophisticated editing by use of cut-on-action and match cuts, well-chosen arenas for location shooting in the Walled City in Lahore combined with spare and haunting dream sequences, and the refusal of typage by casting its characters with specific personality traits, which make them neither heroic nor villainous but quirky, subtle, and flawed. Riaz Shahid's dialogue in the film is agile, humorous, and playful, and the relationships especially between its male characters are laced throughout with everyday levity. Briefly, the plot revolves around the desire of Jeeda, a simpleton who plays the horn in a brass band in the Walled City, to marry, and the complications that ensue in its wake.

The film's opening shots offer establishing views of the Walled City from a high vantage point. The camera rapidly pans 360 degrees, offering a panorama of the setting, and zooms in and out on specific buildings, such as the monumental and iconic Badshahi Mosque, built during the reign of the Mughal emperor Aurangzeb in the seventeenth century. The film is entirely set in the Walled City, and the interior shots provide a mise-en-scène for the film that consists mostly of small spaces, each of which possess distinctive character in their architecture and furnishings that help establish the specificity of the location. The opening credits are beautifully calligraphed in Urdu and proclaim the popular nature of the film. For example, Allauddin, the lead actor, is "the people's actor" (*'avāmī adākār*), and the film title, *Susraal*, is appended with the phrase "your own story" (*āp kī apnī kahānī*). The opening credits segue into a street scene in which a brass band playing wedding music is marching and then stands arrayed by the side of the street. The camera pans across the members of the brass band playing music and comes to rest on the last player, Jeeda, who is playing the horn while eyeing his friend Bhola, a barber by profession, engaged here in stirring *biryani* in an enormous metal cooking vessel as part of the wedding feast. Seeing Jeeda's hunger and his lack of attention to his music, Bhola covers the circular aperture of the vessel.

The next sequence begins with the match cut of a round plate of *biryani*, the camera moving back to show two seated figures speaking to each other. Jeeda notes, "After today's wedding procession, I am convinced that I can never get married. The groom today was very ugly, but he was rich.... If I were a *bābū* [bourgeois], I would have compelled a girl to love me, but I am illiterate and now somewhat past my prime [*javānī kī ḥadd se zarā āge nikal chukā hūṉ*]." Ahmad replies that if Jeeda gave up drinking and gambling, he would save enough money to get married within a year. Jeeda retorts that Ahmad should give up pigeon keeping.[59] Jeeda laments that it is impossible for him to find a young woman to marry because they are either being driven in cars or stay behind the veil. In other words, either eligible women are far above his social class, or they are conservative and are not seen publicly.

In the next sequence, Jeeda enters a hammam, or a public bath. Here he finds his band members stoned, merrily singing together a humorous song with makeshift instruments: "Do not smoke hashish, it will burn up your liver." They see an ad in the newspaper for a firm that offers marriage services, but the business looks somewhat shady, as there is no clear address listed. Meanwhile, Ahmad has gone to the rooftop to attend to his pigeons but also to signal across the rooftops to his beloved Zarina, leading the two of them to sing the first full song of the film, which they sing alternatively from their own roofs across the space that separates them. The song's placement in the rooftop setting is evocative of the importance of this distinctive social space in the dense Walled City (figure 3.2).

Jeeda finds his way to a marriage services business, the Rahnuma Marriage Office. As he is walking down the street and asking for directions, the office's sole assistant spies him coming and quickly tells the manager to spiff up and prepare the office. Jeeda enters the office as the manager and the assistant pretend to be the manager and a client, the manager insisting to the client that he needs to bring with adequate funds before his case will be taken up by Rahnuma Marriage Office. This charade is intended to impress on the new client, Jeeda, the effort and the expense involved in arranging good liaisons. The manager is among the most endearing characters in the film. A fraud through and through, he is endowed with a silver tongue, whose blandishments render even the most ugly and unpalatable realities and the most unattractive marriage prospect into a beautiful fiction. Riaz Shahid's dialogue for the manager's character is among the many pleasures of this film. For example, when the manager asks Jeeda what the source and

FIG. 3.2. Ahmad sings across the rooftops of the Walled City in Lahore to his beloved Zarina. *Susraal* (1962).

amount of his income is, Jeeda replies that while his legal income is close to being nonexistent, he earns extra money through his drinking and gambling pastimes. Upon hearing this, the manager exclaims, "You can never get married, because you are unable to tell a lie! God is my witness, I have arranged hundreds of marriages; every single one of them was based only on deception! . . . Men who had failed their Matric [tenth grade] in school have now become 'BA pass' and 'MA pass.'" And as soon as he hears Jeeda's colloquial name, without missing a beat, he portentously renames him as Abdul Majeed or, even better, Chaudhary Abdul Majeed, baptizing Jeeda with an honorific name worthy of a dignified person.

Right after Jeeda departs, the father of a young woman comes in and asks the manager for help. The manager exaggerates the profile of Jeeda as a wealthy and pious individual when the two make an introductory visit to the prospective bride's house. Jeeda briefly sees the beautiful young woman, Zarina, who is supposed to be his intended bride. He cannot believe his good fortune, even more so as the woman's father appears most eager and anxious to conclude the wedding.

Susraal is almost entirely based on location, shooting in the Walled City, but also includes a fantasy song-and-dance sequence. After Jeeda has seen his promised bride and the wedding date has been fixed, he dozes off and finds himself transposed into a dream world. In a cavernous space that is

FIG. 3.3. Fantasy song sequence in Jeeda's dream, "Ā'e gā ṣanam jab naẓareṇ mileṇ gī tab nah jāne kyā ho gā" (When my lover arrives and our eyes meet, who knows what will happen next?). *Susraal* (1962).

otherwise very dark, he is dressed in a fine wedding *sherwani* and seated on a bed whose canopy is lit up with lights. The camera approaches him from a high angle, evoking the sense of looking down on a miniature scenario. As the camera descends and comes closer, Jeeda is distracted by a singing voice from the left. The camera pans left in the dark space, and he sees Zarina dressed in her bridal dress as she comes forth and dances and sings the seductive song on a floating undulating path, "Ā'e gā ṣanam jab naẓareṇ mileṇ gī tab nah jāne kyā ho gā" (When my lover arrives and our eyes meet, who knows what will happen next?), the lyrics and her bodily movement exciting and enthralling him. As he watches her in rapture in a medium close-up, an elliptical balloon floats up vertically across his chest, an innuendo of his sexual arousal that somehow escaped the scissors of the Censor Board (figure 3.3).

Zarina is shown from various angles, including canted shots of her dancing and close-ups of her face and feet adorned with ankle bells (*ghungroo*). Despite the close-up shots, the theatricality of the sequence, with its shiny and reflective surfaces in darkened space, creates a chiaroscuro effect that is unreal and doll-like.

After the wedding ceremony, Jeeda enters the bridal chamber, and the veil is finally lifted from his bride's face. To Jeeda's horror, it is not the beautiful, young, and physically able Zarina he had seen upon his first visit, and whom he had been fantasizing about, but someone else, who is older, less attractive, and above all physically disabled, unable to walk without crutches. It turns out that the biggest fraud of the film has been perpetuated by someone no less than the dignified-looking and righteous-acting father of the bride, who secretly substituted his elder daughter, Safia, as the bride in a brazen bait and switch maneuver.

Jeeda descends into deep depression and self-pity—he drowns himself in drink and avoids going back to his house so as not to encounter Safia. When he finally confronts his father-in-law, the latter justifies his actions as being forced by circumstances. He explains that he is old and cannot continue to support Safia indefinitely. He wanted his elder daughter to be married before the younger and able Zarina; otherwise, he would have no leverage in getting Safia married off later. Zarina has long been in love with Ahmad, Jeeda's best friend. Initially Ahmad is distraught when he realizes that Zarina is to be married to Jeeda but does not reveal his distress to his friends. But when it dawns on him that Zarina is still available, as his best friend has been duped into a terrible situation, this causes a crisis between him and Jeeda and in the larger diegetic world of the film. To complicate matters further, the father has imposed a precondition on Ahmad that he cannot marry Zarina unless Ahmad convinces Jeeda to be reconciled with Safia. Although Ahmad proposes to elope with Zarina to get out of this bind, she firmly refuses this because she does not want to cause family dishonor.

Safia returns to her father's home in despair, which is expressed in a song that has become among the most popular films songs of Pakistani cinema, "Jā apnī ḥasratoṇ par ānsū bahā ke so jā" (Shed tears for your thwarted desires and fall sleep), whose playback singer is Noor Jehan. The song is a lament picturized on Safia when she is back in her father's home after being repudiated by Jeeda, and its lyrics and camerawork embody her physical and psychological predicaments. While Zarina and her father lie in their respective beds at night, Safia sits upright as the camera frames her from various angles and through and against screens and apertures among the furniture, suggesting her imprisoned state of consciousness. These are interspersed with shots of caged birds, her hennaed hands, her wedding jewelry lying on a table, and the father covering his head with his blanket to block out her lament. As the song progresses, a window closes by itself, and her crutches begin to sway by themselves—the song evidently possesses the pathos to move even inanimate objects but is powerless to transform Safia's circumstances.

Eventually the major male characters offer to make extraordinary sacrifices to resolve the situation—the women in the film have no say in these proposals. The father releases Ahmad from the promise that he can marry Zarina only after Jeeda is reconciled with Safia. Ahmad in turn proposes to Jeeda that he should divorce Safia—instead, Jeeda can then wed Zarina, who was shown to him as his intended bride. In exchange, Ahmad will marry Safia and thus provide her with a home and security. This is a sacrifice Ahmad is willing to make in order to preserve his friendship with Jeeda. Jeeda now also has a change of heart. A canted long shot of the exterior of the building, where Jeeda and Ahmad are conversing on the balcony, mirrors the new circumstances. Jeeda begs forgiveness from Ahmad for trespassing and desiring Zarina, who after all was Ahmad's beloved from well before: "If a friend does not forgive the lapse of another friend, the world will never trust any relationship" (Agar dost ne dost kā quṣūr muā'f nah kiyā to dunyā se har rishte kā i'tibār uṭh ja'e gā), he explains to Ahmad.

Ahmad is finally married to Zarina, shown in a long shot sitting with others in the street and wearing a *sehra* (floral headdress and veil). The brass band plays, with Jeeda, dressed in his uniform, enthusiastically playing his large horn. The camera moves in for a medium close-up of him playing the instrument, very similar to the opening shot, when we first encountered Jeeda. His horn becomes increasingly quieter and more introspective. The camera then pans 180 degrees, lingers for a moment to show Safia's dejected face between the large doors of the front entrance of her father's house, and then pans further for a medium close-up of her father's figure, leaning crestfallen against the wall. A three-way shot–reverse shot sequence follows, with close-ups of Safia, who covers her visage, and the father and Jeeda's conflicted faces, accompanied by dramatic music.

Jeeda arrives at the realization that he needs to accept the disabled Safia as his wife, because hierarchical and unjust expectations of society deny humanity and value to those perceived to be less able. In the next close-up shots, framed from a low angle, Jeeda walks toward the father, first as a small figure in relative darkness, then as an equal in scale to the father's profile, and they stand there facing each other. His visually dramatic approach in

FIG. 3.4. Safia's father and Jeeda reconcile after Zarina's wedding. *Susraal* (1962).

this shot is another indication of the change in consciousness in him but about which the father is still unaware. "Don't avert your eyes from me; let's share our grief," Jeeda exhorts, and they embrace (figure 3.4).

As Jeeda turns after the embrace, the camera moves back for a long shot that shows the veiled Safia through the doorway on the left, Jeeda in the middle, and the father at right. Jeeda continues speaking, first addressing the father: "If you concealed your burden and passed it on to me, you are not to be blamed." Then, turning toward Safia: "If Safia is disabled, it's also not her fault." And next, facing the camera frontally: "And had I refused, I would also be blameless." Approaching the camera frontally, he declares angrily, "The fault lies entirely with society [*samāj*]." Turning now and framed against a dark cloth and festive flags that decorated Ahmad's wedding, he grandly proclaims to the camera, "I became afraid of my circumstances. I am still scared; nevertheless, I have decided to embrace Safia as a companion." Now moving toward the camera to an extreme close-up as his face becomes darkened by a shadow, he continues, "If I lose my resolve now, helpless daughters of poor households will remain confined in darkness forever" (Agar main himmat hār gayā to gharībon kī majbūr betiyān qiyāmat tak andheroṉ meṉ baiṭhī raheṉ gī). The final sequence sees him walking down the alley holding his large horn, and with his hand on Safia's back as she walks alongside him on crutches.

The simple and happy-go-lucky Jeeda certainly cuts an odd figure in his new avatar as a social reformer, a didacticism at the end of a film that otherwise possesses much subtlety, at least in the characterization of its male characters. The film focuses centrally on the social relations between men and ultimately the adjustments and sacrifices they make to accommodate each other. The relations between the men are dynamic and animated. Friendships between Ahmad, Bhola, and Jeeda; the tortured gravitas of Safia's father; and the unctuous loquaciousness of the manager of the Rahnuma Marriage Office constitute the center of the film. The relation between Ahmad and Zarina is fleshed out somewhat and imbued with some nuance. On the other hand, Safia is shown as largely suffering her condition as an unwanted and disabled person living a thwarted and unhappy life due to society's normative ableism. A female side character, the washerwoman Chanda, is given incidental treatment. Chanda offers advice to many people as she delivers their laundry. She is herself interested in Ahmad, but he does not reciprocate. Bhola eventually courts her, and they suddenly elope—together disappearing from the Walled City one night. The only female character accorded some depth is Zarina, but even she eventually becomes a token of exchange among the male characters who are attempting to resolve the dilemmas of their friendship when these bonds run up against an impasse.

In his detailed analysis of the film *Saheli* (Female friend, 1960, dir. S. M. Yusuf), Kamran Asdar Ali has cited Claude Lévi-Strauss on marriage, which Ali summarizes as "constitut[ing] the exchange of women between two male groups. Women in this process figure as objects of exchange, and not as active partners."[60] And while Ali notes that this view has been "severely criticized by feminists," it nonetheless offers a framework for thinking through *Susraal*'s conception of gender dynamics in society.[61] Ali, however, suggests yet another methodological route, that of the figure of the *raqīb* (male friend and rival) in classical and modern Urdu poetry: "In most cases, the two *raqīb* seek the attention of the same (female) beloved, but what remains under-theorized in Urdu literary criticism is the intensity of male bonding that permeates this relationship."[62] This is most evocative in characterizing the dynamic between Jeeda and Ahmad. Overall, however, the handling of gender dynamics in the film does compromise its otherwise sympathetic portrayal of nonelite everyday life. And as Ali's analysis of *Saheli* has demonstrated, imaginative scenarios focusing more centrally on the relationships among women were also emerging at that time, within the very matrix of Lahore's commercial cinema, but this is not the case for *Susraal*. Nevertheless, with its focus on subaltern lives beyond typage and stock characters, the film could have charted a new trajectory for Lahore cinema, and there is no reason why subsequent works in this vein would not have addressed women's lives with subtlety and nuance.

Susraal evokes lifeworlds with characters whose daily habits are wasteful, such as gambling and drinking, pigeon fancying, and consuming marijuana and opium; consequently, they have no savings. They are employed as musicians and barbers and in other petty professions. Most of the male characters are involved to some degree in presenting a fraudulent sense of themselves to others. Indeed, the film suggests that authentic lives are possible only because they are based on a contrived and fraudulent presentation of the self, and a filiation and loyalty toward fellow travelers in one's social world, partly because embracing the quality of duplicity is a recognition of human finitude and thus forms the most enduring basis for kinship. There are therefore no heroes or villains in this film and no stock characters such as the vamp; the corrupt, wealthy, and lecherous industrialist; the saintly mother figure; the girl's bourgeois father dressed in a dressing gown and smoking a pipe; the joker sidekick to the hero; and so on. The complete lack of reliance on typage in *Susraal* is a refreshing change from the wearying homogeneity of such characterization in an endless number of social films from Lahore and Bombay. It also promised to make available for Lahore cinema the possibility that minor lives might become visible in their complexity and yet remain buoyant—rather than their portrayal only as oppressed figures in alternative cinema that takes itself seriously as proffering a diagnostic aesthetic. The possibilities missed by *Susraal*'s commercial failure and its neglect in public memory subsequently were thus enormous for Pakistani cinema, as they were for Riaz Shahid himself. He continued to write original and meaningful stories and scintillating dialogue and directed many important films later in his career, but the subtlety of *Susraal* was subsequently eclipsed by evident anticolonial and anti-imperial messaging and calls for social reform. The film *Zinda Bhaag* (Run for life, 2013, dir. Meenu Gaur and Farjad Nabi), analyzed in chapter 4, also focuses on the lives of young men in a nonelite neighborhood of Lahore and can thus be compared with the ambitions of *Susraal*, from five decades earlier.

BADNAM (1966)

Badnam is a landmark accomplishment in Pakistani cinema, for which it was accorded second place (after *Susraal*) by the Pakistan Television Corporation's jury convened for the country's twenty-fifth anniversary.[63] The film is adapted from a short story by Saadat Hasan Manto, "Jhumke." Manto had been associated with Bombay cinema during the forties and, after the Partition, had moved to Lahore. Many of his stories have been adapted to film in both India and Pakistan.[64] A film titled *Jhumke*, based on the same story, was released in 1946.[65] While this film is now unavailable, Pervez Anjum, author of the book *Manto aur cinema* (Manto and cinema), notes that *Badnam* (1966) is a superior adaption of the short story, as well as having achieved far greater success commercially. *Badnam* was directed by Iqbal Shehzad, who was earlier associated with Eastern Film Studios in Karachi as its chief sound technician.[66] The film was his directorial debut, for which he recruited Riaz Shahid to adapt the short story to full feature length, as well as write the screenplay and the dialogue (figure 3.5).

Badnam adheres fairly closely to the original short story, with some key differences, however. While the original story does not have a morally redemptive ending, in *Badnam*, the film ends with the errant character having achieved moral closure.[67] Alamgir Kabir notes that *Badnam*, along with *Lakhon Mein Aik* (One in a million, 1967, dir. Raza Mir and written by Zia Sarhadi) and *Neela Parbat* (The blue mountain, 1969, dir. Ahmad Bashir), "made unusual twists at points where the spectators anticipated the conventional. In other words, they tried to make the audiences think, even if momentarily, something that is dreaded by other directors as suicidal."[68] Kabir also observes that *Badnam*'s "theme has an unusual boldness for a Pakistani film although a great deal of its power is lost in the 'commercialized' portrayal."[69] Despite these departures from the original story, the film raises the disturbing question of whether sexual transactions permitted by marriage are not in fact a form of legalized prostitution.

Dino is a poor man who owns a tonga (horse carriage) and works long hours to provide for his young wife, Hameeda, and daughter, Saeeda, who is not yet of school-going age. Their home is quite spare, but next to a small mirror on the wall hangs a page from a magazine for an advertisement for Pond's cream, which shows a woman adorned in jewelry with *jhumke*, or bell-shaped pendant earrings. Hameeda desperately craves *jhumke* of her own and is constantly imploring Dino to provide these for her. Dino visits a jeweler, who shows him a design that will cost 150 rupees. Dino plans to

FIG. 3.5. Publicity poster of *Badnam* (1966).

save 5 rupees every day, so that in thirty days he will be able to purchase the jewelry. On the twentieth day, he has a stroke of good fortune: after coming home that night, he scrupulously returns a bag full of cash to a customer who had forgotten it on the back of the tonga, and he receives a reward of 50 rupees, the precise remaining sum he needs. He decides that he will wait no longer and will present the *jhumke* to Hameeda that very night. Fortunately, the jeweler is awake and at his shop late that evening. Dino arrives at the jeweler in a framing shot against shallow background space consisting of a poster from the film *Shaheed*. On that poster is the oversize portrait of the actor Allauddin (who plays the role of Dino in *Badnam* and Sardar in *Shaheed*), and on the poster the text *Riaz Shahed* (sic) is visible, creating a mirrored interfilmic reference to Dino himself and also to the anticolonial films of Khalil Qaiser and Riaz Shahid. Later in the film, a lampooning *qawwali* sung by college boys in their hostel will also reference global anticolonial movements (see figure 3.10).

Above the home of Dino and Hameeda lives their landlord, who has been making overtures to Hameeda, offering his assistance in resolving disputes between Dino and her, and taking care of the young daughter. He seemingly acts in a respectable, albeit nosy, fashion but is a character with an unknown background and dubious motivations, as he seeks to learn about private matters between Dino and Hameeda by enticing their little girl with treats. One day, Saeeda returns from playing at his house with a single earring, or *jhumka*. When Hameeda goes upstairs to return it, the landlord asks her to place it on a fabric that is strewn with jewelry, dazzling Hameeda and tempting her to try on the earrings while he is apparently not paying attention.

On the same night when Dino leaves home with the bag of cash to return it to the passenger who had left it behind in the tonga, Saeeda develops a fever. Hameeda goes upstairs to ask the landlord to fetch her medicine, but he seems to be asleep. The lavish spread of jewelry tempts her again, this time decisively, to finally possess the earrings she has coveted all along. She picks up the earrings and models them on her ears in a close-up shot that has the landlord sleeping in the background. She moves to leave with them from the apartment quietly, accompanied by an ominous percussion score. But to her horror, the landlord has awoken and now jubilantly blocks her path. He pushes her roughly on the bed and audaciously offers her a poisoned choice—either he reports the attempted theft, which would ruin her reputation and Dino's, or she makes herself available to him right then, in which case she can keep the *jhumke*, and what transpires between them that night will remain a secret. Hameeda, in shock, is now like an automaton who gives in to the landlord's coercive actions as he pushes her back on the bed with his arm. Afterward, as she is leaving his home in stupor, the landlord puts the *jhumke* on her ears as payment for the sexual transaction that just took place.

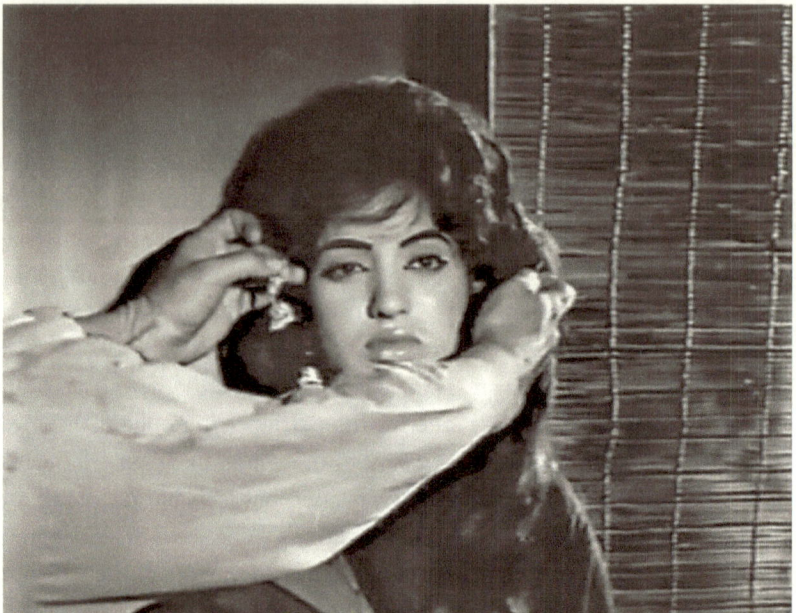

FIG. 3.6. Dino extends his arms to put his newly purchased *jhumke* (bell-shaped pendant earrings) on Hameeda. *Badnam* (1966).

Meanwhile, Dino is back home with his newly purchased *jhumke* and is wondering aloud where Hameeda has gone but assumes that she may have stepped out to purchase medicine for Saeeda. He is preparing to gift her the *jhumke* right away. Hameeda stumbles down the outside stairs and enters the house, disheveled and in a state of shock. In an excited monologue, Dino asks her to stand where she is, so that "the *jhumke* will themselves walk toward you!" His outstretched hands, holding the ornaments, approach her in order to place the earrings on her ears, but as his hands lift her hair to reach her ears, he is shocked to see that she is already wearing pendant earrings (figure 3.6).

The dialogue that follows has become something of a cult classic in Pakistani cinema, or *paisa vaṣūl* (ticket money well spent), according to Zakhmi Kanpuri.[70] Reportedly, audiences would repeatedly return to see *Badnam* just to see and hear this dialogue on screen. Dino walks backward, accompanied with a dissonant score, the camera focusing on his outstretched hands in jerky articulations. He moves back from where he had started, extremely perturbed. Crying out her name, he begins a new monologue of impassioned rage and sorrow, now turning to face the camera, with Hameeda out of focus in the distance in the background in a close-up shot

FIG. 3.7. Dino is shocked to discover the landlord's *jhumke* already on Hameeda. *Badnam* (1966).

of Dino. As the shot progresses, Dino appears to float back toward Hameeda as she slowly comes into focus and he comes nearer to her, both facing the camera (figure 3.7).

> Kis ne pehnā'e haiṇ yeh jhumke
> Kahāṇ se ā'e haiṇ yeh jhumke
> tumhāre khule bāloṇ meṇ kyūṇ aṭke hū'e haiṇ yeh jhumke
> tumhārī āṇkhoṇ se kyūṇ baih rahe haiṇ yeh jhumke

> Who put these *jhumke* on you?
> Where did these *jhumke* come from!
> Why are these *jhumke* entangled in your open tresses?
> Why are these *jhumke* flowing from your eyes?

And turning again toward her, he continues accusingly:

> kyā kaih rahe haiṇ jhumke
> kyā batā rahe haiṇ jhumke

What are these *jhumke* saying?
What is the story of these *jhumke*!

He turns around and strikes the stupefied Hameeda so that she collapses against the charpoy (rope bed) propped against the wall, still in a dazed and silent state. Dino continues his impassioned monologue, berating her for having sold her chastity for the sake of the *jhumke* and saying that she has become a living corpse that he can neither bury nor mourn.[71] And before she realizes what is happening, he picks up Saeeda and leaves the house forever. The popularity of this dialogue is a manifest index to anxieties surrounding conjugal relations and the status of women at a time of accelerating social change in Pakistan. Popular forms manage or repress the repercussions of societal anxieties, "gratifying intolerable, unrealizable, properly imperishable desires only to the degree to which they can again be laid to rest," according to Fredric Jameson.[72] *Badnam* in general, and this dialogue in particular, raises disturbing questions about the all too proximate relation between legal marriage and prostitution, if both relations are ultimately based on a transactional foundation exemplified here by the *jhumke*.

"The film should have ended here but proceeds further in the second half by dealing with their lives after separation," Gazdar has suggested, but in fact, Manto's story also continues on, and the second part of the film is largely faithful to it.[73] It begins with Hameeda going back to the landlord to ask for shelter, but he harshly berates her, telling her that she is not trustworthy even as a domestic servant. He dramatically offers her a lipstick, a premonition of her life to come as a fallen woman and a courtesan. Meanwhile, Dino and Saeeda move to another small home, and he begins working very long hours to provide for her education. Years pass, and Saeeda (played by Neelo; see figure I.2) comes of age as a graceful and accomplished young woman who joins an elite college where mostly sons and daughters of the rich study. Here, she meets Saeed, a young man from a poor rural family, who is initially a social misfit and has been roundly heckled and hazed by his classmates. Saeed and Saeeda begin to fall in love, and Saeed gifts her a pair of *jhumke* one day as a token of his love for her.

When Dino sees Saeeda with the *jhumke*, he imagines that his worst fears are coming to realization and that Saeeda is falling prey to the same overpowering desire for gold and jewelry that had led Hameeda astray. Hari Narayan notes, "Having developed an aversion to jewels, he considers his daughter's *taleem* (education) the best ornament he can give her."[74] Saeeda is unable to explain to him the honorable intentions of Saeed's gift. In desperation, Dino reluctantly sells the horse carriage and his faithful horse and uses the money to immediately buy a handful of jewelry that he brings to Saeeda, as he imagines that this might satisfy her desires and prevent her from straying. Eventually, however, Saeeda is able to convince Dino that the gift that she received was intended not for a sexual transaction but as an expression of true love. A relieved Dino reacquires his tonga.

Dino brings Saeeda to the college every day in his tonga. He has made her promise not to reveal that he is her father, as he does not want her classmates to find out about their poverty and lowly social status. However, one of the heckling students audaciously asks Dino to make Saeeda available to him, as he suspects, without any evidence, that Dino is working as a pimp for a sexually promiscuous Saeeda. In anger, Dino brings him to a lonely spot and gives him a thrashing. Saeed also comes under the mistaken impression now that Dino, the tonga driver, is an unscrupulous man who is leading Saeeda astray. He confronts Dino verbally and physically. Only then does Saeeda confess to her college mates that Dino is indeed her father. Dino also realizes that Saeed is a young man of character, blesses their love, and suggests that they marry right away.

The simple wedding ceremony of Saeeda and Saeed is held at Dino's small home, with Saeed's mother also present from the village. Some guests insist on a dance performance in the courtyard as festive entertainment. In keeping with the conventions of melodrama that abound with improbable chance encounters precisely timed to advance the narrative, the dancer who arrives to perform is none other than Hameeda herself. Upon seeing her after all these years, Dino refuses to let her stay or meet Saeeda. Hameeda now pleads to Dino that she is innocent and offers to bring evidence immediately from the landlord to prove this. When she arrives at the landlord's house, she finds him engaged in forcibly seducing yet another gullible woman who appears to be no older than an adolescent. Hameeda confronts him and shoots him dead but is also injured in the process. Returning back to Dino's house as she is dying, she confesses to Dino that she was tempted toward theft, was then trapped, and was forced to yield to the landlord completely against her wishes. The reason why she never revealed this to Dino was because she was fearful that Dino would have killed the landlord in rage—he would then go to jail, and Saeeda would be left without anyone to look after her. The film ends as the groom and bride depart from Dino's house in his tonga, as Hameeda lies dying in Dino's arms.

Badnam is distinctive as a film on several levels. Riaz Shahid's dialogue for the film is considered to be among the best he ever wrote in their appropriateness, affect, and symbolism. In its "mastery [*chābuk dast*]" and "comprehensiveness [*jama 'andāz*]," it has never been surpassed in Pakistani cinema, claims Pervez Anjum.[75] The dialogue assumes special resonance and density at multiple turns. The film's camerawork and editing break away from the deeply sedimented theatrical conventions that characterize the social film from Lahore (which was acidly criticized by Alamgir Kabir, as discussed earlier in this chapter). Industry observer Zulqarnain Shahid notes that the "making of *Badnam* had a distinct hallmark of somebody who was ready to experiment technically. It had distinctive camerawork, sterling sound, and absolutely astounding editing."[76] For example, the opening shots depict Dino sprucing his tonga at night and riding away after the credits. As the carriage moves toward the camera, the glass lamp held by Dino comes closer to occupying the frame. The lamp moves toward the camera to an extreme close-up out-of-focus shot, then a match cut shows an analogous close-up of a kerosene lamp that Hameeda holds as she walks away from the camera in the interior of the house. This parallelism conveys the sense that the two characters are headed in different directions.

Hameeda, played by the actress Nabila, before her fall is usually dressed in unadorned dark colors. Her movements and gestures are direct and forthright and suggest that the crisis that will make her into an automaton is already latent in her as a corporeal potential. The sequences that depict her internal struggle and crisis are accompanied by dissonant music. Anna Morcom has observed that in Bombay cinema convention, a background score that accompanies disharmony, violence, and disturbance is almost never based on Hindustani ragas.[77] *Badnam* makes effective use of this convention, such as when Hameeda takes hold of both earrings on her first visit to the landlord—she sees herself in the mirror, walks toward it, and holds the ornaments up to her ears in a close-up shot of herself reflected in the mirror. The space is bereft of any other presence, as she becomes totally immersed in a state of inner excitement and turmoil at the thought of possessing her surpassing desire.

The first song in the film is a *lorī*, or a lullaby, that Hameeda sings to put Saeeda to sleep. This comes right after she has encountered the *jhumke* in the landlord's house upstairs, and she is conflicted and troubled inside. As she picks up the sleepy young girl and sings, a crosscut edit shows Dino's tonga moving swiftly and smoothly on the road, accompanied by a musical score that mimics the beat of the horse's gait. As the song proceeds, the song's verses express the desire for a cradle (*jhūlā*) that could put the little girl to sleep more easily, which appears swinging in an imaginary darkened space. The lyrics become stranger, as Hameeda sings to the sleeping girl that her stationary lap can substitute for the cradle. She continues to sing while walking toward the family's small mirror, next to which hangs the Pond's cream advertisement that depicts a woman adorned with earrings. The camera follows Hameeda's gaze to focus on the advertisement. Her disturbed state of mind is symbolized by her continued attraction to the ornaments, which she desires above everything else—the cradle that will bring comfort and joy to the little girl is never a demand that she makes to Dino at any time, for example. The lullaby assumes surreal connotations when Hameeda lifts Saeeda above her head with both hands, singing, "The day will come when compassionate arms will spread out for us, and the world will no longer oppress us" (Din ā'e gā jab phailen ge apne liye sukh ke bāzū, phir chal nah sake gī ham par dunyā kī sīnā zorī), a bizarre lyric in a lullaby meant to comfort a child, and made even stranger by the camera movement that moves quickly to frame her from below in a medium close-up as she holds the child high and somewhat menacingly above her head. The repeated crosscut editing emphasizes the divergence between Dino and Hameeda. As Dino moves smoothly and swiftly in his carriage across Lahore, Hameeda is trapped in her house and in her mind, in a scenario that offers her no way out.

Dino traverses the length and breadth of the city, carrying various passengers across the diverse environments of Lahore's elite and impoverished neighborhoods, commercial plazas, and stately buildings. These are presented as vignettes that dissolve into each other, overlaid at times with close-ups of his face, the jeweler's face, or rotating ornaments that mimic the movement of the tonga wheel, accompanied with a jaunty background score. Gold is the primum mobile animating capitalist urban life.

After Hamida's fall into prostitution, at the *koṭhā* (apartment) of the courtesans who perform for an audience, another haunting song-and-dance sequence was filmed and edited with techniques uncommon in Lahore cinema, such as crane shots, canted and unconventional angles, and montage editing. The sequence evokes a sensorial experience of fragmented theatricality. Dino drives a client to the red light district one night, and the client asks him to wait until he returns. Dino rests in his carriage on the street, as the *mujrā* dance performance begins one floor upstairs at a balcony overlooking the street. The crane shots move alternately from showing Dino close-up to gliding up one floor to a long shot of the balcony from the outside. Inside, Hameeda is singing the lyrics of the *mujrā* song "Baṛe

FIG. 3.8. *Mujrā* (dance) song "Baṛe be-muravvat haiṇ yeh ḥusn wāle" (The exquisite beloved is uncaring). Hameeda plays the *tanpura* (stringed instrument), while actress Zamarrud dances. *Badnam* (1966).

be-muravvat haiṇ yeh ḥusn wāle" (The exquisite beloved is uncaring) and playing the *tanpura* (stringed instrument) with deep pathos, while a dance is performed by the actress Zamarrud (figure 3.8).

As the sound drifts outside the balcony to the street below, the awareness slowly sinks in for Dino that the song is being sung by none other than his estranged wife. In montage shots within the apartment, Zamarrud's rhinestone-encrusted dress and her dance moves and Hameeda's shimmering silvery brocade and jewelry are accentuated by a soft-focus lens that brings out the pathos of Hameeda's visage. Note that a meaning of the word *jhumka* includes a chandelier hanging from a ceiling. Polished mirrors dizzyingly reflect the dancer, and an outsize rotating chandelier frames her in shot compositions that evoke a world of glittering surface effects; across these, the lyrics of the song reverberate in sonic waves, performed by the *kaifi* singer Surayia Multanikar. The song became immensely popular, with a circulation far beyond the ambit of the film itself (figure 3.9).[78]

Badnam's music director was Deebo Bhattacharya, a Bengali who reportedly came to West Pakistan during the midfifties to work with music director Timir Baran, who was also the music director of *Jago Hua Savera*,

FIG. 3.9. Zamarrud's dance accompanying the song "Baṛe be-muravvat haiṇ yeh ḥusn wāle" (The exquisite beloved is uncaring). The word *jhumka* also refers to a chandelier. *Badnam* (1966).

as discussed in chapter 1. Bhattacharya stayed on in West Pakistan throughout the sixties and left only in the early seventies.[79] Another remarkable song sequence is "Bohat be ābrū ho kar tere kūche se ham nikle" (We departed from your street in disgrace), performed by the male students in their college hostel, who lampoon the student who was beaten up by Dino for insinuating that his daughter was a loose woman. The refrain in this *qawwali* is taken from a famous *ghazal* (lyric poem) by Mirza Ghalib (1797–1869) that is ostensibly addressed to a beloved who rejects and humiliates the lover. Symbolism in the *ghazal* form is multivalent, however, and here, its parody addresses anti-imperial geopolitics.[80] Three students—dressed as a Victorian gentleman evidently modeled after Sherlock Holmes to signify the British, a French legionnaire, and an Uncle Sam figure (performed by Saeed)—stand near a large wall map of Africa and mock the defeat of the British in Suez, the withdrawal of France from Algeria, and the retreat of US forces from Korea (figure 3.10).[81]

As seen on the wall poster of *Shaheed* near the jeweler's shop earlier in the film, *Badnam*'s world is punctuated with references to historical and contemporary leftist and anticolonial struggles. The private universe of the

FIG. 3.10. Saeed as Uncle Sam mocking the retreat of the American forces from Korea in the song "Bohat be ābrū ho kar tere kūche se ham nikle" (We departed from your street in disgrace). *Badnam* (1966).

social film is not sealed off from the larger world, even as this world is evoked through melodramatic conventions in Lahore cinema.

The globality of *Badnam* is evoked in the film by circular motifs, which begin at the very opening credits, which show a spinning wheel of the tonga, and in "iris" wipes as the tonga moves from one shot to the next. The circulation of the tonga all over Lahore serves as a local version of the global, which Dino offers as an analogy to Saeeda when she expresses great interest in one of her chosen subjects in college, geography, and explains its importance to him. And when Dino is alarmed at Saeeda's acceptance of the *jhumke*, he directs his monologue to the small globe she has been using in her geography studies. The globe serves as a stand-in for society at large, which denigrates the value of labor and honesty and instead uses gold and lucre to manipulate human needs and weaknesses and takes advantage of this dependence for exploitation (and is also depicted on the film poster; see figure 3.5). This sequence is among the most resonant in the film, shot from multiple angles, including close-up shots of Dino angrily addressing the globe and then him facing the camera in a composition in which the globe is recessed in the background—similar to the shots when Dino discovered the *jhumke* on Hameeda. He finally picks up and attacks the globe, smashing it on the ground. Circularity is also present in the rotating chandelier (also a *jhumka*) in the courtesan's apartment, and it is foregrounded in the vertical shots composed from the top of the chandelier, through which the undulating figure of the dancer on the floor is framed. And it is reiterated in the large paper decorative ornament (which can also be described in Urdu as a *jhumka*) hanging outside Dino's house at Saeeda's wedding, which Hameeda fondles during her conversation with Dino.

Finally, circularity is also generational—Dino is terrified that Saeeda is traversing the same moral arc that her mother did, in their desire for the *jhumke*. This is partly a cinematic convention in Lahore cinema that *Badnam* engages with. Alamgir Kabir has observed that in West Pakistani films, "a good number of the script-writers appear to have a strong faith in some ill-conceived theories of heredity. For them, the son of a respectable father invariably grows up to be respectable and that of a wicked man is almost inevitably condemned to be wicked."[82] The fact that Dino's fears are not borne out by Saeeda suggests that *Badnam* is engaged in a critical retake of this convention, in which individual transformation is not premised upon the prison of biological transmission but is malleable according to circumstances and character, not unlike the value of education for self-cultivation that *Clerk* stresses.

Socially conscious cinema in Lahore during the long sixties consequently needs to be situated within a capacious category encompassing various genres—and indeed the dominant social film itself is largely aligned in this register in the way it evokes the fantasies and nightmares of modernization and its refraction onto issues of gender and class. As exemplified in the film *Zinda Bhaag*, examined in chapter 4, commercial cinema continues to revisit these concerns in present-day Lahore, by drawing on cinematic modes and tropes of earlier films from across South Asia.

4 THE *ZINDA BHAAG* ASSEMBLAGE

Reflexivity and Form

FIVE DECADES AFTER THE LONG SIXTIES, CINEMA IN THE 2010S reveals a profound rupture of memory in contemporary consciousness of forms that were popular prior to 1980. The film *Zinda Bhaag* (Run for life, 2013, dir. Meenu Gaur and Farjad Nabi) was an ambitious attempt to address this cultural and societal amnesia. The long sixties was largely characterized by top-down modernization processes, the promotion of cultural homogeneity, and bourgeois liberal values. It ended with widespread instability and popular mobilization in opposition to Ayub Khan's rule (r. 1958–69). The economic and cultural policies that Pakistan had followed since 1947 had accumulated grievances and a sense of broad political and social disenfranchisement, especially in East Pakistan, which had comprised more than 50 percent of the Pakistani population. This eventually led to the breakup of the country, with Bangladesh becoming an independent nation in December 1971 after a bloody struggle and in the aftermath of war between India and Pakistan, in which the latter was decisively defeated. By 1971, the breakdown of the consensus that had developed during the Ayub years was followed by a greater populist participation in all arenas of life, after the coming to rule of Zulfiqar Ali Bhutto (r. 1971–77). More attention was devoted during the seventies to vernacular, local, and provincial cultural forms. For example, with the founding in 1974 of the organization Lok Virsa, which promoted and documented folk cultural forms, the elite consensus around the singular excellence of Urdu literary forms began to be challenged.[1] In cinema, after 1971, Punjabi-language productions exceeded Urdu productions for the first time (see figure I.1). Pashto-language cinema also saw a rise in the number of films made each year during the 1980s and the 1990s.[2]

Pakistan's economic policies had long been aligned with the American sphere of influence from the 1950s onward. As global developments began to embrace globalization and neoliberalism from the 1980s, these were also adopted by the state in Pakistan without much hindrance. The Afghan War (1978–92) precipitated multiple structural changes in Pakistan, with the inflow of weapons and money, a staggering increase in the domestic consumption of and the export of narcotics and heroin, and the rise of shadowy players wielding power over a growing informalized and urbanized society. Also, from the midseventies onward, expatriate labor left the country for extended temporary stints or permanently, and this included both blue-collar labor and white-collar professionals, with large numbers moving to the Middle East and the Western world. These currents included legalized migration, extended guest-worker movements, and the risky and fraught nonlegal passage—the *dunky* in Lahori slang—whose pursuit is the central subject of the main characters in the film *Zinda Bhaag*.

The Pakistan of the second decade of the twenty-first century is therefore very different from what it was during the long sixties. Nevertheless, the question of memory and cultural lineages of prior popular forms remains an important one for the present. Pakistan lacks a physical and institutional cinema archive, but more importantly, it lacks a presence in the consciousness of the generations of people who came of age after the seventies, whose memory of Pakistani cinema before the eighties is fragmentary and tenuous. With the recent rise of the so-called "New Cinema," the decades-long decline in the quality and number of Urdu films after 1980 finally began to be reversed. Yet critical questions remain pressing regarding the relationship—in formal, thematic, narrative terms—between New Cinema and cinema's golden age from the long sixties and seventies in Lahore, Karachi, and Dhaka.

Zinda Bhaag is an ambitious attempt to engage with the legacies of twentieth-century South Asian cinema for the present. In this respect, it is analogous to the project of *Jago Hua Savera* (A new day dawns, 1959, dir. A. J. Kardar), which also sought to activate thematic and experiential connections across national borders. *Zinda Bhaag*'s broadly leftist orientation in examining issues of disenfranchisement and class via the commercial cinema realm can also be situated with the earlier films of Khalil Qaiser and Riaz Shahid. In particular, both *Susraal* (The in-laws' home, 1962, dir. Riaz Shahid) and *Zinda Bhaag* attend to the lives of subaltern male characters and the dilemmas of male bonding among friends living in Lahore's nonelite neighborhoods. Nevertheless, a temporal and social distance of over fifty years separates the two films. Significantly, unlike all the other films analyzed in this study, *Zinda Bhaag* is primarily a Punjabi-language film. But unlike most Punjabi films made earlier, which are set in rural contexts, *Zinda Bhaag* is fully engaged with urban subaltern life in a contemporary global megacity. The use of mostly Punjabi in this setting is in keeping with the neorealist conception of using the local dialect, which neither *Jago Hua Savera* nor *Susraal* fully followed. The shift in emphasis here to a Punjabi-language production acknowledges the profound transformations that have transpired in the social and cultural life of Lahore since the sixties; it also raises questions of cultural amnesia, as well as the need for reactivating cultural legacies from across South Asia in order to better address the fraught present. The film is also exemplary for the continued salience of the Lahore effect into the present.[3]

NEOLIBERALISM AND CINEMA

The feature-length Punjabi-language film *Zinda Bhaag* (2013), directed by Meenu Gaur and Farjad Nabi and produced by Matteela Films, narrates the story of three young men, Khaldi, Taambi, and Chitta, who desperately attempt to push against the economic and social limitations within which their class background confines them.[4] The various prevalent types of gambling activities, all of which are illegal, are analogues for taking fatal chances with one's own life in order to leave a society that presents little possibility for forward movement. Puhlwan (wrestler), played by noted Indian actor Naseeruddin Shah, is the local don who manages and profits from the gambling, provides a sort of rough-and-ready local governance in the absence of the state, and fondly narrates absorbing moralistic fables as the occasion demands (figure 4.1).

All the young men in the film, as well as Khaldi's love interest, Rubina, are caught in a horizon of aspirations fueled by neoliberal consumerist fantasies. But while Rubina focuses on the steady and persistent entrepreneurial manufacture and guerrilla marketing of soap in the informal locale of nonelite Lahore, the young men perceive themselves to be trapped in a socioeconomic nightmare for which migration to Europe beckons as remedy and fulfillment.[5]

Apart from Naseeruddin Shah, a leading actor in Indian commercial and parallel cinema, *Zinda Bhaag* uses mostly nonprofessional actors and was shot on location in a nondescript lower-middle-class locality in Lahore, which recalls neorealist principles.[6] In its shooting and postproduction, the film also deployed Indian expertise—its production team was mostly Punjabi-speaking, from both sides of the border. That the film deployed a cross-national team and that Matteela Films is now based in Karachi

FIG. 4.1. The Puhlwan mesmerizing his admirers with his fables. *Zinda Bhaag* (2013).

contribute to the possibilities and dilemmas of how media whose reach is increasingly transnational can effectively relate to the specificities of a location that is itself thoroughly permeated by vectors of migration. Despite the grim and serious subject, the film deftly negotiates a narrative arc that traverses realism and fable. It evokes a perceptual space in which the weight and grind of everyday realism are continually traversed by openings that offer glimpses toward possibilities in which the burdened daily existence of the protagonists can be redeemed by levity and success—possibilities that seem to be latent in every moment yet, despite the best efforts of the protagonists, remain unrealizable.

The brief opening sequence establishes the dichotomy between a nostalgic conception of Lahore as a city with a storied history and its famed Punjabi ethos of being a city inhabited by the *zinda dilān* (possessing joie de vivre),[7] on the one hand, and the grim reality faced by its underemployed male youth on the other. It opens with an establishing shot from an elevated perspective of the rooftops and minarets of the old city, accompanied by ambient street noise. Next, close-up shots depict Mughal architecture, street food, colorful fabric, girls laughing together and making henna patterns on their hands, and children bathing in a canal. These joyful touristic shots of everyday life in the city are followed by a shot of neatly arranged piles of cash and a top-down fast-motion shot of narrow lanes, along with frenzied traffic, accompanied with a voiceover by the genial and magisterial Puhlwan. It narrates that all of God's bounties are already available in the city of Lahore; why do fools seek to leave all this behind to venture abroad? The next sequence shows a wide road and medium close-up of the three male friends behind the windshield of a vehicle (figure 4.2). The opening shots

FIG. 4.2. Khaldi, Chitta, and Taambi in the opening scenes. *Zinda Bhaag* (2013).

immediately dangle the allure of the picturesque and touristic Lahore, which is no longer habitable for the three young men.

Zinda Bhaag is an important film whose cinematic, geographical, and moral universe raises a number of critical and analytical questions for independent filmmaking in contemporary Pakistan. These include the considerable history of older Pakistani cinema, its present crisis, and the degraded condition of the older studios and cinema halls; the history of a cinematic form and of its relationship with prior and superseded forms of Pakistani cinema; the tension between vernacular linguistic and cultural forms and international norms; the overwhelming presence of Indian cinema and the difficult task for Pakistani filmmakers to situate themselves both in conflict and in cooperation with this juggernaut; the role of a contemporary imagination that is thoroughly shaped by media and neoliberal consumerist fantasies; the strangely constricted and hallucinatory universe of the protagonists, which is shot throughout with avenues of escape to a thrilling but unfathomable future elsewhere; and the virtual impossibility today of cinematically representing class conflict.

Zinda Bhaag is highly intermedial and reflexive, as it refers to older cinematic tropes and local television soap operas. In terms of form, the film deploys intertextuality with earlier cinematic and theatrical tropes, and it relays between high cinema and commercial mainstream. It utilizes techniques whose lineage goes back to neorealism and Indian parallel cinema: location shooting, nonprofessional actors, local language and dialect. Its fabling also presses on elements of "traditional" imaginative modes—literature, poetry, and theater—to transform them into new, fantastic modes of aspiration promised by entrepreneurial effort, participation in shadowy economic schemes, or physical migration. The film is part of a new wave of cinema emerging from Pakistan, termed New Cinema.[8] But *Zinda Bhaag* completely sidesteps the issue of terrorism and violence, which dominates much of the New Cinema from Pakistan. Nor does it focus on the social and romantic dramas of the elite or the oppression of women, topics that are often revisited by directors and encouraged by the global film festival circuit. Rather, it explores urban subaltern lifeworlds that are not especially concerned with the question of being Muslim and are consequently quite invisible to mainstream reception.

New Cinema has relied on a specific kind of realism that emerges from television serials: the need to grapple with religious "fundamentalism" and offer instead a more moderate and tolerant version of Muslim life for Pakistanis. New Cinema is also under pressure from spectacular commercial mainstream Bollywood, whose influence molds Pakistani New Cinema in its image—in form, narrative, and address. While these provide some cultural resources for Pakistani filmmakers seeking to address their own locale, they are clearly lacking in other ways: the realism of the TV serial follows conventional narrative structures and cinematic styles, the dominant focus on the theme of fundamentalism obscures other contemporary issues, and mainstream Bollywood is compelled to work under market-driven conditions, with many productions simply being variations of formulaic narrative and cinematic tropes. What remains markedly absent in the history of Pakistan's cinema and television is a rich legacy of avant-garde and experimental moving image, critical pedagogy, and viewing practices that foster an environment for experimental and critical approaches to flourish.

In the absence of a tradition of experimental cinema and parallel cinema in Pakistan, New Cinema is tasked with finding new ways forward with narrative and form in order to expand the local vocabulary and range of resources. Its engagement with a much more diverse ensemble of medias is critical if the New Cinema is not to arise in a space filled only by a stereotypical constellation of available tropes and techniques. What is needed is a critical reckoning with the history of the medium in Pakistan and South Asia, and with other disparate mediums and narrative forms that are local, but not in a dogmatic or exclusivist register.

Zinda Bhaag is a cinematic work of considerable ambition in conceiving of itself as an agent that intervenes in numerous cinematic and imaginative domains and traverses both realism and fable. Of primary interest here are its formal and reflexive elements, rather than its charged, socially conscious narrative of the problem of illegal migration. That its form is an assemblage is a more significant intervention in New Cinema than an ostensible adherence to a unified narrative. The following analysis understands *Zinda Bhaag* as an experimental assemblage that marshals a wide ensemble of narrative tropes and visual styles—premodern oral tales and Sufi allegories of the unattainable beloved, Marxist poetry, the influential Pakistani television serials, the golden age of Bombay and Urdu cinema of the 1950s and 1960s, and Pakistani-vernacular action cinema of the 1970s and 1980s. As a montaged ensemble of realism and fable, it flexes the Lahore effect in new ways.[9] The film draws upon multiple resources and subjects them to critical and reflexive translation. It does so not only to narratively address issues of class and masculinity in a crisis-ridden neoliberal present but also to experiment with cinematic form in order to expand the constellation of references for emerging cinema in Pakistan.

The concept of assemblage is helpful for this analysis. "In the work of Gilles Deleuze and Félix Guattari, *assemblage (agencement)* carries connotations of connection, event, transformation, and becoming," notes media theorist N. Katherine Hayles, adding that it is "the notion of an arrangement not so tightly bound that it cannot lose or add parts, yet not so loosely connected that relations between parts cease to matter."[10] Assemblage thus encompasses the ethos of unfolding newness through the dynamic articulation of disparate elements in a specific configuration. Since *Zinda Bhaag* draws tactically and selectively from the media and cultural forms of the premodern and modern eras, it can indeed be usefully seen as the marshaling together of an assemblage. Assemblage also distinguishes *Zinda Bhaag* from earlier art or parallel cinema of South Asia in which a more unified narrative arc subsumes other tropes, and this is the case also for the earlier social film and its melodramatic universe. And if we hold that cinematic form does have an articulation with the social world—keeping in mind that this linkage is not mechanical or simply causal, but overdetermined and marked by fracture and uneven temporality—we can nevertheless posit that while the earlier cinema of relative narrative coherence flourished in expectations of a top-down developmentalist modernity or its failure, *Zinda Bhaag*'s form addresses our neoliberal era and its informalized ethos through its frenetic pace, fractured narrative and editing, permeation of neorealism with fable, and open-ended, nonredemptive ending.

But does Pakistan today face conditions that are dominantly neoliberal, and do the consequences of this "mode of production" characterize its economic, social, and cultural life? This is obviously a proposition that can be bestowed with a kind of magical explanatory power—every consequential transformation since the late 1980s can be easily laid at the feet of an omnipotent neoliberalism. This temptation is especially compelling in the case of Pakistan, which lacks effective and prominent examples in which individuals, communities, or regions have followed other trajectories that could serve as identifiable counters to the alleged hegemony of neoliberalism. Keeping in mind these reservations, and remaining vigilant about totalizing explanations, we can nevertheless note that large areas of governance, economy, and society in Pakistan can indeed be characterized as neoliberal. For our purposes, this means a retrenchment of the state from the kinds of heroic developmental projects from the 1950s to the 1970s that were especially intense during the long sixties; the continued crisis of the national education system at all levels; the privatization of state enterprises and services largely for the benefit of crony capitalism; the unplanned and rapid growth of informal urban housing and employment; a tremendous expansion of the realm of consumer commodities and credit; deepening divides between social groups and classes that have bodily, architectural, and symbolic dimensions, such as gated city enclaves and leisure spaces, including suburban housing, malls, restaurants, and clubs; the stoking of libidinal and material desire in a massive and pervasive capitalist media ecology; and the availability of upmarket accessories and consumer commodities, prominently showcased on glossy billboards and in seductive media advertisements. On the other hand, the hold of the older business elite and the landed aristocratic classes has come under increasing threat from upstarts, in a social economy that is more diversified and far more volatile than during the modernist developmentalist era, and one in which diaspora is no longer a realm cut off from home. In psychic terms, poor education, absence of secure employment opportunities, and immersion in consumer and media images fuel intensified desire for material success and stature via "entrepreneurship," and all this in a society in which breadwinning still remains closely associated with masculinity. This potent realm of crisis and possibility is precisely *Zinda Bhaag*'s contextual mise-en-scène.

THE 2013 JUNCTURE

Cinema in Pakistan experienced major transformations from the late 1970s onward. The arrival of the VCR brought Bombay cinema into the private spaces of middle-class households and, increasingly, lower-class households and communities. Cinema halls showing similar but lesser-quality social and melodramatic Urdu films became less frequented, leading to a vicious cycle of further decline in their number and quality from the eighties into the twenty-first century. The conservative and censorious media policies of the regime of military dictator Muhammad Zia-ul-Haq (1977–88) also created impediments for filmmakers addressing social issues (which television serials arguably addressed more intensively and seriously during the eighties).

The decline in the number of Urdu films was partially made up by the rise of Punjabi and Pashto films that catered to rural and urban working-class constituencies. Ali Nobil Ahmad has cautioned against falling into the prevalent decline-and-fall narrative that romanticizes the golden age of the Urdu social film addressing the middle class, blinding critics to the importance of vernacular cinemas of the eighties and nineties, whose rustic action genres catered to subaltern audiences.[11] Undoubtedly, however, the overall decline in the infrastructure of production and distribution has been dramatic since the late seventies. Ahmad in 2016 noted that "the national industry's hundred-plus features per year in 1980s were regularly projected onto twelve hundred screens nationwide—figures that have dwindled to barely two dozen films and a mere hundred and fifty screens respectively, of which an unknown number are non-functional."[12] This extended crisis has resulted in an infrastructural and thematic discontinuity in Pakistani cinema for three decades, but recent years have witnessed a revival of cinema (aka New Cinema) forged in the crucible of neoliberalism and catering to globally aspirant middle-class tastes.[13]

Several observers have notated 2013 as a landmark year in which several key films were launched. While this number is not large, many of these films were genre-formative and the firsts of their kind for Pakistan. These 2013 developments did not arise in a vacuum, however. After a steep decline in the number and quality of films in Urdu, momentum had been building toward a revival since around 2006. This development was not led by the older filmmakers and studios, whose conditions had deteriorated very badly, as had the conditions of the remaining film theaters.[14] Rather, this revival was spearheaded via new technologies (digital filmmaking), new personnel, new patronage (many supported by the big private news and media networks), and new distribution circuits in newly established multiplex theaters and network television. This meant that this revival of cinema also emerged without an awareness of the not-inconsiderable history of cinema in Pakistan from the 1950s to the late 1970s, a period that saw the release of thousands of commercial feature films.

A milestone in this new turn is the film *Khuda Kay Liye* (In the name of God), a technically well-made 2007 feature film directed by Shoaib Mansoor that elicited considerable publicity domestically and also circulated abroad. Mehreen Jabbar's *Ramchand Pakistani* (2008) is another important film, and one in which the noted Indian actress Nandita Das played a lead role. Its lyrical sensitivity toward the desert landscape and its consciously loose narrative were a welcome departure from the mechanical cause-and-effect scenarios seen in many television serials. Omar Khan's zombie film *Zibahkhana* (Slaughterhouse, 2007), made with fewer resources, has been the subject of a number of scholarly essays.[15] Here, I summarize two of the film's characteristics that are relevant for my study. *Zibahkhana* is salient for its intermediality, as it references *Zinda Laash* (The living corpse, 1967, dir. Khwaja Sarfraz), an Urdu horror film from Lahore, as well as international horror tropes. And it addresses issues of class (although, its take on class is from the vantage of the elite kids and is one in which subalterns are largely monstrous, unlike *Zinda Bhaag*, in which the subaltern urban characters are central). As a horror film, *Zibahkhana*'s reception is evoked via its visceral effects, rather than in the social film, where emotive affect is dominant, and which constitutes the focus of this book. But *Zibahkhana* is partly an exception that proves the rule that most contemporary Pakistani films largely do not address class nor are they engaged with the rich legacy of theatrical, performative, and cinematic fabling that characterized the Lahore effect.

The arrival of the multiplex fueled the desire of middle-class viewers to return to the cinema hall. This was greatly aided by the Pakistani government's decision to legalize the screening of Bollywood films, which enabled the infrastructural development of new cinema theaters that the emerging Pakistani cinema could also utilize.[16] Other recent films that have enjoyed notable publicity include *Bol* (Speak, 2011), directed by Shoaib Mansoor; *Waar* (Strike, 2013), directed by Bilal Lashari; and *Na Maloom Afraad* (Unidentified people, 2014), directed by Nabeel Qureshi. However, gauging New Cinema's commercial success is not easy—neither production budgets nor audiences, nor screening figures, nor returns are fully transparent, given that many films are sponsored in-house by media conglomerates and that some films are aided gratis in their production by the considerable resources of the military. One may note that all these films are in Urdu, and apart from *Ramchand Pakistani*, they all largely follow conventions of mainstream commercial cinema drawn from Hollywood and Bollywood, or realist aspects of earlier parallel cinema in South Asia.[17]

CHAPTER 4

HEGEMONY OF TELEVISION SERIALS

Television serials have been dominant for several decades in the Pakistani mediascape, tackling issues such as the fraught position of women, feudal and gender hierarchies, and other social concerns. Fuller analysis of these serials—including their formal characteristics—is extremely important for understanding their pervasive social influence, a task that is beyond the scope of this study and awaits extended scholarship.[18] For our purposes, it is important to note that the serials are largely made according to specific conventions—linear and steady narrative unfolding; foregrounded but ultimately circumscribed affective and emotional registers; rehearsed dialogue between characters; high-key lighting in staged interiors; little camera movement, with tableau placement of characters facing the camera; and shot-reverse shot and other conventional techniques. Editing is seldom experimental, nor are the placement and movement of the camera or the characters. In this sense, if we posit the quality of being *cinematic* in terms of techniques such as fluid camerawork; montage editing; the deployment of unexpected camera positions; the dilation, compression, and interruption of narrative flow; outdoor mise-en-scène; locations whose ambiance cannot be fully stage-managed; and other aspects of cinematic style, the television serials are *not cinematic*. Even though the television serials might espouse upper-middle-class liberal feminist and anti-authoritarian topics in their overall narrative, the problem with this mode is the reproduction of conventional and commonsense morality, normative temporality, and normalized space, in which events and encounters unfold with a steady regularity in a stable social fabric. And in terms of narrative resolution of issues of gender and class, it largely conforms to mainstream liberal norms. The television serials nevertheless provide an important set of references to New Cinema—the more so as many directors of New Cinema developed their careers in the dozens of television channels that have emerged since the liberalization of media in 2002.[19]

Due to its dominant influence in the Pakistani mediascape, the genre of television serials nevertheless influences many new films, especially those addressing social issues. Notwithstanding their formal and narrative limitations, the serials' undeniable importance for Pakistani society means that *Zinda Bhaag* engages with them, albeit critically and reflexively. The film recognizes the wide viewership of the serials—both Khaldi's mother and Puhlwan are addicted to the fictional television drama serial *Auqat* (Social status), participating in the fashioning of a larger Pakistani "imagined community" that popular media has arguably done more to constitute than uneven official policies have.[20] On the other hand, even from the few clips of the serial that one glimpses in the film, *Auqat* is a parody that lampoons television serials' conservative formal conventions and staged melodramatic bourgeois morality. A wide establishing shot of the rooftops in dim twilight and then ground-level views of the street below connect with a sound bridge to the interior of Khaldi's home, where the theme song of *Auqat* is playing; the sense here is that street life is empty when the popular serial is on. As one watches snippets of *Auqat* throughout the film, it becomes clear that it lampoons the gentility of the television serial with cruel and sadistic dialogue, suggesting that the reality of urban subaltern life is far beyond the ambit of the genteel universe of the television serial.

I believe that the *formal* properties of a genre are more primary and more significant than narrative or thematic content and that the lack of experimentation in Pakistan's moving image production therefore limits development of new approaches in the moving image format. The task of serious artists and filmmakers is then to also reflect on this amnesia and absence. Not only are *Zinda Bhaag*'s rapid editing and quick-paced sequences opposed to the television serials' stodgy temporality but the film also includes an explicit critique of the latter, as when *Auqat* lulls Khaldi's mother into a kind of stupor of inhabiting a parallel universe. This media addiction to what has been commonly understood as a more realist register (as compared with the commercial film) is ironically what is shown here as being unable to keep pace with the quickened, multifarious, intersecting, and clashing challenges of the crisis-ridden present.

Zinda Bhaag also incorporates numerous references to prior cinematic forms. Khaldi's mother recalls but departs from the self-abnegating character of the mother in innumerable commercial Indian and Pakistani films. The mother figure in *Zinda Bhaag* is nevertheless critically bound up in an intertextuality of filmic significations.[21] If the earlier stock mother figure bore enormous personal sacrifices to preserve family honor, such as in *Clerk* (1960), by contrast Khaldi's mother constantly hounds him to become a better breadwinner. Rubina, Khaldi's romantic interest, also refuses the role of the ever-faithful female lover of classic Bombay and Pakistani cinema, walking out of the relationship as Khaldi's desperation grows. This inversion of the conventional codes of femininity nevertheless becomes legible via an interfilmic subtext. These are but two examples of critical reworkings of the cinematic tropes of the past.

This referential strategy was a result of a deliberate set of choices on the part of the filmmakers. According to Meenu Gaur, *Zinda Bhaag* utilizes techniques that were prevalent in 1970s cinema but have now fallen out of fashion, such as flashbacks, voices in the characters' heads, and saturated color that has faded along specific chromatic registers, the way color celluloid unevenly ages.[22] *Zinda Bhaag* integrates and incorporates songs in advancing the narrative, allowing the songs to express emotions or feelings that are difficult to express otherwise. In this sense, it references the golden age of melodramatic films, rather than action genres and more recent Bollywood films, in which songs such as "item numbers" might serve as interruptions that do not necessarily advance the plot.[23] Unlike the violent, nihilistic, and amoral villains in many contemporary films, Puhlwan never deploys brute or muscle power, despite his nickname as a "wrestler." Even this signifier is a chiasma, as his prior career is depicted in flashback not as that of a powerful wrestler or heroic masculine figure but as a "lowly" sanitation worker employed to clean the audience stands at a horse racetrack after the race. And in an incident in which drug addicts have to be removed from a space owned by Puhlwan, he advises using a water hose, sagely observing, "A druggie is already half-dead. Humanity doesn't preach killing of the dead." In his persona as an absorbing, soft-spoken raconteur, Puhlwan takes after an ensemble of villain characters in past films. According to Gaur, one reference is the celebrated Indian actor Pran (1920–2013), who appeared in numerous Bollywood films as a gentleman villain.[24] Pran's character played at the edges of an otherwise functioning society and within a semblance of moral order, rather than transgressing rules completely.[25] A similar character in Pakistani cinema was developed by the actor Aslam Parvez (1932–84).[26] Another inspiration for Puhlwan is the quiet, soft-spoken, and principled Noori Natt character in the hyperviolent, celebrated, and genre-formative Pakistani Punjabi film *Maula Jatt* (1979, dir. Younis Malik).[27]

MISSING LINEAGES OF PARALLEL CINEMA

Barring a few honorable experiments, such as *Jago Hua Savera* (1959), Pakistan does not possess a rich lineage of experimental or avant-garde cinema—certainly nothing of the scope and scale that arose in India from the 1950s onward, associated with directors such as Shyam Benegal, Ritwik Ghatak, Mani Kaul, Satyajit Ray, Aparna Sen, Mrinal Sen, and others.[28] Historically, Italian neorealism was formative in the emergence of parallel cinema in India, where enlightened state funding provided crucial support. Veteran actors such as Naseeruddin Shah (who plays Puhlwan in *Zinda Bhaag*) have been closely associated with Indian parallel cinema for decades—in Shah's role as a young feudal scion in *Nishant* (Night's end, 1975, dir. Shyam Benegal), for example. Avant-garde experiments in India also found another avenue in short films made under the aegis of the Films Division, in which artists such as Akbar Padamsee and Nalini Malani made important formalist experimental work.[29] In Pakistan, the realist feature-length experiment of *Jago Hua Savera* was not repeated in any influential manner until Sabiha Sumar's *Khamosh Pani* (Silent waters, 2003). Even in India, parallel cinema was not *formally* experimental in a cinematic sense, and this is the also case for Sumar's film, which deploys conventional camera and editing and follows a temporally steady realist narrative arc. And while one can analyze commercial and mainstream Pakistani films for occasional experimental and discrepant elements, there is no doubt regarding the larger absence of a legible trajectory of parallel cinema in the country, in theme as well as form.[30] The few experiments that one can recount did not prove to have a lasting impact. Jamil Dehlavi's surrealist political allegory *The Blood of Hussain* (1980) was banned in Pakistan and has not circulated widely.[31] Hasan Zaidi's *Raat Chali Hai Jhoom Ke* (The intoxicated night, 2002), Pakistan's first digitally filmed feature, which Zaidi developed in collaboration with the novelist and critic Mohammad Hanif, was shown only twice on television and has not been released on DVD or the Internet.[32]

Zinda Bhaag reconstructs this missing lineage, by having Naseeruddin Shah play a leading role and by inviting Mohammad Hanif to contribute the lyrics of a key song, which takes after a celebrated poem by Faiz Ahmed Faiz. Faiz was associated with the neorealist experiment *Jago Hua Savera*, was a close friend of Khurshid Anwar's, and contributed lyrics to the films of Riaz Shahid and Khalil Qaiser. Aspects of *Zinda Bhaag* also follow neorealist principles. These include reliance on nonprofessional actors, location shooting in an unremarkable lower-middle-class neighborhood in Lahore, and the challenging task of recording sound on location to render ambiance with a heightened character.

PATRONAGE OF THE NEW CINEMA

The dilemmas faced by contemporary filmmakers in Pakistan in situating their films in a series of overlapping and disrupted traditions have formal implications, beyond the concerns of marketing and distribution. If the missing lineage of parallel and experimental film cannot now be re-created, what is available today, of course, is a much broader palette of options, but they have to be translated into the specific matrix of conditions in which emerging Pakistani cinema is being forged. These resources include mainstream Hollywood and Bollywood genres, such as action, romance, buddy, horror, political thriller, et cetera. And equally significantly, they include the development in Indian cinema of what has been termed the new hybrid, which includes the so-called *hatke* (quirky) films.[33] In his study of "the new indies" in India, Ashvin Devasundaram notes that these films "narrate micro-narratives—the minority and alternative stories of nation excluded from Bollywood film representations ... the discursive contexts and subjective voices in contemporary India, largely elided in academic literature's preoccupation with the majority narrative of Bollywood."[34] These films challenge what Devasundaram has termed Bollywood's "meta-hegemony," which encompasses "monopoly over the Indian film industry's modes of production, distribution, exhibition and capital generation," its "ideological propagation of a post-globalization master narrative," and its investment in "patriarchal, postcolonial, national narrative through gendered and stereotypical representations of women."[35]

Nevertheless, these independent Indian films inhabit a paradoxical landscape. Unlike older parallel cinema that enjoyed state support, these new feature films remain very dependent on precisely the infrastructures of production and distribution that commercial mainstream media and cinema have established.[36] Devasundaram further observes, "This hegemonic configuration often standardizes Bollywood's presence as a seemingly indispensable intermediary for Indies to gain funding or a wider audience ... [and] often deems it necessary for independent film directors to solicit the influence and patronage of Bollywood personalities or producers. The aim is to augment their films' visibility amongst civil society by attaching the associative commercial gravitas of Bollywood to an Indie project. This is part of an idiosyncratic 'godfather' syndrome in the Indian filmmaking firmament."[37]

Independent filmmakers in Pakistan must rely on various "godfathers" as well, even beyond the film industry, given the deteriorated infrastructure of commercial Pakistani cinema. In terms of infrastructure and funding, these include sponsorship by network television media houses, corporate sponsorship and its demands for product placement or attempts to improve its public image by supporting feel-good or conventional themes, and the rise of the multiplex cinema showing Bollywood and mainstream Hollywood films. These neoliberal conditions, and the fact that many new filmmakers have cut their teeth on advertising work, mean that many productions of the New Cinema uncritically embody these aesthetic values.

Zinda Bhaag assumes a reflexive stance toward this infrastructural reality. It focuses centrally on class divisions and antagonisms, a theme that was important in the commercial South Asian cinema of the 1940s to 1970s but is no longer in vogue. And the film has a critical take on product placement and the amplification of desire through capitalist consumerism. For example, the seductive red dress that Rubina admires in the Exist designer store at the Mall of Lahore has a steep sticker price of 4,985 rupees. This dress is also prominently advertised on street billboards, further fueling Khaldi's desire to steal it as a gift for Rubina. Consumerist consumption and branding as lifestyle are thus impossible without the original sin of theft. And Rubina's soap brand, Facelook, would not be dissimilar to what in contemporary art is termed "tactical media" practice.[38] The soap's packaging is branded with a typeface and color lifted from the Facebook logo, exemplary of a highly dominant product placement being waylaid via informal parasitic procedures.

One of the most important patrons of the New Cinema is the powerful and extremely well-resourced Inter Services Public Relations (ISPR), which has provided technical and logistical assistance for some of the most expensive recent feature productions.[39] Since the ISPR is the public face of the Pakistani deep state establishment, this patronage is ideologically fraught for filmmakers who wish to address serious social issues that venture beyond formulaic and mythical resolutions. *Waar* (Strike), a slick action film directed by Bilal Lashari also released in 2013, was made with the extensive support of the ISPR, for example. And Bollywood productions, which have done very well in the new multiplexes in Pakistan, remain a highly influential template for Pakistani aspirants, despite the fact that the budgets and range of professional expertise available to Indian filmmakers are orders of magnitude greater than even the best-financed Pakistani film.[40] Despite calls by critics to develop a less formulaic cinema that is responsive to its local site and to its social and infrastructural conditions, many Pakistani filmmakers remain in thrall to the spectacular big-budget Bollywood extravaganza.[41] Indian commercial cinema thus serves as yet another demanding "godfather" and occasional patron in many ways—for example, Pakistani New Cinema has relied on major Bollywood actors as leads in numerous films, such as *Khamosh Pani, Khuda Kay Liye, Ramchand*

Pakistani, and *Zinda Bhaag*.⁴² *Zinda Bhaag* reflexively foregrounds the structural dependency on these "godfathers." The Puhlwan character, for example, is the very personification of the don who is feared but to whom one also turns to in order to fix one's financial and social difficulties. Puhlwan provides serviceable governance and patronage in a context where the state is absent.⁴³

FABLING AND RECOVERY OF PRECINEMATIC TROPES

One of the most important dimensions of *Zinda Bhaag* is its investment in creating linkages with oral and performance genres from the Punjab and beyond. There are no fewer than four extended flashbacks in the film, each at least eight minutes long, in which Puhlwan recounts stories allegedly from his past in order to provide edifying moral lessons—"*gall vichon gall nikaldi ai*" (one story emerges from another), a phrase he fondly repeats at each flashback. There is, of course, no way of knowing whether these stories are true. In terms of narrative, this nesting structure recalls premodern and early modern genres such as *qiṣṣa* and the *var*, including the story of *Hir-Ranjha*, which incorporated subnarratives that departed from the dominant narrative and offered both entertainment and edification.⁴⁴ Significantly, early cinema in South Asia until the fifties has engaged with the *dāstān*, the Oriental tale and stories of impossible love, such as the Laila-Majnun tale, as film scholar Rosie Thomas has shown.⁴⁵ Codirector Meenu Gaur has observed that many epic oral folktales in Punjabi, Sindhi, and other regional languages are accounts of "death foretold," in which the quest for union with the beloved is all-consuming but impossible, leading toward certain death. These epics depart radically from the narrative arc of modern Western genres, such as the short story or the bildungsroman, for example. This is evident in the closing song of the film, as Gaur notes:

> The lyrics at the end of the film try to communicate that sense of victory in the face of foretold death: *jo haar gayo so paar gayon / sab andhron baharon vaar gayon / sirr dhar tali talwar gayon / haq ticket kata darbar gayon* [you lost and won the passage to eternity / your being was your offering / with your head perched on the tip of a sword / and in your hand clutching the ticket to truth]. . . . These lyrics Farjad and I penned to capture the sense of heroism in failure . . . that to lose is the biggest victory . . . because now there is no place for failure . . . which wasn't the

case when we were growing up ... where the so-called failures amongst us could be renegades and extremely attractive figures.⁴⁶

In *Zinda Bhaag*, the fantasy of the full realization of one's desire is located in the successful *dunky*, the fraught journey to Europe. Despite the bitter experience of Taambi being imprisoned when abroad and then deported, Europe's mythical lure remains undimmed for Chitta, Khaldi, and many other characters as they seek fixes with middlemen who forge passports or who peddle admission in dubious college programs in the United Kingdom as a way to secure visas. Here the realm of *jouissance* is Europe, allegorized as the unattainable, forever-desirable beloved of the *qiṣṣa*, the obsessive quest for whom demands the sacrifice of one's life during the *dunky*. Other references in the film to the performative cultures of the Punjab include skits and comedy acts from popular urban Punjabi theater and "Pānī dā bulbulā" (Bubble of water), a popular song sung by Yaqub Atif "Bulbula" from 1962 onward.⁴⁷

AVANT-GARDISM AND MELODRAMA

Given its dense references to prior cinematic forms as well as to precinematic performative tropes, and the stated intention of the directors to refer to these, we must envision *Zinda Bhaag* as a fable as much as a realist film. In its assemblage, codes of realism are shot throughout with disparate elements of fantasy, which include the nested stories as well as the songs. *Zinda Bhaag*'s innovative and genre-defying assemblage form can be understood in terms of cinematic avant-gardism that intersects with the conventions of the social film. This is evidenced clearly in the song sequences, three of which are briefly analyzed here.

The fantasy sequence choreographed around the song "Kuṛī yes ai" (This girl is yes!) picturizes the inebriated dream of Khaldi as he rides on his motorcycle with Rubina. On a rooftop gathering of young men, who are barbecuing and drinking together, Khaldi on a charpoy (rope bed) slips into an alcohol-fueled fantasy of riding a motorcycle with Rubina, in which the background is completely replaced with computer-generated imagery (figure 4.3).

The lyrics of the song refer to migration, such as "No red signal can stop us from going to the UK" and "I'll take you to London, UK, via Turkey." Decorated heart and dagger motifs in the ornamental background with the words *Matric* and *BA* suggest not only the qualifications one may need to

FIG. 4.3. Computer graphics based on truck art, folk art, and anime constitute the background in the "Kuṛī yes ai" (This girl is yes!) song. *Zinda Bhaag* (2013).

secure a job abroad but also the duplicity involved in enrolling for fake European university programs just to secure a visa, which Khaldi pursues later in the film. (This also recalls the manager of the Rahnuma Marriage Office in *Susraal* from chapter 3, who bragged about grossly inflating the stature of men desiring a good match by bestowing them with imaginary educational qualifications.) The sequence is shot with the couple cavorting on the motorcycle and dancing against a green chroma background that has been replaced with gigantic psychedelic animated graphics based on truck art, folk art, and anime. According to the screenplay, a reference for this song is the celebrated "Ei poth jodi na sesh hoye" (What if this road never ends) from the Bengali film *Saptapadi* (1961), which picturizes a romantic couple riding a motorcycle on a country road in an idyllic landscape.[48] "The Bengali song was a general reference to how we wanted to invert the typical 'romantic' journey of older films, which is usually an urban couple traveling or discovering a semi-rural landscape. But in ours, it's the other way around—moving away and away and eventually out of the country," notes Gaur.[49] And unlike the lyrical but realist black-and-white landscape of the earlier song, *Zinda Bhaag* replaces the background with a hallucinatory dreamworld of eye-popping color. Nevertheless, "every step that Khaldi and Rubina perform is from a famous film song from a Pakistani or Bollywood film."[50] The dance moves are entirely composed of an assemblage of dance moves from numerous films from the past, further underscoring the reflexivity and intermediality of *Zinda Bhaag*.

The intrusion of fantasy song sequences in South Asian cinema is a convention, and this song sequence expresses Khaldi's desire but places it in a realm that is not of this world. The sequence also brings anime graphics into an ostensibly realist film focusing on the serious issue of illegal migration. What is noteworthy about *Zinda Bhaag*'s version is the complete artifice of this fantasy space, which brings together truck art with advanced digital renderings.[51] Gaur observes, "This song is an inversion of commercial film tropes while doing something typically from that world. What constitutes a film song? Rural landscape backdrop, modern couple, and dance. But what's left now of rural beauty and landscape? Instead, we show *one* green leaf and later that too is replaced by a motorway and high buildings, this at a time when Lahore is chopping off its trees to build motorways. Even in older cinema, the rural landscape is a mere (romantic) gesture, but now our hero has no such fantasy about the rural."[52]

The song "Dekhenge" (To witness) was written by Mohammad Hanif. This is the novelist's first film song, and it draws from a famous poem by Faiz Ahmed Faiz whose refrain is *"Ham dekhenge"* (We shall witness). The song sequence in *Zinda Bhaag* is performed by the waiters of the Imperial Punjab Club, who have been humiliated moments before by false accusations of the theft of a mobile phone belonging to an upper-crust anglicized man. Meanwhile, in another corner of the club's hall, an elegant, westernized young woman gushes in admiration as she requests that her male companion play Iqbal Bano's rendition of Faiz's original lyrics. Faiz's poem reflexively borrows powerful Qur'anic apocalyptic and eschatological imagery to foretell a future in which sovereignty will finally belong to the people.[53] Faiz's poem has become very popular in the version performed by the accomplished *ghazal* singer Iqbal Bano.[54] The affective message in Faiz's poem for the call toward dramatic and revolutionary transformation risks being overlooked in the neoliberal era, however, and indeed it plays as soft, ambient music in the Imperial Punjab Club where the elite are socializing. Gaur has noted that this incident is based on observations of a similar scenario from real life. For *Zinda Bhaag*, simply utilizing Faiz's original poetry in the film would no longer be sufficient, as the poem has been tastefully incorporated into upper-class society.[55] Rather, the film's avant-gardist orientation requires a subsumption of the prior form into a new constellation of signification. It rescues Faiz's poetry from its absorption into bourgeois culture as pleasant aesthetic background and extends its call for social transformation into the present era by critically mimicking Faiz's own poetic diction.

Hanif's song's lyrics and declamatory force make for a stirring call for justice that needs be seized by the underprivileged from the elite, who expect

FIG. 4.4. "Dekheṉge" (To witness) song with young male waiters who dance and waltz in pairs. A *jhūmar* (ornamental forehead pendant) made of grapes and leaves briefly adorns Taambi's forehead. *Zinda Bhaag* (2013).

servility from their underlings. The song throughout is a montage of short sequences edited to create a disjunctive effect. Toward the end, the succession becomes increasingly staccato, with rapid shots that assault the screen in bursts and show close-ups of the lips of the elite laughing and consuming food and tobacco and vertical shots of a platter that shows a succession of hors d'oeuvres, as well as jewelry, and blood pressure medical gear to take care of those who consumed too much. The speed of editing and the frenetic pace is much more rapid than the *qawwali* in the film *Clerk* (1960), in which exploited office workers also dance and sing together about the difficulties they face financially. And the homosocial bonds in *Zinda Bhaag*'s song "Dekheṉge" are more overt, as the young male waiters waltz in pairs and a *jhūmar* (ornamental forehead pendant) made of grapes and leaves adorns Taambi's forehead briefly, held up by one of his friends (figure 4.4).

Finally, let us consider the remarkable Punjabi *qawwali* written by the New York–based poet Hasan Mujtaba. The poem, originally several pages long, was edited by the directors and rendered by Rahat Fateh Ali Khan, who is affiliated with the *gharana* (household/atelier) of the celebrated Nusrat Fateh Ali Khan (1948–97). Even though Rahat Fateh Ali Khan is regarded as an accomplished *qawwal* who has created numerous playback songs for Bombay films, this is among his first original renditions.[56] Set at the fictitious shrine of a Shah Muqeem that is nevertheless reminiscent of Lahore's many Sufi shrines, the *qawwali* juxtaposes traditional tropes of the unattainability of the beloved with new imagistic symbols: the mulberry, the silkworm's labor, the sensuality of silk fabric on skin, and the fetishization of kohl-lined eyes. One can designate this an experimental, avant-gardist *qawwali*, at least on the level of its symbolism, which fuses the traditional imagery of the traditional lyrics with startling and unexpected tropes. Its refrain includes the lyrics "The waves in love's ocean surge and crash," but "It's not easy to find a path to the Beloved." As the *qawwali* builds in intensity toward a state of *hāl* (spiritual immersion), the sequence cuts to a grim-faced government official traveling by car, who arrives at the shrine and informs Chitta's father that his son perished while attempting the *dunky*, as the *qawwali* reaches a crescendo. The beloved remains an elusive ideal, in whose quest many young men have sacrificed themselves in succession during the course of the film.

REVISITING THE LAHORE EFFECT

Contemporary Pakistani cinema continues to suffer from multiple crises: not simply those of infrastructure, patronage, and distribution, which may be resolved as the industry grows in scale, but more fundamental predicaments of form, memory, and critical reception. As Ali Nobil Ahmad has wryly noted, by sidestepping these crucial issues, much of what passes for New Cinema is "unabashed about looking good without burdening audiences with unnecessary brain activity."[57] Much of New Cinema ends up relying on, and even quoting verbatim, Bollywood, Hollywood, and advertising stereotypes or at best re-creating the stodgy temporality and upper-middle-class liberalism of the television serial as a feature film.

But what form of critical cinema is adequate for contemporary local *and* global predicaments? Which historical media and cultural forms remain salient for addressing today's increasingly urbanized subjectivity in Pakistan, shaped unevenly as it is by neoliberal forces but also through lived and remembered familial habitus and from cultural memories inherited and learned from widely disparate media? This is hopefully where filmmakers will venture beyond the hackneyed manner in which they have addressed a rather limited number of themes so far—feudal patriarchy, women's oppression, fundamentalism and terrorism, and thwarted individualist aspiration—which all repeatedly find mythic resolution in accordance with the pervasive liberal upper-class norms of the New Cinema.

The analysis above delineates only some of the distinctive features of *Zinda Bhaag*, but even this cursory engagement should underscore the considerable critical ambition of the film. It deploys diverse registers of historical and contemporary forms from the long sixties and beyond to marshal a new self-reflexive cinematic assemblage. *Zinda Bhaag* is itself perhaps engaged in a kind of *dunky*, a consequential and risky journey charting a critical future for Pakistani cinema itself. This is a future in which narrative form is critically rethought, where a fuller range of social, cultural, and media references from across South Asia and beyond are engaged reflexively and in resonance with the lifeworlds of its intended audience, and where aesthetic and social issues are addressed in their emergent complexity.

Made five decades after the other films examined in the previous chapters, *Zinda Bhaag* serves as an important instantiation of the Lahore effect in the present era, in which the narration of realism is inextricable from the foray into the imagination that is enacted by the considerable legacy of South Asian theatrical and mediatized forms. Ashish Rajadhyaksha has suggested that in the Lahore effect, "films quote one other, fold inside each other, or hover over each other. Every film, thus seen, becomes a history of the cinema. Remakes, along with other forms of a haunting cultural survival ... become crucial here."[58] This modality has incorporated reflexivity and recursivity within the commercial feature film itself, rather than seeking these primarily in art, alternative, or avant-garde cinema—which did not have a substantial legacy in Pakistan's cinema.

If cinema associated with Pakistan is to move forward beyond congealed stereotypes to embrace new technological, infrastructural, social, and aesthetic terrains, one way to do so might be to critically reexamine the present moment with awareness of the extensive formal, narrative, and imaginative resources of earlier media forms from South Asia. The Lahore effect was never confined to the city of Lahore itself but was expressed as a modality across South Asia, especially in Bombay cinema, during the mid-twentieth century. A significant potentiality for future South Asian cinemas from various locations and contributors is one that activates cross-border linkages—in production arrangements, distribution circuits, and formal and narrative audience appeal—and that remains indifferent or at an angle to the blandishments of majoritarian and nation-state ideologies. This is a cinematic mode that imbricates realism and fable and resonates with the affective moral universe of multiple publics. Its extended and episodic unfolding has constituted among the most significant developments in popular culture in the modern era, in South Asia and beyond, and its capacious potential awaits future realizations.

NOTES

PREFACE

1. A useful overview of the economic and political history of Pakistan is Talbot, *Pakistan*, especially chs. 4–7 on the 1947–71 period.
2. Vasudevan, *The Melodramatic Public*; Vasudevan, "Film Genres, the Muslim Social, and Discourses of Identity c. 1935–1945."
3. Aarti Wani's account of the importance of the trope of romantic love in midcentury golden-era Bombay cinema, which was amplified by the lyrics of its celebrated songs, Wani, *Fantasy of Modernity*; Manishita Dass's book tracing the formation of a cinematic public sphere between 1920 and 1940 that cut across social and genre hierarchies and did not comfortably inhabit national space, Dass, *Outside the Lettered City*; and Debashree Mukherjee's study of colonial-era Bombay cinema that focuses on industrial and labor practices, D. Mukherjee, *Bombay Hustle*. Noteworthy as well are Madhuja Mukherjee's essay on cinema in Calcutta that include discussions of Hindi productions during the thirties in which many personnel originally from Lahore were involved, M. Mukherjee, "Arriving at Bombay"; and Rosie Thomas's work that emphasizes the ascendance of the melodramatic social film as the highest genre in Bombay cinema from the 1940s onward, even as other genres such as the Oriental fantasy film, and themes based on Hindu and Islamicate oral and folk legends, continued to be popular, Thomas, *Bombay before Bollywood*.
4. The writings of Neepa Majumdar and Moinak Biswas that track the consequences of the encounter of neorealism in South Asian cinema during the fifties have informed this study, especially my reading of a neorealist film from Lahore set in East Bengal (ch. 1). N. Majumdar, "Importing Neorealism, Exporting Cinema"; Biswas, "In the Mirror of an Alternative Globalism."
5. Rajadhyaksha, *Indian Cinema*, 122. For example, see the special issue of *Film History* on "South by South/West by West," edited by Kaveh Askari and Samhita Sunya, *Film History* 32, no. 3 (2020); Rajagopalan, *Indian Films in Soviet Cinemas*; Larkin, *Signal and Noise*; Fair, *Reel Pleasures*; Vasudevan, "Film Genres, the Muslim Social, and Discourses of Identity c. 1935–1945," 31; Hoek, "Cross-Wing Filmmaking."
6. Rajadhyaksha, "The Lahore Effect."
7. The use of "Bombay" and not "Mumbai" to designate the city's cinema production before Indian economic liberalization of the nineties is an accepted

8. Critical studies of the development of Pakistani cinema are relatively few. For instance, Mushtaq Gazdar's *Pakistan Cinema, 1947–1997* is an informative survey of the first fifty years but does not discuss films in depth, while Alamgir Kabir's *The Cinema in Pakistan*, published in 1969, provides a significant contemporary critical account from an avant-gardist and realist perspective. Apart from these, there is not a single monograph in English devoted to Pakistani cinema. Anthologies include Zamindar and Ali, eds., *Love, War & Other Longings*; and Khan and Ahmad, eds., *Cinema and Society*. Chowdhury and De, eds., *South Asian Filmscapes* has several essays on Pakistani cinema, as do special issues of *Screen* 57, no. 4 (December 2016); *BioScope: South Asian Screen Studies* 5, no. 2 (July 1, 2014); and *BioScope: South Asian Screen Studies* 10, no. 2 (December 1, 2019).

9. For example, on the subject of film music and song, there are several book-length studies and research essays on Bombay, whereas for Pakistani cinema there is not yet a single scholarly essay on the subject. Morcom, *Hindi Film Songs and the Cinema*; Beaster-Jones, *Bollywood Sounds*; Booth, *Behind the Curtain*. Essays include Booth, "A Moment of Historical Conjuncture in Mumbai"; and Shope, "Latin American Music in Moving Pictures and Jazzy Cabarets in Mumbai, 1930s to 1950s."

10. Very few articles critically engage with the 1947–80 period. Those on Urdu cinema include K. Ali, "Cinema and Karachi in the 1960s"; K. Ali, "On Female Friendships & Anger"; K. Ali, "Female Friendship and Forbidden Desire"; Dadi, "Registering Crisis"; Dadi, "Lineages of Pakistan's 'Urdu' Cinema"; Hoek, "Cross-Wing Filmmaking"; Siddique, "Meena Shorey"; Siddique, "'Someone to Check Her a Bit'"; N. Rehman, "Pakistan, History, and Sleep." On film music and poetry, see Afzal-Khan, *Siren Song*; Chaudhari, *Jahan-i fan*; Gorija, *Malikah-yi Tarannum Nur Jahan fan ke a'ine men*; Kanpuri, *Dabistan-i film ke nagmahnigar*; Kanpuri, *Gaye ja git milan ke*; A. Parvez, *Melody Makers of the Subcontinent*. Nate Rabe has published several articles in his blog *Lolly Pops* and in Scroll.in on film music from Pakistani cinema, including on films or filmmakers discussed in this book. Anthologies and essays by industry observers in Urdu include Gorija, *Lakshmi Chowk*; Kanpuri, *Kahan tak suno ge*; Kanpuri, *Mujhe sab hai yad zara zara*; Kanpuri, *Pari chehre*; Kanpuri, *Yeh baten teri yeh fasane tere*; Kanpuri, *Zikr e fankar chale*; Sajjad, *Filmon ki dunya ke ek sau gyara sal*;. A compendium of one hundred important films from 1947 to 2000 with useful summaries is Gorija, *Pakistan ki 100 shahkar filmen*; Kanpuri, *Yadgar filmen* is another compendium with over two hundred films summarized but is less informative and less reliable than Gorija's summaries.

11. An important study is by Wani, *Fantasy of Modernity*. The paucity of work on this topic is partly because most scholars working on Bombay cinema lack the ability to read the Urdu script or fully explore the symbolic and metaphorical universe of the midcentury Hindi film from Bombay, which draws heavily from Urdu's cultural and rhetorical tropes.

12. The Urdu films from Karachi and Dhaka are an important subject for further research, which this study is unable to address. Karachi and Dhaka filmmaking did not start until the midfifties, and they consequently did not develop a dense, decades-long exchange with Bombay from the 1920s onwards, unlike Lahore. They share many characteristics of the Lahore film, however, although they also depart from the latter in several important aspects that require further analysis. The formal and thematic concerns of the Urdu films from Dhaka in particular remain less studied. On the Karachi film, see K. Ali, "Cinema and Karachi in the 1960s." On the Dhaka Urdu film, see Hoek, "Cross-Wing Filmmaking." On vernacular language films from West Pakistan made during 1947–80, which this study also does not address, see, for example, Kirk, "This Is London, Not Pakistan!"; Levesque and Bui, "Umar Marvi and the Representation of Sindh"; Sevea, "'Kharaak kita oi!'"; Siddique, "Rustic Releases." And because the focus of this study is the films of the fifties and sixties, I have not traced Lahore's earlier exchanges with Calcutta, which was a significant production node where many film personnel from Lahore worked during the 1920s and 1930s. But this is not the case from the forties onward, as unsettled conditions in Calcutta led to the exodus of many personnel to Bombay and Lahore. M. Mukherjee, "Arriving at Bombay," 111. Calcutta and Bengal were also significant sites for Urdu literary production during the first half of the twentieth century. See, for example, the books by Shanti Ranjan Bhattacharya on the subject available in digital form at Rekhta, "All Writings of Shanti Ranjan Bhattacharya," Rekhta, accessed June 26, 2021, www.rekhta.org/authors/shanti-ranjan-bhattacharya/all; Amstutz, "Finding a Home for Urdu."
13. Recognition of agency via cinematic representation of characters, or lack thereof, is one mode of analysis, but other approaches include an evaluation of the considerable affective charge of this cinema. This was well understood and capitalized on by the industry itself, by its categorization of many social films as "family" or "household" films (the Urdu term in the industry for this genre is *gharelū*), and was intended to especially appeal to women audiences.

    For existing work on cinema and gender, see K. Ali, "Female Friendship and Forbidden Desire"; N. Rehman, "Pakistan, History, and Sleep"; Siddique, "Meena Shorey"; Siddique, "'Someone to Check Her a Bit.'"
14. For example, we have no evidence that *Jago Hua Savera* was shown in India in 1959 or soon after, even though many personnel from India were involved in its making.
15. Dass, *Outside the Lettered City*, 32–34, 105, 186–92.
16. On this concept, see Rajadhyaksha, "The Lahore Effect," 324–25.

INTRODUCTION

1. Lahiri, "An Idiom for India"; Lunn, "The Eloquent Language."
2. I. Ahmed, "The Lahore Film Industry," 60; Shifai, "San'at-e filmsazi men Sarhad ka hissa."
3. Rajadhyaksha, "The Lahore Effect," 334–39. Also see Debashree Mukherjee's account of the role speculative capital from various sources played in the Bombay film industry. D. Mukherjee, *Bombay Hustle*, 45–97.

4. Gazdar, *Pakistan Cinema*, 6, 29; Shuja, *Lahore ka Chelsea*; Rajadhyaksha, *Indian Cinema*, 84.
5. I. Ahmed, "The Lahore Film Industry," 59.
6. For a listing that provides details as well as publicity images, see Rahi, *Punjab ki filmi tarikh*.
7. I. Ahmed, "The Lahore Film Industry," 59.
8. Many film industry personnel had faced an increasingly communalized environment in India. The case of Manto is well known in this regard. Another example is W. Z. Ahmed, who had directed a film on the Bhakti poet Meera titled *Meera Bai* (1947), which came under attack in *Filmindia* magazine on communal grounds. Rachel Dwyer notes, "Baburao Patel's *Filmindia* was known for its eccentricity but the review of this film, 'Muslim "Meerabai" grossly slanders Hinduism!' attacks the film on the basis of its misrepresentation of Hindu marriage but largely because its director was a Muslim who migrated to Pakistan." *Filmindia*, September 1947, 53–57, cited in Dwyer, *Filming the Gods*, 175, note 58.
9. Siddique, "Rustic Releases."
10. On the early years, see Gorija, *Lakshmi Chowk*, 19–50.
11. Gazdar, *Pakistan Cinema*, 36.
12. Gazdar, *Pakistan Cinema*, 28.
13. "Prominent amongst the first batch of migrants were producers and directors like Nazir, Daud Chand, Zahoor Raja, Shaukat Hussain Rizvi, W. Z. Ahmed, Sibtain Fazli, Munshi Dil, Luqman, and Attaullah Shah Hashmi. Stars from the silver screen included Noor Jehan, Swaranlata, Shamim Bano, Khurshid, Ragni, Charlie, Himaliyawala, M. Ismail, Shahnawaz, Ajmal, Ghulam Mohammad, Santosh Kumar, and Nasir Khan. Music composers of the calibre of Ghulam Haider, Feroz Nizami, Rashid Attre and Khurshid Anwar; writers and lyricists of the likes of Saadat Hasan Manto, Nazir Ajmeri, Tanvir Naqvi, and Arsh Lakhnavi; and a number of better known technicians including Bhayaji A. Hameed, Pyare Khan, Murtaza Jilani, A. Z. Baig and C. G. C. Mandody opted for Pakistan." Gazdar, *Pakistan Cinema*, 24.
14. W. Z. Ahmed's full name is Wahiduddin Ziauddin Ahmed. As Gazdar notes, "Except for Sardari Lal, the custodian of Pancholi Studios, there was hardly anyone left to initiate a film project. The onus of reinvigorating the film movement fell on the shoulders of those who came from across the border. W. Z. Ahmed, Nazir, Sibtain Fazli, and Shaukat Hussain [Rizvi]." Gazdar, *Pakistan Cinema*, 25.
15. Gazdar, *Pakistan Cinema*, 24.
16. Gul, "A Short History of Pakistani Films."
17. Gazdar, *Pakistan Cinema*, 38, 41–42.
18. *Roohi* was banned from being shown and has not been available to view. For an account, see Gazdar, *Pakistan Cinema*, 72–73; Gorija, *Pakistan ki 100 shahkar filmen*, 26–28; Sajjad, *Filmon ki dunya ke ek sau gyara sal*, 129–37; Z. Shahid, "Early Corruption in Pakistan Film Industry."
19. "Pakistani Film History from 1954," Pakistan Film Magazine, accessed July 18, 2020, https://pakmag.net/film/history.php?gid=1954%20reg=1954; "Pakistani Film History from 1956," Pakistan Film Magazine, accessed July 18, 2020,

https://pakmag.net/film/history.php?gid=1956%20reg=1956; Ishtiaq Ahmed mentions a total of thirty-one releases for 1956. "The Lahore Film Industry," 65. Also see Gazdar, *Pakistan Cinema*, 52.
20. On the *Jaal* agitation, see Gazdar, *Pakistan Cinema*, 49–50.
21. For an official chronology of events in 1954 and 1955 published in a film report in 1957, see Anwar, *Film Industry in West Pakistan*, 221. The issue of Indian film imports is discussed on pp. 73–78.
22. "Film Industry's Protest at Dacca, Lahore, Karachi against Recertification of Indian Films"; Haroon, "Editorial: After the 'Injunction,'" 5.
23. Gazdar, *Pakistan Cinema*, 54.
24. S. Ahmed, "W. Z. Ahmed Passes Away"; Siddique, "Archive Filmaria," 204.
25. Usman, "Portrait of a Film-Maker."
26. For an assessment from 1957, see J. Khan, "The Film Industry in West Pakistan."
27. I. Ahmed, "The Lahore Film Industry," 65. In industry terminology, a *silver jubilee* means a film that has had a continuous run in the same city for twenty-five weeks.
28. "Pakistani Film History from 1969," Pakistan Film Magazine, accessed July 30, 2020, https://pakmag.net/film/history.php?gid=1969%20reg=1969. Also see the annual assessments published in *Eastern Film*. Nasarullah, "The Year 1964"; Nasarullah, "The Year 1965"; Nasarullah, "The Year 1966"; Nasarullah, "The Year 1967."
29. Gazdar, *Pakistan Cinema*, 49, 66–68. *Eastern Film*, a monthly film magazine in English with good production values, was launched in 1959.
30. Gorija, *Pakistan ki 100 shahkar filmen*, 127. On the film *Aag* (1967), Gazdar remarks that audiences had difficulty following one of the characters, who was portrayed with the use of flashbacks, noting the limitations of cinematic language and its public legibility. Gazdar, *Pakistan Cinema*, 142. Other late-sixties films that Gorija remarks on as being fast-paced include *Mera Ghar Mere Jannat* (My home is my heaven, 1968); *Behan Bhai* (Brother and sister, 1968); *Aashiq* (Lover, 1968); and *Buzdil* (The coward, 1969). Gorija, *Pakistan ki 100 shahkar filmen*, 151, 157, 160, 166.
31. Kanpuri, *Yadgar filmen*, 191. On *Nagin*, see Sajjad, "Lollywood ki sanpon kay mauzu par banai gai film *Nagin* 1959."
32. Gazdar notes that "whenever a Peoples Party government is in office, film censorship laws are relaxed. This happened between 1971–1977." Gazdar, *Pakistan Cinema*, 217.
33. Gazdar, *Pakistan Cinema*, 239.
34. For a brief overview, see Mumtaz, "The Best of Times, the Worst of Times."
35. Gopalan, *Cinema of Interruptions*.
36. Bhaskar, "Expressionist Aurality."
37. For an account of early theater in Urdu, see Suvorova, *Early Urdu Theatre*. The work includes an expansive bibliography of writings in Urdu on the subject.
38. Hansen, "Languages on Stage."
39. Hansen, "Languages on Stage," 396; Hansen, "The *Indar Sabha* Phenomenon." Also see Hansen, "Heteroglossia in Amanat's *Indar Sabha*"; Taj, *The Court of Indar and the Rebirth of North Indian Drama*.

40. Kathryn Hansen has discussed how, when the Irish play *Colleen Bawn* was translated and performed in India, it incorporated songs that were not part of the original play. Hansen, "Boucicault in Bombay."
41. Hansen, "The *Indar Sabha* Phenomenon," 105–6.
42. Hansen, "Boucicault in Bombay," 66.
43. Hansen, "Languages on Stage," 402.
44. Lunn, "The Eloquent Language." With the arrival of the talkies in 1931, the cinema of the 1930s confronted additional challenges. These included the problem of recording sound live in settings beyond the stage. Now that the camera could bring to the viewer locations, sites, and situations that were not necessarily confined to the theater stage, what would be the role of the song in such situations?
45. N. Majumdar, "Between Rage and Song"; D. Mukherjee, *Bombay Hustle*, 143–82.
46. Aziz, *Light of the Universe*, 8.
47. Aziz, *Light of the Universe*, 9.
48. Booth, "A Moment of Historical Conjuncture in Mumbai," 21–22.
49. Morcom, *Hindi Film Songs and the Cinema*, 11–12.
50. Morcom, *Hindi Film Songs and the Cinema*, 239.
51. B. Sen, "The Sounds of Modernity," 85.
52. For a good overview of the economic dimensions of the Ayub Khan era, see S. A. Zaidi, *Issues in Pakistan's Economy*, 110–23. Zaidi finds that "between 1958 and 1968 . . . growth rates continued to impress, and a substantial industrial and economic base was established" (110). He argues that the "Ayub Khan era was in fact highly progressive and dynamic, and that despite some negative consequences of its economic strategy, it was overall a resounding success" (110).
53. Gazdar, *Pakistan Cinema*, 78. On the Censor Board's role during the midsixties, see Haroon, "Editorial: The Curse"; Haroon, "Editorial: Censor Board"; Haroon, "Editorial: The Cloud without Silver Lining."
54. *Report of the Film Fact Finding Committee*, 9.
55. *Report of the Film Fact Finding Committee*, 8.
56. *Report of the Film Fact Finding Committee*, 259.
57. Gazdar, *Pakistan Cinema*, 113.
58. Gazdar, *Pakistan Cinema*, 73–78.
59. Gazdar, *Pakistan Cinema*, 77.
60. Gazdar, *Pakistan Cinema*, 74–75. I have been unable to find a viewing copy of *Nai Kiran*.
61. Shahab, *Shahabnama*.
62. M. Khwaja, "'Shahab nama' ka maqsad akhfai'yi zat hai"; Parekh, "Shahabnama, Its Creator and Critics."
63. On the takeover of Progressive Papers, see for example, M. Khan, "Ayub's Attack on Progressive Papers." Shahab's disingenuous recollection in the *Shahabnama* is in his chapter on the National Press Trust (781–94).
64. The Harvard Advisory Group economists had charted a policy of "Functional Inequality" for Pakistan, which focused on industrial development, concentrating wealth in a small number of business houses. Zaidi, *Issues in Pakistan's Economy*, 121–22.

65. Shahab, *Shahabnama*, 746.
66. Shahab, *Shahabnama*, 747–48.
67. Kamran Asdar Ali on Ayub Khan's cultural policies: "The state recruited a cultural leadership of artists, poets, journalists, writers, and film producers to 'tame' and 'harness' particularistic identities (to produce sameness, a unified Pakistani identity in a country that had multiple ethnic and linguistic groups). In this regard, the formation of the National Press Trust and the Pakistan Writers Guild were attempts to bring the intelligentsia around to supporting the cultural policies of the regime." K. Ali, "Cinema and Karachi in the 1960s," 392.
68. Jalib has been widely known as the "people's poet" (*'avāmī shā'ir*). Jalib, *Jalib biti*, 227–29; Ahmad Bashir, "Main nahin manta," 73.
69. Jalib, *Jalib biti*, 89.
70. Jalib, *Jalib biti*, 93.
71. On Habib Jalib's participation in the film industry, see Jalib's interview in Barelvi, *Habib Jalib*, 148–52. For a more detailed account, see S. Parvez, *Habib Jalib: shakhsiyyat aur fann*, 191–204; Jalib's verse for the cinema is compiled in Jalib, *Is shahr-i kharabi men*, 103–71.
72. I. A. Rehman, "'Somehow the Authorities Never Found a Non-farcical Reason for Arresting Me'—Habib Jalib."
73. Jalib's reminiscence on the charged context of 1962 public recitation of the poem at a poetry gathering in Murree is in Jalib, *Jalib biti*, 48–51. Jalib's oral account on the poem's context accompanied by a recitation in *tarannum* (melody) in his own voice is available on YouTube: Akbar, *Habib Jalib*. Also see Gardezi, "Qafas dar qafas," 44–45. For the text of "Dastoor," see *Habib Jalib: fann aur shakhsiyyat*, 142–43. This book was published by Jalib's supporters in 1978 to celebrate his fiftieth birthday, with a title cover design by the artist Sadequain and the back cover consisting of verses by Jalib calligraphed by the artist. S. Parvez, *Habib Jalib: sha'ir-i sh'ulah nava*, 26–27.
74. Rahman, "Habib Jalib, His Dastoor"; S. Ali, "Habib Jalib, Pakistan's Poet of Dissent Whose Lines Are Now Chanted on Both Sides of Border."
75. Bashir, "Main nahin manta," 73.
76. Barelvi, *Habib Jalib*, 152. It's unclear whether Jalib meant *lyricism*; I prefer to transliterate the Urdu as *lyric-ism* as this retains the sense of Jalib's own interpretation of the term and is specific to his poetry.
77. Gazdar, *Pakistan Cinema*, 72.
78. The *Report of the Film Fact Finding Committee* notes, "Unlimited freedom which now exists in this field . . . enables the unscrupulous adventurer to enter the industry at will and start doubtful enterprises which hardly ever reach their conclusion and swallow up considerable portions of limited technical facilities and adversely affect the time, effort and reputation of artistes, writers, technicians and other workers in this field. The exploits of such shady individuals whom the possession of a small capital entitles to a free entry into the field of film production brings disgrace and degradation to the industry which already suffers from bad name due to its uncertain commercial prospects and unsatisfactory working conditions" (8). Also see M. Mukherjee, "The Public in the Cities."

79. "To reap golden harvests of box-office receipts, Sex, Crime Horror and Action of the 'Western' type are glorified by Producers. Mass taste is easily corrupted and all decent ideals or values of life are lost sight of. It is a sad reflection on the achievements of our Film Industry that it has failed to make capital out of appealing even to the crude instincts of the Mob and films specifically made to 'catch' the public have flopped miserably. This failure, illustrates both the lack of technical and artistic skills in the Industry and lack of true insight into mass psychology. Mass Taste has been too under-rated and the Industry has sacrificed moral, spiritual and artistic values to little purpose by stopping [sic] to the production of some very crude films which even the masses have rejected 'en masse.'" *Report of the Film Fact Finding Committee*, 258–59.
80. The increase in economic disparity between East and West Pakistan at the end of the Ayub era is summarized in Zaidi, *Issues in Pakistan's Economy*, 116–23.
81. Akhter, "*Jibon Thekey Neya* (Glimpses of life, 1970)"; Nitol, "Jibon Theke Neya, an Emblem of Political Satire."
82. See chapter 3 for a discussion of *Zerqa*. Also see Petiwala, "*Falasteen ka matlab kya?*"
83. Barelvi, *Habib Jalib*, 148.
84. Gazdar, *Pakistan Cinema*, 49–56; Siddique, "From Gandhi to Jinnah"; Z. Shahid, "Early Corruption in Pakistan Film Industry." Gorija lists several films that he characterizes as *charba*, Gorija, *Pakistan ki 100 shahkar filmen*.
85. *Eastern Film* took a strong stance against plagiarism. See, for example, Amrohi, "The Censor Problem"; Haroon, "Editorial: Censor Board"; Haroon, "Editorial: The Cloud without Silver Lining"; Haroon, "Editorial: The Curse"; Noorani, "*Ek Tera Sahara.*"
86. For a summary account, see I. Ahmed, "The Lahore Film Industry," 67–69.
87. "They refused to compromise on principles and invested their talent in authentic art. Khwaja Khurshid Anwar, Masood Pervaiz, and Anwar Kamal Pasha were towering personalities of this group of idealists who sowed the seeds of a genuine Pakistani cinema in the days of its infancy," notes Mushtaq Gazdar. Gazdar, *Pakistan Cinema*, 56.
88. Gorija, *Pakistan ki 100 shahkar filmen*.
89. Rajadhyaksha, *Indian Cinema in the Time of Celluloid*, 330.
90. Gazdar, *Pakistan Cinema*, 64; Siddique, "From Gandhi to Jinnah."
91. Bhaskar Sarkar's in-depth study on the effects of Partition on Indian cinema is very suggestive for examining this phenomenon in Lahore cinema. Sarkar, *Mourning the Nation*.
92. "Nasir Khan Profile," cineplot.com, June 24, 2011, http://cineplot.com/nasir-khan-profile; Bali, "Most Pakistani Hindu Filmmakers Fled after 1947, but Not JC Anand." A blog entry lists no less than 185 Bombay cinema personnel with familial connections with the territories that became (West) Pakistan. Amir, "Bollywood's Pakistan Connection."
93. Rajadhyaksha identifies "*cinema-effects*" as "tangible narrative productions with economic and political existence analogous to the economic production of a film. Such an effect can be produced as much *within* the cinema as by ancillary practices

defined *by* the cinema but going beyond and *outside* it. A film narrative, seen as an ongoing process of sequencing and negotiating such effects (recognizing, consuming, and resisting them), may also develop a distinct political edge when this effect *also* produces a means to account for—and thence to navigate through— diverse extra-textual boundaries including, but not limited to, distribution circuits, national borders and firewalls." Rajadhyaksha, "The Lahore Effect," 324–25.

94. On the Indian serpent film, see M. Sen, *Haunting Bollywood*. Pakistani films from the fifties with serpent themes include *Nagin* (1959, dir. Khalil Qaiser) and *Zehr-e Ishq* (1958, dir. Masood Pervaiz). For a reading of *Zehr-e Ishq*, see Dadi, "Lineages of Pakistan's 'Urdu' Cinema."
95. Alonso, "Radio, Citizenship, and the 'Sound Standards' of a Newly Independent India."
96. For an important study on the cassette player's impact on music in India, see Manuel, *Cassette Culture*.
97. Gazdar, *Pakistan Cinema*, 5–6.
98. Rajadhyaksha, "The Lahore Effect," 332.
99. Rajadhyaksha, "The Lahore Effect," 332.
100. Rajadhyaksha, "The Lahore Effect," 332.
101. "Lahore had clearly started something. If Hollywood developed, in the first two decades of the twentieth century a 'mode,' of performance, camera work, editing, and even celluloid-processing, that was founded upon what Janet Staiger identified as a 'Hollywood Mode of Production' premised on interchangeability, standardization, and assembly, what Lahore may have done was equally astonishing: a *counter-mode*, we may call it, that opened a way of making, showing and seeing films and indeed something resembling an industrial practice—or at least a functioning substitute for it—that produced a market ranging through the subcontinent. The "Hindi" cinema has been historically wedded to this mode. It has required an adherence to a cultural memory that has transcended borders and challenged nationalist domestication across the subcontinent. And it has come at a cost: its disqualification from becoming a national cinema." Rajadhyaksha, "The Lahore Effect," 334.
102. Dass, *Outside the Lettered City*, 105.
103. Rajadhyaksha, "The Lahore Effect," 341–42.
104. Gazdar, *Pakistan Cinema*, 24.
105. *Report of the Film Fact Finding Committee*, 8.
106. The trope of the "backward but proud Muslim" emerged in the colonial era from the later nineteenth century. See Seth, "Governmentality and Identity."
107. In January 1949, the renowned literary critic Muhammad Hasan Askari described the Muslim social film in India in his characteristically acerbic manner. "In truth, most filmmakers were Hindu and thus incapable of feeling any enthusiasm for the political or social aspirations of Muslims. But if you retain your own sense of self-worth then the Other has no choice but to alter their conduct: filmmakers had to bow before the demands of Muslims and thus the entity known as the 'Muslim Social' came into being. . . . The very earliest social films about Muslims depict the

social world of wealthy families in Lucknow, in contrast to the hero of 'Hindu Socials'—a man of the people who, in order to pursue an education or in order to improve a village would go and live there to work; he would fall in love with the feudal landlord's daughter in his free time. The main occupation of the hero in the Muslim Social was 'lover' (he spent his free time flying kites). Art cannot flourish without a vibrant political life: no conception of service for the nation among Muslims had existed for the 15 or so years previous to this time, so how could it be represented on screen? Unsurprisingly, the Muslim Social remained the sort of film that featured splendid princely Lucknow pyjamas, paandaans [ornamental betel nut and leaf containers], and a few Id-ul-Azha [Islamic festival] scenes." Askari, "Building Pakistan and Filmmaking," 177–78.

108. Vasudevan, "Film Genres, the Muslim Social, and Discourses of Identity," 28. For an account of the Oriental film and the stunt film, as well as the persistence of the Oriental film into the fifties in Bombay, see Thomas, *Bombay before Bollywood*. On Bombay films that draw from Islamicate legends and lyric tropes, see A. G. Roy, *Cinema of Enchantment*. For a study of the relation between Urdu literary forms and Bombay cinema, see Haq, *Urdu fiction aur cinema*.
109. Vasudevan, "Film Genres, the Muslim Social, and Discourses of Identity," 31.
110. Vasudevan, "Film Genres, the Muslim Social, and Discourses of Identity," 29.
111. S. F. Hasnain was part of the Fazli Brothers duo, whose other member is Sibtain Fazli.
112. Vasudevan, "Film Genres, the Muslim Social, and Discourses of Identity," 35.
113. Vasudevan, "Film Genres, the Muslim Social, and Discourses of Identity," 40.
114. A summary account is available by M. Ramnath, "The Progressive Writers Association." Also see Jalil, *Liking Progress, Loving Change*; Coppola, *Urdu Poetry, 1935–1970*; Coppola, *Marxist Influences and South Asian Literature*.
115. Dass, "Cinetopia," 109.
116. Dass, "Cinetopia," 109.
117. Film scholar Debashree Mukherjee has observed that Urdu progressive writers "took to film writing with such gusto, when their Hindi peers consciously shunned this supposedly lowly form." D. Mukherjee, "The Lost Films of Sa'adat Hasan Manto."
118. Dass, "Cinetopia," 109. For an example of an event where affiliative leftist aesthetics traverse the high-low cultural registers, see "Pak Film Industry Meets Afro-Asian Delegates."
119. "The Muslim social of the 1940s emerges from a particular moment in this discourse of cultural difference, and sought to negotiate a space on the screen, which was distinctive and new, a space for the Muslim in the contemporary world, and as part of a national imagination. It was very much a political product of its times. However, it lived alongside more durable forms, ones that could continue a promiscuous engagement with the hybridity of languages, dress, décor, and setting despite large-scale changes in the formation of nations and states." Vasudevan, "Film Genres, the Muslim Social, and Discourses of Identity," 42.
120. Rajadhyaksha, "The Lahore Effect," 342. For the purposes of this study, it is important to note here that the leading actress and singer Noor Jehan, the star of

Khandan (Family, 1942), *Anmol Ghadi* (Precious watch, 1946), and *Jugnu* (Firefly, 1947), was among the industry personnel who moved to Lahore, along with directors Shaukat Hussain Rizvi and Sibtain Fazli, after 1947. The poet Tanvir Naqvi had written the lyrics for *Anmol Ghadi*, whose songs became very popular. Beaster-Jones, *Bollywood Sounds*, 43–46.
121. Aujla, "Khurshid Anwar."
122. K. Ali, "On Female Friendships & Anger"; K. Ali, "Cinema and Karachi in the 1960s."
123. However, Salma Siddique strikes a note of caution: "The fact that India has a national film archive does not imply robust preservation or straightforward access: even where films survive, they are often not digitized or made available to researchers because of copyright regulations." Siddique, "Archive Filmaria," 197.
124. T. Cooper, "Raddi Infrastructure"; Siddique, "Archive Filmaria"; Zamindar, *"Ek Haseen* Archive."
125. Among these archival resources, I have found the online *Pakistan Film Magazine* to be most useful, as it includes a complete database of films produced every year; provides extensive factual information, such as the names of the key personnel involved, titles of songs, screening history, et cetera; and is openly accessible digitally. "Pakistan Film Magazine," *Pakistan Film Magazine*, accessed July 19, 2020, https://pakmag.net/film.
126. Kuhu Tanvir, "Pirate Histories," 115–36.
127. Some of the reasons for the decline are summarized in Mumtaz, "The Best of Times, the Worst of Times."
128. On Urdu poetry, especially by Faiz, and the Partition, see Mufti, *Enlightenment in the Colony*. For a reading that emphasizes Sufi tropes in Urdu poetry and in tales such as the *qiṣṣa* from North India, see Satia, "Poets of Partition."
129. Mumtaz, "The Best of Times, the Worst of Times."
130. Kirk, "'A Camera from the Time of the British.'"
131. For the importance of the *Hir-Ranjha qiṣṣa* in the Punjab during the colonial era, see Mir, *The Social Space of Language*.

1. BETWEEN NEOREALISM AND HUMANISM

1. *Jago Hua Savera* can nevertheless be situated on the horizon of progressive cultural politics of midcentury. In the Urdu cinema of Pakistan, writers and directors associated with progressivism played a key role in feature films during the fifties and even the sixties. These individuals include many of the leading writers and directors: W. Z. Ahmed, Riaz Shahid, Khalil Qaiser, Zia Sarhadi, and many more. Serious films made in Dhaka in Bengali during this period include *Asiya* (1960, dir. Fateh Lohani). For a discussion, see Raju, *Bangladesh Cinema and National Identity*, 84, 132–39. Many of Zahir Raihan's Bengali-language films from the 1960s are widely regarded as ambitious aesthetic and political ventures, most notably *Jibon Theke Neya* (Glimpses of life, 1970). For an analysis, see Akhter, "*Jibon Thekey Neya* (Glimpses of life, 1970)." Raihan had served as assistant director for *Jago Hua Savera*, and its lead actor Khan Ataur Rahman also plays a

central role in *Jibon Theke Neya* as actor, music composer, and singer. For a discussion of the collaborative work between Raihan, Khan Ataur Rahman, and fellow travelers, see Hoek, "The Conscience Whipper."
2. A short profile of A. J. Kardar was published as "Introducing A. J. Kardar."
3. The novel and its author remain unacknowledged in the film's opening credits. Overall, the story is far more ambitious and complex in its narrative scope than *Jago Hua Savera*. For example, the story has Hindu and Muslim characters, but the film does not depict a mixed community. The middleman in the story is Housain Miya, who has multiple preoccupations, one of them being an attempt to reclaim a low-lying deltaic island, settling it and making it agriculturally productive. All this is absent in *Jago Hua Savera*, which has a more streamlined and unified narrative that moves forward toward a cinematic denouement. For an English translation of *Padma nadir majhi*, see Bandyopadhyay, *Padma River Boatman*. Bandopadhyay himself was sensitive to the need for realism in cinema: "The common audience may not apply conscious judgment . . . but with the times their taste is changing. They want the story of real life and living humans in film . . . cinema cannot satisfy people any longer by resorting to romance, thrills, mythology and religion." Quoted and translated in Biswas, "In the Mirror of an Alternative Globalism," 83.
4. Raihan was disappeared and killed in 1972, probably by collaborators associated with the Pakistani Army.
5. For further discussion on Zahir Raihan and Khan Ataur Rahman, see Hoek, "The Conscience Whipper."
6. Lassally, *Itinerant Cameraman*, 44–55, 164–68.
7. "Santi Chatterjee," IMDb, accessed July 17, 2017, www.imdb.com/name/nm0154155.
8. "With Faiz himself contributing the lyrics, the music for the film was composed by Timir Baran, who was part of a New Theatres triumvirate that included R. C. Boral and Pankaj Mullick," noted Saibal Chatterjee in "A Treasure Regained."
9. "Movies & Music of India—Timir Baran."
10. Damodaran, *The Radical Impulse*; M. Bhattacharya, "The Indian People's Theatre Association"; Bhatia, "Staging Resistance"; Bharucha, "The Indian People's Theatre Association (IPTA)."
11. On the making of *Dharti Ke Lal*, see the primary documents assembled in Pradhan, "The All India People's Theatre Association." On Tripti Mitra's work with IPTA (as Tripti Bhaduri) in the 1944 play *Jabanbandhi*, see pages 254 and 372. Hiren Mukherjee writes of her performance, "No praise, however, can be adequate for Tripti Bhaduri and Anoo Das Gupta, who in their roles of peasant women could beat any professional hallow [sic]." H. Mukherjee, "Bengal Anti-fascist Writers and Artists 1944," 372.
12. Jamil, *Zikr-e-Faiz*, 501. Jamil notes that A. J. Kardar had proposed adapting the story to film. Faiz liked the idea; enthusiastically wrote the script, screenplay, and dialogue; and even helped out with the direction.
13. Indian cinema was increasingly restricted for distribution in Pakistan beginning in the midfifties and completely prohibited within a decade. Protests by filmmakers in Lahore against the import of Indian cinema in 1954 are termed the "*Jaal*

agitation," because the lightning rod for this protest was the import of the Indian film *Jaal* (1952) to West Pakistan. Mushtaq Gazdar observes that "the restriction on Bombay cinema opened a new free and non-competitive market for local productions. 1956 proved to be the most fruitful year of the first decade in terms of box-office returns from indigenous cinema" (52). See Gazdar, *Pakistan Cinema*, 49–53. On exchanges of film, personnel, and themes between Indian and Pakistan, also see Siddique, "Meena Shorey" and "Archive Filmaria."

14. The concept of "global neorealism" is a recent one in cinema studies, emphatically not one where the Italian development serves as a master template and all others are secondary but precisely the opposite—it takes each local articulation seriously in its own right, sees all of them as fully legitimate, and situates them in the post–Second World War period and the onset of decolonization, when varieties of neorealism were developed in many locations. Ruberto and Wilson, *Italian Neorealism and Global Cinema*; Giovacchini and Sklar, *Global Neorealism*. For an overview account, see Nowell-Smith, "The Second Life of Italian Neo-realism."
15. On the concept of the "studio *Social*," see Biswas, "In the Mirror of an Alternative Globalism."
16. "Moscow International Film Festival (1959)," IMDb, accessed March 13, 2022, www.imdb.com/event/ev0000450/1959/1.
17. Lassally, *Itinerant Cameraman*, 55.
18. Raj, "Pakistan's First Oscar Submission 'Jago Hua Savera' Goes to Cannes."
19. Thanks to Tariq Omar Ali for this observation and for the citations below that span the years 1914 to 1952. These describe jute cultivators, but may well also characterize the general economic scenario of rural East Bengal during the early to mid-twentieth century:

> The crores of rupees paid for the raw article have had no visible effect on the manliness or contentedness of the agricultural classes or even on their material prosperity. They have no idea of saving, and in most cases their earnings from jute are frittered away on profitless extravagances long before the next crop is on the ground. By increasing their credit the inflated prices of jute have deepened rather than diminished their general indebtedness. (F. A. Sachse, Settlement Officer, Mymensingh to Revenue Dept., Government of Bengal, February 21, 1914. Proceedings A, Agriculture Dept., Agriculture Branch, List 14, Bundle 28, National Archives Bangladesh)

> There is a kind of poverty, which while not amounting to insolvency, nevertheless makes for precarious and uncertain living. It is this latter class of poverty, which is the real cause of indebtedness among agriculturists in Bengal. (Bengal Provincial Banking Enquiry Committee, vol. I, 1933, 73–74)

> Poverty, illiteracy, indebtedness, love of litigation have however all combined to reduce many cultivators to the position of landless labourers. He neither can realize the importance nor can he afford to take recourse to

improved methods of intensive farming for cultivating the small holding which he might yet own. ("Note by Cooperative Directorate for the Agricultural Enquiry Committee," 1952, MSS EUR F235/303, India Office Records, British Library)
20. According to Lassally, the interior shots were done in Dhaka in a set constructed outdoors. Lassally, *Itinerant Cameraman*, 48–49.
21. Gazdar, *Pakistan Cinema*, 78.
22. *Jago Hua Savera* (booklet).
23. Raj, "Pakistan's First Oscar Submission 'Jago Hua Savera' Goes to Cannes."
24. Zaheer, *The Times and Trial of the Rawalpindi Conspiracy, 1951*.
25. Husain, *Chiraghon ka dhuan*.
26. Chatterjee, "A Treasure Regained."
27. "The India-Pakistan Masterpiece That Fell through the Cracks."
28. N. Ramnath, "Made in Pakistan with Some Help from India, Lost and Found Again."
29. "1954–57 were particularly good years for India's cinematic morale." N. Majumdar, "Importing Neorealism, Exporting Cinema," 181.
30. Ray, *Our Films, Their Films*, 42–43.
31. Jamil, *Zikr-e-Faiz*, 501–3.
32. On the "*Jaal* agitation" of 1954, which started to see Indian films being screened less in Pakistan, see note 13, above. Nevertheless, the realist social film *Aadmi* (1958) was directed by Lahore-based Luqman, who was close to celebrated Indian actor Dilip Kumar. The story was written by Ayub Sarwar, elder brother of Dilip Kumar, who wanted Dilip to star in it initially. See Gazdar, *Pakistan Cinema*, 70; Lanba, *Life and Films of Dilip Kumar*.
33. N. Majumdar, "Importing Neorealism, Exporting Cinema," 187.
34. Biswas, "In the Mirror of an Alternative Globalism"; N. Majumdar, "Importing Neorealism, Exporting Cinema."
35. Biswas, "In the Mirror of an Alternative Globalism," 77.
36. Biswas, "In the Mirror of an Alternative Globalism," 78. For an overview of the development of IPTA, see Bhatia, "Staging Resistance."
37. Sunderason, *Partisan Aesthetics*.
38. Bharucha, *Rehearsals of Revolution*, 49.
39. Biswas, "In the Mirror of an Alternative Globalism," 81. Also see Dass, "Cinetopia."
40. N. Majumdar, "Importing Neorealism, Exporting Cinema," 178.
41. Biswas, "In the Mirror of an Alternative Globalism," 81.
42. It was released the same year as Vittorio De Sica's landmark neorealist film *Ladri di Biciclette* (The bicycle thief, 1948).
43. Younger, "The River," 166.
44. S. Cooper, "Henfi Agel's Cinema of Contemplation," 322–23.
45. Jaikumar, *Where Histories Reside*, 155–69.
46. S. Cooper, "Henfi Agel's Cinema of Contemplation," 323–24. The highly influential postwar cinema critic André Bazin proclaimed *The River* a "pure masterpiece" whose achievement was nothing less that the revelation of reality itself: "In The

River the screen no longer exists; there is nothing but reality. Not pictorial, not theatrical, not anti-expressionist, the screen simply disappears in favor of what it reveals." Bazin, "A Pure Masterpiece," 118. For an assessment of Bazin's influence in the postwar era, see R. Majumdar, "Art Cinema," 588.
47. For a summary of these criticisms, see Younger, "The River."
48. Such that by the mid-1950s, "one can find a continuum of films ranging from mainstream studio products such as Zia Sarhadi's *Footpath* (1953) to hybrid independent and studio films such as Bimol [Bimal] Roy's *Do Bigha Zamin* (Two Acres of Land, 1953) to state-supported independent films such as *Pather Panchali*." N. Majumdar, "Importing Neorealism, Exporting Cinema," 179.
49. Ray, *Our Films, Their Films*, 9.
50. Biswas, "In the Mirror of an Alternative Globalism," 85.
51. Manishita Dass also examines these questions in "Look Back in Angst."
52. Biswas, "In the Mirror of an Alternative Globalism," 72–73.
53. Here I also note the analysis of realism in the Indian novel offered by Ulka Anjaria, which bears relevance for our discussion. In her analysis of realism's purported belatedness and its ambivalences in South Asia, Anjaria observes, "Although a realist novel may seem to support colonial or nationalist hegemony, its instability allows it to elude any rigid ideology . . . a realist representation of the rural poor is not solely a means of incorporating that population into the universal fold of the nation, but can simultaneously show the *inability* of realism to capture the reality of social inequality. . . . Realism is sometimes complicit with dominant ideology, sometimes resistant, but mostly neither—or somewhere in between. This ambivalence is not always aesthetically pleasing but sometimes clumsy, reading at times more like inconsistency and hesitation." Anjaria suggests that realism in its awkward silences and contradictions offers an aesthetic and social critique that cannot be neatly folded into a national register. See Anjaria, *Realism in the Twentieth-Century Indian Novel*, 8.
54. N. Majumdar, "Importing Neorealism, Exporting Cinema," 190.
55. Biswas, "In the Mirror of an Alternative Globalism," 78.
56. As Neepa Majumdar notes in "Importing Neorealism, Exporting Cinema," 181, "If success abroad was the measure of pride in a national cinema, then 1954–57 were particularly good years for India's cinematic morale. At the Cannes Film Festival in each of these years, an Indian film won either an award or a special mention."
57. Ray, *Our Films, Their Films*, 42.
58. Biswas, "In the Mirror of an Alternative Globalism," 76. Biswas perceptively remarks that the impact of neorealism "helped Indian cinema break away from a set of restrictions and lay the basis of modern ways of working with its own material . . . its reality lying outdoors . . . its people living out there . . . its novels, poems, and pictures" (89).
59. Dass, "Cinetopia," 109.
60. For a good discussion of the intellectual genealogy of neorealism, including a discussion of Bazin and Zavattini, see Haaland, *Italian Neorealist Cinema*, ch. 2.
61. Zavattini, "Some Ideas on the Cinema," 125.

62. "Neorealism... rejects all those canons, which... exist only to commodify limitations. Reality breaks all the rules, which you can discover if you walk out with a camera to meet it." Zavattini, "Some Ideas on the Cinema," 131.
63. Zavattini, "Some Ideas on the Cinema," 126,
64. Zavattini, "Some Ideas on the Cinema," 133.
65. Zavattini, "Some Ideas on the Cinema," 126.
66. Zavattini, "Some Ideas on the Cinema," 130, 132.
67. "*La Terra Trema* is a great bore, a colossal aesthetic blunder and a monumental confusion of styles," noted Satyajit Ray in his damning critique. See Ray, *Our Films, Their Films*, 122.
68. Bazin, *What Is Cinema?*, 43.
69. P. Thomas, "Gone Fishin'?," 22.
70. Steimatsky, *Italian Locations*, 90.
71. "Visconti endows the suffering of his characters with an aura of grace and grandeur... [and] boldly grafts diverse visions, scales, spaces, narrative and historical orders in a resonant chorale.... [The] cinematographic grasp of the location as an enframed chorale suggests a conception of nature as a contained, determinant, humanized stage—and a conception of reality as itself such a set." Steimatsky, *Italian Locations*, 105, 115.
72. "Its opening sequence that portrays the homecoming of the fishermen just before sunrise after a whole night's fishing in the river has been overwhelmingly influenced by a surprisingly similar sequence from Luchino Visconti's 'La Terra Trema,' a masterpiece based on the plight of the Sicilian fishermen. Whether this was a conscious imitation or an accidental coincidence is not really important. The scene certainly added a lyrical quality to the severely austere mood of the story." Kabir, *The Cinema in Pakistan*, 71–72.
73. Zavattini, "Some Ideas on the Cinema," 126–27.
74. Haaland, *Italian Neorealist Cinema*, 52.
75. Haaland, *Italian Neorealist Cinema*, 53.
76. Haaland, *Italian Neorealist Cinema*, 53,
77. Pucci, "History, Myth, and the Everyday," 434.
78. Rajput, "River Life in East Pakistan," 42. Also see Layli Uddin's discussion as to how the Kagmari Festival in 1957 enacted a transformed understanding of rural Bengal. Uddin, "Kagmari Festival, 1957."
79. In her analysis on the film *Akaler Sandhaney* (In search of famine, 1980, dir. Mrinal Sen), Manishita Dass observes how urban leftist Indian filmmakers repeatedly misconstrued and romanticized rural conditions in West Bengal even as late as in 1980. Dass, "Look Back in Angst."
80. Raju, *Bangladesh Cinema and National Identity*, 138. His extended discussion on the files and their aesthetics is on pages 132–38.
81. Doss, *Looking at LIFE Magazine*.
82. Back and Schmidt-Linsenhoff, *The Family of Man 1955–2001*; Stimson, *The Pivot of the World*; Staniszewski, *The Power of Display*, 235–59. Roland Barthes's influential critique of this exhibition is in his *Mythologies*, 196–99.
83. Sunderason, *Partisan Aesthetics*.

84. Another example is an article taxonomizing various types of boats in Bengal. M. A. Ahmed, "River Craft in Modern Bengal," 37–39.
85. "[In 1958] during three and a half months lies the story of one of the great pioneering efforts in cinema history.... Every single item necessary for the intricate requirements of a feature film had to be packed and taken to the location.... The whole operation was planned and tackled with the precision of a military objective." *Jago Hua Savera* booklet.
86. Lassally, *Itinerant Cameraman*, 44–55.
87. See Lotte Hoek on how critic Alamgir Kabir positioned *Jago Hua Savera* as an influential but troubling exemplar for socially committed cinema in Bangladesh. Hoek, "The Conscience Whipper."
88. The long take and cinematic immersion in the riverine landscape is also celebrated in early Bengali-language productions from Dhaka, *Mukh o Mukhosh* (The face and the mask, 1956, dir. Abdul Jabbar Khan), and *Asiya* (1960, dir. Fateh Lohani). Zakir Hossain Raju observes that both films combine "images and sounds that quite ably represent East Bengal's traditional lifestyle and the beauty of rural nature. Lohani himself admits that he was accused of using long takes of the natural scenery of rural East Pakistan.... I argue that the 'unnecessarily' long sequences of natural beauty and of folk culture in rural East Bengal actually portrayed the relationship of Bengali-Muslim identity within its local setting.... *Asiya* also repeatedly presents long shots of boats, rivers and clouds, and medium shots of water lilies. Moreover, it combines various scenes such as a snake-play by a snake-charmer in a rural market and women singing folk songs whilst thrashing paddy. These images are only remotely connected with the narrative development of the film, but are significant constituents of the rural culture of the Bengal delta. East-Bengali folk literature also plays [an] important role in the film. Not only are there a number of folk songs in the film, but sometimes the protagonists, the two young lovers, converse using folk riddles." Raju, *Bangladesh Cinema and National Identity*, 138.
89. Lotte Hoek and Sanjukta Sunderason, email communication, October 31, 2016.
90. "The engagement with the indigenous saw a wide variety, ranging from presenting indigenous artists or their music, to using indigenous forms and tunes with political lyrics, to interpreting, mixing and borrowing between different forms, involving substantial aesthetic transformations." Damodaran, *The Radical Impulse*, 153. Also see page 119, where she notes that the singer Hemanga Biswas included *bhatiali* songs in his performances.
91. Pradhan, "The All India People's Theatre Association," 251. Also cited in Anuradha Roy, *Cultural Communism in Bengal, 1936–1952*, 202.
92. Damodaran, *The Radical Impulse*, 153.
93. Anuradha Roy, *Cultural Communism in Bengal*, 202–4.
94. "Timir Baran's own classical training and work/travels with Uday Shankar and the milieu of the IPTA in the 1940s and 1950s does open up a new mode of producing (and affirming) a lyrical scape, at once classical and folk." Sanjukta Sunderason, email communication, October 4, 2017.
95. *Folk Music of Pakistan*. Songs available online for streaming at www.aspresolver.com/aspresolver.asp?GLMU;71822.

96. "Regional genres came to be appreciated across the region, such as the wistful love songs from the north—bhaoaya . . . and the haunting boat songs—bhatiali . . . from the east and south." Schendel, *A History of Bangladesh*, 156. Also see Zakir Hossain Raju's discussion of the first film made in Dhaka, *Mukh o Mukhosh* (The face and the mask, 1956, dir. Abdul Jabbar Khan), specifically the lyrics and picturization of the "song by the boatman." Raju, *Bangladesh Cinema and National Identity*, 137.
97. Jasimuddin, "The Folk Songs of East Bengal." *Bhatiali* is discussed on page 50.
98. The poem was written in 1952. For the Urdu text of poem with a gloss on its context, see Nasir, *Ham jite ji masruf rahe*, 139–43. The poem recited by Faiz is available on YouTube: "Shishon ka masiha koi nahin (Faiz Ahmad Faiz)."
99. Nasir, *Ham jite ji masruf rahe*, 260–61 (translation mine). Also quoted in Jamil, *Zikr-e-Faiz*, 502–3. On the dancer Rakhshi, see A. Parvez, "Rakhshi."
100. Lassally, *Itinerant Cameraman*, 50.
101. On the "item number," see, for example, Weidman, "Voices of Meenakumari."
102. Morcom, *Hindi Film Songs and the Cinema*, 85.
103. Haaland, *Italian Neorealist Cinema*, 151.
104. Haaland, *Italian Neorealist Cinema*, 151.
105. Ray, *Our Films, Their Films*, 122.
106. Haaland, *Italian Neorealist Cinema*, 151–52.
107. Sanjukta Sunderason comments: "The question of dialect in *Jago Hua Savera* had struck me while watching the film. The minimal smattering of Bengali used in the film seems to have a sharp west Bengali accent. It could be an evident slip from the actresses from Calcutta, showing further how the local in the film was pastiche formulation." Email communication, October 4, 2017.
108. Kabir, *The Cinema in Pakistan*, 43, 71.
109. Mohaiemen, "Simulation at War's End," 35.
110. Shahidullah, "Common Origin of Urdu and Bengali."
111. For an overview, see Schendel, *A History of Bangladesh*.
112. "Hamari Zaban," Motion Picture Archive of Pakistan, accessed August 8, 2017, www.mpaop.org/mpaop/pak-film-database/chronological-of-films/1955-2/hamari-zaban. I have been unable to find a copy of *Hamari Zaban*.
113. Mufti, Enlightenment in the Colony, 230–31.
114. Lahiri, "An Idiom for India"; Lunn, "The Eloquent Language."
115. Lahiri, "An Idiom for India," 78.
116. "Movies from East Pakistan, Dacca," *Pakistan Film Magazine*, accessed April 4, 2021, https://pakmag.net/film/db/EastPakistanFilms.php. Bengali/Urdu double versions number thirteen, while another forty-one are Urdu-only releases through 1971. Moreover, industry personnel would move across Dhaka, Lahore, and Karachi from the 1950s onward, and this continued after 1971, as exemplified by the team involved in the blockbuster Lahore film *Aina* (Mirror, 1977, dir. Nazrul Islam). See Hoek, "Mirrors of Movement." Alamgir Kabir notes that the release of the Dhaka-made Urdu film *Chanda* (1962, dir. Ehtesham) marked a shift in films made in Dhaka for a few years until about 1965, with more emphasis on Urdu-language productions. Kabir, *Film in Bangladesh*, 27. Also see Raju, *Bangladesh Cinema and National Identity*, 84–85.

117. Hoek, "Cross-Wing Filmmaking," 105.
118. "The Pakistan period was not only a time of political and economic struggle; it was also a time of crucial cultural change. After 1947 the inhabitants of the Bengal delta had a lot of rethinking to do. What did it mean to be a Bengali now that the old centre of Bengali culture, Kolkata (Calcutta), had become inaccessible.... What set this emerging elite apart was that they were not bilingual (Bengali–English or Bengali–Urdu) and that their frame of reference was the Bengal delta, not the entire subcontinent or all of Pakistan. Their new cultural style was ... popular rather than aristocratic, open-minded rather than orthodox and delta-focused rather than national. Most importantly, it was expressed in the Bengali language. Dhaka and other rapidly growing towns in East Pakistan became centres of this cultural renewal." Schendel, *A History of Bangladesh*, 152. Also cited in Raju, *Bangladesh Cinema and National Identity*, 116.
119. Despite a generally unfavorable environment in Pakistan for experimental cinema, leftist intellectuals continued their association with cinema, mostly in a commercial register. For example, Faiz wrote lyrics for the film *Sukh Ka Sapna* (Distant dream, 1962, dir. Masood Pervaiz). The leftist journalist and writer Hamid Akhtar (1924–2011) contributed its dialogue. I have been unable to find a copy of this film. On Akhtar, see K. Ali, *Communism in Pakistan*. Faiz also contributed lyrics to the Khalil Qaiser–directed films *Shaheed* (1962) and *Farangi* (1964), as well as *Qaidi* (Prisoner, 1962, dir. Najam Naqvi) and *Ghoonghat* (The veil, 1962, dir. Khurshid Anwar). On Faiz's involvement in cinema, see Jamil, *Zikr-e-Faiz*, 500–509.
120. Kabir, *The Cinema in Pakistan*, 71. Also see Hoek, "The Conscience Whipper."

2. LYRIC ROMANTICISM

1. For a profile of Anwar from 1964, see Jaffery, "Khursheed Anwar."
2. *Anarkali* is credited with popularizing the romantic myth of Anarkali, the dancing girl who fell in love with the Mughal prince Salim, the future Emperor Jahangir (1569–1627). This story was adapted numerous times for films produced both in Bombay and elsewhere. Taj himself adapted the play as a cinema screenplay, which served as the basis for a number of films in India, culminating in *Mughal-e-Azam* (1960), considered one of the greatest films of Bombay cinema. Desoulieres, "Historical Fiction and Style."
3. Naushahi and Shibli, *Syed Imtiaz Ali Taj*.
4. See, for example, the Bombay film *Mirza Ghalib* (1954).
5. Naushahi and Shibli, *Syed Imtiaz Ali Taj*.
6. Films directed by Taj include *Swarg Ki Sidhi* (1935). Taj and Anwar had worked together on *Pagdandi* (1947), *Intezar* (1956), and *Zehr-e Ishq* (1958). For the latter two, Anwar wrote the story and screenplay, while Taj contributed the dialogue.
7. Khurshid Anwar's interviews with Asghar Ali Kausar provide valuable biographical information on his early years. They were published in the Urdu newspaper *Imroze*, in fifteen parts, between June 10 and September 30, 1983. Kausar, "Khawaja Khurshid Anwar ki kahani." I have henceforth used the following

abbreviations to cite these: KAK1 (part 1, June 10, p. 6); KAK2 (part 2, June 17, p. 6); KAK3 (part 3, June 24, p. 9); KAK4 (part 4, July 1, p. 10); KAK5 (part 5, July 8, p. 6); KAK6 (part 6, July 15, p. 14); KAK7 (part 7, August 5, p. 9); KAK8 (part 8, August 12, pp. 6, 15); KAK9 (part 9, August 19, p. 11); KAK10 (part 10, August 26, p. 6); KAK11 (part 11, September 2, pp. 7, 8); KAK12 (part 12, September 9, pp. 8, 10); KAK13 (part 13, September 16, p. 13); KAK14 (part 14, September 23, p. 6); KAK15 (part 15, September 30, p. 9).

8. "The primary musical influence on my mind was that of classical music. As a child and as a young man I had the privilege to be present at the twice-a-week soirees at my father's house which were graced with performances by such great names of the day as Ustad Waheed Khan, Ustad Ashiq Ali Khan, Ustad Bade Ghulam Ali Khan and my own teacher, Ustad Tawakkal Hussain Khan. My father was simply mad about music. He had a collection of close to ten thousand records, mostly classical music." Usman, "Portrait of a Film-Maker"; KAK4.

9. "In the weekly soirees of music which were held in . . . [Anwar's father's] house, renowned masters used to perform, and it was here that the young Khurshid Anwar developed a taste for classical music. Seeing Khwaja Khurshid Anwar's keen love for learning music, Khan Saheb Tawakkal Hussain took him under his tutelage in 1934." A. Parvez, *Melody Makers of the Subcontinent*, 98.

10. Usman, "Portrait of a Film-Maker."

11. Usman, "Portrait of a Film-Maker."

12. KAK2.

13. KAK1. Taj evidently also wrote for *Swami* (1941, dir. A. R. Kardar), *Khandan* (Family, 1942, dir. Shaukat Hussain Rizvi), and *Zamindar* (Landlord, 1942, dir. Moti Gidwani). Anarkali renditions include *The Loves of a Mughal Prince* (1928, dir. Prafulla Roy and Charu Roy), *Anarkali* (1953, dir. Nandlal Jaswantlal), and *Mughal-e-Azam* (The great Mughal, 1960, dir. K. Asif) in India, and *Anarkali* (1958, dir. Anwar Kamal Pasha) in Pakistan. Taj and Anwar worked on *Pagdandi* (The path, 1947, dir. Ram Narayan Dave).

14. KAK2.

15. KAK2.

16. KAK10; Aujla, "Khurshid Anwar."

17. Shakur, "Khurshid Anwar"; Chaudhari, *Jahan-i fan*, 75; Siddiqi, "Khawaja Khurshid Anwar." Anwar had hired Roshan Lal Nagrath (1917–67, "Roshan") as his assistant, who later became a renowned music director in Bombay cinema (and is the grandfather to the Indian star Hrithik Roshan). Roshan had composed the celebrated *qawwalis* for the 1960 film *Barsaat Ki Raat* (A night of the rainy season), which include "Na to karavan ki talaash hai."

18. Aujla, "Khurshid Anwar."

19. KAK14; KAK15.

20. According to Aujla, "if you are a good poet and you have taken training in classical ragas, you automatically have a head start over your contemporaries. Khurshid Anwar's stint at All India Radio Delhi gave him a much-needed experience to start a new life as a film music director." Aujla, "Khurshid Anwar."

21. Aujla, "Khurshid Anwar."

22. The flute and the violin play an important role in evoking a haunting affect in Anwar's compositions: "Anwar composed 76 tunes during his Mumbai stint.... His tune in raag Pahadi, *Papi papiha re pi pi na bol*, sung by Suraiya, featured flute accompaniment played by the legendary Bengali flautist, Pannalal Ghosh [also in *Parwana*]. The extraordinary flair of flute accompaniment irreversibly convinced Anwar to rank the flute as the [instrument] most expressive of human feelings, much like he rated the violin being the closest to human vox, a conviction that is manifest in all his compositions." Siddiqi, "Khawaja Khurshid Anwar."
23. A. Parvez, "Khwaja Khurshid Anwar," 99.
24. I. Ahmed, "The Lahore Film Industry," 59–61.
25. Aziz, *Light of the Universe*, 6, also see 6–12; Rajadhyaksha, "The Lahore Effect." For an elaboration of the concept of the Lahore effect for this study, see the introduction.
26. I. Ahmed, "How Pakistani Film Music Has Declined over the Decades"; Aujla, "Khurshid Anwar."
27. These were a "small group of musicians-composers, singers, and arrangers . . . Naushad Ali, Shankar-Jaikishan, C. Ramchandra, Lata Mangeshkar, Antonio Vaz, and Sebastian D'Souza." Booth, "A Moment of Historical Conjuncture in Mumbai," 22. Booth notes, "The transformation of the Hindi song scene from a relatively static emotional soliloquy or staged performance to a component with the potential to serve as a unifier of both cinematic and narrative content was implemented during the 1948–1952 period." Booth, "A Moment of Historical Conjuncture in Mumbai," 35. Anwar's reminiscences of his Bombay years are in KAK12. Also see Aujla, "Khurshid Anwar."
28. Elam, "Commonplace Anti-colonialism." According to historian K. C. Yadav, Bhagat Singh was possessed of "a giant of a brain." Quoted in Moffat, *India's Revolutionary Inheritance*, 60.
29. Moffat, *India's Revolutionary Inheritance*, 48.
30. Moffat, *India's Revolutionary Inheritance*, 66.
31. Moffat, *India's Revolutionary Inheritance*, 55.
32. Quoted in Moffat, *India's Revolutionary Inheritance*, 90.
33. Moffat, *India's Revolutionary Inheritance*, 90.
34. Moffat, *India's Revolutionary Inheritance*, 90–97.
35. Moffat, *India's Revolutionary Inheritance*, 91.
36. Moffat, *India's Revolutionary Inheritance*, 106.
37. Moffat, *India's Revolutionary Inheritance*, 125.
38. Moffat, *India's Revolutionary Inheritance*, 117; Rekhta, "#BhagatSingh ' Hand-Written Letter from Jail in #Urdu to His Younger Brother Kultar Singh on March 3, 1931.Pic.Twitter.Com/TOPQRInj9G," Tweet, @*rekhta* (blog), March 23, 2016, https://twitter.com/rekhta/status/712563730530177024?lang=en.
39. These images have continued to proliferate in Indian bazaar and calendar arts for many decades into the present. They often show Bhagat Singh in a frontal portrait pose, dressed in European attire with a fashionable trilby hat, which he had famously donned in order to disguise himself while on the run from the British authorities. The image of a bare-chested Chandrashekhar Azad twirling his

mustache often accompanies Bhagat Singh. Azad had died in a shootout with the police in 1931 in Allahabad. Pinney, "Photos of the Gods," 123–33.

40. One facet of reexamining the legacy of Bhagat Singh seeks to understand how HSRA's legacy continues to reverberate in subsequent decades in subaltern and counterpublic spheres, beyond the safe borders of official nationalist history. In an exemplary recent study, Kama Maclean discusses the popular visuality associated with the HSRA members during their trial and after their passing. Maclean, *A Revolutionary History of Interwar India*.
41. Elam, "Commonplace Anti-colonialism," 597.
42. Moffat, *India's Revolutionary Inheritance*, 19. Moffat draws upon and expands Jacques Rancière's theorization of dissensus. Moffat, *India's Revolutionary Inheritance*, 17.
43. Moffat, *India's Revolutionary Inheritance*, 223–45.
44. U. Khan, "Khawaja Khurshid Anwar."
45. Usman, "Portrait of a Film-Maker."
46. Usman, "Portrait of a Film-Maker."
47. U. Khan, "Khawaja Khurshid Anwar."
48. "In legal parlance, revolutionaries who took to the stand to testify were known as 'approvers,' or King's witnesses. Crucially, an approver was both an informer and an accuser, who simultaneously confessed to his crime while accusing others in the court.... The legal presumption was that an approver's testimony was a voluntary confession which required a certain measure of self-implication to hold judicial value. However, not all approver confessions were 'voluntary.'" Vaidik, "History of a Renegade Revolutionary," 218. The novelist Yashpal was considered unreliable after he had married. See Yashpal, *Yashpal Looks Back*, 160–62, 170–71. I am grateful to J. Daniel Elam for this reference and for his advice on the life and work of Bhagat Singh and the HSRA. On Yashpal's memoir, see Elam and Moffat. "On the Form, Politics and Effects of Writing Revolution," 517–18.
49. On Faiz Ahmed Faiz, see KAK1 and KAK10; on Mulk Raj Anand, see KAK1; on theater, see KAK2; on All India Radio, see KAK11 and KAK15; on Radio Pakistan, see KAK3 and KAK15; on classical musicians, see KAK4 and KAK13; on musical directors and playback singers, see KAK14. Regarding music scholarship, Anwar notes that Bhatkhande's book classifies music in ten *thaats* but that a number of Muslim musicians had classified them well before him, such as Sadiq Ali, who also has ten *thaats* in his book *Sarmaya-i ishrat*. KAK13. For an appreciation of Vishnu Narayan Bhatkhande (1860–1936), see Nayar, *Bhatkhande's Contribution to Music*. For a critical reading in broad alignment with Anwar's views, see Bakhle, *Two Men and Music*. In a video interview, Anwar also positively mentions this study: Acharyah, *Musalman aur barr-i saghir ki mausiqi*.
50. KAK12.
51. Anwar dwells on this extensively in his interviews KAK1, KAK5, KAK6, KAK7, KAK8, and KAK9. In KAK10, he discusses communism, socialism, and fascism. He discusses his music in Bombay only in KAK12.
52. The presence of two attractive young women, the sisters Mohini Zutshi and Shyama Zutshi, lent a powerful aura of romance to these gatherings: "I was about

17, which is an impassioned age [*tez ṭarrār 'umr*]." KAK5. On the Zutshi sisters, see Sahgal, *An Indian Freedom Fighter Recalls Her Life*; "The Fearless Zutshi Sisters of Lahore." Anwar also attended the Indian National Congress session in late 1929, encountering Indira Gandhi (the future prime minister of India) as an enchanting teenager in the girl's camp "whose presence mesmerized us for hours on end." KAK5.

53. KAK5. I have not been able to trace a Central Revolutionary Party. Perhaps Anwar meant the Central Committee of the HSRA. There is mention of a "Central Committee of the Revolutionary Party, meaning the inner circle of the HSRA" in Maclean, *A Revolutionary History of Interwar India*, 106. However, in his memoirs, Anwar went to great lengths to disassociate himself from any of Bhagat Singh's associates.
54. KAK7.
55. KAK6.
56. KAK8.
57. KAK1.
58. KAK7. "'Approvement' was an old but effective instrument of judicial pacification in British India." Vaidik, "History of a Renegade Revolutionary," 218.
59. KAK7.
60. "Jab main ne apne vālid kī bāt kā javāb diyā to sab ke ṭoṭe uṛ ga'e" (When I refuted my father's request, everyone was flabbergasted). KAK8.
61. KAK8.
62. KAK9.
63. U. Khan, "Khawaja Khurshid Anwar."
64. KAK1. However, according to Faiz's recollection, Anwar was among two or three close friends who were involved with Bhagat Singh's movement: "The leader [*sarghana*] of this group was Khawaja Khurshid Anwar, now a famous music director, who had converted my hostel room into a center [*aḍḍā*] for distributing underground literature. These texts were mostly on Karl Marx, Lenin, and the Russian Revolution. At times, I would also glance at them in a cursory way [*kabhī kabhār sarsarī naẓar se main bhī dekh liyā kartā thā*]." Faiz, *Mah o sal-i ashna'i*, 10. However, in his interviews, Anwar contests this: "I am astonished as to why Faiz wrote such a thing. Yes, I used to visit his room, but I don't remember any details. Why would I distribute communist literature when I was never impressed by communism?" KAK1.
65. Anwar mentions "ultimate values" in English and also uses the Urdu phrase *ḥatmī aqdār*. KAK1.
66. KAK5.
67. The latter is especially difficult to pin down, given that Bhagat Singh was only twenty-three years old when he was put to death and his ideological views were in a process of formation. Maclean, *A Revolutionary History of Interwar India*, 6. Recent scholarship has argued for an understanding of Singh's close reading of diverse texts and affiliation with them as enabling a sense of openness toward the future. For example, for J. Daniel Elam, Bhagat Singh's Jail Notebook reveals that his "reading practices, especially in the face of death, suggest a new way to theorize

68. Anwar sarcastically observes, "This musician's love for Pakistan was so encompassing that he soon abandoned it and returned to India." KAK3. Z. A. Bukhari discusses the musician's return to Delhi in his autobiography, Bukhari, *Sarguzasht*. Also see Kapuria, "Music and Its Many Memories."
69. Bukhari was a veteran of All India Radio in Delhi. Lelyveld, "Talking the National Language"; Bukhari, *Sarguzasht*.
70. KAK15.
71. *Ahang-e-Khusravi: Raag mala*; *Ahang-e-Khusravi: Gharanon ki gaiki*. W. A. Khwaja, "Khawaja Khurshid Anwar." Also see A. Parvez, "Khwaja Khurshid Anwar," 99; Siddiqi, "Khawaja Khurshid Anwar."
72. On the question of genre in the Gothic and horror films in Bombay cinema, see M. Sen, *Haunting Bollywood*, 9.
73. The threat of Indic myths and lifeworlds to modern bourgeois life in *Zehr-e Ishq* (1958) is analyzed in Dadi, "Lineages of Pakistan's 'Urdu' Cinema."
74. Sarkar, *Mourning the Nation*, 30.
75. The quote "figural sublimations and displacements" is from Bhaskar Sarkar in describing Indian films and their relation to the Partition. Sarkar, *Mourning the Nation*, 30. On Bombay cinema's tropes of reincarnation in its midcentury films, see M. Sen, *Haunting Bollywood*, 25 and passim.
76. M. Sen, *Haunting Bollywood*, 42.
77. Jameson, "Reification and Utopia in Mass Culture."
78. The two films from the 1930s are *Swarg Ki Sidhi* (1935, dir. Imtiaz Ali Taj) and *Suhag Ka Daan* (1936). "Imtiaz Ali Taj," Pakistan Artists Database, accessed April 4, 2020, https://pakmag.net/film/artists/details.php?pid=1441; "*Swarg Ki Sidhi* (1935)," IMDb, accessed July 24, 2020, www.imdb.com/title/tt0232745. Among Master Ghulam Haider's first film compositions were those for Taj's *Swarg Ki Sidhi*. "Master Ghulam Haider," Pakistan Artists Database, accessed April 4, 2020, https://pakmag.net/film/artists/details.php?pid=1164. Zakhmi Kanpuri seems to conflate *Gulnar* with *Zehr-e Ishq* and mentions that it was based on Lakhnavi culture. He notes that Qateel Shifai, although writing lyrics for films for ten years, made a breakthrough in this film in terms of the popularity of his songs. Kanpuri perhaps confuses this with *Zehr-e Ishq*, because Qateel Shifai's first film is *Teri Yaad* (1948). Kanpuri, *Yadgar filmen*, 163.
79. "Gulnar (1953)," Pakistan Film Database—Lollywood Movies, accessed May 29, 2020, http://pakmag.net/film/details.php?pid=45. On Haider's work for *Humayun* (1945), Gregory D. Booth writes, "The musical results of the freelance/studio musician collaboration, the presence of specialist arrangers, and improving sound technology and expertise can all be heard in Mehboob Productions' *Humayun* (1945). In the early 1940s, Mehboob Productions employed roughly fifteen musicians on salary, who were complemented in this film by the small group of freelance musicians who were associated regularly with the film's music director, Ghulam Haider. Six of Haider's musicians had come with him to Mumbai from

Lahore and many, like Haider himself, did not read Western notation. . . . *Humayun*'s soundtrack illustrates how far music had progressed in the nine years since *Amar Jyoti*, both musically and technologically. The playback-singer system was now firmly in place; the voices of Shams Luckhnavi and Shamshad Begum (whose name is mysteriously absent from the title credits) dominate the soundtrack. . . . *Humayun* has an effective background music score that demonstrates increased range and flexibility and that continues under dialogue when appropriate, supporting the emotional content. In films such as *Humayun*, all the primary elements of the Bollywood sound fall into place; composers expand and develop these elements in subsequent decades until, by the 1970s at the latest, they had become almost totally subject to conventional treatment." Booth, "That Bollywood Sound," 90–91.
80. "Noor Jehan," IMDb, accessed April 4, 2020, www.imdb.com/name/nm0420451. On Noor Jehan's accomplishments as a singer in Mehboob Khan's *Anmol Ghadi* (1946), see Beaster-Jones, *Bollywood Sounds*, 43–46.
81. I. A. Rehman, "Intezar."
82. Anwar's classicizing approach can perhaps be situated alongside Naushad Ali in India. On the latter, see Booth, *Behind the Curtain*, 264.
83. On "winking" as a strategy in the Hollywood musical *Singin' in the Rain* (1952) that acknowledges the film's artifice, see Feuer, "Singin' in the Rain (1952), Stanley Donen and Gene Kelly."
84. Booth, *Behind the Curtain*, 264.
85. On port cities, see Denning, *Noise Uprising*. A jazz musician named Micky Correa, "Karachi's leading saxophonist," performed in Bombay, as reported in "Personalities in Pictures," *Indian Listener* 2, no. 15 (July 22, 1937): 664. Thanks to Harleen Singh for this reference.
86. Siddiqi, "Khawaja Khurshid Anwar." Gregory D. Booth includes Sebastian D'Souza among the small group of industry professionals who between 1948 and 1952 codified the modern Hindi film song. See Booth, "A Moment of Historical Conjuncture in Mumbai."
87. Booth, "A Moment of Historical Conjuncture in Mumbai," 32. Also, "[Sebastian] D'Souza had been playing and arranging for his uncle's jazz band in Lahore prior to Partition in 1947," according to Gregory D. Booth, "That Bollywood Sound," 93.
88. Anwar offers a detailed explanation of the technical problems in shooting this scene. Usman, "Portrait of a Film-Maker."
89. Booth, "A Moment of Historical Conjuncture in Mumbai," 32.
90. B. Sen, "The Sounds of Modernity," 91.
91. Gregory Booth observes that the "newly created governments of India and Pakistan each had their own reasons for not encouraging foreign popular musical styles. It is perhaps ironic that many dance-band musicians chose to work in the Hindi film industry despite their preference for other musical styles. Many of these musicians were Goans, who spoke little Hindi and who rarely (if ever) watched for pleasure the films whose music they played for profit." Booth, "That Bollywood Sound," 92.
92. Morcom, *Hindi Film Songs and the Cinema*, 67.

93. Morcom, *Hindi Film Songs and the Cinema*, 170–71. She further notes, "Western music's particular emphasis on the sense of 'dynamic passage through time' may have made it especially attractive to music directors. That Indian music is strongly identified with stasis but less so with transition and progression—whether at the level of structure or popular essentialist notions of the 'mythical,' 'eternal' nature of India—would lead to more borrowing of Western music in Hindi movies in scenes of progression than in scenes of stasis. These conceptions can perhaps be seen as factors justifying the use of music heavily laden with Western techniques in highly Indian scenes and contexts, given that Western music was and is anyway fashionable and one of the unique selling points of Hindi films, especially in the early days" (172).
94. On the significance of the opera *Indar Sabha* (The assembly of King Indar), composed by Agha Hasan Amanat in 1853, see Hansen, "The *Indar Sabha* Phenomenon." Also see Hansen, "Heteroglossia in Amanat's *Indar Sabha*."
95. In fact, the renowned classical musician Bade Ghulam Ali Khan, whose hometown was in Kasur, West Pakistan, came to Pakistan after 1947 but left the country permanently in 1957 to return to India.
96. For accounts of the transition to sound and its implications for playback singing, see N. Majumdar, "Between Rage and Song"; D. Mukherjee, *Bombay Hustle*, 143–82.
97. But see Neepa Majumdar's discussion of the difference between the value of authenticity in Hollywood exemplified by *Singin' in the Rain* and Indian cinema of the period. N. Majumdar, *Wanted Cultured Ladies Only!*, 177–78.
98. For an analysis of *Singin' in the Rain*, see Wollen, *Singin' in the Rain*; Feuer, "Singin' in the Rain (1952), Stanley Donen and Gene Kelly," 440–54.
99. On the stardom of Lata Mangeshkar, see N. Majumdar, *Wanted Cultured Ladies Only!*
100. The celebration of the playback singer as a star in her own right contrasts markedly to the phenomenon of the "ghost voice" just a few years before. Meheli Sen observes, "Playback singing, for example, overlays a prerecorded music track atop the image track and imbues the form with an added layer of spectrality; not only do ghostly forms flicker via the apparatus, but ghostly voices of absent others (and shards of times past) accompany them in the present of the projected moment." M. Sen, *Haunting Bollywood*, 5. A film magazine editor had remarked in 1944 that off-screen singing voices accompanying on-screen bodies constituted "artistic fraud." N. Majumdar, *Wanted Cultured Ladies Only!*, 185.
101. Shikha Jhingan remarks on Noor Jehan's career in Bombay cinema, "What made Noor Jehan stand apart from the other singers was the embodied nature of her performance. She retained the *mehfil* style of singing in which the live presence of the singer was underscored by heightened emotionality, corporeality, clear enunciation of lyrics, and the projection of an intense investment in performance." Jhingan, "Sonic Ruptures," 215–16. Also see Sundar, "Meri Awaaz Suno."
102. A widely shared view is that Mangeshkar's rise became possible only due to the place vacated by Noor Jehan. Jhingan notes, "There has been intense speculation that had Noor Jehan not left for Pakistan, Lata Mangeshkar may not have achieved

the kind of hegemonic status that she did." Jhingan, "Sonic Ruptures," 215–16. And Neepa Majumdar observes, "The shift to the dominance of a few recognizable voices is explained in the Bombay film industry as a monopoly engineered by shrewd individuals such as Lata Mangeshkar, who were able to take advantage of the migration of several singers (such as the equally popular Noor Jehan) to Pakistan after the partition of India in 1947" (187). According to Majumdar, Mangeshkar's playback status as a fully realized star text emerges in the wake of the release of *Mahal* (1949) and the demand by fans to know the name of the singer when its songs were played on radio: "Lata's song from *Mahal* may be said to mark the transition from 'ghost voices' to the aural stardom of 'playback singers,' a transition forced by fans" (189). N. Majumdar, *Wanted Cultured Ladies Only!*
103. Rajamani, Pernau, and Schofield, *Monsoon Feelings*.
104. "[Sebastian] D'Souza's professionalism (oral accounts emphasize the speed at which he could work, together with his flexibility) and the commercial success of the Kapoor-Shankar-Jaikishan films established a musical, professional, and economic framework that effectively normalized the use of a larger and more diverse film orchestra in the productions of scores in which harmony, sectional playing, and counterpoint figured prominently." Booth, "That Bollywood Sound," 93.
105. "Indiancine.ma: A Project by Pad.ma," Indiancine.ma, accessed April 4, 2020; "Aankh Ka Nasha," Pakistan Film Database—Lollywood Movies, accessed April 4, 2020, https://pakmag.net/film/details.php?pid=120.
106. Hansen, "Boucicault in Bombay," 65–66. On Agha Hashr Kashmiri's popular play *Yahudi ki larki* (The Jew's daughter), see Hansen, "Staging Composite Culture."
107. "Hollywood films and Latin-themed cabarets in Mumbai inspired a number of enterprising Hindi film song composers and arrangers, including C. Ramchandra, the composer duo Shankar-Jaikishan, O. P. Nayyar, and Naushad Ali." Shope, "Latin American Music in Moving Pictures and Jazzy Cabarets in Mumbai, 1930s to 1950s," 202.
108. For an extended analysis of this *Albela* song and its links with Carmen Miranda's song in *Week-End in Havana* (1941, dir. Walter Lang), see Shope, "Latin American Music in Moving Pictures and Jazzy Cabarets in Mumbai, 1930s to 1950s," 212–13.
109. Dass, *Outside the Lettered City*, 124–25.
110. I. A. Rehman, "Intezar."
111. Dadi, "Lineages of Pakistan's 'Urdu' Cinema."
112. Malik, "Ghunghat (1962) Review."
113. One of the film's opening titles notes that idea of the ghost was adapted from a short story by Ghulam Mohammad titled "Dosheeza."
114. Also a Lahore film released in 1965.
115. According to Arif Rahman Chughtai (son of the artist), this work is *Lilly of the Fields*. Email communication, July 4, 2020.
116. For a detailed discussion of Chughtai, see Dadi, *Modernism and the Art of Muslim South Asia*.
117. Faiz, "Musavvir-i Mashriq," 73. The *ghazal* form had come under criticism by reformers during the later nineteenth century for its purported artifice and lack of

118. Chughtai, *Maqalat-i Chughtai*, vol. 1, 147.
119. Faiz is listed in IMDb and in www.pakmag.net as a lyricist but not mentioned in the title credits, which only list Tanvir Naqvi. "Ghoonghat (1962) - Pakistani Urdu Film," Pakistan Film Magazine, accessed March 13, 2022, https://pakmag.net/film/details.php?pid=308. But see this note by M. A. Siddiqi: "Faiz's song for the film *Ghoonghat*, *More piyā ko ḍhūṇḍ ke lā'o sakhī*, sung by Noor Jahan, was written in a traditional Purbi vernacular (Western Standard Bhojpuri) embellished by poignant *shehnai* pieces with rhythmic adjustments in *antarās*." Siddiqi, "Khawaja Khurshid Anwar."
120. A. Parvez, "Three Uniquely Shot Pakistani Film Songs." Jayson Beaster-Jones notes that Tanvir Naqvi had written lyrics for the Bombay film *Anmol Ghadi* (Precious watch, 1946, dir. Mehboob Khan) with Noor Jehan as star and playback singer. Many songs of this film "are still considered evergreen (i.e., classic) hits." Beaster-Jones, *Bollywood Sounds*, 43.
121. M. Sen, *Haunting Bollywood*, 38.
122. For an excellent discussion of the modalities and significance of *darshan*, see Eck, *Darśan*.
123. Waheed, "Beyond the Wounded Archive," 7–8.
124. As Meheli Sen notes in her analysis of Bombay Gothic films from the midcentury, "The phallic and moral economy of the investigative thriller is . . . constitutively aligned to the expulsion, or at least marginalization, of the female ghost—the rejection of the irrational-supernatural-feminine, which had heretofore insistently haunted and enslaved the male subject. This reorganization of narrative material would also come to be a generic convention of the Hindi Gothic during the 1950s and beyond." M. Sen, *Haunting Bollywood*, 43.
125. "Āp hī jaise adīboṇ ne bahāroṇ ke naghme, sitāroṇ kī kirneṇ, phūloṇ kī khushbū, ko'il kī kūkū, aur na jāne kyā alā balā milā kar 'aurat ko devī banā kar chabūtre par rakh choṛā hai. Āp bhūl jāte haiṇ keh voh bhī āp kī ṭarah insān hai, us ke honṭ muskurā sakte haiṇ, us kī āṇkheṇ āṇsū bahā saktī haiṇ, us ke pā'ūṇ thokar bhī khā sakte haiṇ, khāmiyāṇ us meṇ bhī hotī haiṇ, phir āp us bechārī ko devī kyūṇ samajh baiṭhte haiṇ?"
126. These include technical issues, such as from where do the temple bell sounds emanate? From the swinging bells at the temple themselves, whose cause of movement is never explained, or from the organ in Sunder Nivas?
127. Gorija, *Pakistan ki 100 shahkar filmen*, 72.
128. Meheli Sen has noted that in her analysis of midcentury Bombay Gothic films, "Historical and ideological imperatives necessitate that the narrative cannot remain in disarray, mired in returns and repetitions, either. Hereafter, the films deploy a tricky sleight of hand to accomplish virtually an impossible task— recuperate the impaired/imperiled masculinity of the hero and reinstate him to the helm of narrative agency. This recuperative gesture, then, will also reinscribe him within the modern time-consciousness of the nation-state. The universe of meanings that have gathered around the 'ghost story' must be, figuratively speaking, put to rest." M. Sen, *Haunting Bollywood*, 42.

129. Usman, "Portrait of a Film-Maker." "According to Khawaja Irfan Anwar, this interview is dated December 2015 (but of course it must originally date back to Anwar's lifetime)." Comment in Facebook post by Ikrumul Haq, dated October 30, 2015, in Khwaja Khurshid Anwar (public group) on Facebook.
130. Shaina Anand notes, "Tellingly, that's not how one would generally spell Usha. It's not entirely wrong, but the 'sh' would be a different one." Personal communication, June 10, 2019.
131. Sarkar, *Mourning the Nation*, 68.
132. Dadi, "Lineages of Pakistan's 'Urdu' Cinema."
133. Sarkar, *Mourning the Nation*.
134. Moffat, *India's Revolutionary Inheritance*, 19.

3. CINEMA AND POLITICS

1. For a study of the disruptive role of romantic love in Indian commercial cinema, see Wani, *Fantasy of Modernity*. Manishita Dass has examined the relay of filmmakers and writers affiliated in the forties with the Indian People's Theatre Association (IPTA) who moved to work in the commercial Bombay film industry. Their engagement with Bombay transformed the latter during the forties and fifties by bringing questions of social exploitation to the social film. She notes, "The cinematic legacy of the IPTA is usually discussed (if at all) in terms of an impulse toward social realism and often in terms of failure—the failure to inject a dose of social realism into Bombay cinema and the inevitable dilution of radicalism in the cauldron of mass culture. However, a focus on the failure of the social realist agenda makes us lose sight of the fact that social realism was one of the many strands of the IPTA movement in the 1940s; it also prevents us from exploring the ways in which the IPTA experience and aesthetic actually left their mark on Bombay cinema. As several scholarly and eyewitness accounts indicate, songs, dances, tableaux, and shadow plays—all of which relied on stylization and a fusion of entertainment and edification—as well as nonnaturalistic modes of staging and acting formed an integral part of leftist street theater performances right from the beginning." Dass, "Cinetopia," 110.
2. Rajadhyaksha, "The Lahore Effect," 332.
3. In his critically insightful book published in 1969, Alamgir Kabir has perceptively remarked on the vast scale of Lahore's film production: "Lahore now has 8 film studios, and a large number of directors . . . confidently turning out money-spinners, often with amazing frequency." Kabir further notes, "Of course, the 'gold rush' forced a good number of them to abandon any artistic ambition. But directors like S. M. Yusuf and Masud Parvez [Masood Pervaiz] have proved that, at times, they too can be aware of the true needs of their medium and produce films that could pass for 'bold attempts.' And that may mean quite something under the circumstances. And there are other directors who have taken great pains to show that they are far from happy at the state of the art in Pakistan and have tried, however modestly, to bring about a fusion of 'commercial' appeal and the needs of culture and art in their efforts. They include directors like Anwar Kamal [Pasha],

Khalil Kaiser [Qaiser], . . . Hasan [Hassan] Tariq, Qadir Ghouri, Sharif Nayyar, W. Z. Ahmed, Ahmed Bashir and S. Suleman." Kabir, *The Cinema in Pakistan*, 58–59.

4. Mushtaq Gazdar provides a useful overview: "Khalil Qaiser and Riaz Shahid . . . became known for their exploration of a cinematic verism that dealt with both the historical freedom movement and the contemporary struggle against autocracy. . . . [Qaiser directed] *Clerk*, a down-to-earth story in which he also played the title role. It was a bold attempt that caught the attention of the Press but not that of film-goers. Next was *Shaheed*. This was the pinnacle of Khalil's achievement both as director and producer. It was written by Riaz Shahid, a progressive journalist who was aspiring to change the world through cinema." Gazdar, *Pakistan Cinema*, 90.

5. Their fellow travelers include the directors Jamil Akhtar and Hassan Tariq.

6. For profiles of Tanvir Naqvi and Himayat Ali Shair from the sixties, see "Men and Ideas: Tanveer Naqvi"; Noorani, "Himayat Ali Shair," 26.

7. Kanpuri, *Zikr e fankar chale*, 173.

8. On *Nagin*, see Sajjad, "Lollywood ki sanpon kay mauzu par banai gai film *Nagin* 1959."

9. According to Kanpuri, the failure of *Clerk* at the box office was due to Khalil Qaiser playing an uncharismatic lead role. Kanpuri, *Zikr e fankar chale*, 178.

10. In an interview, industry observer Aijaz Gul reiterates the popular perception of this group of industry stalwarts: "Khalil Qaisar was rebellious because he was against corruption in the political system, whether it was the British Raj or the Pakistani government. Riaz Shahid was a writer and also became a director but essentially he was collaborating with director Khalil Qaisar. Tanvir Naqvi was their lyricist, Faiz Ahmed Faiz their poet and Rashid Attre their music composer. So it was a whole team. Riaz Shahid kept on writing against the vices of the system and the corruption in the establishment. . . . They took the subject of Palestine, Andalus, Kashmir. *Shaheed* deals with British corruption in the Middle East. Khalil Qaisar did not live long. He made *Shaheed*, *Farangi*, *Nagin*, *Haveli*, and two or three more films, and passed away in a very tragic way. So, Riaz Shahid took over and did continue with his revolutionary scripts and films. His film *Zerqa* deals with the independence of Palestine, *Gharnata* with Muslims in Spain and *Yeh Aman* with Kashmir. Gul and Amanullah, "Aijaz Gul on Cinema in Pakistan," 180–81.

11. On the life and work of Jalib, see, for example, "Habib Jalib: The People's Poet and Historian"; Jalib, *Jalib biti*; *Habib Jalib: fann aur shakhsiyyat*; S. Parvez, *Habib Jalib: ghar ki gavahi*; Barelvi, *Habib Jalib*; S. Parvez, *Habib Jalib: sha'ir-i sh'ulah nava*.

12. Kanpuri, *Zikr e fankar chale*, 175.

13. R. Shahid, *Hazar Dastan*.

14. Kanpuri, *Zikr e fankar chale*, 175–83.

15. Kanpuri, *Zikr e fankar chale*, 176–77.

16. For a reading of *Neend*, see N. Rehman, "Pakistan, History, and Sleep."

17. Shakur, "Riaz Shahid."

18. Gazdar, *Pakistan Cinema*, 92.
19. Kabir, *The Cinema in Pakistan*, 170.
20. Kabir, *The Cinema in Pakistan*, 89.
21. On Pakistani cinema's relation to Bombay cinema: "Pakistan began with a micro film industry based at Lahore inheriting all that was bad in the filmart dispensed from the subcontinent's erstwhile film capital, Bombay." Kabir, *The Cinema in Pakistan*, 81. On cultural awareness: "Any artistic upliftment of the cinema must be preceded by radical changes in the social outlook particularly in that of the new middle-class of West Pakistan. Education and culture are synonymous. Without the participation of socially conscious and truly 'cultivated' individuals, no artistic development is possible in the state of the cinema. At present, needless to say, this participation is insignificant." Kabir, *The Cinema in Pakistan*, 60. On plagiarism: "Lahore discovered a surprisingly easy but ethically indefensible way out—plagiarism. Story elements, treatments, musical scores including songs, even the titles from Bombay productions began to be plagiarized. One producer went for even greater 'perfection' and imported a plagiarism-expert from India who could reproduce latest 'hits' of Indian screen with greater authenticity except for the cast which just had to be Pakistani." Kabir, *The Cinema in Pakistan*, 82. On stereotypes: "Generally, there is no story without the romantic trio—two girls (one of whom is usually poor) and one boy. Rarely do two boys fight over the same girl unless one is a copy-book villain. In no story is the heroine allowed to confront the problem of having to choose from two equally attractive suitors because it is not nice for an oriental girl to have such a dilemma. She is, however, allowed to fall headlong for the one and only who is to be her husband in the end. Nearly the same goes for the hero. He, too, is never told to choose from two equally pretty, homely, and devoted maidens. The theme is usually divided into three parts. In the first, the trio let out their overtures. In the second, the feudal father or a dominating mother or whoever is the boss lets loose the strains and stresses in the intra-trio relationship. In the last, the climax arrives; the good and the lovables triumph and the trouble-makers either die off or become sincerely repentant. The values that are loudly glorified are the dignity of the poor (this often amounts to a glorification of poverty), right of the poor girl to love and marry the rich boy, the real evil is money and not quite its hoarder, benevolent aristocracy is preferable to its other varieties, sanctity of law and order and nationalism (this is often mistaken for patriotism and frequently reduced to chauvinism). Elements denounced are high society life (portrayed with parties, night-clubs, bars etc.) and westernization of the womenfolk." Kabir, *The Cinema in Pakistan*, 85–87. On realism: "The basic pattern of the themes of Lahore or Karachi productions is more or less fixed and few directors would dare to venture into variations outside it. All stories have a built-in fairy-tale-like quality. Problems of various kinds are created without regard for realism. As unreal problems do not call for realistic solutions, the 'problems' created in the films are solved just as extraordinarily so that in the end the audiences can go home without anything to think about." Kabir, *The Cinema in Pakistan*, 85. On sexuality: "Sex still remains the earner of bread and butter, by and large. In Punjabi films this is often stretched to newer and wider limits of vulgarity

(sex in the Pakistani cinema usually means a display of the vital parts of a plump actress). No director would dare to think in terms of telling a story that has some resemblance with reality without songs sung in the play-back and those voluptuous hip-shaking dances that do not contribute at all to the development of the theme." Kabir, *The Cinema in Pakistan*, 83. Also see 171.

22. Kabir, *The Cinema in Pakistan*, 87.
23. Kabir, *The Cinema in Pakistan*, 171.
24. Gazdar, *Pakistan Cinema*, 114.
25. K. Ali, *Communism in Pakistan*.
26. On the arbitrary and heavy-handed character of the Censor Board, see Gazdar, *Pakistan Cinema*, 72–73, 93. Also see the cartoon lampooning the Censor Board published in the film magazine *Nigar* in 1961 and reproduced in Siddique, "Nigar hai toh industry hai," 201.
27. Aijaz Gul notes, "As he [Riaz Shahid] had to face serious problems with the censor board, many people think that he died because of the system. His son Shaan, who is now a leading man in films, says: 'Mere baap ko cancer ne nahin, censor ne maara' (My father was killed not by cancer but by the censor)." Gul and Amanullah, "Aijaz Gul on Cinema in Pakistan," 181. Also see Kanpuri, *Zikr e fankar chale*, 181; Gazdar, *Pakistan Cinema*, 93.
28. Jameson, "Reification and Utopia in Mass Culture," 137.
29. Jameson, "Reification and Utopia in Mass Culture," 140.
30. Jameson, "Reification and Utopia in Mass Culture," 141.
31. Wani, *Fantasy of Modernity*, 24.
32. Hall, "Notes on Deconstructing the Popular [1981]," 348.
33. Hall, "Notes on Deconstructing the Popular [1981]," 356.
34. Barelvi, *Habib Jalib*, 148.
35. Jaffery, "Lahore Calling"; Barelvi, *Habib Jalib*, 152.
36. Jalib uses the term "biggest S.H.O." (The station house officer is the officer in charge of a police station in Pakistan.) Jalib, *Jalib biti*, 71.
37. Barelvi, *Habib Jalib*, 151.
38. Z. Shahid, "How Habib Jalib and Riaz Shahid Forged the Way for Socialist Cinema in Pakistan."
39. For example, see Gazdar, *Pakistan Cinema*, 92–93 and 113; Rabe, "Raqs zanjeer pehen kar bhi kiya jata hai"; Mehmood, "Flashback."
40. Faiz, "Film."
41. Jameson, "Reification and Utopia in Mass Culture," 141.
42. Rajadhyaksha, "The Lahore Effect."
43. For a recitation in his own voice of Habib Jalib's poem "Dastoor," which he wrote against Ayub Khan's new constitution, see Akbar, *Habib Jalib*. At demonstrations in India in 2019 and 2020, the poetry of Jalib and Faiz has been recited. See, for example, Rahman, "Habib Jalib, His Dastoor"; S. Ali, "Habib Jalib, Pakistan's Poet of Dissent Whose Lines Are Now Chanted on Both Sides of Border."
44. I thank Aamir Mufti for his advice with this translation. For the full poem and translation, see Faiz, *Poems by Faiz*, 230–32.

45. See Manishita Dass's reading of the bazaar in her discussion of cinema and the public sphere in late colonial India. Dass, *Outside the Lettered City*, 96–97.
46. Bhaumik, "The Emergence of the Bombay Film Industry, 1913-1936."
47. While *Zerqa* champions Palestinian resistance, it also veers into stereotyping Africans and Jews. Ahmad, "Birth of a (Muslim) Nation." For an enthusiastically affirmative reading of the film, see Petiwala, "*Falasteen Ka Matlab Kya*?"
48. A. Parvez, "Neelo"; Lone, "Memorable Romance."
49. Christians and Hindus have played a key role in cinema in Pakistan. For example, see Rabe, "Five Pakistani-Christian Singers."
50. For a discussion of the language politics among the leftists in West Pakistan and the widespread sense of racial superiority, see K. Ali, *Communism in Pakistan*, 107–9, 200–205.
51. Alamgir Kabir's book, which was also published in 1969, just two years before the break of the country, and his sustained criticism of the Lahore and Karachi filmmakers can therefore also be read in the context of the growing estrangement and the divergence of the trajectory of cinema between the two wings of the country. Kabir, *The Cinema in Pakistan*.
52. Manishita Dass, "Cinetopia," 111.
53. Aijaz Gul notes, for example, that *Clerk* is "a good example of a film that deals with the poverty of an ordinary clerk who resists corruption, bribery and palm greasing, and who lives by his own rules ... a good subject, but didn't do very well at the box-office because it was very sad and grim." Gul and Amanullah, "Aijaz Gul on Cinema in Pakistan," 181.
54. On the roles played by Kumar in Bombay, see Siddique, "From Gandhi to Jinnah."
55. Gorija, *Pakistan ki 100 shahkar filmen*; Kanpuri, *Yadgar filmen*.
56. Adnan, "As a Young Man, I Wanted to Write Short Stories, Not Dramas and Films."
57. Faiz, "Film."
58. As Mushtaq Gazdar puts it, "Though their work lacked artistic and technical finesse, its impact on the common people was direct and unambiguous." Gazdar, *Pakistan Cinema*, 90.
59. On traditional leisure activities in Lahore, see Frembgen and Rollier, *Wrestlers, Pigeon Fanciers, and Kite Flyers*.
60. K. Ali, "On Female Friendships & Anger," 125.
61. K. Ali, "On Female Friendships & Anger," 125.
62. K. Ali, "On Female Friendships & Anger," 125.
63. Faiz, "Film."
64. Documents and reflections on Manto's contribution to cinema are compiled in Abbas, *Manto filmen (mubahis)*.
65. D. Mukherjee, "The Lost Films of Sa'adat Hasan Manto"; Anjum, *Manto aur cinema*.
66. For a profile of Iqbal Shehzad from 1966, see "Men and Ideas: Iqbal Shahzad."
67. "The film, unlike the original story, is forcibly injected with principles of probity." Narayan, "The Forbidden Jhumke."
68. Kabir, *The Cinema in Pakistan*, 87–88.

69. Kabir, *The Cinema in Pakistan*, 88.
70. Kanpuri, *Yadgar filmen*, 51–52.
71. "From this point, the wife becomes a zombie, a *ṭhanḍā gosht* (cold meat [or a corpse]), to use the title of another Manto story," notes Hari Narayan in his review. Narayan, "The Forbidden Jhumke."
72. Jameson, "Reification and Utopia in Mass Culture," 141.
73. Gazdar, *Pakistan Cinema*, 98–100.
74. Narayan, "The Forbidden Jhumke."
75. Anjum, *Manto aur cinema*, 459.
76. Z. Shahid, "Iqbal Shehzad."
77. "Hindi movies virtually never use *rag* or any other kind of Indian melody including folk or film melody, in scenes of disturbance. Moreover . . . many of the Western sounding techniques for creating disturbance, extensive chromatic movement, whole tone scales, diminished sevenths, and unmelodic motifs, apparently do so by virtue of being altogether out of the musical logic of any kind of Indian melody." Morcom, *Hindi Film Songs and the Cinema*, 173.
78. According to Hari Narayan, the film's "commercial success owed greatly to its music." Narayan, "The Forbidden Jhumke."
79. "Deebo Bhattacharya"; A. Parvez, "Deebo Bhattacharya—a Captivating Composer." For a profile from 1966, see "Men and Ideas: Deboo Bhatacharjee."
80. Mirza Ghalib, "Hazaron khwahishen aisi ki har khwahish pe dam nikle," Rekhta, accessed July 13, 2020, www.rekhta.org/ghazals/hazaaron-khvaahishen-aisii-ki-har-khvaahish-pe-dam-nikle-mirza-ghalib-ghazals; Frances Pritchett, "219_03 [Ghalib, Ghazal 219, Verse 3]," Divan-e Ghalib, accessed July 13, 2020, www.columbia.edu/itc/mealac/pritchett/00ghalib/219/219_03.html.
81. Narayan, "The Forbidden Jhumke."
82. Kabir, *The Cinema in Pakistan*, 87.

4. THE *ZINDA BHAAG* ASSEMBLAGE

1. "History—Lok Virsa," Lok Virsa, accessed July 25, 2020, https://lokvirsa.org.pk/history. In 2019, Lok Virsa Museum screened *Susraal* (1962) as part of its "initiative to revive the classical cinema," according to Radio Pakistan. "Lok Virsa Screens Film Susral," Radio Pakistan, March 10, 2019, www.radio.gov.pk/10-03-2019/lok-virsa-screens-film-susral. For an assessment of Lok Virsa and its promotion of "folk" culture, see Gilmartin and Maskiell, "Appropriating the Punjabi Folk."
2. Gazdar, *Pakistan Cinema*, 240.
3. See the introduction for a discussion of the Lahore effect. For Rajadhyaksha's elaboration, see his "The Lahore Effect."
4. Matteela's website is http://matteela.org.
5. The film was made as part of a project on masculinity titled Let's Talk Men, supported by Partners for Prevention, a joint program of four United Nations agencies for the prevention of gender-based violence. Directors Gaur and Nabi note, "The project came our way in 2010. . . . The commissioning editor was

very open about it and didn't try to introduce any particular agenda into the film.... That was fantastic because the story of *Zinda Bhaag* deals with 'issues' at a subterranean level and not in a very obvious way.... The commissioning editor of the series was Rahul Roy, himself a very well-known documentary film-maker.... Part of the funds for *Zinda Bhaag* were covered by this project, and the rest we raised privately." Meenu Gaur, personal communication, July 7, 2017.

6. Gaur notes that the casting process was in some ways the opposite of the use of experienced actors and involved a development of method acting: "These were non-actors ... What we did was look for particular personalities in the open auditions, and then during the rehearsal period develop the character further according to the personality of the person playing the role, e.g., Khurram Patras matched Khaldi's personality in the auditions." Meenu Gaur, personal communication, July 2, 2017.

7. W. Masood, "Down the River of Windfall Lights."

8. Ahmad, "New Cinema from Pakistan," 343–72; Hamid, "The Birth of a Cinema in Post-9/11 Pakistan"; Hamid, "Behind the Scenes."

9. Rajadhyaksha, "The Lahore Effect."

10. Hayles, "Cognitive Assemblages." For Kajri Jain, in her earlier work on bazaar aesthetics in India and her more recent study of monumental cement sculpture in India, the word *assemblage* denotes "a confluence of heterogeneous systems and processes whose combination exceeds the acts and putative ends of its individual elements, and that enter further combinations with other assemblages." K. Jain, "Post-reform India's Automotive-Iconic-Cement Assemblages."

11. Ahmad, "Film and Cinephilia in Pakistan"; Ahmad, "Explorations into Pakistani Cinema."

12. Ahmad, "New Cinema from Pakistan," 360–61.

13. Hoad, "Is Pakistani Film Experiencing a Revival?"

14. Ahmad, "Film and Cinephilia in Pakistan," 90–92. See also Kirk, "'A Camera from the Time of the British.'"

15. On *Zibahkhana*, see Khan and Ahmad, "From Zinda Laash to Zibahkhana"; Kirk, "Working Class Zombies and Men in Burqas"; and S. Masood, "Visions of Queer Anarchism."

16. Ahmad, "New Cinema from Pakistan," 358–63.

17. See Ahmad, "New Cinema from Pakistan"; Paracha, "New-Wave of Pakistani Cinema."

18. The television serial since the late 1970s is arguably a more influential medium in contemporary Pakistan than its cinema, but the limited number of studies of the serials have largely not focused on their formal characteristics. Recent publications include Kothari, "From Genre to Zanaana." The recent special issue of *BioScope: South Asian Screen Studies* 10, no. 2 (2019) on "Televisual Pakistan" includes essays on the television serial by Aisha Malik and Eliot Montpellier and an interview with serial writer Haseena Moin. And the inaugural issue of the online journal *Reel Pakistan: A Screen Studies Forum* 1 (2020) includes several student essays on Pakistani cinema and television serials. https://reelpakistan.lums.edu.pk/volumes.

19. For an account of the reforms enacted under President Pervez Musharraf, see Kazi, *Religious Television and Pious Authority in Pakistan*, 36–43.
20. The importance of media in constituting a sense of community follows and updates Benedict Anderson's influential account of the rise of the concept of the modern nation through print capitalism. Anderson, *Imagined Communities*.
21. Zahid Chaudhary and the author interviewed Gaur at Princeton University on April 27, 2017.
22. Meenu Gaur, personal communication, April 27, 2017. The making of the film poster also referred to the making of publicity for earlier films. S. Iqbal created the poster art for *Zinda Bhaag* in a traditional hand-painted style that has now become virtually extinct. *Zinda Bhaag's Hand Made Poster*.
23. On the formal and theoretical significance of narrative interruption in Indian action cinema, see Gopalan, *Cinema of Interruptions*. On the rise of "item numbers," see Brara, "The Item Number."
24. For a biographical account of Pran, see Reuben, *—And Pran*.
25. For example, see the compilation *Pran—Villain of the Millennium—Best Dialogues*, YouTube, 2012, www.youtube.com/watch?v=jIhB4NYNKlw.
26. Nadeem Paracha's recapitulation of the citational typage of such characters is noteworthy: "If you ever catch a Pakistani film of the 1960s and 1970s . . . you will notice that most films shared visual and contextual commonalities regarding their portrayal of rich people. . . . A rich father would almost always be in a suit or a nightgown and thick glasses, holding a walking stick and chewing on a pipe. His daughter could often be seen skipping down from the twisty staircase in a white miniskirt, rolling a badminton racket in her hands and announcing, 'Daddy, I go keelub and play badminton.' At the keelub (club) she would venture from the badminton court to the bar where the lecherous owner of the club (usually played by the late great Aslam Parvez) would make her sip some whiskey. A mere sip would suffice for the girl to go dashing towards the dance floor to do the most anarchic version of the 'hippie shake' this side of the '70s, before passing out. She would then usually wake up to realise that the lewd club owner had raped her in her drunken state." Paracha, "New-Wave of Pakistani Cinema."
27. "Directors of Pak's Oscar Entry Zinda Bhaag Talk about Its Universal Appeal."
28. R. Majumdar, "Art Cinema."
29. A. Jain, "The Curious Case of the Films Division"; Deprez, "The Films Division of India, 1948–1964"; Adajania, "New Media Overtures before New Media Practice in India"; Jhaveri, "Building on a Prehistory."
30. According to veteran media professional Javed Jabbar, an organization named Pakistan Institute for the Study of Film Art showed Satyajit Ray films in 1977. Jabbar, "The Little Road." The Kara Film Festival from 2001 to 2009 promoted critical viewership of thoughtful cinema in Karachi. More work is needed to understand the role of film societies and viewing practices for alternative and world cinema in Pakistan.
31. See H. Zaidi, "Herald Exclusive."
32. "Jamil Dehlavi's *Blood of Hussain*, released in England . . . was banned under martial law and remains effectively proscribed." "A. J. Kardar's *Door Hey*

Sukh Ka Gaon [Faraway village of peace], funded during the rule of Zulfiqar Ali Bhutto (1973–1977), never left the English laboratory it was sent to for post-production due to financing problems." Ahmad, "Film and Cinephilia in Pakistan," 82.
33. On the new hybrid, see Devasundaram, *India's New Independent Cinema*. On *hatke* films, see the interviews by Elahe Hiptoola, Rucha Pathak, and Anurag Kashyap in Dwyer and Pinto, *Beyond the Boundaries of Bollywood*.
34. Devasundaram, *India's New Independent Cinema*, 2.
35. Devasundaram, *India's New Independent Cinema*, 6–7.
36. "The traditional Western conception of Indie cinema as films created outside the studio system is not necessarily applicable to Indian Indies, which often solicit the financial and infrastructural support of big corporate studios and Bollywood in order to survive." Devasundaram, *India's New Independent Cinema*, 271.
37. Devasundaram, *India's New Independent Cinema*, 242.
38. Rubina practices "shop giving" rather than "shoplifting" in order to create demand for her soap. The term "shop giving" was deployed by the artist collective The Yes Men, who in their Barbie Liberation Organization project switched the voice boxes of several Barbie dolls and G.I. Joe action figures and then placed the altered toys back on the shelves for unsuspecting consumers to purchase. Firestone, "While Barbie Talks Tough, G. I. Joe Goes Shopping."
39. Siddiqa, *Military Inc*. As Ali Nobil Ahmad memorably notes, "New Cinema's best financed, most technologically advanced and highest-grossing films are also those most likely to warm the miniscule hearts of ISPR . . . ideologues and censors." Ahmad, "New Cinema from Pakistan," 347; "How Well Did Movies with ISPR Backing Do at the Box Office?"; Bokhari, "I Finally Watched Kaaf Kangana and Instantly Wished I Hadn't."
40. Ahmad, "New Cinema from Pakistan," 361.
41. See Paracha, "Whatever Happened to Pakistan's Film Industry?"; Ahmad, "New Cinema from Pakistan."
42. "*Zinda Bhaag* also contracted production and post-production assistance from across the border, a common practice in Pakistani New Cinema, where the lack of technical infrastructure and personnel in Pakistan compels filmmakers to work with Indian or Thai expertise. In the case of *Zinda Bhaag*, the fact that many of the Indian personnel were familiar with Punjabi was an additional asset in terms of their being familiar with the site and context of the film." Meenu Gaur, personal communication, April 27, 2017; July 2, 2017.
43. Meenu Gaur, personal communication, April 27, 2017.
44. Farina Mir has noted that the *Hir-Ranjha* story "surfaces repeatedly in Punjab's history in places one would least expect to find it or any other love story," such as being embedded in a Sikh dynastic history from 1849 and used as a "sacred" book upon which anticolonial revolutionaries took oath in court in 1940. Mir, *The Social Space of Language*, 1–3. On the *var*, see p. 38.
45. For an analysis of the persistence of the Oriental film into the fifties in Bombay, see R. Thomas, *Bombay before Bollywood*. On Bombay films that draw from Islamicate legends and lyric tropes, see A. G. Roy, *Cinema of Enchantment*. For an account of

Sufi tropes in Urdu poetry and in the *qiṣṣa* from North India, see Satia, "Poets of Partition."

46. Meenu Gaur, personal communication, July 2, 2017.
47. Zinda Bhaag, *The Genius behind Pani Da Bulbula*; "Zinda Bhaag Revives 'Pani Da Bulbula.'" Significantly, these popular references depart from the crisis-ridden role of Punjabiyat as a living subaltern form of comedy and theater as much as of Sufi verse, albeit one without any purchase on power.
48. "'Ei poth jodi na sesh hoye' (Bangla Song), 2011," YouTube, accessed June 8, 2017, www.youtube.com/watch?v=lEzqQNh7oKY. "This Kumar/Sen hit . . . including their characteristic low-angle, soft-focus close-ups and stylized movements, yielded one of the most popular song picturizations of the decade, the classic motor bike scene number *'Ei path jadi na shesh hoi.'*" "Saptapadi (Ajoy Kar) 1961," Indiancine.ma, accessed April 4, 2020.
49. Meenu Gaur, personal communication, July 17, 2017.
50. Meenu Gaur, personal communication, July 17, 2017.
51. Elias, *On Wings of Diesel*; Paracha, "Beyond 'Horn OK Please.'"
52. Meenu Gaur, personal communication, July 17, 2017.
53. "*Wa-Yabqa-Wajh-o-Rabbik*—Faiz Ahmad Faiz," *Rekhta*, accessed June 8, 2017, https://rekhta.org/nazms/va-yabqaa-vajh-o-rabbik-faiz-ahmad-faiz-nazms.
54. An article from 1965 in *Eastern Film* magazine titled "Pak Film Industry Meets Afro-Asian Delegates" notes that "Iqbal Bano . . . stole the show with Faiz Ahmed Faiz's ghazal." It is unclear as to which specific poem by Faiz was presented there. "Pak Film Industry Meets Afro-Asian Delegates."
55. However, Faiz's poem, along with lyrics of Habib Jalib's poetry (as noted in chapter 3), have been deployed in street demonstrations in India against the government in 2019 and 2020. See, for example, Daniyal, "The Art of Resistance"; Rahman, "Habib Jalib, His Dastoor"; S. Ali, "Habib Jalib, Pakistan's Poet of Dissent Whose Lines Are Now Chanted on Both Sides of Border."
56. S. Khan, "Zinda Bhaag's Music Is Quintessentially Pakistani."
57. Ahmad, "New Cinema from Pakistan," 364.
58. Rajadhyaksha, "The Lahore Effect," 332.

BIBLIOGRAPHY

Abbas, Tahir, ed. *Manto filmen (mubahis)*. Lahore: Aks, 2019.

Acharyah, Barhaspati. *Musalman aur barr-i saghir ki mausiqi*. Lahore: Idarah-i Tahqiq Klasiki Mausiqi, 1980.

Adajania, Nancy. "New Media Overtures before New Media Practice in India." *Domus* 4, no. 3 (January 2015): 34–37.

Adnan, Ally. "As a Young Man, I Wanted to Write Short Stories, Not Dramas and Films: Faseeh Bari Khan." *Daily Times* (blog), May 13, 2018. https://dailytimes.com.pk/239215/as-a-young-man-i-wanted-to-write-short-stories-not-dramas-and-films-faseeh-bari-khan.

Afzal-Khan, Fawzia. *Siren Song: Understanding Pakistan through Its Women Singers*. Karachi: Oxford University Press, 2020.

Ahang-e-Khusravi: Gharanon ki gaiki. 20 vols. Karachi: EMI, 1978.

Ahang-e-Khusravi: Raag mala. 10 vols. Karachi: EMI, 1978.

Ahmad, Ali Nobil. "Birth of a (Muslim) Nation." *Caravan*, November 2019, 8–10.

———. "Explorations into Pakistani Cinema: Introduction." *Screen* 57, no. 4 (December 2016): 468–79.

———. "Film and Cinephilia in Pakistan: Beyond Life and Death." *BioScope: South Asian Screen Studies* 5, no. 2 (July 1, 2014): 81–98.

———. "New Cinema from Pakistan: Film, Technology and Media in Transition." In *Cinema and Society: Film and Social Change in Pakistan*, edited by Ali Khan and Ali Nobil Ahmad, 343–72. Karachi: Oxford University Press, 2016.

Ahmed, Ishtiaq. "How Pakistani Film Music Has Declined over the Decades." *Herald Magazine*, November 8, 2017. http://herald.dawn.com/news/1153897.

———. "The Lahore Film Industry: A Historical Sketch." In *Travels of Bollywood Cinema: From Bombay to LA*, edited by Anjali Gera Roy and Beng Huat Chua, 55–77. New Delhi: Oxford University Press, 2012.

Ahmed, M. A. "River Craft in Modern Bengal." *Pakistan Quarterly* 4, no. 2 (Summer 1954): 37–39.

Ahmed, Shoaib. "W. Z. Ahmed Passes Away." dawn.com. April 17, 2007. www.dawn.com/news/242776/w-z-ahmed-passes-away.

Akbar, Tariq. *Habib Jalib: Dastoor (the Constitution)*. YouTube. March 11, 2010. www.youtube.com/watch?v=8AKf1SSIWRE.

Akhter, Fahmida. "*Jibon Thekey Neya* (Glimpses of life, 1970): The First Political Film in Pre-liberation Bangladesh and a Cinematic Metaphor for Nationalist Concerns." *Journal of the Asiatic Society of Bangladesh* 59, no. 2 (2014): 291–303.

Ali, Kamran Asdar. "Cinema and Karachi in the 1960s: Cultural Wounds and National Cohesion." In *Handbook of Religion and the Asian City: Aspiration and Urbanization in the Twenty-First Century*, edited by Peter van der Veer, 387–402. Oakland, California: University of California Press, 2015.

———. *Communism in Pakistan: Politics and Class Activism, 1947–1972*. London: I. B. Tauris, 2015.

———. "Female Friendship and Forbidden Desire: Two Films from 1960s Pakistan." In *South Asian Filmscapes: Transregional Encounters*, edited by Elora Halim Chowdhury and Esha Niyogi De, 43–59. Seattle: University of Washington Press, 2020.

———. "On Female Friendships & Anger." In *Love, War & Other Longings: Essays on Cinema in Pakistan*, edited by Vazira Zamindar and Asad Ali, 114–30. Karachi: Oxford University Press, 2019.

Ali, Sajid. "Habib Jalib, Pakistan's Poet of Dissent Whose Lines Are Now Chanted on Both Sides of Border." ThePrint. November 28, 2019. https://theprint.in/features/habib-jalib-pakistans-poet-of-dissent-whose-lines-are-now-chanted-on-both-sides-of-border/326475.

Alonso, Isabel Huacuja. "Radio, Citizenship, and the 'Sound Standards' of a Newly Independent India." *Public Culture* 31, no. 1 (January 1, 2019): 117–44.

Amir, Tariq. "Bollywood's Pakistan Connection." *Pakistan Geotagging* (blog), August 27, 2014. http://pakgeotagging.blogspot.com/2014/08/bollywoods-pakistan-connection.html.

Amrohi, Izhar. "The Censor Problem." *Eastern Film* 7, no. 9 (April 1966): 7.

Amstutz, Andrew McKinney. "Finding a Home for Urdu: Islam and Science in Modern South Asia." PhD diss., Cornell University, 2017.

Anderson, Benedict R. O'G. *Imagined Communities: Reflections on the Origin and Spread of Nationalism*. Rev. ed. London: Verso, 2006.

Anjaria, Ulka. *Realism in the Twentieth-Century Indian Novel: Colonial Difference and Literary Form*. New York: Cambridge University Press, 2012.

Anjum, Pervez. *Manto aur cinema*. Lahore: Sang-e-Meel, 2014.

Anwar, Abdul Aziz. *Film Industry in West Pakistan*. Lahore: Board of Economic Inquiry Punjab (Pakistan), 1957.

Askari, Muhammad Hasan. "Building Pakistan and Filmmaking." Translated by Ali Nobil Ahmad. *BioScope: South Asian Screen Studies* 5, no. 2 (July 1, 2014): 175–81.

Aujla, Harjap Singh. "Khurshid Anwar, a Prince among the Music Directors of the Sub-continent and His Exploits in British and Independent India." *Academy of the Punjab in North America* (blog), accessed June 12, 2020. www.apnaorg.com/articles/aujla-7.

Aziz, Ashraf. *Light of the Universe: Essays on Hindustani Film Music*. New Delhi: Three Essays Collective, 2003.

Back, Jean, and Viktoria Schmidt-Linsenhoff, eds. *The Family of Man 1955–2001: Humanismus und Postmoderne: Eine Revision von Edward Steichens Fotoausstellung* [Humanism and postmodernism: A reappraisal of the photo exhibition by Edward Steichen]. Marburg: Jonas Verlag, 2004.

Bakhle, Janaki. *Two Men and Music: Nationalism in the Making of an Indian Classical Tradition*. Oxford: Oxford University Press, 2005.

Bali, Karan. "Most Pakistani Hindu Filmmakers Fled after 1947, but Not JC Anand." Scroll.in. May 10, 2016. https://scroll.in/reel/807775/most-pakistani-hindu-filmmakers-fled-after-1947-but-not-jc-anand.
Bandyopadhyay, Manik. *Padma River Boatman*. Translated by Barbara Painter and Yann Lovelock. St. Lucia: University of Queensland Press, 1973.
Barelvi, Mujahid, ed. *Habib Jalib: shakhsiyyat, sha'iri*. Quetta: Goshah-yi Adab, 1991.
Barthes, Roland. *Mythologies: The Complete Edition, in a New Translation*. Translated by Richard Howard and Annette Lavers. 2nd ed. New York: Hill and Wang, 2013.
Bashir, Ahmad. "Main nahin manta." In *Habib Jalib: shakhsiyyat, sha'iri*, edited by Mujahid Barelvi, 73–75. Quetta: Goshah-yi Adab, 1991.
Bazin, André. "A Pure Masterpiece: The River." In *Jean Renoir*, 104–19. New York: Simon and Schuster, 1973.
———. *What Is Cinema?* Vol. 2. Translated by Hugh Gray. Berkeley: University of California Press, 1971.
Beaster-Jones, Jayson. *Bollywood Sounds: The Cosmopolitan Mediations of Hindi Film Song*. New York: Oxford University Press, 2015.
Bharucha, Rustom. "The Indian People's Theatre Association (IPTA)." In *In the Name of the Secular: Contemporary Cultural Activism in India*, 26–51. Delhi: Oxford University Press, 1998.
———. *Rehearsals of Revolution: The Political Theater of Bengal*. Honolulu: University of Hawaii Press, 1983.
Bhaskar, Ira. "Expressionist Aurality: The Stylized Aesthetic of Bhava in Indian Melodrama." In *Melodrama Unbound: Across History, Media, and National Cultures*, edited by Linda Williams and Christine Gledhill, 253–72. New York: Columbia University Press, 2018.
Bhatia, Nandi. "Staging Resistance: The Indian People's Theatre Association." In *The Politics of Culture in the Shadow of Capital*, edited by Lisa Lowe and David Lloyd, 432–60. Durham: Duke University Press, 1997.
Bhattacharya, Malini. "The Indian People's Theatre Association: A Preliminary Sketch of the Movement and the Organization, 1942–47." In *Modern Indian Theatre: A Reader*, edited by Nandi Bhatia, 158–81. Delhi: Oxford University Press, 2009.
Bhaumik, Kaushik. "The Emergence of the Bombay Film Industry, 1913–1936." PhD diss., Oxford University, 2001.
Biswas, Moinak. "In the Mirror of an Alternative Globalism: The Neorealist Encounter in India." In *Italian Neorealism and Global Cinema*, edited by Laura E. Ruberto and Kristi M. Wilson, 72–90. Contemporary Approaches to Film and Television Series. Detroit: Wayne State University Press, 2007.
Bokhari, Haiya. "I Finally Watched Kaaf Kangana and Instantly Wished I Hadn't." dawn.com. November 15, 2019. https://images.dawn.com/news/1184022.
Booth, Gregory D. *Behind the Curtain: Making Music in Mumbai's Film Studios*. New York: Oxford University Press, 2008.
———. "A Moment of Historical Conjuncture in Mumbai: Playback Singers, Music Directors, and Arrangers and the Creation of Hindi Song (1948–1952)." In *More than Bollywood: Studies in Indian Popular Music*, edited by Gregory D. Booth and Bradley Shope, 21–37. New York: Oxford University Press, 2014.

———. "That Bollywood Sound." In *Global Soundtracks: Worlds of Film Music*, edited by Mark Slobin, 85–113. Music/Culture. Middletown, CT: Wesleyan University Press, 2008.

Brara, Rita. "The Item Number: Cinesexuality in Bollywood and Social Life." *Economic and Political Weekly* 45, no. 23 (June 5, 2010): 67–74.

Bukhari, Syed Zulfiqar Ali. *Sarguzasht*. Lahore: Al-Hamd, 2013.

Chatterjee, Saibal. "A Treasure Regained: A Neo-realist Gem Shows Pakistani Cinema in a New Light." DNA India. June 11, 2016. www.dnaindia.com/analysis/column-a-treasure-regained-2222123.

Chaudhari, Zahoor. *Jahan-i fan*. Lahore: Fiction House, 2005.

Chowdhury, Elora Halim, and Esha Niyogi De, eds. *South Asian Filmscapes: Transregional Encounters*. Seattle: University of Washington Press, 2020.

Chughtai, Abdur Rahman. *Maqalat-i Chughtai*. Edited by Shima Majid. 2 vols. Islamabad: Idarah-yi Saqafat-i Pakistan, 1987.

Cooper, Sarah. "Henfi Agel's Cinema of Contemplation: Renoir and Philosophy." In *A Companion to Jean Renoir*, edited by Alastair Phillips and Ginette Vincendeau, 313–27. Chichester, West Sussex, UK: Wiley-Blackwell, 2013.

Cooper, Timothy P. A. "Raddi Infrastructure: Collecting Film Memorabilia in Pakistan: An Interview with Guddu Khan of Guddu's Film Archive." *BioScope: South Asian Screen Studies* 7, no. 2 (December 1, 2016): 151–71.

Coppola, Carlo. *Marxist Influences and South Asian Literature*. South Asia Series, occasional paper no. 23. East Lansing: Asian Studies Center, Michigan State University, 1974.

———. *Urdu Poetry, 1935–1970: The Progressive Episode*. The Platinum Series. Karachi, Pakistan: Oxford University Press, 2017.

Dadi, Iftikhar. "Between Neorealism and Humanism: Jago Hua Savera." In *Forms of the Left in Postcolonial South Asia: Aesthetics, Networks and Connected Histories*, edited by Sanjukta Sunderason and Lotte Hoek, 97–134. London: Bloomsbury Academic, 2021.

———. "Lineages of Pakistan's 'Urdu' Cinema: Mode, Mood and Genre in Zehr-e Ishq / Poison of Love (1958)." *Screen* 57, no. 4 (December 2016): 480–87.

———. *Modernism and the Art of Muslim South Asia*. Chapel Hill: University of North Carolina Press, 2010.

———. "Registering Crisis: Ethnicity in Pakistani Cinema of the 1960s and 1970s." In *Beyond Crisis: Re-evaluating Pakistan*, edited by Naveeda Ahmed Khan, 145–76. New Delhi: Routledge, 2010.

———. "The Zinda Bhaag Assemblage: Notes on Reflexivity and Form." In *Love, War & Other Longings: Essays on Cinema in Pakistan*, edited by Vazira Zamindar and Asad Ali, 86–113. Karachi: Oxford University Press, 2019.

Damodaran, Sumangala. *The Radical Impulse: Music in the Tradition of the Indian People's Theatre Association*. New Delhi: Tulika Books, 2017.

Daniyal, Shoaib. "The Art of Resistance: How Faiz's 'Hum Dekhenge' Has Battled Tyranny across Time and Place." Scroll.in. January 1, 2020. https://scroll.in/article/948419/the-art-of-resistance-how-faizs-hum-dekhenge-has-battled-tyranny-across-time-and-place.

Dass, Manishita. "Cinetopia: Leftist Street Theatre and the Musical Production of the Metropolis in 1950s Bombay Cinema." *Positions: Asia Critique* 25, no. 1 (February 2017): 101–24.

———. "Look Back in Angst: Akaler Sandhaney and the Afterlife of the IPTA Movement." In *Forms of the Left: Left-Wing Aesthetics and Postcolonial South Asia*, edited by Lotte Hoek and Sanjukta Sunderason, 213–35. London: Bloomsbury, 2021.

———. *Outside the Lettered City: Cinema, Modernity, and the Public Sphere in Late Colonial India*. New York: Oxford University Press, 2016.

"Deebo Bhattacharya." Cineplot.com. October 24, 2011. https://cineplot.com/deebo-bhattacharya.

Denning, Michael. *Noise Uprising: The Audiopolitics of a World Musical Revolution*. London: Verso, 2015.

Deprez, Camille. "The Films Division of India, 1948–1964: The Early Days and the Influence of the British Documentary Film Tradition." *Film History: An International Journal* 25, no. 3 (2013): 149–73.

Desoulieres, Alain. "Historical Fiction and Style: The Case of Anarkali." *Annual of Urdu Studies* 22 (2007): 67–98.

Devasundaram, Ashvin Immanuel. *India's New Independent Cinema: Rise of the Hybrid*. New York: Routledge, 2016.

"Directors of Pak's Oscar Entry Zinda Bhaag Talk about Its Universal Appeal." Firstpost. October 3, 2013. www.firstpost.com/entertainment/directors-of-paks-oscar-entry-zinda-bhaag-talk-about-its-universal-appeal-1150553.html.

Doss, Erika, ed. *Looking at LIFE Magazine*. Washington, DC: Smithsonian Institution Press, 2001.

Dwyer, Rachel. *Filming the Gods: Religion and Indian Cinema*. London: Routledge, 2006.

Dwyer, Rachel, and Jerry Pinto, eds. *Beyond the Boundaries of Bollywood: The Many Forms of Hindi Cinema*. South Asian Cinema. New Delhi: Oxford University Press, 2011.

Eck, Diana L. *Darśan: Seeing the Divine Image in India*. 3rd ed. New York: Columbia University Press, 1998.

Elam, J. Daniel. "Commonplace Anti-colonialism: Bhagat Singh's Jail Notebook and the Politics of Reading." *South Asia: Journal of South Asian Studies* 39, no. 3 (July 2, 2016): 592–607.

Elam, J. Daniel, and Chris Moffat. "On the Form, Politics and Effects of Writing Revolution." *South Asia: Journal of South Asian Studies* 39, no. 3 (July 2, 2016): 513–24.

Elias, Jamal J. *On Wings of Diesel: Trucks, Identity and Culture in Pakistan*. Oxford: Oneworld, 2011.

Fair, Laura. *Reel Pleasures: Cinema Audiences and Entrepreneurs in Twentieth-Century Urban Tanzania*. Athens, OH: Ohio University Press, 2018.

Faiz, Faiz Ahmed. "Film." In *Mata'-i lauh o qalam*, 249–53. Karachi: Maktabah-yi Daniyal, 1973.

———. *Mah o sal-i ashna'i: yadon ka majmu'ah*. Karachi: Maktabah-yi Daniyal, 1981.

———. "Musavvir-i Mashriq." In *Abdur Rahman Chughtai: shakhsiyyat aur fan*, edited by Vazir Agha, 68–74. Lahore: Majlis-i Taraqqi-yi Adab, 1980.

———. *Poems by Faiz*. Translated by Victor Kiernan. London: Allen & Unwin, 1971.

"The Fearless Zutshi Sisters of Lahore . . . Shyama, Manmohini and Janak." *Chinar Shade* (blog). August 29, 2016. http://autarmota.blogspot.com/2016/08/the-fearless-zutshi-sisters-of-lahore.html.

Feuer, Jane. "Singin' in the Rain (1952), Stanley Donen and Gene Kelly." In *Film Analysis: A Norton Reader*, edited by Jeffrey Geiger and R. L. Rutsky, 440–54. New York: W. W. Norton, 2005.

"Film Industry's Protest at Dacca, Lahore, Karachi against Recertification of Indian Films." *Eastern Film* 4, no. 9 (April 1963): 19–21.

Firestone, David. "While Barbie Talks Tough, G. I. Joe Goes Shopping." *New York Times*, December 31, 1993. www.nytimes.com/1993/12/31/us/while-barbie-talks-tough-g-i-joe-goes-shopping.html.

Folk Music of Pakistan: Recorded in Pakistan with the Cooperation of the Government of Pakistan. Program notes by John Gonella ([4]p.). New York: Folkways Records, 1951.

Frembgen, Jürgen Wasim, and Paul Rollier. *Wrestlers, Pigeon Fanciers, and Kite Flyers: Traditional Sports and Pastimes in Lahore*. New Delhi: Oxford University Press, 2014.

Gardezi, Kasur. "Qafas dar qafas." In *Habib Jalib: shakhsiyyat, sha'iri*, edited by Mujahid Barelvi, 37–51. Quetta: Goshah-yi Adab, 1991.

Gazdar, Mushtaq. *Pakistan Cinema, 1947–1997*. Karachi: Oxford University Press, 1997.

Gilmartin, David, and Michelle Maskiell. "Appropriating the Punjabi Folk: Gender and Other Dichotomies in Colonial and Post-colonial Folk Studies." In *Pakistan at the Millennium*, edited by Charles H. Kennedy, Kathleen McNeil, Carl W. Ernst, and David Gilmartin, 40–64. Karachi: Oxford University Press, 2003.

Giovacchini, Saverio, and Robert Sklar, eds. *Global Neorealism: The Transnational History of a Film Style*. Jackson: University Press of Mississippi, 2011.

Gopalan, Lalitha. *Cinema of Interruptions: Action Genres in Contemporary Indian Cinema*. London: British Film Institute, 2002.

Gorija, Yasin. *Lakshmi Chowk: Filmi dunya ke dilchasp vaqiat*. Edited by Tufail Akhtar. Lahore: Prime Time, 2000.

———. *Malikah-yi Tarannum Nur Jahan fan ke a'ine men*. Lahore: Jan Book Depot, 2000.

———. *Pakistan ki 100 shahkar filmen*. Islamabad: Alhamra, 2000.

Gul, Aijaz. "A Short History of Pakistani Films." FIPRESCI—the international federation of film critics. Accessed June 12, 2020. http://fipresci.hegenauer.co.uk/world_cinema/south/south_english_asian_cinema_pakistan_history.htm.

Gul, Aijaz, and Arshad Amanullah. "Aijaz Gul on Cinema in Pakistan." In *Filming the Line of Control: The Indo-Pak Relationship through the Cinematic Lens*, edited by Meenakshi Bharat and Nirmal Kumar, 179–85. New Delhi: Routledge, 2008.

Haaland, Torunn. *Italian Neorealist Cinema*. Edinburgh: Edinburgh University Press, 2012.

Habib Jalib: fann aur shakhsiyyat. Lahore: Shaikh Ghulam Ali and Sons, 1978.

"Habib Jalib: The People's Poet and Historian." *Daily Times*, March 25, 2018. https://dailytimes.com.pk/219119/habib-jalib-the-peoples-poet-and-historian/.

Hall, Stuart. "Notes on Deconstructing the Popular [1981]." In *Essential Essays*. Vol. 1, *Foundations of Cultural Studies*, edited by David Morley, 347–61. Durham: Duke University Press, 2019.

Hamid, Zebunnisa. "Behind the Scenes: The Women Filmmakers of New Pakistani Cinema." *BioScope: South Asian Screen Studies* 11, no. 1 (2020): 15–26.

———. "The Birth of a Cinema in Post-9/11 Pakistan." In *South Asian Filmscapes: Transregional Encounters*, edited by Elora Halim Chowdhury and Esha Niyogi De, 216–30. Seattle: University of Washington Press, 2020.

Hansen, Kathryn. "Boucicault in Bombay: Global Theater Circuits and Domestic Melodrama in the Parsi Theater." In *Melodrama Unbound: Across History, Media, and National Cultures*, edited by Linda Williams and Christine Gledhill, 49–67. New York: Columbia University Press, 2018.

———. "Heteroglossia in Amanat's *Indar Sabha*." In *The Banyan Tree: Essays on Early Literature in New Indo-Aryan Languages*, edited by Mariola Offredi, 97–112. New Delhi: Manohar, 2000.

———. "The *Indar Sabha* Phenomenon: Public Theatre and Consumption in Greater India (1853–1956)." In *Pleasure and the Nation: The History, Politics, and Consumption of Public Culture in India*, edited by Rachel Dwyer and Christopher Pinney, 76–114. New Delhi: Oxford University Press, 2001.

———. "Languages on Stage: Linguistic Pluralism and Community Formation in the Nineteenth-Century Parsi Theatre." *Modern Asian Studies* 37, no. 2 (May 1, 2003): 381–405.

———. "Staging Composite Culture: Nautanki and Parsi Theatre in Recent Revivals." *South Asia Research* 29, no. 2 (July 1, 2009): 151–68.

Haq, Rizwanul. *Urdu fiction aur cinema*. Delhi: Educational Publishing House, 2008.

Haroon, Said A. "Editorial: After the 'Injunction.'" *Eastern Film* 4, no. 2 (June 1963): 5.

———. "Editorial: Censor Board." *Eastern Film* 7, no. 8 (March 1966): 5.

———. "Editorial: The Cloud without Silver Lining." *Eastern Film* 8, no. 8 (March 1967): 5.

———. "Editorial: The Curse." *Eastern Film* 5, no. 9 (April 1964): 5.

Hayles, N. Katherine. "Cognitive Assemblages: Technical Agency and Human Interactions." *Critical Inquiry* 43, no. 1 (September 1, 2016): 32–55.

Hoad, Phil. "Is Pakistani Film Experiencing a Revival?" Al Jazeera. February 3, 2017. www.aljazeera.com/features/2017/2/3/is-pakistani-film-experiencing-a-revival.

Hoek, Lotte. "The Conscience Whipper: Film Criticism and the Political Velocity of Cinema in 1960s East Pakistan." In *Forms of the Left: Left-Wing Aesthetics and Postcolonial South Asia*, edited by Lotte Hoek and Sanjukta Sunderason, 185–212. London: Bloomsbury, 2021.

———. "Cross-Wing Filmmaking: East Pakistani Urdu Films and Their Traces in the Bangladesh Film Archive." *BioScope: South Asian Screen Studies* 5, no. 2 (July 1, 2014): 99–118.

———. "Mirrors of Movement: *Aina*, Afzal Chowdhury's Cinematography and the Interlinked Histories of Cinema in Pakistan and Bangladesh." *Screen* 57, no. 4 (Winter 2016): 488–95. https://doi.org/10.1093/screen/hjw052.

"How Well Did Movies with ISPR Backing Do at the Box Office?" Samaa TV. August 21, 2018. www.samaa.tv/culture/2018/08/how-well-did-movies-with-ispr-backing-do-at-the-box-office.

Husain, Intezar. *Chiraghon ka dhuan: Yadon ke pachas baras*. Lahore: Sang-e-Meel, 2003.

"The India-Pakistan Masterpiece That Fell through the Cracks—BBC News." BBC News. Accessed June 5, 2016. www.bbc.com/news/world-asia-india-36417007?SThisFB.

"Introducing A. J. Kardar." *Eastern Film* 5, no. 5 (June 1963): 44.

Jabbar, Javed. "The Little Road: A Large Vision." In *Snapshots: Reflections in a Pakistani Eye*, 222–28. Lahore: Wajidalis, 1982.

Jaffery. "Khursheed Anwar: The Creative Rebel." *Eastern Film* 5, no. 12 (July 1964): 13.

———. "Lahore Calling: The Truth about the Neelo Affair." *Eastern Film* 6, no. 8 (March 1965): 21.

Jaikumar, Priya. *Where Histories Reside: India as Filmed Space*. Durham: Duke University Press, 2019.

Jain, Anuja. "The Curious Case of the Films Division: Some Annotations on the Beginnings of Indian Documentary Cinema in Postindependence India, 1940s–1960s." *Velvet Light Trap* 71, no. 1 (2013): 15–26.

Jain, Kajri. "Post-reform India's Automotive-Iconic-Cement Assemblages: Uneven Globality, Territorial Spectacle and Iconic Exhibition Value." *Identities: Global Studies in Culture and Power* 23, no. 3 (2016): 327–44.

Jalib, Habib. *Is shahr-i kharabi men*. Karachi: Maktabah-yi Daniyal, 1989.

———. *Jalib biti: 'avami sha'ir Habib Jalib ki kahani khud un ki zabani*. Edited by Asghar Tahir. Lahore: Jang, 1993.

Jalil, Rakhshanda. *Liking Progress, Loving Change: A Literary History of the Progressive Writers' Movement in Urdu*. New Delhi: Oxford University Press, 2014.

Jameson, Fredric. "Reification and Utopia in Mass Culture." *Social Text*, no. 1 (January 1, 1979): 130–48.

Jamil, Sayyid Mazhar. *Zikr-e-Faiz*. Karachi: Department of Culture, Government of Sindh, 2013.

Jasimuddin. "The Fisherman." Translated by Winfred Holmes. *Pakistan Quarterly* 4, no. 2 (1954): 40.

———. "The Folk Songs of East Bengal." *Pakistan Quarterly* 6, no. 3 (1956): 45–50.

Jhaveri, Shanay. "Building on a Prehistory: Artists' Film and New Media in India, Part 1." LUX. May 2, 2014. https://lux.org.uk/writing/building-prehistory-artists-film-new-media-india-part-1.

Jhingan, Shikha. "Sonic Ruptures: Music, Mobility and the Media." In *Media and Utopia: History, Imagination and Technology*, edited by Arvind Rajagopal and Anupama Rao, 209–34. New Delhi: Routledge India, 2016.

Kabir, Alamgir. *The Cinema in Pakistan*. Dacca: Sandhani, 1969.

———. *Film in Bangladesh*. Dacca: Bangla Academy, 1979.

Kanpuri, Zakhmi. *Dabistan-i film ke nagmahnigar*. Edited by Shahid Moin Faruqi. Karachi: Bazm-i Funun, 2002.

———. *Gaye ja git milan ke*. Karachi: City Book Point, 2011.

———. *Kahan tak suno ge*. Karachi: City Book Point, 2011.
———. *Mujhe sab hai yad zara zara*. Karachi: City Book Point, 2007.
———. *Pari chehre*. Karachi: City Book Point, 2007.
———. *Yadgar filmen*. Karachi: City Book Point, 2012.
———. *Yeh baten teri yeh fasane tere*. Karachi: City Book Point, 2010.
———. *Zikr e fankar chale*. Karachi: City Book Point, 2009.
Kapuria, Radha. "Music and Its Many Memories: Complicating 1947 for the Punjab." In *Partition and the Practice of Memory*, edited by Churnjeet Mahn and Anne Murphy, 17–42. Cham, Switzerland: Palgrave Macmillan, 2018.
Kausar, Asghar Ali. "Khawaja Khurshid Anwar ki kahani." *Imroze*, June 10–Sep 30, 1983.
Kazi, Taha. *Religious Television and Pious Authority in Pakistan*. Bloomington: Indiana University Press, 2021.
"Khalil Kaiser Murdered." *Eastern Film* 8, no. 3 (October 1966): 19.
Khan, Ali, and Ali Nobil Ahmad, eds. *Cinema and Society: Film and Social Change in Pakistan*. Karachi: Oxford University Press, 2016.
Khan, Ali, and Ali Nobil Ahmad. "From Zinda Laash to Zibahkhana: Violence and Horror in Pakistani Cinema." *Third Text* 24, no. 1 (January 2010): 149–61.
Khan, Jehangir A. "The Film Industry in West Pakistan." *Pakistan Quarterly* 7, no. 2 (Summer 1957): 56–64.
Khan, Mazhar Ali. "Ayub's Attack on Progressive Papers." dawn.com. November 13, 2017. www.dawn.com/news/1370051.
Khan, Sher. "Zinda Bhaag's Music Is Quintessentially Pakistani." Express Tribune, May 30, 2013. https://tribune.com.pk/story/556490/zinda-bhaags-music-is-quintessentially-pakistani.
Khan, Ustad Ghulam Haider. "Khawaja Khurshid Anwar." *Friday Times* 22, no. 52 (February 11, 2011): n.p.
Khwaja, Mushfiq. "'Shahab nama' ka maqsad akhfai'yi zat hai." In *Khamah bagoshiyan: Mushfiq Khvajah ke adabi kalam*, 230–40. Islamabad: Purab Academy, 2010.
Khwaja, Waqas A. "Khawaja Khurshid Anwar: A Brief Biography." Academia.edu. n.d. Accessed October 22, 2021. www.academia.edu/29542638/Khawaja_Khurshid_Anwar_A_Brief_Biography.
Kirk, Gwendolyn S. "'A Camera from the Time of the British': Film Technologies and Aesthetic Exclusion in Pakistani Cinema." *Screen* 57, no. 4 (December 2016): 496–502.
———. "This Is London, Not Pakistan! Articulations of the Diaspora in Pakistani Punjabi Film." In *South Asian Filmscapes: Transregional Encounters*, edited by Elora Halim Chowdhury and Esha Niyogi De, 197–215. Seattle: University of Washington Press, 2020.
———. "Working Class Zombies and Men in Burqas: Temporality, Trauma, and the Specter of Nostalgia in Zibahkhana." *BioScope: South Asian Screen Studies* 5, no. 2 (July 1, 2014): 141–51.
Kothari, Shuchi. "From Genre to Zanaana: Urdu Television Drama Serials and Women's Culture in Pakistan." *Contemporary South Asia* 14, no. 3 (September 2005): 289–305.
Lahiri, Madhumita. "An Idiom for India: Hindustani and the Limits of the Language Concept." *Interventions: International Journal of Postcolonial Studies* 18, no. 1 (2016): 60–85.

Lanba, Urmila. *Life and Films of Dilip Kumar, the Thespian*. New Delhi: Vision Books, 2002.

Larkin, Brian. *Signal and Noise: Media, Infrastructure, and Urban Culture in Nigeria*. Durham: Duke University Press, 2008.

Lassally, Walter. *Itinerant Cameraman*. London: J. Murray, 1987.

Lelyveld, David. "Talking the National Language: Hindi/Urdu/Hindustani in Indian Broadcasting and Cinema." In *Language and Politics in India*, edited by Asha Sarangi, 351–67. New Delhi: Oxford University Press, 2009.

Levesque, Julien, and Camille Bui. "Umar Marvi and the Representation of Sindh: Cinema and Modernity in the Margins." *BioScope: South Asian Screen Studies* 5, no. 2 (July 1, 2014): 119–28.

Lone, Maliha. "Memorable Romance: Neelo & Riaz Shahid." *Good Times*. April 16, 2016. www.goodtimes.com.pk/memorable-romance-neelo-riaz-shahid.

Lunn, David. "The Eloquent Language: Hindustani in 1940s Indian Cinema." *BioScope: South Asian Screen Studies* 6, no. 1 (January 1, 2015): 1–26.

Maclean, Kama. *A Revolutionary History of Interwar India: Violence, Image, Voice and Text*. New York: Oxford University Press, 2015.

Majumdar, Neepa. "Between Rage and Song: Voice, Performance, and Instrumentation in Shanta Apte's Films of the 1930s." In *Indian Sound Cultures, Indian Sound Citizenship*, edited by Laura Brueck, Jacob Smith, and Neil Verma, 229–43. Ann Arbor: University of Michigan Press, 2020.

———. "Importing Neorealism, Exporting Cinema: Indian Cinema and Film Festivals in the 1950s." In *Global Neorealism: The Transnational History of a Film Style*, edited by Saverio Giovacchini and Robert Sklar, 178–93. University Press of Mississippi, 2011.

———. *Wanted Cultured Ladies Only! Female Stardom and Cinema in India, 1930s–1950s*. Urbana: University of Illinois Press, 2009.

Majumdar, Rochona. "Art Cinema: The Indian Career of a Global Category." *Critical Inquiry* 42, no. 3 (March 1, 2016): 580–610.

Malik, Q. Z. "Ghunghat (1962) Review." *Hindi Movies Films Songs Books* (blog), n.d. Accessed March 21, 2020. http://hindi-movies-songs.com/joomla/index.php/khurshid-anwar/14-khurshid-anwar/121-ghunghat-1962-review.

Manuel, Peter. *Cassette Culture: Popular Music and Technology in North India*. Chicago: University of Chicago Press, 1993.

Masood, Syeda Momina. "Visions of Queer Anarchism: Gender, Desire, and Futurity in Omar Ali Khan's *Zibahkhana*." *BioScope: South Asian Screen Studies* 10, no. 1 (2019): 75–90.

Masood, Wajahat. "Down the River of Windfall Lights." *Newsweek Pakistan*, February 24, 2014. www.newsweekpakistan.com/down-the-river-of-windfall-lights.

Mehmood, Yousuf. "Flashback: Riaz Shahid Remains Pakistan's Revolutionary Filmmaker." PakistaniCinema.net. October 1, 2019. https://pakistanicinema.net/2019/10/01/flashback-riaz-shahid-remains-pakistans-revolutionary-filmmaker.

"Men and Ideas: Deboo Bhatacharjee." *Eastern Film* 8, no. 4 (November 1966): 37.

"Men and Ideas: Iqbal Shahzad." *Eastern Film* 8, no. 3 (October 1966): 22.

"Men and Ideas: Tanveer Naqvi." *Eastern Film* 9, no. 8 (March 1968): 37.

Mir, Farina. *The Social Space of Language: Vernacular Culture in British Colonial Punjab*. Berkeley: University of California Press, 2010.
Moffat, Chris. *India's Revolutionary Inheritance: Politics and the Promise of Bhagat Singh*. Cambridge, United Kingdom: Cambridge University Press, 2019.
Mohaiemen, Naeem. "Simulation at War's End: A 'Documentary' in the Field of Evidence Quest." *BioScope: South Asian Screen Studies* 7, no. 1 (2016): 31–57.
Morcom, Anna. *Hindi Film Songs and the Cinema*. Aldershot: Ashgate, 2007.
"Movies & Music of India—Timir Baran." Movies & Music of India. March 29, 2012. https://iyerbhaskar.wordpress.com/2012/03/29/movies-music-of-india-timir-baran.
Mufti, Aamir. *Enlightenment in the Colony: The Jewish Question and the Crisis of Postcolonial Culture*. Princeton, NJ: Princeton University Press, 2007.
Mukherjee, Debashree. *Bombay Hustle: Making Movies in a Colonial City*. Columbia University Press, 2020.
———. "The Lost Films of Saʻadat Hasan Manto (May 11, 2012)." *Phar'aat* (blog), May 23, 2012. http://pharaat.blogspot.com/2012/05/debashree-mukherjee-lost-films-of.html.
Mukherjee, Hiren. "Bengal Anti-fascist Writers and Artists 1944." In *Marxist Cultural Movement in India: Chronicles and Documents*, edited by Sudhi Pradhan, 368–71. Calcutta: Santi Pradhan, 1979.
Mukherjee, Madhuja. "Arriving at Bombay: Bimal Roy, Transits, Transitions, and Cinema of Intersection." In *Industrial Networks and Cinemas of India: Shooting Stars, Shifting Geographies and Multiplying Media*, edited by Monika Mehta and Madhuja Mukherjee, 108–23. Abingdon, Oxon: Routledge, 2021.
———. "The Public in the Cities: Detouring through Cinemas of Bombay, Calcutta, and Lahore (1920s–1930s)." In *South Asian Filmscapes: Transregional Encounters*, edited by Elora Halim Chowdhury and Esha Niyogi De, 119–39. Seattle: University of Washington Press, 2020.
Mumtaz, Khusro. "The Best of Times, the Worst of Times: Pakistan Cinema in the Seventies." In *Pakistan's Radioactive Decade: An Informal Cultural History of the 1970s*, edited by Amin Gulgee, Niilofur Farrukh, and John McCarry, 272–83. Karachi: Oxford University Press, 2019.
Narayan, Hari. "The Forbidden Jhumke." *Hindu*, September 19, 2016, sec. Cinema. www.thehindu.com/features/cinema/The-forbidden-jhumke/article14988512.ece.
Nasarullah, Nusrat. "The Year 1964." *Eastern Film* 6, no. 9 (April 1965): 22–23.
———. "The Year 1965." *Eastern Film* 7, no. 7 (February 1966): 20–21, 30.
———. "The Year 1966." *Eastern Film* 8, no. 7 (February 1967): 44–45.
———. "The Year 1967." *Eastern Film* 9, no. 7 (February 1968): 38–39.
Nasir, Agha. *Ham jite ji masruf rahe*. Lahore: Sang-e-Meel, 2008.
Naushahi, Gauhar, and Muhammad Siddiq Khan Shibli. *Syed Imtiaz Ali Taj: shakhsiyyat aur fann*. Islamabad: Academy Adabiyat-i Pakistan, 1999.
Nayar, Sobhana. *Bhatkhande's Contribution to Music: A Historical Perspective*. Bombay: Popular Prakashan, 1989.
Nitol, Afsana Aziz. "Jibon Theke Neya, an Emblem of Political Satire." Daily Observer. March 23, 2017. www.observerbd.com/details.php?id=64848.
Noorani, Asif. "*Ek Tera Sahara*: Another Feather in the Cap of Plagirists." *Eastern Film* 5, no. 6 (January 1964): 43.

———. "Himayat Ali Shair." *Eastern Film* 5, no. 2 (September 1963): 26.
Nowell-Smith, Geoffrey. "The Second Life of Italian Neo-realism." *Journal of the Moving Image* (2014): 46–58.
"Pak Film Industry Meets Afro-Asian Delegates." *Eastern Film* 6, no. 9 (March 1965): 7.
Paracha, Nadeem F. "Beyond 'Horn OK Please': The Elusive History and Politics of Pakistan's Truck Art." Scroll.in. August 20, 2016. http://scroll.in/article/814433/beyond-horn-ok-please-the-elusive-history-and-politics-of-pakistans-truck-art.
———. "New-Wave of Pakistani Cinema: Zinda and Kicking." dawn.com. September 26, 2013. www.dawn.com/news/1045365.
———. "Whatever Happened to Pakistan's Film Industry?" Dw.com. August 29, 2015. www.dw.com/en/whatever-happened-to-pakistans-film-industry/a-18681029.
Parekh, Rauf. "Shahabnama, Its Creator and Critics." dawn.com. July 20, 2009. www.dawn.com/news/970096/shahabnama-its-creator-and-critics.
Parvez, Amjad. "Deebo Bhattacharya—a Captivating Composer." *Daily Times*, January 30, 2019, sec. Lifestyle. https://dailytimes.com.pk/349542/deebo-bhattacharya-a-captivating-composer.
———. "Khwaja Khurshid Anwar." In *Melody Makers of the Subcontinent*, 97–102. Lahore: Sang-e-Meel Publications, 2013.
———. *Melody Makers of the Subcontinent*. Lahore: Sang-e-Meel, 2013.
———. "Neelo—the Iconic Filmstar of Yesteryears." *Daily Times*, May 29, 2019. https://dailytimes.com.pk/403175/neelo-the-iconic-filmstar-of-yesteryears.
———. "Rakhshi—the First Vamp/Dancer of Lollywood." *Daily Times*, April 14, 2020. https://dailytimes.com.pk/595320/rakhshi-the-first-vamp-dancer-of-lollywood.
———. "Three Uniquely Shot Pakistani Film Songs." *Daily Times*, February 16, 2019. https://dailytimes.com.pk/355422/three-uniquely-shot-pakistani-film-songs.
Parvez, Saeed. *Habib Jalib: ghar ki gavahi*. Karachi: Maktabah-yi Daniyal, 1994.
———. *Habib Jalib: sha'ir-i sh'ulah nava*. Karachi: Maktabah-yi Daniyal, 1996.
———. *Habib Jalib: shakhsiyyat aur fann*. Islamabad: Pakistan Academy of Letters, 2009.
Petiwala, Ada. "*Falasteen ka matlab kya*? (What does Palestine mean?) In Riaz Shahid's *Zerqa* (1969)." *Film History* 32, no. 3 (2020): 75–104.
Pinney, Christopher. *"Photos of the Gods": The Printed Image and Political Struggle in India*. London: Reaktion, 2003.
Pradhan, Sudhi, ed. "The All India People's Theatre Association: Annual Report—1946." In *Marxist Cultural Movement in India: Chronicles and Documents*, 236–304. Calcutta: Santi Pradhan, 1979.
Pritchett, Frances W. *Nets of Awareness: Urdu Poetry and Its Critics*. Berkeley: University of California Press, 1994.
Pucci, Lara. "History, Myth, and the Everyday: Luchino Visconti, Renato Guttuso, and the Fishing Communities of the Italian South." *Oxford Art Journal* 36 (2013): 417–35.
Rabe, Nate. "Five Pakistani-Christian Singers Who Were the Mainstay of Lollywood's Golden Years." Scroll.in. July 5, 2015. http://scroll.in/article/738597/five-pakistani-christian-singers-who-were-the-mainstay-of-lollywoods-golden-years.
———. "Lollywood Music Special: 'Ae roshiniyon ke shahar bata' from the 1964 Film 'Chingari.'" Scroll.in. March 25, 2017. https://thereel.scroll.in/832767/sound-of

-lollywood-jazz-wanton-women-and-a-deeply-horrified-man-in-ae-roshiniyon-ke-shahar-bata.

———. "Raqs zanjeer pehen kar bhi kiya jata hai." *Lolly Pops* (blog), March 16, 2017. https://dailylollyblog.wordpress.com/2017/03/16/raqa-zanjeer-pehen-kar-bhi-kiya-jata-hai.

———. "Sound of Lollywood: In Pakistan's Version of 'Lawrence of Arabia,' a Stirring Lament for Love." Scroll.in. August 5, 2017. https://thereel.scroll.in/846182/sound-of-lollywood-in-pakistans-version-of-lawrence-of-arabia-a-stirring-lament-for-love.

Rahi, Parvez. *Punjab ki filmi tarikh*. Lahore: Rahi, 1998.

Rahman, Saba. "Habib Jalib, His Dastoor—Why the People's Poet and His Verse Are Inspiring India's Youth." *Indian Express*, January 2, 2020. https://indianexpress.com/article/lifestyle/art-and-culture/habib-jalib-his-dastoor-why-the-peoples-poet-and-his-verse-are-inspiring-indias-youth-6194746.

Raj, Ali. "Pakistan's First Oscar Submission 'Jago Hua Savera' Goes to Cannes." *Express Tribune*, May 1, 2016. http://tribune.com.pk/story/1095386/pakistans-first-oscar-submission-jago-hua-savera-goes-to-cannes.

Rajadhyaksha, Ashish. *Indian Cinema: A Very Short Introduction*. Oxford: Oxford University Press, 2016.

———. *Indian Cinema in the Time of Celluloid: From Bollywood to the Emergency*. Bloomington: Indiana University Press, 2009.

———. "The Lahore Effect." In *The Lahore Biennale Reader 01*, edited by Iftikhar Dadi, 324–55. Milan: Skira, 2022.

Rajagopalan, Sudha. *Indian Films in Soviet Cinemas: The Culture of Movie-Going after Stalin*. Bloomington: Indiana University Press, 2008.

Rajamani, Imke, Margrit Pernau, and Katherine Butler Schofield. *Monsoon Feelings: A History of Emotions in the Rain*. New Delhi: Niyogi Books, 2018.

Rajput, A. B. "River Life in East Pakistan." *Pakistan Quarterly*, Summer 1964, 40–42.

Raju, Zakir Hossain. *Bangladesh Cinema and National Identity: In Search of the Modern?* London: Routledge, 2015.

Ramnath, Maia. "The Progressive Writers Association." *Oxford Research Encyclopedia of Asian History*. April 26, 2019. https://doi.org/10.1093/acrefore/9780190277727.013.337.

Ramnath, Nandini. "Made in Pakistan with Some Help from India, Lost and Found Again: The Story of 'Jago Hua Savera.'" Scroll.in. Accessed May 8, 2018. https://scroll.in/reel/817995/made-in-pakistan-with-some-help-from-india-lost-and-found-again-the-story-of-jago-hua-savera.

Ray, Satyajit. *Our Films, Their Films*. 3rd ed. Bombay: Orient Longman, 1976.

Rehman, I. A. "Intezar: A Successful Experiment." *Pakistan Times*, May 18, 1956. Accessed at *Hindi Movies Films Songs Books* (blog), December 28, 2018. http://hindi-movies-songs.com/joomla/index.php/component/content/article/14-khurshid-anwar/118-intezar-1956-review.

———. "'Somehow the Authorities Never Found a Non-farcical Reason for Arresting Me'—Habib Jalib." *Herald Magazine*, February 6, 2019. https://herald.dawn.com/news/1398806.

Rehman, Nasreen. "Pakistan, History, and Sleep: Hassan Tariq, a Progressive Patriarch, and Neend." In *South Asian Filmscapes: Transregional Encounters*, edited by Elora

Halim Chowdhury and Esha Niyogi De, 97–115. Seattle: University of Washington Press, 2020.

Report of the Film Fact Finding Committee, Govt. of Pakistan, Ministry of Industries, April 1960–April 1961. Karachi: Manager of Publications, 1962.

Reuben, Bunny. *—And Pran: A Biography.* New Delhi: HarperCollins, 2005.

Roy, Anjali Gera. *Cinema of Enchantment: Perso-Arabic Genealogies of the Hindi Masala Film.* New Delhi: Orient BlackSwan, 2015.

Roy, Anuradha. *Cultural Communism in Bengal, 1936–1952.* Delhi: Primus Books, 2014.

Ruberto, Laura E., and Kristi M. Wilson, eds. *Italian Neorealism and Global Cinema.* Detroit: Wayne State University Press, 2007.

Sahgal, Manmohini Zutshi. *An Indian Freedom Fighter Recalls Her Life.* Edited by Geraldine Hancock Forbes. Armonk, NY: M. E. Sharpe, 1994.

Sajjad, Sajjad Ahmad. *Filmon ki dunya ke ek sau gyara sal.* Karachi: Tawakkul Academy, 2016.

———. "Lollywood ki sanpon kay mauzu par banai gai film *Nagin* 1959." In *Filmon ki dunya ke ek sau gyara sal*, 154–59. Karachi: Tawakkul Academy, 2016.

Sarkar, Bhaskar. *Mourning the Nation: Indian Cinema in the Wake of Partition.* Durham: Duke University Press, 2009.

Satia, Priya. "Poets of Partition." *Tanqeed* no. 10 (January 2016). www.tanqeed.org/2016/01/poets-of-partition/6.

Schendel, Willem van. *A History of Bangladesh.* Cambridge: Cambridge University Press, 2009.

Sen, Biswarup. "The Sounds of Modernity: The Evolution of Bollywood Film Song." In *Global Bollywood: Travels of Hindi Song and Dance*, edited by Sangita Gopal and Sujata Moorti, 85–104. Minneapolis: University of Minnesota Press, 2008.

Sen, Meheli. *Haunting Bollywood: Gender, Genre, and the Supernatural in Hindi Commercial Cinema.* Austin: University of Texas Press, 2017.

Seth, Sanjay. "Governmentality and Identity: Constituting the 'Backward but Proud Muslim.'" In *Subject Lessons: The Western Education of Colonial India*, 109–27. Durham: Duke University Press, 2007.

Sevea, Iqbal. "'Kharaak kita oi!': Masculinity, Caste, and Gender in Punjabi Films." *BioScope: South Asian Screen Studies* 5, no. 2 (July 1, 2014): 129–40.

Shahab, Qudratullah. *Shahabnama.* Lahore: Sang-e-Meel, 1987.

Shahid, Riaz. *Hazar Dastan: Riaz Shahid ka vahid navil.* Karachi: Maktabah-yi Shahkar, 1982.

Shahid, Zulqarnain. "Early Corruption in Pakistan Film Industry." *Qalam Dawaat* (blog), August 19, 2014. https://qalamdawaat.wordpress.com/2014/08/19/early-corruption-in-pakistan-film-industry.

———. "How Habib Jalib and Riaz Shahid Forged the Way for Socialist Cinema in Pakistan." Dawn Images. March 24, 2017. https://images.dawn.com/news/1177311.

———. "Iqbal Shehzad." Cineplot.com. September 19, 2009. https://cineplot.com/iqbal-shehzad.

Shahidullah, Muhammad. "Common Origin of Urdu and Bengali." *Pakistan Quarterly* 9, no. 3 (Autumn 1959): 52–53.

Shakur, Anis. "Khurshid Anwar: A Lasting Legacy." Anis Shakur. Accessed December 28, 2018. http://anisshakur.tripod.com/id71.html.

——. "Riaz Shahid: Extraordinary Accomplishments." Anis Shakur. Accessed July 5, 2020. http://anisshakur.tripod.com/id20.html.

"Sheeshon ka maseeha koi nahin (Faiz Ahmed Faiz)." YouTube. Accessed June 1, 2020. www.youtube.com/watch?v=97Nkozycokc.

Shifai, Qateel. "San'at-e filmsazi men Sarhad ka hissa." *Sang-e Mil* 7–8 (January 1950): 469–75.

Shope, Bradley. "Latin American Music in Moving Pictures and Jazzy Cabarets in Mumbai, 1930s to 1950s." In *More than Bollywood: Studies in Indian Popular Music*, edited by Gregory D. Booth and Bradley Shope. New York: Oxford University Press, 2014.

Shuja, Hakim Ahmed. *Lahore ka Chelsea*. Lahore: Packages Limited, 1988.

Siddiqa, Ayesha. *Military Inc.: Inside Pakistan's Military Economy*. 2nd rev. ed. London: Pluto Press, 2017.

Siddiqi, M. A. "Khawaja Khurshid Anwar: Serenading on the Silver Screen." *Herald Magazine*, November 12, 2017. https://herald.dawn.com/news/1398586.

Siddique, Salma. "Archive Filmaria: Cinema, Curation, and Contagion." *Comparative Studies of South Asia, Africa and the Middle East* 39, no. 1 (May 1, 2019): 196–211.

——. "From Gandhi to Jinnah: National Dilemmas in the Stardom of Rattan Kumar." In *Indian Film Stars: New Critical Perspectives*, edited by Michael Lawrence, 109–23. London: British Film Institute, 2020.

——. "Meena Shorey: The Droll Queen of Partition." *BioScope: South Asian Screen Studies* 6, no. 1 (January 1, 2015): 44–66.

——. "Nigar hai toh industry hai: Notes on the Morale and Mortality of Pakistani Film." *BioScope: South Asian Screen Studies* 11, no. 2 (December 1, 2020): 187–206.

——. "Rustic Releases: Vernacular Cinema and Partition Temporality in Lahore." *Third Text* 31, no. 2–3 (May 4, 2017): 477–96.

——. "'Someone to Check Her a Bit': Feminine Abandon and the Abducted Woman in Shorey Comedies." *Feminist Media Histories* 3, no. 2 (April 1, 2017): 36–56.

Staniszewski, Mary Anne. *The Power of Display: A History of Exhibition Installations at the Museum of Modern Art*. Cambridge, MA: MIT Press, 1998.

Steimatsky, Noa. *Italian Locations: Reinhabiting the Past in Postwar Cinema*. Minneapolis: University of Minnesota Press, 2008.

Stimson, Blake. *The Pivot of the World: Photography and Its Nation*. Cambridge, MA: MIT Press, 2006.

Sundar, Pavitra. "Meri Awaaz Suno: Women, Vocality, and Nation in Hindi Cinema." *Meridians* 8, no. 1 (January 1, 2008): 144–79.

Sunderason, Sanjukta. *Partisan Aesthetics: Modern Art and India's Long Decolonization*. Stanford, CA: Stanford University Press, 2020.

Suvorova, Anna. *Early Urdu Theatre: Traditions and Transformations*. Lahore: National College of Arts, 2009.

Taj, Afroz. *The Court of Indar and the Rebirth of North Indian Drama*. New Delhi: Anjuman Taraqqi Urdu (Hind), 2007.

Talbot, Ian. *Pakistan: A Modern History*. London: Palgrave Macmillan, 2005.

Tanvir, Kuhu. "Pirate Histories: Rethinking the Indian Film Archive." *BioScope: South Asian Screen Studies* 4, no. 2 (2013): 115–36.

Thomas, Paul. "Gone Fishin'? Rossellini's *Stromboli*, Visconti's *La Terra Trema*." *Film Quarterly* 62, no. 2 (Winter 2009): 20–25.

Thomas, Rosie. *Bombay before Bollywood: Film City Fantasies*. New Delhi: Orient Black Swan, 2014.

Uddin, Layli. "Kagmari Festival, 1957: Political Aesthetics and Subaltern Internationalism in Pakistan." In *Forms of the Left: Left-Wing Aesthetics and Postcolonial South Asia*, edited by Lotte Hoek and Sanjukta Sunderason, 65–95. London: Bloomsbury, 2021.

Usman, Javed. "Portrait of a Film-Maker: An Interview of Khurshid Anwar." *Hindi Movies Films Songs Books* (blog), accessed June 16, 2018. http://films.hindi-movies-songs.com/portrait-interview.html.

Vaidik, Aparna. "History of a Renegade Revolutionary: Revolutionism and Betrayal in Colonial India." *Postcolonial Studies* 16, no. 2 (June 1, 2013): 216–29.

Vasudevan, Ravi S. "Film Genres, the Muslim Social, and Discourses of Identity c. 1935–1945." *BioScope: South Asian Screen Studies* 6, no. 1 (January 1, 2015): 27–43.

———. *The Melodramatic Public: Film Form and Spectatorship in Indian Cinema*. New York: Palgrave Macmillan, 2011.

Waheed, Sarah. "Beyond the Wounded Archive: Partition's Hauntings and Bombay Cinema." *Postcolonial Text* 12, no. 1 (2017): 1–19.

Wani, Aarti. *Fantasy of Modernity: Romantic Love in Bombay Cinema of the 1950s*. Delhi: Cambridge University Press, 2016.

Weidman, Amanda. "Voices of Meenakumari: Sound, Meaning, and Self-Fashioning in Performances of an Item Number." *South Asian Popular Culture* 10, no. 3 (October 2012): 307–18.

Wollen, Peter. *Singin' in the Rain*. 2nd ed. London: BFI, 2012.

Yashpal. *Yashpal Looks Back: Selections from an Autobiography*. Edited by Corinne Friend. New Delhi: Vikas, 1981.

Younger, Prakash. "The River: Beneath the Surface with Andre Bazin." In *A Companion to Jean Renoir*, edited by Alastair Phillips and Ginette Vincendeau, 166–75. Chichester, West Sussex, UK: Wiley-Blackwell, 2013.

Zaheer, Hasan. *The Times and Trial of the Rawalpindi Conspiracy, 1951: The First Coup Attempt in Pakistan*. Karachi: Oxford University Press, 1998.

Zaidi, Hasan. "Herald Exclusive: In Conversation with Jamil Dehlavi." dawn.com. July 25, 2014. www.dawn.com/news/1120888.

Zaidi, S. Akbar. *Issues in Pakistan's Economy: A Political Economy Perspective*. 3rd ed. Karachi: Oxford University Press, 2015.

Zamindar, Vazira. "*Ek Haseen* Archive: Notes on Love & Longing in a Film Archive." In *Love, War & Other Longings: Essays on Cinema in Pakistan*, edited by Vazira Zamindar and Asad Ali, 132–58. Karachi: Oxford University Press, 2019.

Zamindar, Vazira, and Asad Ali, eds. *Love, War & Other Longings: Essays on Cinema in Pakistan*. Karachi: Oxford University Press, 2019.

Zavattini, Cesare. "Some Ideas on the Cinema (Italy, 1953)." In *Film Manifestos and Global Cinema Cultures: A Critical Anthology*, edited by Scott MacKenzie, 124–33. Berkeley: University of California Press, 2014.

Zinda Bhaag. *The Genius behind Pani Da Bulbula*. YouTube. 2013. www.youtube.com /watch?v=BZMxG3XheFE.

"Zinda Bhaag Revives 'Pani Da Bulbula.'" dawn.com. August 12, 2013. www.dawn.com /news/1035426.

Zinda Bhaag's Hand Made Poster. YouTube. 2013. www.youtube.com/watch?v =pROXggnv8GM.

INDEX

Aadmi (1958), 178n32
Aag (1967), 169n30
Aankh ka nasha (Intoxication for the eyes), 81–82
Aashiq (Lover, 1968), 169n30
Abbas, Khwaja Ahmad, 22, 30, 37, 38
"Ab kyā dekheṇ rāh tumhārī" (Still waiting for your return; song in *Jago Hua Savera*), 47
ableism, 124–27
Academy Awards (US), 87
Aci Trezza (Sicilian village), 41–42, 44
advertising, 25, 107, 129, 137, 149, 163; employment in, 27, 157; film posters, 18, 24, 75*fig.*, 76, 107, 115*fig.*, 116, 130*fig.*, 131, 139, 140, 200n22
"Ā'e gā ṣanam jab naẓareṇ mileṇ gī tab nah jāne kyā ho gā" (When my lover arrives and our eyes meet, who knows what will happen next?; song in *Susraal*), 123, 123*fig.*
aesthetics, xi, 5–6, 15–16, 107–8; binaries and, 86–87; documentary, 28, 38, 43, 45; immersive, 42–44, 47, 76, 87, 181n88; neorealist, 39–40, 42; New Cinema, 156–57, 164; realist, 38–39, 160; in television serials, 152–53; theatrical conventions, 104, 107, 123, 136
Afaqi, Ali Sufyan, 105
affect, x, xi, 120, 136, 151–52, 167n13; film song and, 7, 24, 49, 60, 87, 94, 185n22; language and, 52, 102; melodrama and, 68–69; memory and, 28, 103; Partition and, 17; popular politics and, 111–13, 161, 164
Afghan War (1978–92), 143
Afzal-Khan, Fawzia, 166n10
Ahmad, Ali Nobil, 150, 163, 201n39
Ahmad, Ashfaq, 119
Ahmad, Farid, 5
Ahmad, Nabi, 71
Ahmad, Shaikh Riaz. *See* Shahid, Riaz
Ahmed, Ishtiaq, 1–2, 169n19
Ahmed, Wahiduddin Ziauddin (W. Z.), 2–4, 40, 168n8,14, 175n1, 194n3
Aina (Mirror, 1977), 182n116
Ajab Khan (1961), 105
Ajmeri, Nazir, 3, 105
Akaler Sandhaney (In search of famine, 1980), 180n79
Akbar, Emperor, 19
Akhtar, Hamid, 183n119
Akhtar, Jamil, 105, 106, 194n5
Alam Ara (1931), 9
Albela (Stylish, 1951), 85–86, 191n108
Ali, Kamran Asdar, ix, x, 109, 127, 166n10, 167nn12–13, 171n67, 197n50
Ali, Naushad, 185n27, 189n82, 191n107
Ali, Sadiq, 186n49
Ali, Tariq Omar, 177n19
Allauddin, 120, 131
All-India Progressive Writers' Association (PWA), xii, 22, 36, 53, 113
All India Radio (AIR), 18, 57, 59, 65, 184n20
All Pakistan Progressive Writers Association, 35

alternative cinema, 29, 104, 113, 119, 128, 164, 200n30
Amanat, Agha Hasan, 7, 190n94
American cinema: realism in, 40–41. See also Hollywood
Amrohi, Kamal, 95
Anand, Chetan, 22
Anand, Jagdish Chand (J. C.), 3, 17
Anand, Mulk Raj, 65, 67
Anand, Shaina, 193n130
Anarkali (mythical figure), 19–20, 56–57, 184n13
Anarkali film versions, 19, 71, 183n2, 184n13
Anarkali play (1922), 56, 70–71, 183n2
Andaleeb (1969), 5
Anderson, Benedict, 200n20
Anjaria, Ulka, 179n53
Anjum, Pervez, 129, 136
"Ānkh se ānkh milā le" (Let your eyes meet mine; song in *Intezar*), 86
Anmol Ghadi (Precious watch, 1946), 23, 192n120
Anokhi (Singular, 1956), 30
anti-colonialism, xii, 61–69, 139, 186n48
anti-imperialist films, 105–6, 110, 111, 131
Anwar, Khurshid, xii, 2, 4, 9, 55–69, 172n87, 186n49, 186n51, 188n68, 189n82, 189n88; Bombay years, 60–61, 184n20, 185n27; compositions with flute and violin, 185n22; early years, 57–60, 183n7, 184nn8–9, 184n20, 186n52; Faiz and, 155; film song and, 9; on gender roles, 100–101; *Hamraz*, 119; lyric romanticism and, 55; Partition and, 17, 23; photograph of, 57*fig.*; political activism, 4, 61–69, 187n53, 187nn64–65; Roshan and, 184n17; Taj and, 183n6, 184n13. See also *Ghoonghat* (The veil, 1962); *Intezar* (The awaiting, 1956)
Anwar, Naseer, 87
Apu Trilogy, 38
Ara, Shamim, 69
Arabian Nights themes, 21

archives, 24–28, 142–43, 175n123, 175n125
Arora, Prakash, 38, 116
art cinema, 29, 40, 113, 148, 164
Asif, K., 19, 184n13
Asiya (1960), 175n1, 181n88
Askari, Muhammad Hasan, 173n107
assemblage, 148, 199n10; *Zinda Bhaag* and, 159, 163–64
Atif, Yaqub "Bulbula," 159
Attre, Rashid, 194n10
Aujla, Harjap Singh, 23, 59, 60, 184n20
Aurat (Woman, 1940), 37
Aur Bhi Gham Hein, 11
authoritarian rule, 10–11, 13–14, 113
'avāmī adākār (people's actor), 120. See also Allauddin
'avāmī shā'ir (people's poet), 171n67. See also Jalib, Habib
avant-garde cinema, 28, 109, 112, 147, 164; film song and, 7; in India, 154–55; melodrama and, 159–63. See also parallel cinema, Indian
Ayaz (1960), 58
Ayub Khan era (1958–69): authoritarianism, vii, 10–11, 13–14, 113, 115; cultural politics, xi, 10–18, 35–36, 109, 142, 171n67; economy, 170n52; modernization, vii, 5; resistance against, 106, 142, 196n43
Azad, Chandrashekhar, 185n39
Aziz, Ashraf, 9, 61
Azmi, Kaifi, 22

Bachchan, Amitabh, 26
Badnam (Disgraced, 1966), 105, 106, 119, 129–41, 130*fig.*, 132–33*fig.*, 138–40*fig.*
Badshahi Mosque, 120
Baji (Sister, 1963), 81
Baksh, Rahim, 66
Bandopadhyay, Manik, 29, 176n3
Bangladesh, 11, 52, 181n87; independence, 113, 142; national archives, 24
Bano, Iqbal, 48, 161, 202n54
Baran, Timir, 30, 48, 138, 176n8, 181n94

"Baṛe be-muravvat haiṉ yeh ḥusn wāle" (The exquisite beloved is uncaring; song in *Badnam*), 137–38, 138–39*fig.*
Barsaat Ki Raat (A night of the rainy season, 1960), 184n17
Barthes, Roland, 45
Barua, P. C., 30, 100–101
Bashir, Ahmad, 14, 129, 194n3
bazaar public sphere, 112–13
Bazin, André, 41–43, 178n46
Beaster-Jones, Jayson, 166n9, 175n120, 189n80, 192n120
Bedari (1957), 17
Bedi, Rajinder Singh, 22
Begum, Naseem, 87
Begum, Shamshad, 189n79
Behan Bhai (Brother and sister, 1968), 169n30
Benegal, Shyam, 154, 155
Bengal: folk music in, 48; Hindi-Urdu films in, 53. *See also bhatiali* songs; East Bengal; West Bengal
Bengal Famine (1943), 37
Bengali language: denigration of, 113; in films, vii, 8, 45, 51–54, 107, 160, 175n1, 181n88; in *Jago Hua Savera*, 182n107; after Partition, 183n118
Beqarar (Restless, 1950), 3
B-genres, 21–22
Bhaduri, Tripti. *See* Mitra, Tripti
Bhakti, 7
Bharosa (Trust, 1958), 106
Bharucha, Rustom, 37
bhatiali songs, 47–48, 50, 181n90, 182n96
Bhatkhande, Pandit Vishnu Narayan, 65, 186n49
Bhattacharya, Bijon, 37
Bhattacharya, Deebo, 138–39
Bhatti Gate (in Lahore), 1
Bhaumik, Kaushik, 113
Bhojpuri, 48, 50, 93
"Bhor hū'ī ghar āo maṉjhī" (It's dawn, return home boatman; song in *Jago Hua Savera*), 47
Bhutto, Zulfiqar Ali, 6, 142, 201n32

The Bicycle Thief (1948), 38, 40, 178n42
BioScope: South Asian Screen Studies (journal), viii, 199n18
Bismil, Ram Prasad, 63
Biswas, Hemanga, 181n90
Biswas, Moinak, 37, 38–39, 165n4, 177n15, 179n58
The Blood of Hussain (1980), 30, 155, 200n32
"Bohat be ābrū ho kar tere kuche say hum nikle" (We departed from your street in disgrace; song in *Badnam*), 139–40, 140*fig.*
Bol (Speak, 2011), 151
Bollywood: genres, 156; globalization of, 26; indie films and, 201n36; music in, 189n79; Pakistani New Cinema and, 147, 156–57, 163. *See also* Bombay cinema; Indian cinema
Bombay cinema: aesthetics, 108; Anwar and, 60–61; film song, 9; Lahore cinema and, viii, x–xi, 1–2, 15–18, 60–61, 71, 172n92, 195n21; "Lahore effect" and, viii, 18–20, 23, 26–28, 164; languages and, 8–9, 53; leftist politics in, 104, 113–14; memory and, 26; musical conventions, 136; Parsi theater and, 7; realism in, 39; scholarship on, vii–ix; singers in, 191n102; social realism and, 193n1; Urdu and, ix–x; use of term, 165n7; Western music in, 79. *See also* Bollywood; Indian cinema
Booth, Gregory, 9, 61, 76–78, 185n27, 188n79, 189n86, 189n91, 191n104
Boot Polish (1954), 116
bourgeois liberal values, 11, 142, 161; domesticity, 90–92, 102
Bukhari, Jafar, 106, 188nn68–69
Bukhari, Patras, 59
Bukhari, Z. A., 68
Buzdil (The coward, 1969), 169n30

Calcutta: Bengali culture in, 183n118; film production in, x, 1–2, 53–54, 167n12
Cannes Film Festival, 31, 179n56

Censor Board, 11, 14, 109, 123
censorship, 150, 169n32, 200n32, 201n39
"Chan chan chan merī pāyal kī dhun" (My ankle bracelets sing chan chan chan; song in Ghoonghat), 94, 95fig.
Chanda (1962), 182n116
"Chānd hanse duniyā base royay merā piyār" (The moon smiles, the world flourishes, but only my love weeps; song in Intezar), 77
characterization, x, 10, 18, 69, 127–28
charba films, 15–16, 172n84. See also plagiarism
Chatterjee, Saibal, 176n8
Chatterjee, Sarat Chandra, 101
Chatterji, Shanti Kumar, 30
Chawla, Juhi, 17
Chingari (Spark, 1964), 58, 69, 102
Chinnamul (The uprooted, 1950), 37
Chittoprasad, 45
Christians, 197n47
Chughtai, Abdur Rahman, 91–92
Chughtai, Arif Rahman, 191n115
Chughtai, Ismat, 22
"cinema-effects," 18, 172n93. See also "Lahore effect"
cinematic immersion, 42–44, 47, 76, 87, 181n88
cinematic techniques, 5, 152–55
circular motifs, 140–41
class divides, 71, 79, 93, 105–6, 108–10, 121, 135, 141, 143–46, 148–52, 157. See also elite; middle-class viewers; poverty
classical music. See Indian classical music
Clerk (1960), 11, 105, 114–20, 141, 153, 162, 194n4, 194n9, 197n53; publicity poster, 115fig.
Cold War, 10–11, 13; cyclical time and, 45; realist cinema and, 40
colonialism: affective burden of, 68. See also anti-colonialism
color film, xii, 5–6, 29, 31, 34, 48–50, 104, 154, 160

commercial cinema: aesthetics of, 39; conventions of, 151; East-West divide, 56; genres and techniques, 5; government control and, 12, 14; influence of, 28; leftist politics in, 104, 113; musical forms in, 78; nationalism in, 20–21, 39–40; recursivity and reflexivity in, 164; scholarship on, viii–ix
communal strife, 23, 52, 103, 168n8
communism, 67–68, 187n64
Communist Party of Italy, 41
Communist Party of Pakistan, 35
consumerism, 157
conventional forms, 152–53, 155
Cooper, Sarah, 38
Cooper, Timothy, 24
corporate sponsorship, 156–57
Correa, Micky, 189n85
courtship, 117, 120–28, 195n21
Cuban music, 73, 85. See also Latin American music
cultural awareness, 195n21
cultural politics, 10–18, 35–36, 109, 142, 171n67
cultural studies, ix, 109
cyclical time, 38; humanism and, 44–46

Damodaran, Sumangala, 47–48, 181n90
dancing, 73fig., 79, 84fig., 138–39fig., 162fig.; in chains, 111–12; Latin, 85–86. See also mujra (dance song); song-and-dance sequence
darshan (beholding the deity), 94, 95fig.
Das, Nandita, 151
Dasi (The maid, 1944), 2
Dass, Manishita, 20, 22, 39, 86, 114, 180n79, 193n1
dāstān, 21, 158
dastanic films, 22, 105
"Dastoor" (Constitution, 1962), 14
Dave, Ram Narayan, 71, 184n13
"death foretold" tales, 158–59
Decade of Reformation (1957–66), 4

"Deewana yeh parwana" (This intoxicated moth; song in *Albela*), 86
Dehlavi, Jamil, 30, 155, 200n32
"Dekhenge" (To witness; song in *Zinda Bhaag*), 161–62, 162*fig.*
Deleuze, Gilles, 41, 148
Department of Film and Publications, 12
Dervi, Danish, 11
De Sica, Vittorio, 38, 40, 178n42
detective film genre, 26, 97–99
Devanagari script, 95, 96*fig.*, 102
Devar Bhabi (Brother-in-law and sister-in-law, 1967), 5
Devasundaram, Ashvin, 156, 201n33, 201n36
Devdas films, 30, 91, 101
devotional poetry, 7
Dhaka: Bengali films from, 175n1, 181n88; film industry personnel, 182n116; films from, vii, x, 5, 26, 45, 53, 107, 143, 167n12, 182n116; language in, 52–53
Dharti Ke Lal (Children of the earth, 1946), 30, 37, 176n11
Dhoop Aur Saey (1968), 119
dialects, 37, 41, 144, 146, 182n107
disability, 124–27
distribution networks, viii, 2–3, 16–18, 36, 150, 156, 163–64, 173n93; local, 50, 104; restrictions on Indian films, 16, 54, 176n13
Do Aansoo (Two tears, 1952), 3
Do Bigha Zamin (Two Acres of Land, 1953), 179n48
documentary aesthetic, 28, 38, 43, 45
Door Hey Sukh Ka Gaon (Faraway village of peace), 200n32
Dosheeza (Damsel, 1962), 105
"Dosheeza" (Mohammad), 191n113
doubling trope, 17, 69, 83, 95, 98–99
D'Souza, Sebastian, 77–78, 81, 185n27, 189n86–87, 191n104
"Duets with Dialogues" (radio program), 59–60
dunky, 143, 159, 163, 164. *See also* labor migration; migration

Dupatta (Scarf, 1952), 3
Dutt, B. K., 62
Dutt, Guru, 3, 26, 39
Dwyer, Rachel, 168n8

East Bengal, xii, 47–48, 51, 53–54, 113, 177n19, 181n88
Eastern Film (magazine), 5, 6*fig.*
Eastern Film Studios, 5, 129
East Pakistan: filmmakers, 15; Indian films shown in, 4; language in, 52; political instability in, 11, 113, 142; relations with West Pakistan, 15, 44–46, 54, 113; river life in, 44–46. *See also* Bangladesh
East-West divide, 56, 70; musical styles and, 70–86
education, 118–19, 134–35, 140, 149
Ehtesham, 182n116
"Ei poth jodi na sesh hoye" (What if this road never ends; song in *Saptapadi*), 160, 202n48
Elaan (Proclamation, 1948), 22
Elam, J. Daniel, 63, 187n67
elite: cultural values of, 11, 142, 183n118; decadence among, 21; Jameson on elite cultural forms, 109; language, x; neighborhoods in *Badnam*, 137; social groups, 149, 151, 161–62; versus popular culture, 22, 109–10, 112–13, 142; views on commercial cinema, 20, 22. *See also* high culture; nonelite neighborhoods
emotive affect, 151. *See also* affect; melodrama
English-language theater, 8
epic oral folktales, 158. See also *Hir-Ranjha* story; Laila-Majnun tale
Europe: film festivals, 36; films produced in, 39; migration to, 144, 159–60; nationalist movements in, 61. *See also* Italian neorealism
Evernew Studios, 3, 27
everyday life, portrayals of. *See* realism
exoticism, 41, 44, 46, 54

experimental cinema, vii, ix; conventions of, 152; in India, 154–55; *Jago Hua Savera* as, 46, 52, 54; leftists and, 183n119; lineage of, 155–56; New Cinema and, 147–48; realism and, 34, 38. *See also* parallel cinema, Indian

exploitation, 140; leftist progressive writers on, 52, 54, 105; realist depictions of, 40–42, 44–46, 50, 114; of rural poor, xii–xiii, 29, 33; sexual, 105–6, 110, 118, 131–35, 200n26; of workers, 78, 114–19, 140, 193n1

fable, vii–ix, xi, xiii, 20, 104, 112; *Intezar* and, 85–87; "Lahore effect," 151; realism and, ix, xiii, 145, 147–48, 164; *Zinda Bhaag* and, 144–45, 145*fig.*, 158–63. *See also* "Lahore effect"

Faiz, Faiz Ahmed: All-India Progressive Writers' Association and, xii, 13, 36; Anwar and, 58, 65, 67, 186n49, 187n64; Chughtai and, 91; dissidents and, 196n43; *Ghoonghat* and, 192n119; high cultural forms and, 22, 112; *Jago Hua Savera* and, 29–30, 47–50, 52, 176n8, 176n12, 182nn98–99; poems and lyrics by, xv, 15, 105, 155, 161, 175n128, 183n119, 196n43, 202nn54–55; politics and, 13, 35, 67–68; Qaiser and, 194n10; Shahid and, 106, 119, 194n10

family film (*gharelū*), 167n13

The Family of Man (exhibition), 45

Fankar (Artist, 1956), 30

fantasy, vii, 122–24; genre, 21–22; realism and, 28, 112, 159; social melodramatic film and, 7, 24; song sequences, 159–61. *See also* fable

Farangi (The European, 1964), 105–6, 183n119, 194n10

Fazli, Sibtain, 2–4, 168nn13–14, 175n120

femininity, 153, 192n124. *See also* gender

Fernandez, Cynthia Alexander. *See* Neelo (actor)

film festivals, 31, 36, 37, 39, 179n56, 200n30

filmi, 50

Filmindia (magazine), 21–22, 168n8

Films Division, 155

film song, 7–10; affect and, 7, 24, 49, 60, 87, 94, 185n22; in Bombay cinema, 61; circulation of, 18; conventions of, 161; high culture and, 31; in *Intezar*, 70; in *Jago Hua Savera*, 47–50; lullabies, 136–37; melodrama and, 69; modernity and, 69; musical instruments and, 185n22; narrative and, 154; neorealism and, 29; popularity of, 14; in *Susraal*, 121–25; in *Zinda Bhaag*, 154. *See also bhatiali* songs; *ghazal* (lyric poem); *gīt*; *kaifī*; playback singing; *qawwali*; song-and-dance sequence

fishing villages, 31–33, 41–44

flashbacks, 158

folk culture: documentation of, 142; of East Bengal, 181n88; epic oral folktales, 158; music, 47–48, 50, 78; theater, 7

Folk Music of Pakistan (Smithsonian, 1951), 48

Footpath (1953), 179n48

form: aesthetic problems of, xi; genre and, 153; in New Cinema, 147–48. *See also* aesthetics

Foucault, Michel, 13

funding, 156–58

Gandhi, Indira, 187n52

Gandhi, Mahatma, 62

Gaur, Meenu, xiii, 27, 128, 142, 144, 154, 158, 160–61, 198n5, 199n6, 201n42

Gazdar, Mushtaq, 4, 11, 12, 17, 20, 34, 107, 108–9, 134, 166n8, 168nn13–14, 168n18, 169n30, 169n32, 172n87, 177n13, 178n32, 194n4, 196n26, 197n58

gender, x; Gothic films and, 192n124; modernity and, 97, 100–101; in television serials, 152. *See also* femininity; homosocial bonds; marriage; masculinity; patriarchy; women

INDEX   227

gender-based violence, 198n5
genres, 21–22, 26, 141, 156; formal properties of, 153; politics and, 113. *See also specific genres*
Ghalib, Mirza, 139
gharana (hereditary musical lineage), 68, 162
Gharnata, 194n10
"Ghar se chiṭṭhī ā'ī" (A letter from home has arrived; song in *Clerk*), 116
Ghatak, Ritwik, 154
ghazal (lyric poem), 58, 82, 92–93, 139, 191n117, 202n54; singers, 48, 87, 106, 110, 112, 161
Ghaznavi, Shatir, 2
Ghoonghat (The veil, 1962), 17, 58, 69, 87–103; analysis of, 99–101; lyrics in, 183n119; as Partition allegory, 101–3; plot summary, 88–99; songs in, 93–94, 192n119; stills from, 90*fig.*, 95–96*fig.*, 98*fig.*
Ghosh, Nemai, 37
Ghouri, Qadir, 194n3
Gibran, Khalil, 107
Gidwani, Moti, 184n13
gīt, 10, 93
globalization, 142–43
global neorealism, ix, 177n14
Global South: film production in, 104. *See also* Indian cinema; Pakistani cinema; South Asian cinema
Goan musicians, 76–79, 189n91
goddess figures, 94, 95*fig.*, 97, 98
Golden Era (1956–66), 4, 143, 150
Gopalan, Lalitha, 200n23
Gorija, Yasin, 5, 99, 119, 166n10, 169n30, 172n84
Gothic suspense films, 69, 87–99, 192n124, 192n128
Government College, 57, 59, 66, 67
Guattari, Félix, 148
guest workers, 143
Gujarati theater, 7–8
Gul, Agha A. G., 3
Gul, Aijaz, 119, 194n10, 196n27, 197n53

Gulnar (1953), 71, 188nn78–79
Gulzar (poet), 17

Haaland, Torunn, 42, 50–51
Hagen, Jean, 80
Haider, Master Ghulam, 9, 71, 188–89nn78–79
Haider Ali (1978), 105
Hall, Stuart, 110, 113
Hamari Zaban (Our language, 1955), 52, 182n112
Hamraz (The confidant, 1967), 58, 69, 119
Hanif, Mohammad, 155, 161
Hansen, Kathryn, 8, 82, 170n40, 190n94, 191n106
Harvard Advisory Group, 170n64
Hasnain, S. F., 22
Hassan, Mehdi, 87, 106, 110, 112
Hassan, Mohammad, 30
hatke (quirky) films, 156
Haveli (Mansion, 1964), 58, 194n10
Hayles, N. Katherine, 148
Hazar dastan (Shahid), 106
Heer Ranjha (1970), 56, 58
high culture, ix, 22, 109, 112. *See also* elite
Hindavi, 93
Hindi films: Bombay cinema and, 1, 8–9, 16, 53; genres, 26; Lahore cinema and, x, 173n101
Hindi plays, 7
Hindi songs, 9–10, 94, 185n27, 189n86, 189n91, 190n93, 198n77
Hindi/Urdu divide, 23, 52
Hindi-Urdu films, x, 1, 8–9, 16, 23, 52–53
Hindu mythology, 28, 38, 101–3
Hindus, in Pakistani cinema, 197n47
Hindustani, x, 1, 53
Hindustani classical music, 68–69. *See also* Indian classical music
Hindustan Republican Association (HRA), 61, 63
Hindustan Socialist Republican Association (HSRA), 61–65, 186n40, 187n53
Hir-Ranjha story, 158, 201n44

history, vii, 1. *See also* archives; Ayub Khan era (1958–69); Lahore cinema; memory; Pakistan
Hoek, Lotte, ix, 47, 53, 167n12, 181n87
Hollywood: Bombay cinema and, 16; conventions of, vii, 151, 156, 173n101; musicals, 70, 80, 82, 189n83; Oscars, 31, 87; Pakistani New Cinema and, 156–57, 163; realism, 37, 38. *See also* American cinema
Homeric epics, 42
homosocial bonds, 125–28, 143, 162
horror films, 26, 151. *See also* Gothic suspense films
humanism, 42, 44–47
Humayun (1945), 188n79
Husain, Abdullah, 13

Imroze (newspaper), 35, 59, 65, 67
Indar Sabha (film, 1931), 8
Indar Sabha (opera), 7
independent filmmakers, 156, 201n36
India: national archives, 24, 175n123; nationalism, 23
Indian cinema: awards, 179n56; budgets, 157; independent, 201n36; neorealism in, 29–31; parallel cinema, 29, 54, 144, 146–48, 151, 154–56; regulation of films shown in Pakistan, 3–4, 16, 54, 149, 151, 176n13. *See also* Bollywood; Bombay cinema
Indian Civil Service (ICS), 59
Indian classical music, 68–87, 184nn8–9, 184n20, 190n93
Indian Mutiny (1857), 20
Indian National Congress, 62, 187n52
Indian parallel cinema, 29, 54, 144, 146–48, 151, 154–56
Indian People's Theatre Association (IPTA), 22, 30, 36–37, 39, 45, 181n94, 193n1; folk music and, 47–48, 50; leftist politics and, 113–14
India-Pakistan War (1965), 12, 142
infrastructures: in Pakistani film industry, vii, 5, 11–12, 26–27, 46, 150, 151; New Cinema and, 156–58; realism and, 41. *See also* theaters, cinema
International Film Festival, 37
Inter Services Public Relations (ISPR), 157
intertextuality, 146, 153, 160
Intezar (The awaiting, 1956), 17, 56, 58, 69, 70–87, 183n6; characters and performance, 76–85; fable and, 85–87; modernity and, 102; plot summary, 71–76; publicity poster, 75*fig.*; stills from, 73–74*fig.*, 83–84*fig.*
Iqbal, S., 200n22
Irish Republican Army, 61, 68
Ishq Par Zor Nahin (Love cannot be coerced, 1963), 119
Islam, Nazrul, 182n116
Islamization, 26
Italian neorealism, ix, 29, 31, 37–38, 154–55, 177n14; form and style in, 40–44; language and, 50–51
"item number" songs, 49, 154

"*Jaal* agitation" (1952), 3–4, 177n13
"Jā apnī ḥasratoṇ par ānsū bahā ke so jā" (Shed tears for your thwarted desires and fall sleep; song in *Susraal*), 124–25
Jabbar, Mehreen, 151
Jago Hua Savera (A new day dawns, 1959), xii, 11, 27–36, 119, 138; awards, 31, 87; cyclical time in, 38; distribution, 167n14; as experimental, 54; humanism and, 29, 42, 44–47, 50, 54; international version, 34; language in, 50–55, 182n107; local authenticity and, 41–44; on location, 181n85; narrative, 176n3; neorealism in, 29, 34–36, 42–44, 50, 54–55, 104, 144, 155; plot summary, 31–33; production team, 29–30; progressive cultural politics and, 175n1; reception, 35–36, 54; social film genre and, 49–50; songs, 47–50; stills from, 32*fig.*, 34–35*fig.*, 43*fig.*; style, 29, 34–35, 108; themes in, 29, 104, 143

Jagriti (1954), 17
Jahangir, Emperor, 19, 183n2
Jain, Kajri, 199n10
Jalib, Habib, xii, 13–16, 22, 106, 110–12, 171n68, 171n71, 171n73, 171n76, 196n36, 196n43, 202n55; "Dastoor," 196n43
Jameson, Fredric, 109, 134
Jasimuddin, 48
Jaswantlal, Nandlal, 184n13
"Javānī kī rāten javānī ke din" (Days and nights of youthful passion; song in *Intezar*), 73*fig.*
Jawab (Question, 1942), 100–101
Jehan, Noor, 9; in *Anmol Ghadi*, 189n80, 192n120; Anwar and, 56, 58, 61, 69, 71; Bombay cinema and, 2, 190n101; in *Ghoonghat*, 87; in *Intezar*, 69, 80–81; Lahore cinema and, 2, 71, 168n13, 174n120; Mangeshkar and, 80–81, 190n102; in *Nai Kiran*, 12; in *Susraal*, 124
Jhoomer (The jeweled forehead pendant, 1959), 58, 69, 70
Jhumke (film, 1946), 129
"Jhumke" (story, Manto), 129, 134
Jibon Theke Neya (Glimpses from life, 1970), 15, 175n1
Jog Biyog (1970), 30

Kabir, Alamgir, 42, 51, 54, 107–9, 129, 136, 141, 166n8, 181n87, 182n116, 193n3, 195n21, 197n51
kaifī, 138
Kaiser, Shahidullah, 13
Kanpuri, Zakhmi, 5, 119, 132, 166n10, 188n78, 194n9
Kapoor, Raj, 26, 38, 39
Karachi: audiences, 200n30; film industry personnel, 182n116; films from, vii, x, 5, 26, 52–53, 107, 129, 143, 144, 167n12; Western music in, 76–77
Kara Film Festival, 200n30
Kardar, Abdul Rashid, 1, 23, 29, 53, 60

Kardar, Akhtar Jung (A. J.), 176n2, 176n12; director of *Door Hey Sukh Ka Gaon*, 200n32; director of *Jago Hua Savera*, xii, 11, 29–30, 143; Faiz and, 48, 176n12; *Jago Hua Savera*'s lost song sequence and, 49; A. R. Kardar and, 53, 60
Kartar Singh, 11
Kashmiri, Agha Hashr, 8, 16, 57, 81–82, 191n106
Kaul, Mani, 154
Kausar, Asghar Ali, 183n7
Khalid, Leila, 106
Khamosh Pani (Silent waters, 2003), 155, 157
Khamosh Raho (Remain silent, 1964), 105, 106
Khan, Faseeh Bari, 119
Khan, Mehboob, 22, 23, 26, 37, 192n120
Khan, Nasir, 17
Khan, Nusrat Fateh Ali, 162
Khan, Omar, 151
Khan, Rahat Fateh Ali, 162
Khan, Shah Rukh, 26
Khan, Ustad Ashiq Ali, 184n8
Khan, Ustad Bade Ghulam Ali, 58, 68, 184n8, 190n95
Khan, Ustad Ghulam Haider, 64–65, 67
Khan, Ustad Tawakkal Hussain, 58, 184nn8–9
Khan, Ustad Waheed, 184n8
Khan, Yahya, 113
Khandan (Family, 1942), 2, 22, 71, 184n13
Khanum, Zubeida, 56
Khazanchi (The treasurer, 1941), 2
Khuda Kay Liye (In the name of God, 2007), 151, 157
Koel (Nightingale, 1959), 56, 58, 69–71, 80, 82, 86–87
Krishna, 7
Kumar, Amar, 38
Kumar, Dilip, 17, 178n32
Kumar, Rattan, 6*fig.*, 17, 115*fig.*, 116
Kumar, Santosh, 72, 88

"Kuṛī yes ai" (This girl is yes!; song in *Zinda Bhaag*), 159–60, 160*fig*.
"Kyūṇ jagāte ho mere sīne meṇ armānoṇ ko" (Why do you awaken desires in my breast?; song in *Clerk*), 117

labor exploitation, xii–xiii, 29, 33, 78, 114–19, 140, 193n1
labor migration, 143–45, 147, 159–61
Lahiri, Madhumita, 53
Lahore: nostalgic conceptions of, 145–46; Walled City, 106, 120–22, 127
Lahore cinema: Bombay cinema and, viii, x–xi, 1–2, 15–18, 60–61, 71, 172n92, 195n21; "Lahore effect," xiii, 18–20, 23, 26–28, 61, 104, 112, 148, 151, 163–64, 173n101; languages in, ix–x, 53; in the long sixties (1956–69), vii, x–xiii, 4–7, 143, 150; before 1947, 1–2; post-1947, 2–7; post-1971, 6–7, 150–51; size of, 193n3. *See also* aesthetics; language
Lahore Conspiracy Case, 62
"Lahore effect," xiii, 18–20, 23, 26–28, 61, 104, 112, 148, 151, 163–64, 173n101
Laila-Majnun tale, 97, 158
Lakhnavi, Behzad, 59–60
Lakhnavi culture, 188n78
Lakhon Mein Aik (One in a million, 1967), 11, 129
Lal, Deewan Sardari, 2
language: aesthetic problems of, xi; affect and, 52, 102; artifice and, 29; dialects, 37, 41, 144, 146, 182n107; subalternity and, 50–55; vernacular, 52. *See also* Punjabi language; Sindhi; Urdu
Lashari, Bilal, 151, 157
Lassally, Walter, 30, 31, 46, 49, 178n20
Latif, Shaheed, 22, 23
Latin American music, 73*fig*., 77, 85, 191n107
legendary stories, 21. *See also* Anarkali (mythical figure); *dāstān*; Oriental tales; *qiṣṣa* genre
Lévi-Strauss, Claude, 127
liberal values. *See* bourgeois liberal values

Life (magazine), 45
literary domain, 13–14; neorealism and, 39–40; Urdu, 142, 167n12
literary journals, 58, 104, 106
local cultural forms, 142, 144
Lok Virsa, 142
long sixties (1956–69), vii–xii, 3–4, 142–43, 149, 163; Anwar and, 61, 63, 69; Ayub Khan era and, 10, 14, 108; cinema and, viii, xii, 16, 22, 24–26, 61, 114, 141; *Jago Hua Savera* and, 29; Jalib and, 13; Kabir and, 108; leftist culture and, 104, 113; literature and, 14; rising film production during, 3*fig*., 5, 104
The Loves of a Mughal Prince (1928), 184n13
Luckhnavi, Shams, 189n79
Lucknow, 7
Ludhanvi, Sahir, 22
Lunn, David, 53
Luqman, 40, 178n32
lyric, vii, x, 137. *See also* film song; poetry; *specific films and songs*

Maa Baap (Mother and father, 1967), 105
Maclean, Kama, 186n40, 187n53, 187n67
magical effects, 8
Mahal (The mansion, 1949), 95, 191n102
Majumdar, Neepa, 39, 165n4, 179n56, 190nn96–97, 191n102
Malani, Nalini, 155
Malik, Aisha, 199n18
Malik, Younis, 154
Mangeshkar, Lata, 80–81, 185n27, 190n102
Mansoor, Shoaib, 151
Manto, Saadat Hasan, xiii, 2, 16, 22, 106, 168n8, 168n13, 174n117, 197n64; "Jhumke," 129, 134, 198n71
Marathi, 8
marginalization, 38. *See also* poverty
marriage, 17, 120–35, 141
Marxism, 45, 61, 67–69, 187n64
masculinity, 100–101, 148, 149, 154, 192n128, 198n5

Masoom (Innocent, 1942), 22
Matteela Films, 144
Maula Jatt (1979), 154
Meera Bai (1947), 168n8
Mehboob Productions, 188n79
mehfil style, 190n101
melodrama, ix, 7, 15, 55; affect and, 68–69; in Anwar's films, 69; avant-garde cinema and, 159–63; conventions of, 135, 140; in mainstream Pakistani cinema, 34; modernity and, 109–10; social films and, 105, 109, 111, 114, 148; songs and, 9, 154. *See also* social films
memory, xi, xiii, 19, 101–3; affect and, 28, 103; archives and, 24–28, 143; cultural amnesia, 86, 142–44
Mera Ghar Mere Jannat (My home is my heaven, 1968), 169n30
"Meray dil ki ghadi kare tick tick tick" (The clock of my heart beats tick tick tick; song in *Albela*), 85
middle-class viewers, 108–9, 149–52, 195n21
migration, 143–45, 147, 159–61. *See also dunky*
Mir, Farina, 201n44
Mir, Raza, 11, 129
Miranda, Carmen, 85, 191n108
Mirza, Diljeet, 119
Mirza, Humayun, 105
misidentification trope, 69, 99. *See also* doubling trope
Mitra, Naresh, 101
Mitra, Tripti, 30, 48, 176n11
modernity and modernization, 5, 23–24; accelerating temporality, x, 5, 9, 71, 78, 134; cinematic Gothic and, 94; Cold War humanism and, 45–46; commercial film and, x, 108–9; corruption and, 70; female body and, 86; gender roles and, 97, 100–101; Partition allegories and, 101–3; popular music and, 78; top-down processes, 142

Moffat, Chris, 64, 103, 185n28, 186n42
Mohaiemen, Naeem, 51
Mohammad, Ghulam, 168n13, 191n113
Moin, Haseena, 199n18
Montpellier, Eliot, 199n18
morality, 34, 85, 108, 118, 120, 129; contemporary Pakistani films and, 146, 154, 158, 164; East-West opposition, 69–70, 76, 84, 172n79; in Gothic films, 192; heredity and, 141; neoliberalism and, 144; neorealism and, 41; playback singing and, 80–81; in television serials, 152–53
Morcom, Anna, 9–10, 50, 79, 136, 166n9, 190n93, 198n77
Moscow Film Festival, 31
mother figure, 114, 117, 153
Mufti, Aamir, 52, 175n128
Mughal-e-Azam (1960), 19, 183n2, 184n13
Mughal historical films, 56
mujra (dance song), 48–49, 137–38, 138*fig.*, 139*fig.*
Mujtaba, Hasan, 162
Mukherjee, Debashree, 165n3, 167n3, 174n117
Mukherjee, Hiren, 176n11
Mukherjee, Madhuja, 165n3, 191n78
Mukh o Mukhosh (The face and the mask, 1956), 181n88
Multanikar, Surayia, 138
multiplex theaters, 150, 151, 157
musicals, 7, 70. *See also* social films
musical scores, 136–37, 188n79. *See also* film song
musical styles: East-West opposition, 70–76. *See also* Indian classical music; Western music
music directors, 1–2, 9, 22, 60, 138, 184n17. *See also* Anwar, Khurshid; Baran, Timir; Bhattacharya, Deebo; D'Souza, Sebastian; Haider, Master Ghulam; Shankar-Jaikishan
Muslims, 147, 173n106; filmmaking and, 20–21

"Muslim social" film, viii, xi, 21–22, 173n107, 174n119. *See also* social films
mythology, 18–20, 98. *See also* Anarkali (mythical figure)

Nabanna (New harvest, 1944), 37
Nabi, Farjad, xiii, 27, 128, 142, 144, 158, 198n5
Nabila, 136
Nagin (Serpent, 1959), 5, 105, 194n10
Nagrath, Roshan Lal, 184n17
Nai Kiran (A new ray of light, 1960), 12
Nairang-i-Khayal (journal), 58
Najma (1943), 22
Na Maloom Afraad (Unidentified people, 2014), 151
Naqvi, Najam, 183n119
Naqvi, Tanvir, 56, 105, 168n13, 194n6, 194n10; Anwar and, 58, 71; lyrics for *Anmol Ghadi*, 175n120, 192n120; lyrics for *Ghoonghat*, 93, 192n119; Taj and, 71
Narayan, Hari, 134, 197n67, 198n71
narrative, vii; aesthetic problems of, xi; form, 164; genre and, 153; humanist, 29; in New Cinema, 147–48; originality and plagiarism, 4, 15–17, 108, 172n85, 195n21; premodern genres and, 158; progressive, 29; temporal structures of, 5; tropes, x, 70
Nasir, Agha, 48–49
national cinema, 19–20, 173n101; realism and, 39
nationalism, xii, 20–24, 56, 102. *See also* anti-colonialism; revolutionary movements
National Press Trust, 13
Natyashastra, 7
Naujawan Bharat Sabha (NJBS), 61, 66
Nawaz, Shah, 30, 168n13
Nayyar, O. P., 191n107
Nayyar, Sharif, 119, 194n3
Nazir, Musarrat, 114, 115*fig.*
Neelam Pari (The sapphire fairy, 1952), 58, 60
Neela Parbat (The blue mountain, 1969), 129

Neelo (actor), 6*fig.*, 92, 111, 113, 134
Neend (Sleep, 1959), 11, 105, 106
neoliberalism, 142–50, 157, 163
neorealism, ix, 29, 144, 180n62; global, 30–31; Indian cinema and, 179n58; language and, 144
New Cinema, 27, 143, 150, 163; censorship and, 201n39; commercial success of, 151; patronage of, 155–58; realism in, 147; television serials and, 152
News Pictorial, 12
newsreels, 12
Niazi, Naheed, 56, 87
Nigar film awards, 5
Nishant (Night's end, 1975), 155
nonelite neighborhoods, 120–21, 128, 137, 143–44

"O jāne wāle re, ṭhero zarā ruk jā'o" (Pause a bit, don't leave yet; song in *Intezar*), 74
oral performing traditions, vii, 7, 158
Oriental tales, 21, 26, 158

Padamsee, Akbar, 155
Padma nadir majhi (The boatman on the river Padma, Bandopadhyay), 29, 176n3
Pagdandi (The path, 1947), 60, 71, 183n6, 184n13
Pakistan: cultural politics in the long sixties (1956–69), 10–18, 35–36, 108–9, 142; economy, 24, 149, 170n52, 170n64; neoliberalism in, 142–50, 157, 163; tensions between India and, 54; in twenty-first century, 142–49; United States alliance, 10–11, 13, 35, 45–46, 142–43. *See also* Ayub Khan era (1958–69); East Pakistan; Pakistani cinema; West Pakistan
Pakistan Film Magazine, 175n125
Pakistan Film Producers Association, 119
Pakistani cinema: archives, 24–28, 143; films released between 1947 and 1980, 3*fig.*; government control over, 11–12; industry personnel, viii–xii, 2, 17, 23,

29–30, 53, 138–39, 182n116; overview of, 1–24; scholarship on, viii–ix, 166n8. *See also* art cinema; avant-garde cinema; Ayub Khan era (1958–69); censorship; commercial cinema; Dhaka; experimental cinema; Karachi; Lahore cinema; New Cinema
Pakistan Institute for the Study of Film Art, 200n30
Pakistan Quarterly (journal), 44, 46, 48, 51
Pakistan Television Corporation, 48, 111, 119, 129
Pakistan Writers' Guild (PWG), 13
Palestinian resistance, 110–12, 197n47
Pancholi, Dalsukh M., 2, 22
Pancholi Studios, 2, 71
"Pānī dā bulbulā" (Bubble of water; song in *Zinda Bhaag*), 159
Paracha, Nadeem, 200n26
parallel cinema, Indian, 29, 54, 144, 146–48, 151, 154–56
Parsi theater, 7–8, 16, 57
Partition allegories, 17, 69, 87, 95–96, 98, 101–3
Partition of 1947, 20–24; affect and, 17; Anwar's films and, 60; cinema and, 81; communal strife and, 23, 52; cultural separatism and, 79; Hindi-Urdu divide, 52; plagiarism and, 17; trauma of, 56, 95–96
Parvez, Amjad, 93, 184n9
Parvez, Aslam, 154, 200n26
Parwana (The moth, 1947), 23, 60
Pasha, Anwar Kamal, 2, 3, 105, 172n87, 184n13, 193n3
Pashto films, vii, 142, 150
Patel, Baburao, 101, 168n8
Pathan diaspora, 16
Pather Panchali (Song of the little road, 1955), 30, 38–39, 42
Patras, Khurram, 199n6
patriarchy, 100, 102, 156, 163
Peer, Rafi, 59
people's actor ('avāmī adākār), 120. *See also* Allauddin

people's poet ('avāmī shā'ir), 171n67. *See also* Jalib, Habib
performance, 76–85
performance genre, 158–59
Pervaiz, Masood, 56, 58, 87, 105, 119, 172n87, 183n119, 193n3
plagiarism, 4, 15–17, 108, 172n85, 195n21. See also *charba* films
playback singing, 79–81, 124, 189n79, 190n100
poetry: by Khurshid Anwar, 58; film song and, 7; male bonding in, 127; Urdu, xii, 16, 22, 63. *See also* Faiz, Faiz Ahmed; Gaur, Meenu; Ghalib, Mirza; Hanif, Mohammad; Jalib, Habib; Mujtaba, Hasan; Nabi, Farjad; Naqvi, Tanvir; Saif, Saifuddin; Shair, Himayat Ali; Shifai, Qateel
politics: affect and, 111–13, 161, 164. *See also* Ayub Khan era (1958–69); revolutionary movements
popular culture, ix, 22, 164; criticality and, 109; elite culture and, 112; leftist politics and, 110–14. *See also* commercial cinema
popular music, 10, 78, 189n91
Posley, Asha, 2
posters: film, 18, 24, 75*fig.*, 76, 107, 115*fig.*, 116, 130*fig.*, 131, 139, 140, 200n22; political, 63
poverty, 33, 38, 135, 197n53; as resource for filmmakers, 41
Prakrit, 51
Pran (actor), 154
press censorship, 13
product placement, 156–57
progressive/leftist politics, 35, 63, 139; humanism and, 44–47; in Lahore cinema, 54; modernization and, 45, 108–9; popular culture and, 110; repression of, 35; social films and, 104–14; writers and poets, vii, xii–xiii, 22, 52, 63, 104, 174n117, 175n1. *See also* Marxism; Qaiser, Khalil; Shahid, Riaz
Progressive Papers, 13, 35, 170n63

propaganda, 12, 17
prostitution, 113, 129, 134, 137, 139, 141
provincial cultural forms, 142
public sphere: bazaar as, 112–13; cinematic, vii, ix–xii, 20, 27, 164; mediatized, 27, 200n20
Punjab: film industry and, 1; performative cultures of, 158–59
Punjabi diaspora, 16
Punjabi language, vii, 1, 6–7, 107, 142–45, 150, 201n42
Punjabiyat, 202n47
Purbi, 48, 50, 93, 192n119

Qaidi (Prisoner, 1941), 22
Qaidi (Prisoner, 1962), 183n119
Qaiser, Khalil, xii, 5, 11, 40, 54, 68, 105–6, 110, 115*fig.*, 120, 131, 155, 175n1, 194nn3–4; *Clerk*, 114, 194n9; politics, 194n10
Qasmi, Ahmad Nadeem, 13
Qatil (Murderer, 1955), 3
qawwali, 116, 131, 139, 140*fig.*, 162–63, 184n17
Qismat (Fate, 1956), 105, 119
Qismat Ke Her Pher (The twists of fate, 1931), 1
qiṣṣa genre, 21, 158–59
Qureshi, Nabeel, 151

Raat Chali Hai Jhoom Ke (The intoxicated night, 2002), 155
Rabe, Nate, 166n10, 196n39, 197n49
Radio Ceylon, 18
Radio Pakistan, 65, 68
Rahguzar, 11
Rahi, Younus, 114
Rahman, Khan Ataur, 30, 175n1
"Rāhoṇ meṇ ṭhārī maiṇ naẓareṇ jamā'e" (With my gaze affixed on the road; song in *Ghoonghat*), 93
Raihan, Zahir, 5, 13, 15, 29–30, 175n1, 176nn4–5
Rajadhyaksha, Ashish: on "cinema-effects," 18, 172n93; on the "Lahore effect," viii, xv, 18–19, 23, 61, 104, 112, 164; on midcentury cinema, viii, xi, 16, 23, 173n101. *See also* "Lahore effect"
Raj Kapoor dynasty, 17
Rajput, A. B., 44, 46
Raju, Zakir Hossain, 45, 180n80, 181n88
Rakhshi (dancer), 49
Ramchand Pakistani (2008), 151, 157–58
Ramchandra, C., 85, 185n27, 191n107
Rancière, Jacques, 186n42
"Raqṣ zanjīr pahan kar bhī kiyā jātā hai" (You can dance even in fetters; song in *Zerqa*), 110–12
Rashid, Noon Meer, 58
Rawalpindi Conspiracy Case, 35
Ray, Satyajit, 30, 37, 38–39, 42, 50, 154, 180n67, 200n30
Raz (The secret, 1959), 105
realism, vii; aesthetics, 38–39, 160; in American cinema, 40–41; audience and, 176n3; fable and, ix, xiii, 145, 147–48, 164; fantasy and, 28; ideologies and, 179n53; Kabir on, 195n21; national cinema and, 39; portrayals of everyday life, xii–xiii, 31–34, 38, 40–44, 87, 105, 114, 128, 145; romanticism and, 104; social melodramatic films and, 7, 105; television serials and, 153
Reel Pakistan: A Screen Studies Forum (online journal), 199n18
reflexivity, xi, 146–48, 157, 160, 161, 163–64
Rehman, I. A., 71, 86
Rehman, Nasreen, x, 166n10
reincarnation, 69, 93, 95, 102
religious fundamentalism, 147
religious minorities, 113
remakes, 16, 19, 164
Renoir, Jean, 37–38, 44
Report of the Film Fact Finding Committee (Govt. of Pakistan), 11–12, 171n78, 172n79
revolutionary movements, 20, 45; film song and, 161. *See also* anti-colonialism

The River (1951), 37–38, 44, 178n46
"River Life in East Pakistan" (Rajput), 44
Riwaaj (Custom, 1965), 119
Rizvi, Shaukat Hussain, 2, 4, 23, 71, 168nn13–14, 175n120, 184n13
romanticism, 56, 58; in Anwar's films, 69; colonialism and, 68; music and, 60, 81; Partition allegories and, 102–3
Roohi (1954), 3, 168n18
Roy, Bimal, 22, 38, 101, 179n48
Roy, Rahul, 199n5
rural life, 161; in *Jago Hua Savera*, 31–33

Saheli (Female friend, 1960), 127–28
Saif, Saifuddin, 11, 105
Saigal, Kundan Lal, 61
Salam e Mohabbat (Salutations of love, 1971), 58
Salim (later, Emperor Jahangir), 19
Sangam (Confluence, 1964), 5
Saptapadi (1961), 160
Sarfraz, Khwaja, 151
Sarhad (Border, 1966), 58
Sarhadi, Zia, 11, 17, 22, 38, 129, 175n1, 179n48
Sarkar, Bhaskar, 69, 102, 172n91, 188n75
sarqa films, 15. See also *charba* films; plagiarism
Sarwar, Ayub, 178n32
"Sāvan kī ghanghor ghatā'eṇ" (Cloudy breezes of the rainy season; song in *Intezar*), 84, 84*fig.*
Sawaal (The question, 1966), 105
Schendel, Willem van, 48, 54, 183n118
Sen, Aparna, 154
Sen, Biswarup, 10, 78
Sen, Meheli, 69, 94, 190n100, 192n124, 192n128
Sen, Mrinal, 154, 180n79
serious cinema, 54–55; neorealist, 39–40
serpent film genre, 5, 18, 26, 105, 173n94
sexual exploitation, 118, 131–35, 200n26
sexuality, 49, 195n21
Shah, Naseeruddin, 144, 155
Shahab, Qudratullah, 12–13, 170n63

Shahabnama (Shahab), 12–13
Shaheed (Martyr, 1962), 105–6, 131, 139, 183n119, 194n10
Shaheed Minar, 52
Shahid, Riaz, xii; censorship and, 109, 196n27; color films, 5; Faiz and, 155; *Hazar dastan* (novel), 106; Jalib and, 15; leftist politics, 105–7, 110–11, 131, 175n1, 194n4; marriage, 111, 113; politics, 40, 54, 68, 194n10; writing style, 107, 121, 135–36. See also *Badnam* (Disgraced, 1966); *Clerk* (1960); *Susraal* (The in-laws' home, 1962); *Zerqa* (1969)
Shah of Iran, 111
Shair, Himayat Ali, 105, 194n6
Shaitnol (village on Meghna River), 31–33, 36, 42, 43*fig.*
Shalimar Recording Company, 24
Shankar, Uday, 181n94
Shankar-Jaikishan, 185n27, 191n104, 191n107
Shehzad, Iqbal, xii–xiii, 105, 106, 129
Sherani, Akhtar, 58
Shifai, Qateel, 2, 56, 58, 71, 105, 188n78
Shikwa (Complaint, 1963), 105
"Shīshoṇ kā masīḥa ko'ī nahīṇ" (The shattered glass has no savior; song in *Jago Hua Savera*), 48–50, 182n98
Shope, Bradley, 85, 166n9, 191nn107–8
Shorey studio owners, 2
Shuja, Hakim Ahmed, 2
Siaposh, Baba Alam, 2
Siddique, Salma, ix, x, 24, 175n123
Siddiqui, Shaukat, 13
silent films, vii, 1, 8, 57, 80, 101
Simon Commission, 65
Sindhi: disaspora, 16; films, vii, 16; oral folktales, 28, 158
Singh, Bhagat, xii, 61–69, 185n28, 185n39, 187n67; afterlife of, 63–64, 103, 186n40; Anwar and, 67–69, 187n53, 187n64; iconology of, 63, 185n28,39; trial of, 20, 61–62, 66–67

Singin' in the Rain (1952), 80–81, 83, 189n83
social films: affect and, 167n13; in Bombay cinema, 193n1; courtship rituals in, 117; decline in, 150; film song and, 7–10; *Ghoonghat* as, 99; influence of, 28; leftist politics and, 104–14; modernization and, 141; "Muslim social," viii, xi, 21–22, 173n107, 174n119; national cinema and, 20–24; theater and, 82. *See also* melodrama
social hierarchies, 104, 125
social issues, 40; inequality, 104, 108–9, 160–61, 179n53; in New Cinema, 164; state funding and, 157–58
"So jā so jā dard bhare dil ab to so jā" (O mournful heart, sleep at last!; song in *Clerk*), 117
song. *See* film song
song-and-dance sequence, xii, 5, 18, 22, 69, 111–12; in *Badnam*, 137–39; in *Clerk*, 116–17; "item number," 49, 154; in *Jago Hua Savera*, 31, 34, 48–50; in *Susraal*, 122–23. *See also* dancing; film song; *mujra* (dance song)
sound films: languages and, 8–9; live settings, 170n44; songs in, 9–10; Urdu and, 1. *See also* film song; language
South Asian cinema, 18, 28; neorealism (after 1952), 30–31, 38–40; realism in (before 1952), 36–38; scholarship on, vii–ix. *See also* Bombay cinema; Indian cinema; Lahore cinema; Pakistani cinema
Soviet Union, 11
special effects, 8
spectral figures, 87–90, 93–97, 102–3
stardom, 2, 18; in Bombay cinema, 80–81; female body and, 86; in Lahore Urdu cinema, 4–5
Steichen, Edward, 45
Steimatsky, Noa, 42, 180nn71–72
stereotypical works, 108, 163, 195n21, 197n47. *See also* typage
Stop Genocide (1971), 30
"studio *Social*," 37, 38
stunt films, 21
style. *See* aesthetics
subalternity, 128, 143, 147, 151; language and, 50–55; in Punjabi films, 144; vernacular cinema and, 150
Sufi traditions, 7, 28, 148, 162, 202n47
Suhag Ka Daan (1936), 188n78
Sukh Ka Sapna (Distant dream, 1962), 119, 183n119
Suleman, S., 194n3
Sultana, Nayyar, 88, 90*fig.*, 95–96*fig.*
Sumar, Sabiha, 155
Sunderason, Sanjukta, 47, 182n107
suspense films, Gothic, 69, 87–99, 192n124, 192n128
Susraal (The in-laws' home, 1962), 106, 107, 111, 119–28, 122–23*fig.*, 126*fig.*, 143–44, 160, 198n1; neorealism in, 144; themes in, 143
Swami (1941), 184n13
Swarg Ki Sidhi (1935), 183n6, 188n78

Taj, Syed Imtiaz Ali: author of *Anarkali* play, 19, 56–57, 183n2; dialogue writer for *Intezar*, 70, 82, 86; involvement in cinema, 2, 56, 71, 87, 183n6, 184n13, 188n78; as a literary figure, 57; as a playwright, 16, 70; producer of Anwar's first radio play, 59. *See also Anarkali* play (1922)
Talish, Agha, 91
Tamil, 8
Tanvir, Kuhu, 25
Tariq, Hassan, 5, 11, 40, 105, 106, 194n3, 194n5
Taseer, Anjum, 36
technological changes, 5–6; digital, 27, 150; videocassette recorders (VCR), 26, 149. *See also* color film; sound films
television serials, 25, 27, 147, 150, 152–54, 163, 199n18
Teri Yaad (1948), 188n78
La Terra Trema (The earth trembles, 1948), 37, 41–42, 44, 50–51, 180n67, 180nn71–72

terrorism, 147
theater: Anwar and, 59; colonial-era, vii; within film, 76, 80, 82, 84; Gujarati, 7–8; Parsi, 7–8, 16, 57; playback singing, 79–81. *See also* Indian People's Theatre Association (IPTA)
theaters, cinema, 149–51, 157
theatrical conventions, 104, 107, 123, 136
theatricality, 8, 37, 42
themes: genre and, 153; transformations in, 6
Thomas, Rosie, 158, 165n3, 174n108, 201n45
traditional societies, 44–46
transnational media, 144–45
Triumph of the Will (1935), 12
typage, viii, x, 18, 104, 105, 107–9, 200n26; refusal of, 120, 128. *See also* stereotypical works

United States: Pakistan's alliance with, 10–11, 13, 35, 45–46, 142–43. *See also* Hollywood
Urdu: Bengali and, 51–52; idioms and metaphors in, 106–7; linguistic conception of, ix–x; poetry and writing in, xii, 16, 22, 63; politics and, 113; scholarship on Bombay cinema and, 166n11; songs in *Jago Hua Savera*, 48
Urdu films: archive and memory, 24–28, 142–43; from Bombay, 1, 8–9, 17; decline in number of, 150; in Dhaka, 53; from Lahore, 3–7; New Cinema, 151; restrictions on, 26. *See also* social films
Urdu literary production, 142, 167n12
Urdu plays, 7–8, 16
Usman, Javed, 64, 100–101, 184n8

var genre, 158
Vasudevan, Ravi, vii–viii, xi, 21–23, 174n119
Vaz, Antonio, 185n27
VCR (videocassette recorder), 26, 149

Verga, Giovanni, 42
vernacular cinema, 150
vernacular cultural forms, 142
Vertigo (1958), 99
Visconti, Luchino, 37, 41–42, 44, 50–51, 180n71

Waar (Strike, 2013), 151, 157
Waheed, Sarah, 95
Walled City (Lahore), 106, 120–22, 127
Wani, Aarti, 109, 165n3, 166n11, 193n1, 196n31
West Bengal, 54, 180n79, 182n107
Western music, 70–86, 190n93, 191n107, 198n77
West Pakistan: Bombay films and, 17; cinematic style in, 107, 141; film industry personnel, 138–39; Indian films shown in, 3–4; language in, 52; relations with East Pakistan, 15, 44–46, 54, 113
women: employment, 116–18; marriage and, 127–28; self-presentation, 91–92; sexual exploitation of, 105–6, 110, 118, 131–35, 200n26; sexuality, 49, 195n21; social roles, 97, 100; status of, 134. *See also* gender; marriage

Yadav, K. C., 185n28
Yashpal, 186n48
Yeh Aman (1971), 109, 194n10
The Yes Men, 201n38
Yusuf, S. M., 17, 127, 193n3

Zaidi, Hasan, 155
Zaidi, S. A., 170n52
Zamindar (Landlord, 1942), 184n13
Zamindar, Vazira, 24
Zavattini, Cesare, 40–43, 180n62
Zehr-e Ishq (Poison of love, 1958), 56, 58, 70, 87, 102, 183n6, 188n73, 188n78
Zerqa (1969), 5, 15, 105–7, 110–11, 113, 194n10, 197n47
Zia-ul-Haq, Muhammad, 26, 150

Zibahkhana (Slaughterhouse, 2007), 151
Zinda Bhaag (Run for life, 2013): assemblage form, 159–60, 163–64; awards and, 87; casting, 199n6; cinematic lineages and, 141, 155; cinematic techniques, 152–55; class issues in, 128, 143–44, 151; as fable, 158–63; funding for, 198n5, 201n42; infrastructure and, 157; "Lahore effect" and, xiii, 27, 164; neoliberalism and, 144–49; publicity poster, 200n22; realism, 159, 164; song-and-dance sequences, 159–63; stills from, 145–46*fig.*, 160*fig.*, 162*fig.*; television serials and, 152–53
Zinda Laash (The living corpse, 1967), 151
Zorba the Greek (1965), 30
Zutshi, Mohini and Shyama, 186n52

GLOBAL
SOUTH
ASIA

Padma Kaimal
K. Sivaramakrishnan
Anand A. Yang
SERIES EDITORS

Global South Asia takes an interdisciplinary approach to the humanities and social sciences in its exploration of how South Asia, through its global influence, is and has been shaping the world.

Lahore Cinema: Between Realism and Fable, by Iftikhar Dadi

Adivasi Art and Activism: Curation in a Nationalist Age, by Alice Tilche

New Lives in Anand: Building a Muslim Hub in Western India, by Sanderien Verstappen

Mumbai Taximen: Autobiographies and Automobilities in India, by Tarini Bedi

Outcaste Bombay: City Making and the Politics of the Poor, by Juned Shaikh

The Ends of Kinship: Connecting Himalayan Lives between Nepal and New York, by Sienna Craig

Making Kantha, Making Home: Women at Work in Colonial Bengal, by Pika Ghosh

A Secular Need: Islamic Law and State Governance in Contemporary India, by Jeffery A. Redding

Making the Modern Slum: The Power of Capital in Colonial Bombay, by Sheetal Chhabria

History and Collective Memory in South Asia, 1200–2000, by Sumit Guha

Climate Change and the Art of Devotion: Geoaesthetics in the Land of Krishna, 1550–1850, by Sugata Ray

Bhakti and Power: Debating India's Religion of the Heart, edited by John Stratton Hawley, Christian Lee Novetzke, and Swapna Sharma

Marrying for a Future: Transnational Sri Lankan Tamil Marriages in the Shadow of War, by Sidharthan Maunaguru

Gandhi's Search for the Perfect Diet: Eating with the World in Mind, by Nico Slate

Mountain Temples and Temple Mountains: Architecture, Religion, and Nature in the Central Himalayas, by Nachiket Chanchani

Creating the Universe: Depictions of the Cosmos in Himalayan Buddhism, by Eric Huntington

Privileged Minorities: Syrian Christianity, Gender, and Minority Rights in Postcolonial India, by Sonja Thomas

High-Tech Housewives: Indian IT Workers, Gendered Labor, and Transmigration, by Amy Bhatt

Making New Nepal: From Student Activism to Mainstream Politics, by Amanda Thérèse Snellinger

The Rebirth of Bodh Gaya: Buddhism and the Making of a World Heritage Site, by David Geary

Mobilizing Krishna's World: The Writings of Prince Sāvant Singh of Kishangarh, by Heidi Rika Maria Pauwels

Banaras Reconstructed: Architecture and Sacred Space in a Hindu Holy City, by Madhuri Desai

Displaying Time: The Many Temporalities of the Festival of India, by Rebecca M. Brown

The Gender of Caste: Representing Dalits in Print, by Charu Gupta

Sensitive Space: Fragmented Territory at the India-Bangladesh Border, by Jason Cons

The Afterlife of Sai Baba: Competing Visions of a Global Saint, by Karline McLain

A Place for Utopia: Urban Designs from South Asia, by Smriti Srinivas

www.ingramcontent.com/pod-product-compliance
Lightning Source LLC
Chambersburg PA
CBHW030616230426
43661CB00053B/2019

GREYSCALE
BIN TRAVELER FORM

Cut By _Manuel_ Qty _#44_ Date _5-1-26_

Scanned By _____ Qty _____ Date _____

Scanned Batch IDs _____

Notes / Exception _____